D1552619

CHARLES AUSTIN BEARD

CHARLES AUSTIN BEARD

THE RETURN OF THE MASTER HISTORIAN OF AMERICAN IMPERIALISM

RICHARD DRAKE

CORNELL UNIVERSITY PRESS
Ithaca and London

First published 2018 by Cornell University Press

Printed in the United States of America

Library of Congress Cataloging-in-Publication Data

Names: Drake, Richard, 1942– author.
Title: Charles Austin Beard : the return of the master historian of American imperialism / Richard Drake.
Description: Ithaca [New York] : Cornell University Press, 2018. | Includes bibliographical references and index.
Identifiers: LCCN 2018024044 (print) | LCCN 2018025891 (ebook) | ISBN 9781501715136 (e-book epub/mobi) | ISBN 9781501715143 (e-book pdf) | ISBN 9781501715167 | ISBN 9781501715167 (cloth alk. paper)
Subjects: LCSH: Beard, Charles A. (Charles Austin), 1874–1948. | Historians—United States—Biography. | United States—Foreign Relations—20th century—Historiography. | United States—History—20th Century—Historiography.
Classification: LCC E175.5.B38 (ebook) | LCC E175.5.B38 D73 2018 (print) | DDC 973.07202 [B] —dc23
LC record available at https://lccn.loc.gov/2018024044

In homage to Leonardo Bruni, who in the fifteenth century observed that the fundamental lesson to be found in the pages of history concerns the eternal struggle between the rich and the poor.

Contents

PREFACE

        I began graduate work on American history in 1963 at a school where Charles Beard survived on seminar reading lists mainly as an example of how not to think about the field. As an undergraduate, I had read *An Economic Interpretation of the Constitution of the United States.* It had stayed in my mind as a humanly credible alternative to the celebratory American pageant approach then typical of history textbooks and, in that era of burgeoning consensus about the country's exceptional ideals and virtues, leading monographs as well.

With what Beard later acknowledged were some overstatements, he identified the economic forces responsible for the American political system at its founding. At the same time, his book provided a historical primer for understanding how American politics continued to work on one of its many levels, as a natural conduit for the advancement of people and interests with the money to pay for the entitlements bestowed by Washington. His thesis had the enormous advantage of explaining historically one of the most obviously true aspects of American political life, its reliance on money. The system worked in the main as its designers had intended, Beard argued, to create a country suited as much as possible to the economic needs of the business and landowning classes. That the Founders were in many ways praiseworthy men of exceptional brilliance and learning did not take away from the thrust of his argument in the book about the natural inclination for them to look out for their own interests. He admired them, not least for the forthrightness with which in *The Federalist* and other sources they freely acknowledged their economic motives in designing the Constitution.

I kept wondering in graduate school why, despite the arguments I heard in seminars and lectures, Beard seemed to me to be right in his principal judgments. In his great book, he had claimed only to be advancing an interpretation and invited historians to test it. Books had appeared to refute aspects of his interpretation, in fulfillment of Beard's own expectations about the likely course of research developments following the publication of *An Economic Interpretation.* Though critics only partially had succeeded in their attack against him, his entire argument had come to be associated with a false start in the study of American history, as a point of view at odds with current developments in the field and national attitudes generally. I later came to understand that I had been a witness to what Peter Novick would call in *That Noble Dream: The "Objectivity Question" and the American Historical Profession* (1988) the containment, trivialization, and rejection of dissident currents in American historiography. A new celebratory consensus about America's past and present had excluded Beard. To be within the consensus was to be objective and not disqualified by Beard's subjective critical approach in tracing the social, economic, and political problems of the present back to their historical origins. Beard, it seemed, had written propaganda, something that no real historian ever would do.

Thinking that there was something wrong with my way of understanding American history, I left graduate school. Some years later, I would receive a PhD specializing in the history of Europe. In the process of making this field shift, I spent a year in Italy, where I began to read about Italian political theory. The theorists who interested me the most were the Italian realists: Gaetano Mosca, Vilfredo Pareto, and Roberto Michels. Their ideas would lead me to my dissertation and first book. Applying the insights of Niccolò Machiavelli and Francesco Guicciardini to the study of modern politics, these late nineteenth- and early twentieth-century writers developed theories that I thought bore a striking resemblance in some key respects to Beard's interpretation of history.

Mosca's *Teorica dei governi e governo parlamentare* (1884) and *Elementi di scienza politica* (2 vols., 1895 and 1922) contain the most succinct summaries of this school's essential points about the controlling role that elites play in every society for which historical records exist. The essence of government always consisting of a monopoly on using and sitting in judgment on legitimate force, new ruling elites never differ essentially from the old and invariably dominate the weak and disorganized masses no matter what the political system of a country might be. A classic nineteenth-century liberal writing from a frankly anti-democratic and anti-socialist viewpoint, Mosca asserted that contemporary republics, such as the United States, do not constitute an exception to the elitist rule. They have their own elites, which through lobbying interventions inevitably develop effective strategies for the transmission of their political and economic power. Henry George's *Progress and Poverty* (1879) made clear to him the plutocratic essence of American politics. Moreover, Mosca felt certain that the socialists—the group he dreaded most of all—would fare even worse in their attempts to create an authentic rule of the people than the democrats had in theirs. He lived long enough to perceive in the enormities of Stalin a ghastly confirmation of his predictions about the way the Marxist dictatorship of the proletariat system would work in practice.

Pareto, a liberal political economist also claiming to be writing as a realist in scientific pursuit of the truth, came to the same central conclusion that Mosca had: the granite foundation of historical reality was not class conflict, but conflict between reigning and contesting elites. A rallying point for anti-socialists in Italy, his *Systèmes socialistes* (1902) presented the case that every political establishment throughout history had come into existence in the service of elites who differed only in their methods of securing and maintaining power. In his turn-of-the-century political journalism for Enrico Corradini's anti-socialist *Il Regno*, Pareto sided wholeheartedly with the ruling class and vehemently opposed the socialists because of what he judged to be their fantastically moronic clichés about human equality. If the socialists won their revolution, he warned, they only would succeed in creating an elite of their own, which would govern in the same exploitative way of all elites, with the refinements of Marxism added as an evil bonus. Liberal elites because of their theory of limited government seemed to him the best guarantee for civilization's survival, but they did not rule democratically. No government did or could. Very small groups of men made all the power decisions, no matter where or when.

Michels, a German-Jewish sociologist long-resident in Italy, actively participated in the Italian Socialist Party congresses of 1902, 1904, and 1906. He noted in *Storia critica del movimento socialista italiano dagli inizi fino al 1911* (1926) that the party leaders almost invariably came from elite socioeconomic circles. Michels reported that whenever someone from a working-class background appeared at these congresses, it was an occasion for wonder and excited comment by the delegates, as if a rare and seldom-seen animal had approached the speaker's rostrum and miraculously had acquired powers of speech. Even before he spoke at his first Socialist congress, Benito Mussolini, a blacksmith's son without university training, dazzled the delegates because he possessed just this kind of exotic pedigree. A glaring exception in socialist politics, Mussolini at the same time confirmed the rule in that culture. In keeping with their counterparts across the ideological spectrum, socialist leaders had nearly identical class and educational backgrounds, underscoring for Michels the elitist character of politics even on the left.

In the March 1917 issue of the *Political Science Quarterly*, Beard reviewed *Political Parties: A Sociological Study of Oligarchical Tendencies in Modern Democracy* by Michels. Beard often reviewed books on European politics and history, displaying a special interest in the rise of Italian fascism. He praised Michels as a major figure in the realist school to which Mosca and Pareto had made vital contributions. He knew the work of all three of them and in the review traced their ideas about politics and history beyond Machiavelli and Guicciardini to the unsurpassed genius of Aristotle, the primal inspiration for his own ideas on these subjects. What he said about Michels could be repeated about him and any book of his: "He has told more truth than most of us can endure and his volume will prove to be stimulating to all students of democratic institutions."

Beard's reading of the Italian realists cannot be dated with precision, but *An Economic Interpretation of the Constitution of the United States* calls to mind their way of thinking about history. What had he said in that book, if not that elites had established the American Republic as a control system for the preservation of their interests? Put another way, it would have been most unusual if they had created a political order injurious to their interests. Acting as they did, the Founding Fathers had conformed to the eternal laws of politics and economics, as the Italian realists had said always happened in history. Beard's *The Rise of American Civilization* (1927) made the same case for the entire course of American history. His notorious anti-Roosevelt books of the 1930s and 1940s belonged to the same realistic and elite-focused approach that Beard habitually had taken in his work. In good European fashion, he doubted the sufficiency of mere rhetoric about ideals as a serious explanation of any important historical event, in peace or in war. Something more solid than words, particularly when they came from officialdom, had to be found as a basis for understanding the meaning of history. Actions and the real outcomes of wars and revolutions would be more reliable points of entry for the historian in analyzing the true meaning of the past.

My study of Italian history led me back to Beard for another reason as well. The presence of some fifty American military bases in Italy seventy years after the end of World War II and twenty-five years after the end of the Cold War renders palpable the actual relationship between the two countries. The bases had appeared to be necessary during the Cold War, when the Soviet Union and its Warsaw Pact allies, sworn enemies of democratic freedoms, stood in martial vigor on the other side of the Iron Curtain. The bases, however, survived in augmented form the collapse and disappearance of the Soviet Union. Their survival and the existence of eight hundred or more others ringing the globe raised the question of why they should remain at all, if the reason given for their construction had vanished. Evidently, some other motive explained the need for America's global presence. Italy's lot in the American empire was one of the factors that inspired my return to the study of United States history. It became impossible to understand Italy without accounting for the country's presence in the orbit of American military and economic power. The reality of life in Italy and Europe generally today stems from long-term consequences of the Marshall Plan and the North Atlantic Treaty Organization, both deemed by Beard at the time of their formulation as transparently imperialist initiatives designed to assemble a lineup of European vassal states under the direction of what in so many words American leaders even then characterized as the indispensable nation.

My book title, *Charles Austin Beard: The Return of the Master Historian of American Imperialism*, is misleading to the extent that he never has been away. In 2013, the centenary of the publication of *An Economic Interpretation of the Constitution of the United States*, many academic conferences were held to mark the occasion. I spoke at two of them, one at Oxford University and the other at the University of Virginia. People came from all over the world to have their say about Beard. Not everyone in attendance came to pay tribute to him. If these two conferences be any guide, his work continues to spark contentious debates. He still offends people. Indeed, at the Virginia conference I thought that the most enthusiastically applauded paper was one in which Beard was criticized for his failure to acknowledge the power and efficacy of American ideals. The Beardians at Virginia might have been outnumbered by the anti-Beardians, who were strongly represented at Oxford as well. Nevertheless, it is a rare historian whose work continues to receive this kind of international attention a century after its publication. *An Economic Interpretation* remains a classic work. If he had published nothing else, this book would be sufficient to secure for him enduring fame as one of the most influential American historians who ever lived. The books of his later years, however, all but destroyed his reputation. From that oblivion his work deserves to be rescued.

The book necessarily takes essay form. When Beard and his wife decided to burn all their papers, they severely restricted the scope of an archive-based systematic study of how they had lived and worked. They intended just such an outcome. Beard explained for his part that he did not want to be interpreted based on what he had for breakfast. Many of their letters do survive in scattered collections, but everyone who has written about the Beards recognizes the necessity of relying heavily on their published work. The documentation typically found in historical archives of necessity can shed only a limited amount of light in the case of the Beards. Limited light, however, means something different from no light. Wherever possible, archival sources form the basis of this book's interpretation of the origin and development of Beard's ideas and the signal role that he played as a scholar, critic, and activist in the defining historical events of his time.

Acknowledgments

It would require a long essay for me to thank adequately all the people who helped me to complete this book. The format imposed on me here by necessity calls for a degree of brevity that does not do justice to the assistance I received.

I can never repay the kindness and support that Walter LaFeber, Andrew H. and James S. Tisch Distinguished University Professor Emeritus at Cornell University, gave me at the outset of this project. He placed at my disposal his profound knowledge of Beard and read portions of the manuscript with an unerring instinct for its weaknesses and a generous appreciation for what I was trying to do. I am indebted to other historians as well for their critical comments: Woody Holton, Peter and Bonnie McCausland Professor of History at the University of South Carolina; Andrew Bacevich, Professor Emeritus of International Relations and History at Boston University; and the late Joyce Appleby, who for many years taught history at UCLA. They all read portions of the manuscript, saving me from numerous errors and misjudgments. Thanks go as well to Bill Kauffman, a political writer, who with great perceptiveness read the chapter on the America First Committee.

Many stimulating conversations with students and colleagues in the Department of History at the University of Montana deepened my understanding of imperialism and militarism. A graduate seminar on the American Empire that I taught in the spring of 2016 gave me the opportunity to review classic works of scholarly literature on these two themes. I also had the pleasure of teaching several courses at the Osher Lifelong Learning Institute (MOLLI) where several faculty members from across the campus participated. I benefited enormously from their comments and those of other members of my MOLLI courses. David Emmons, Professor Emeritus in the Department of History and my dear friend, was one such faculty member, and he also provided me with helpful reading suggestions.

Other scholars helped me to gain information that I needed or access to archival collections: Eric Foner, DeWitt Clinton Professor of History at Columbia University; David Vine, Associate Professor of Anthropology at

American University; William Robbins, Emeritus Distinguished Professor of History at Oregon State University; and David S. Brown, Professor of History at Elizabethtown College.

Librarians and archivists gave me unstinting assistance. From the Mansfield Library at my home institution, the University of Montana, I have special reason to thank the following individuals: Donna McCrea, Head of Archives and Special Collections who always heeded my calls for research assistance; Pamela Marek, Interlibrary Loan Specialist and Supervisor, who brought me the riches of countless libraries; and Glenn Kneebone, Manager of the Paw Print and indispensable provider of technical support. At Columbia University, Thai Jones and Tom McCutchon gave me a gracious welcome and expert guidance in the Rare Book and Manuscript Library. I wish to thank Sarah Hofstadter for giving me permission to quote from her father's papers, which are housed at Columbia. Professor Nina Howe, literary executor for the estate of Irving Howe, gave me permission to quote from a letter by her father to Richard Hofstadter. Bonnie B. Coles, Senior Searcher Examiner helped me to track down documents at the Library of Congress. Amanda M. Stow, Assistant Archivist at the University of Wyoming's American Heritage Center, aided me in navigating the Harry Elmer Barnes Papers. I received similar help for the Merle Curti Papers from the staff at the State Historical Society of Wisconsin in Madison, Wisconsin; for the Herbert Hoover Papers from Carol A. Leadenham, Assistant Archivist for Reference at the Hoover Institution Archives in Stanford, California; for the Herbert Hoover Papers from Matthew Schaefer, archivist, and Spencer Howard, archivist technician at the Herbert Hoover Presidential Library-Museum in West Branch, Iowa; for the William Appleman Williams Papers from Rachel Lilley, Public Services Archivist in the Special Collections Archives Research Center at Oregon State University in Corvallis, Oregon; for the Oswald Garrison Villard Papers from Susan Halpert, Reference Librarian in the Houghton Library at Harvard University in Cambridge, Massachusetts; for the Edwin Montefiore Borchard Papers from Claryn Spies, Public Services, Manuscripts and Archives at the Yale University Library in New Haven, Connecticut; and for Charles A. Beard documents and images from Wesley W. Wilson, Coordinator of Archives and Special Collections, DePauw University Archives in Greencastle, Indiana. I am grateful to Audrey Mullender, Principal of Ruskin College in Old Headington, Oxford, for access to the Ruskin College Archives and a tour of Beard's haunts during his Oxford University days. Raymond King, Learning Resources Manager at Ruskin College, aided me in finding many Beard documents and images. Mr. King also performed vital fact-checking services for me. In this same category of individuals who provided me with important research assistance are Jess Pernsteiner and Norman Stockwell, Office Manager and Publisher respectively of *The Progressive* magazine. For generously supplied instruction about the life and work of poet Robinson Jeffers, I am indebted to James Karman, Emeritus Professor of English and Religious Studies at California State University, Chico, and pillar of the Robinson Jeffers Association (RJA). Through Professor Karman's encouragement, I delivered a paper at the RJA conference on February 24, 2018, in Carmel, California: "Politics and History in the Poetry of Robinson Jeffers" in which I analyzed Beard's influence on him.

An article that I published in *Constitutional Commentary*, "Charles Beard and the English Historians" (vol. 29, no. 3, 2014), contains an argument that I make in this book. I wish to thank the editors for giving me permission to republish excerpts of that article.

By expressing interest and enthusiasm, senior editor Michael McGandy at Cornell University Press heartened me to think that I might have a project worth publishing. He expertly saw me through all the stages of the project's progress from manuscript to book. Meagan Dermody, Acquisitions Assistant, also provided editorial assistance. Carmen Torrado Gonzalez, Marketing Assistant, attended patiently to my questions about ways to arouse public interest in the fate of a long-dead historian. Kate Gibson, Production Editor at Westchester Publishing Services, vigilantly oversaw copyediting, which was expertly provided by Adriana Cloud. I am fortunate to have had the services of a seasoned indexer, David Prout, who brings a deep interest in history to his work. Two anonymous readers commissioned by the Press put me on my mettle to strengthen the manuscript. I hope that they will find the published book up to the professional standards laid out in their excellent reader reports.

I wish to acknowledge the funding support and friendship that I have received from the five University of Montana presidents I have worked for in my capacity over the past thirty-one years as the coordinator of the President's Lecture Series: James V. Koch, the late George M. Dennison, Royce Engstrom, Sheila Stearns, and Seth Bodnar. In return for my services as the lecture series coordinator, they have provided me with funding that facilitated my research, most recently for this book. Additional support in the form of release time from teaching has come from the anonymous donor who in April 2017 funded the Lucile Speer Research Chair in Politics and History and thought to put me forward as its inaugural holder.

For the completion of this book, I owe many personal debts. I only can mention a few of them here. Andrea Anderson, a devoted cousin, and Joel Brandzel of Alexandria, Virginia, generously gave me hospitality and a host of kindnesses on my research trips to Washington, D.C. My former student and now dear friend, Leland Buck, gave me the benefit of his vast knowledge of computers and repeatedly saved me from technical mishaps. My wife, Laure Pengelly Drake, combines skill as an editor with a love of history. Her imprint on this book is the greatest of all the personal debts that must be recorded here.

CHARLES AUSTIN BEARD

Introduction

The Beardian Interpretation of American History

The decline of Charles Austin Beard's professional reputation occurred with a sharpness remarkable for someone who had enjoyed an unparalleled popular and critical success in the history of American scholarly life. No American historian before Beard could match his sales record. His dozens of textbooks and monographs sold in the millions of copies. As a measure of the esteem in which scholars held him, he served as the president of the American Historical Association and the American Political Science Association, a rare double honor. For more than three decades, from the publication in 1913 of *An Economic Interpretation of the Constitution of the United States* to his death in 1948, Beard's work set the terms of the debates among American historians and informed popular understanding of the nation's past.

The 1,600-page *The Rise of American Civilization*, which he wrote with his wife, Mary Ritter Beard, ranks as one of the most amazing success stories in the history of publishing. It became a Book-of-the-Month Club selection and by 1954 had sold over 130,000 copies. Samuel Eliot Morison, one of Beard's harshest critics in the great controversies that enveloped him late in life, called it the most profound survey of its kind ever written. The book's astonishing appeal to the general reading public is difficult to fathom today. It is an intellectually rigorous text with a powerful thesis about the decisive role economics played in all the turning points in American history. Part of the explanation for its phenomenal sales can be attributed to Beard's immense prestige. With the publication of his seminal *An Economic Interpretation of the Constitution of the United States*, he redefined the field of American history. Others before Beard had written about the historical salience of economics, but none with his impact.

A generation of historians followed Beard's lead in search of the money trail snaking from the counting houses of the financial elites to Washington, D.C., where the power decisions were made about the nation's domestic policies and its wars. He did not always argue such points with a becoming subtlety and nuance. His initial characterization of the Founding Fathers as a group of landed and commercial elites concerned primarily about safeguarding their wealth with an anti-democratic political system underwent considerable modification in later writings he published. As he grew older, Beard wrote about these men with increasing respect, though he never abandoned his main contention in *An Economic Interpretation*, that human nature is so constituted as strongly to incline men toward a tender solicitude for their material well-being. He went to his grave firm in the conviction that the Constitution of the United States had come into being predominantly because of the normal economic motives associated with politics.

Beard's growth as a thinker is sometimes interpreted as his retreat from the economic interpretation of history; it should be seen instead as an organic advance toward greater understanding of how politics and economics interact with each other. Recognizing the state's capacity to act as an independent variable, he did not in his mature works oversimplify American politics by presenting the leaders in Washington as mere helpers running errands up and down Pennsylvania Avenue for their superiors on Wall Street. Nevertheless, he left no doubt regarding the existence of a complexly functioning economic and political power elite lording over the underlying masses. American democracy, to him, lay in the future, if it ever could be achieved against the oligarchy that always had ruled the country and ruled it still. For millions of readers in the 1930s, the decade of Beard's greatest influence, his work explained the Depression-era world in which they lived.

More than anything else, Beard's opposition to America's entry into the Second World War cost him his reputation. Even after Pearl Harbor, he continued to question what became known as the "good war," thus alienating much of the historical profession, as the comments about him in reviews and surviving correspondence show to an overwhelming degree. Conservatives by and large always had found him offensive over his seldom-resisted inclination to write skeptically about American idealism, which he thought by itself explained nothing significantly true and meaningful about the country's past. Marxists with a passable knowledge of *Das Kapital* would have seen from the first that Beard had nothing in common with them, except perhaps a shared loathing of what capitalism had become. Marxist solutions for the problems created by capitalism held no appeal for him, and he, in fact, opposed them. Progressive liberals had recognized Beard for what he was, as one of their own, and they had been with him as allies until he attacked the supreme icon of liberalism, President Franklin Delano Roosevelt. Beard's refusal to get right with American policy in the Second World War and his bitter condemnation of Roosevelt cost him his natural constituency. Thus, in the end Beard became isolated for failing to appreciate the gallantly led and high-souled integrity of the crusade against Nazi tyranny, which conservatives, liberals, and Marxists all agreed had been the real stake for the Allies in the Second World War.

The defection of the liberals injured Beard the most. Historians who had admired him and had looked to his writing as the master work of the profession began to turn away from him in bewilderment and then in anger. When he published vitriolic denunciations of Roosevelt for deceiving the American people about the real reasons for our intervention in the Second World War, he became something like an enemy of the people. In these books and articles, he argued that, as with all wars, the Second World War had to do fundamentally with economics and only at the level of marketing with high-sounding ideals and principles. Beard's thesis about the war infuriated the history profession by and large, although the reading public still bought his books. The kinetic energy of past achievements carried his reputation forward some ways, but the combined weight of conservative, liberal, and Marxist disapproval inevitably took its toll until, among most historians, Beardianism became a label for a bygone era in the writing of history. The University of Wisconsin history department, most famously in the work of William Appleman Williams, kept faith with Beard's economic interpretation of history, but did so as an exception to the rule of the research and the graduate work under way in most history departments by the 1950s and 1960s.

Beard died on September 1, 1948. In his last years, he commented about America's true motives in the Second World War and in the then-aborning Cold War. He viewed both conflicts with a complete absence of romantic nationalism about their causes and likely consequences. It seemed highly unlikely to him that something other than the old game was being played. American history had some exceptional features, but Beard did not think that we could get very far in understanding American history, especially the country's foreign policy and wars, by indulging in self-congratulatory illusions about how the country worked. It was bad enough for presidents to rhapsodize about America's exceptionally virtuous character, but for historians to do it seemed like a dereliction of duty that would be fatal for the country. The *histor* was supposedly the man who knew. If he did not tell the truth about the always-corrupting exercise of power, there could be no way to prevent the country from drifting into the senility that foreshadows the decline and fall of peoples, nations, and civilizations.

Although during his lifetime Beard would continue to have a strong following, in the 1930s he began to engage in what the post–World War II generation would view as transgressive behavior. Beard did not think that with those books he had changed anything basic in his approach to writing history. European thinkers during that decade indeed had added theoretical refinements to his repertoire. Although he acquired fluency in the language of advanced European theorizing about historiography, the core insight of Beardianism— the persistent success of economic elites in gaining the political ends that mattered most to them—ever remained at the center of his work. He had not changed at all on that point, except in the increasingly variegated way he wrote about it.

Beard's attacks on the war policies of FDR, however, produced so much shock and consternation that an impression gained currency about how a drastic change had taken place in his thought, caused either by mental deterioration or by the fanaticism of an anti-government vendetta said to be waged from what his critics often referred to as the pastoral torpor and isolation of his Connecticut dairy farm. That he lived in suburban comfort in New Milford some twenty miles from the farm others worked for him failed to inhibit the growth of legends about the failing powers of "Farmer Beard."

Beard remained extremely alert to the very end and steadfast in his convictions about how the American political and economic systems worked and for whose benefit. Amidst stacks of books, newspapers, and historical documents, he studied and wrote at home in his customary way, trying to furnish a realistic interpretation of the country's past and present. A lifetime spent in arduous study convinced him that competing imperialisms made the world what it was. At bottom, all wars had an economic driver, which invariably coexisted with subsidiary motives used ideologically by warring governments to ennoble the fighting, to make it appear as if war were the only way honor, safety, and the future of the race could be secured. Professing to make good the promise of a nation's philosophy is a time-honored and depressingly effective way for governments to prepare peoples for war, Beard lamented.

The Second World War seemed to Beard the best example yet produced by American history of how Washington beguiled the nation into fighting for empire. The assiduity with which he advanced such a contrarian thesis in the nationalist glow of America's wartime victory bore an inverse relationship to how the scholarly critics received it. Even *American Foreign Policy in the Making, 1932–1940: A Study in Responsibilities* (1946) and *President Roosevelt and the Coming of the War, 1941: A Study in Appearances and Realities* (1948), Beard's last two anti-FDR books, which like twin grave markers would come to overtop his reputation, sold well—some thirty thousand copies each by 1954. For university press publications, such sales figures stand out as a reminder of Beard's continuing power with a large public, no matter what critics said about him. He possessed iconic status with Depression-era readers as a ruggedly independent-minded thinker who could be counted on to unmask the antagonists of the people.

The mood of the country, however, had changed dramatically with the war. The Depression era gave way to the postwar era, a time of triumphalism. The onset of the American Century required a new perspective derived from a proper appreciation of America's exceptional qualities, as a nation shining the light of democracy and freedom on a world recovering from one form of totalitarianism and confronting another. Beard had no use for celebratory exercises. He found many achievements in America to celebrate, but not its wars, which required critical analysis, especially regarding the all-but-universally hailed good war. Beard begged to differ with the consensus regarding that war, and in so doing alienated the main body of the history profession. His books about the Second World War and its aftermath attracted less and less attention among scholars and soon achieved the status of conspiracy theory tracts. They nonetheless merit further consideration, in the light of their prophetic power.

The return of Charles Beard will not be welcomed in the manner of the Bible's prodigal son. Not everyone will be pleased to see him turn up again. With Beard the debate is not merely a matter of liberal progressives clashing with Marxists and conservatives, nor does it concern only the causes and character of the Second World War. Columbia University president Nicholas Murray Butler, with whom Beard often clashed, once lamented that he was a redhead inside and out. He meant by this remark that with Beard everything was a fight. He wrote as a fighter, too, contrasting his ideal vision of America as a workers' republic with the country's appalling inequities and its addiction to imperialism, which in presenting itself as an earth-liberation movement concealed what in truth it was: a supreme illustration of the ideological mystifications ever attendant upon the exercise of military and financial power. His critique of American imperialism penetrated to the heart of the country's value system. America always had been inclined toward violence and greed. The country exhibited from its infancy a large capacity for self-deception about its motives. Beard devoted the best part of his career to the cause of laying bare the country's soul, an inquiry for which he never has been forgiven.

Eugene Genovese, a Marxist critic who thought that Beard's refusal to accept a dialectical view of class conflict limited his overall effectiveness as an historian, nevertheless described him as an express train. This was one great historian's tribute to another. Beard had roared through the history profession as no one had before him. Recovering his legacy today matters in direct proportion to the extent of our concerns over the fulfillment of the predictions he made regarding the bankruptcy and dissolution that would befall the United States if it continued its vocation in the world as an imperialist oligarchy rather than becoming a democratic republic in accordance with its highest nature.

CHAPTER 1

Discovering the Economic Taproot of Imperialism

To the question of where Charles Beard discovered the economic interpretation of history, his wife, Mary Ritter Beard, offered some authoritative answers in her book about him, *The Making of Charles A. Beard*. Born in 1874 into a solidly Republican family, he started out in life with conservative views about politics. Following a rural boyhood near Knightstown, Indiana, and a turn at local journalism, he left in 1894 for nearby DePauw University. A teacher at the school, Colonel James Riley Weaver, sparked his interest in social critics. Beard began reading Henry George and other authors irreverent in their attitudes toward Republican orthodoxies. A veteran of the Civil War and a man of substantial international background with postings in the American consulates in Brindisi, Antwerp, and Vienna, Weaver introduced the young student to the world of European culture and thought.[1] Mary emphasized the importance in Beard's political formation of a Weaver course he took on practical sociology, which required him to spend time at Jane Addams's Hull House in Chicago. Ravaged by the depression of the 1890s, the city shocked him with its extremes of poverty and luxury. The contrast between the rich and the poor, she observed, "made a deep and lasting imprint on his mind and influenced his future activities."[2]

Only after going to Oxford as a graduate student in 1898, however, did Beard acquire a historical understanding of the economic forces that shaped politics and culture. His father, a wealthy farmer and businessman, provided financial support for his son's education in England. Although the young man would not sit for a single examination at Oxford, the approximately three years that he spent in England proved to be decisive in his intellectual formation. With high enthusiasm Beard arrived in Oxford late in the summer of 1898. About his preparation for graduate work he declared: "My ignorance was, as American movie magnates might say, 'colossal,' but my enthusiasm was high."[3] He had resolved to make his way as a scholar of English constitutional and political history.

Although Beard met many outstanding scholars at Oxford, the author who influenced him the most was the art historian and social critic John Ruskin, formerly an Oxford professor but by then retired and in his dotage. According to Mary, Ruskin gave her husband his first real understanding of how the world worked and in whose interests. She wrote, "Beard regarded Ruskin's philosophy as set forth in his small book, *Unto This Last*, as the acme of wisdom and usually had it in his hand or pocket as a bracer."[4] He had read the book while still in college, but his life experiences in England fully brought home its lessons to him. As Beardianism begins in Ruskinism, it becomes necessary here to examine this singularly influential book in his young life.

Originally published in 1862, *Unto This Last* took its place in a long line of anti-modernist British preachments dating back to Oliver Goldsmith's "The Deserted Village," including William Wordsworth's preface to *Lyrical Ballads*, Thomas Carlyle's *Past and Present*, and Charles Dickens's *Hard Times*. To this imposing body of work, Ruskin brought distinctive rhetorical gifts and the acclaimed insights of the most erudite and influential art historian of the age. He thought that a disastrous confusion afflicted the modern world, where genuine art and even basic decency could lead only a fugitive existence. In a prefatory essay to the book, titled "Political Economy of Art," he considered the questions of how artists are produced and maintained for the lasting advantage of society and civilization. Ruskin lamented that modern men had forgotten what their medieval forebears had understood fully in providing for the education, training, and advancement of creative talent, with the result that Gothic civilization could boast the spires of a hundred magnificent cathedrals throughout Europe, whereas "I am sorry to say, the great tendency of this age is to expend its genius in perishable art." Ruskin thought, as Wordsworth had before him, that modern literature also proclaimed the vulgarity and stupidity of contemporary man. The books of the present day showed that "the world is, generally speaking, in calamitous disorder."[5]

Unto This Last proper consists of four essays that Ruskin originally published as articles in William Thackeray's *Cornhill Magazine* in 1860. He recalled how they "were reprobated in a violent manner." In these essays he had undertaken to give, "as I believe for the first time in plain English . . . a logical definition of WEALTH." In the first of the essays, "The Roots of Honour," he criticized modern political economy for its neglect of moral criteria in determining the wealth of society. All that modern economists concerned themselves with was the creation and sale of goods and services, as if justice and the well-being of society had nothing to do with the economy. Ruskin called such an approach to economics "this negation of a soul."[6]

In "The Veins of Wealth," Ruskin ruled out socialism as a solution for the problems of industrial society. He saw nothing wrong with wealth in and of itself: "Any given accumulation of commercial wealth may be indicative, on the one hand, of faithful industries, progressive energies, and productive ingenuities; or, on the other, it may be indicative of mortal luxury, merciless tyranny, ruinous chicane." Wealth could not be separated from the moral character of the ways in which it had been acquired. Commercial dealings had to be just and faithful. Indeed, every economic question "merged itself ultimately in the great question of justice." The actual wealth of society had to do fundamentally with the number of "full-breathed, bright-eyed, and happy-hearted human creatures" in it. Ruskin thought that contemporary ideas about wealth excluded human values, with disastrous results for society. Surveying the scene around him, he found the English population generally to be sunk in "a dim-eyed and narrow-chested state of being."[7]

The third essay, "Qui Judicatis Terram," concerned the relationship between the rich and the poor. They had a perpetual bond in history, and in a good society both sides would act from a sense of charity, love, and justice. The Latin aphorism inspiring the title of this essay read "Diligite Justiam Qui Judicatis Terram," which he translated as "Ye who judge the earth give (not, observe, merely love, but) diligent love to justice." This passion for justice defined righteousness. Ruskin stands at an infinite remove from Marx, who claimed that class conflict drove the historical process. Ruskin, however, preached a message of class harmony, with the workers and the owners striving together to bring society ever closer toward "the sun of justice." He wanted nothing to do with the socialists. As he would write in the final essay of the book, not socialism but Christianity offers man safe passage out of the quagmire in which he now finds himself, bereft and friendless: "until the time come, and the kingdom, when Christ's gift of bread and bequest of peace shall be Unto this last as unto thee." The central meaning of his writings, "if there be any one point insisted on throughout my works more frequently than another, that one point is the impossibility of Equality." He took the eternal superiority of some individuals to be a given in history. They are the leaders and should lead, "on occasion even to compel and subdue their inferiors, according to their own better knowledge and wiser will."[8] Anarchy, the greatest evil imaginable to Ruskin, loomed as the only alternative to the time-honored hierarchical arrangement in human affairs.

In the last essay, "Ad Valorem," he attacked the leading economists of the day, especially John Stuart Mill and David Ricardo, for their intellectual justifications of the economic practices and institutions that had laid waste to the earth and most of its inhabitants. On the principle that the economy should have as its only aim the creation of meaningful work for every able-bodied member of society, he condemned economic liberalism as a monstrous system of exploitation from which only the investors stood to gain. Economics should be the science of life enhancement for humanity, or "that which teaches nations to desire and labour for the things that lead to life; and which teaches them to scorn and destroy the things that lead to destruction." A true political economy should be instructive about the differences between vanity and substance "and how the service of Death, the Lord of Waste, and of eternal emptiness, differs from the service of Wisdom, the Lady of Saving, and of eternal fullness." Wealth, in short, is "the possession of the valuable by the valiant," and not at all a row of dividend numbers on the stock-and-bond statements of financial elites whose valor, Ruskin thought, could not be guaranteed, given the greed and obscene consumption habits that generally marked them as a class. Things not only should be consumed, but consumed nobly and serviceably, in a way that made the welfare of all "the end and aim of consumption." The distilled essence of Ruskinism, "There is no wealth but life," became the mantra of young Beard and his circle of friends at Oxford.[9]

Beard found in Ruskin's book not only a compelling interpretation of modern social problems, but also a call to action. With another American who also admired Ruskin, Walter Vrooman, he founded Ruskin Hall as a college of the people, a workmen's university. In so doing, they followed the example of Ruskin himself, who had taught in the Working Men's College founded by Christian Socialists in 1854 and had worked assiduously to establish schools that would promote his educational principles. Vrooman had come to study philosophy at Oxford, but, like Beard, became distracted by the Ruskin Hall project and did not get very far with his formal studies. Vrooman's wife Amne, a Baltimore heiress, provided funding for the college.[10] The historian Harold Pollen wrote: "The idea was to educate workingmen in order to achieve social change."[11] The incorporation agreement stated that Ruskin Hall would provide for instruction in science, history, modern languages, "and generally in the duties of a citizen, and in practical industrial work, and for the delivery of lectures to them and others upon such subjects," but not "for the purpose of teaching the Latin, Greek, or Hebrew languages, metaphysics, theology, or party politics."[12] A memorandum from the Executive Committee read, "Ruskin College is required to be absolutely neutral in all matters of theology and party politics."[13] The insistence on political neutrality would have no practical effect at the historically left-wing school.[14]

In an article that Beard wrote in 1936 for the *New Republic*, he explained how Ruskin Hall, which in 1907 formally would become Ruskin College, acquired its name. The organizational meeting had taken place in a little room in Beard's lodgings at 11 Grove Street. Referring to himself, Beard wrote, "An American 'from the wilds of Indiana' who had read Ruskin in the library of 'a freshwater college' proposed that the new institution be called 'Ruskin Hall.'"[15] The debate that ensued among the founders involved a discussion of *Unto This Last*: "That was the book that furnished a frame of reference for the students who started Ruskin College."[16] Other books also had influenced them, most notably by John Stuart Mill, Herbert Spencer, Alfred Marshall, and Karl Marx, "but 'Unto This Last' served to give unity and purpose to their enterprise. Despite all the wrangling battles and deviations, Ruskin's teachings furnished a kind of anchor against storms, in the early days of the labor college."[17]

After the formal opening of Ruskin College on February 22, 1899, Beard continued to be engaged actively with the school, serving as its secretary, recruiting students as well as full-time and part-time teachers for the faculty, and winning the support of prominent union leaders. He also created Ruskin Hall correspondence courses for students. Beard had not yet made a definite career choice between university scholarship and social activism. He sought to do both. Amidst a whirl of Ruskin Hall–related activities, by the end of his first year at Oxford he managed to write a 50,000-word draft on the evolution of the office of the justice of the peace in England. Returning then to America with a hazy plan to spread the Ruskin Hall idea there, he continued to follow a dual career path. He spent a term doing graduate work at Cornell University with Moses Coit Tyler, the eminent historian of American literature, while still being deeply committed to the cause of worker education.[18] In a vain effort to keep Beard, Tyler offered him a fellowship and then lamented, "It is with extreme regret that I now yield him up to the superior claims and attractions of the mission which calls him to educational work in the United Kingdom."[19]

Beard decided at the end of 1899 to resume his life in England, but not before making Mary his wife. Following their wedding, Charles and Mary settled in Manchester, which as the center of England's textile boom had become the greatest industrial city in the world. There he headed the extension department of Ruskin Hall. He also taught various courses of his own and gave many public lectures. Their daughter, Miriam, was born in that city two years later. Beard continued to study the British trade union movement and explored the Black Country—the industrial districts around Birmingham, which were named for the soot of the heavy industries that covered the area.[20] He felt revolted by the squalor and the waste of these places. His wife recalled this period of their lives as an endless round of political and educational activity, with Beard addressing workers' assemblies and rallies of the English wholesale cooperative movement. The young couple moved in a wide circle of radical intellectuals and activists that included Prince Peter Kropotkin, Keir Hardie, and Emmeline Pankhurst, whose feminist ideas appealed to them both.

Beard's continued affiliation with Ruskin Hall included the writing that he did for *Young Oxford: A Monthly Magazine Devoted to the Ruskin Hall Movement*, which published its first issue in October 1899. When Ruskin died the following year, the magazine celebrated his legacy. Above all, he had striven "to implant in men's minds a love for the beautiful—so conspicuously wanting in our towns and cities." No one more eloquently than Ruskin had exposed the blighting effects of the modern industrial order and its terrible failure to produce a civilized society. The *Young Oxford* tribute to Ruskin quoted from his critique of modern industrial cities as "mere crowded masses of store, warehouse, and counter . . . in which the object of man is not life but labour . . . and the streets not the avenues for the passing and procession of a happy people but the drains for the discharge of a tormented mob, in which the only object in reaching any spot is to be transferred to another." Ruskin Hall had been founded to perpetuate this great man's "There is no wealth but life" legacy.[21]

From its beginnings in October 1899, *Young Oxford* published many Beard articles, signed and unsigned. Writing in the 1970s, his daughter, Miriam, thought that all the many "Hotspur" articles in the magazine were written by him: "they sound so much like father and seem very American."[22] Restricting our examination only to those articles that he signed with his real name, we discover images that later would be seen to be both characteristically Beardian and extremely uncharacteristic of him. From this early date in his career, Beard identified, as he always would, with the workers. For example, in the magazine's maiden issue he likened their current condition to that of the serfs and slaves of the past: "It was habit that bound the toiling serf to the soil through the ages past; it was habit that kept the negroes from generation to generation beneath the slave owners' lash; and it is habit which chains the workers of today to slavery under the greatest of all tyrants—ignorance."[23]

On the question of imperialism, though, the Beard of *Young Oxford* interpreted the "white man's burden" essentially the way Ruskin did, giving no hint of his anti-imperialist views of the future. In "A Living Empire," which appeared in October 1901, he claimed that the history of the entire world for the past three hundred years, and most of all American history, was the result of imperialism. What did people think had been played out in America from the founding of the colonies on the Atlantic seaboard to the conquest of the West and the eradication of the frontier, if not, in its most thoroughgoing form, the dialectic of imperialism? The historical process in America involved the conquest and occupation of the land by white settlers at the expense of Indians, who suffered displacement where they were not annihilated. Beard, however, viewed American imperialism favorably: "the imperialism which produced the United States is good." Americans, bad as they might be, are better than the Comanches. Thus, "the ultimate result has been relatively good."[24]

Indeed, race, not class, mattered most to Beard at this time. He faulted contemporary American imperialism abroad precisely over the failure of Washington to consider the impact of its policies on white people: "Americans, sending at an enormous expense 600 teachers equipped to the Philippines to instruct naked natives while thousands of white children in American cities are underfed and undereducated, are not brute imperialists but self-destructive lunatics." From Beard's perspective, "an imperial victory will not be planting a flag over a collection of negro huts, or the organization of cannibals for commercial exploitation, but the planting of a new colony of rationally organized white men." To be sure, wasteful, parasite-ridden, and immoral empires were as bad as the anti-imperialists said they were, but for Beard "organized, healthy, sober, industrious, flesh and blood empires withstand the wreck of nations and the chaos of revolutions."[25] The British Empire seemed to him yet another relatively good historical outcome.

In a second installment of "A Living Empire," published in the same issue of *Young Oxford*, Beard explained further what he meant in stressing the connection between race and imperialism: "A truly imperial people cannot be reared under the economic conditions which prevail in western civilization today." Empires required morally, mentally, and physically fit rulers. He had extreme measures in mind for the accomplishment of this requirement: "Parasites, wasters, luxury consumers, idle rich, gamblers, and all enemies of man must be ruthlessly eliminated." Racism he could not condone, but then he professed two bewildering principles to show his aversion to it. First, "the only sane attitude which statesmen can adopt toward other races is that of non-mixture." The second principle he italicized for emphasis: "*Some life shall be repressed.* Which shall it be?"[26] Drawing upon the lessons of the boyhood that he spent in an Indiana farming community, he queried that if we do not leave cattle breeding to chance, why would we fail to take similar care with the breeding of children? Imperialism itself could not be condemned on principle, but racially heedless imperialist policies would harm the white race, he feared.

Meanwhile, Beard already had published his first book, *The Industrial Revolution*. Arthur W. Macmahon, a former student at Columbia who would become a law professor there, in 1950 called *The Industrial Revolution* Beard's "first and almost forgotten book."[27] It was published in England in January 1901. Priced at a shilling, the book was intended as a primer for the adult education and labor cooperative movements. The book included a preface by Frederick York Powell, Regius Professor of Medieval and Modern History at Oxford and Beard's tutor there. He shared and reinforced Beard's commitment to Ruskin's ideas. In an in memoriam tribute to Ruskin, Powell celebrated him as a prophetic social and cultural critic who had mounted a campaign of heroic opposition to "all the meaningless, deceptive buzzing of the ephemerals." He had been everlastingly right to say, "the people who possesses the greatest number of healthy, honourable, cheerful, and wise men and women is, and must be, the greatest nation on earth."[28] Although the intellectually idiosyncratic Powell, who had steeped himself in the literature of Iceland and a plethora of other arcane subjects, did not generally find favor with students as a lecturer and published nothing of scholarly distinction, as a true believer in the Ruskinian creed, he had Beard's full attention.[29]

Of all the professors Beard might have had as Oxford mentors, the eclectic and restless Powell would have been the most understanding of his indisposition at this time for regular and disciplined study. He turned Beard loose to find his own way. The two men developed a close relationship, attested on Beard's side by his choice of Powell to write the preface for *The Industrial Revolution*, and on Powell's side by his description of Beard as "the nicest American I ever knew."[30] In the manner of Ruskin, Powell generally detested Americans as a crass and ignorant people who all by themselves had demonstrated the falsity of democratic theory. The country itself seemed to him a gigantic mistake. A timely hanging of George Washington, he thought, might have spared the world some of its biggest headaches and disappointments. Jefferson he dismissed as a French revolutionary with a southern drawl. It is not as if the country, for Powell, were a total loss. He admired John Brown, Abraham Lincoln, Walt Whitman, and Charles Beard. The Ruskin bond no doubt constituted the major element of Powell's approval in this last case.

Powell, at Beard's request, served as the presiding officer at the inaugural meeting of Ruskin Hall on February 22, 1899. He would die of heart disease in 1904 at age fifty-four, but right to the end he maintained an undiminished interest in the school. Shortly before his death, he would write to a friend, "Ruskin Hall is doing a deal of good. I know its work. The big Trades Unions are making levies and sending their best men up to it for education."[31] His biographer recounted how he threw himself into the cause of Ruskin Hall "as something of an antidote to the worst Oxford tendencies" of snobbery and dilettantism, which in 1895 had found immortal literary expression in Thomas Hardy's *Jude the Obscure*.[32] The novel recounts the tragic story of working-class Jude Fawley's attempt to become a student at Christminster, Hardy's alias for Oxford. For such an aspiration in Victorian England, Jude has the wrong parents, the wrong clothes, and the wrong accent. He also has too passionate and generous a nature, for a man without advantages "should be as cold-blooded as a fish and as selfish as a pig to have a really good chance of being one of the country's worthies." Despite his genuine love of learning and relentless efforts to acquire it, he cannot overcome the obstacles of class in his path. The novel ends in Jude's total defeat and death.

The very Oxford tendencies to which Powell alluded became a central theme in *Jude the Obscure*. Hardy lampooned the Christminster curriculum as little more than a pedagogical exercise in social distancing, designed to furnish the master class with an outward show of cultural superiority. He made it clear that Jude's reverence for Christminster was misplaced. The character of Sue Bridehead, the great love of Jude's life, expressed Hardy's views of the higher learning in Britain. Referring to Jude, she said: "He still thinks it is a great centre of high and fearless thought, instead of what it is, a nest of commonplace schoolmasters whose characteristic is timid obsequiousness to tradition." Even Jude eventually recognized that despite his love for the school, "I know how it hates all men like me." In a 1912 postscript to the novel, Hardy took appreciative notice of Ruskin College, repeating the comment of some readers: "It should have been called the College of Jude the Obscure."[33]

In a May 1, 1899 letter to Beard, playwright George Bernard Shaw had made a Hardy-like argument about the futility of the idea animating Ruskin College. Beard had invited him to give a lecture at the school, but he could not understand why any workman would want to attend Oxford University. An Oxford degree might have a certain commercial and social value for the middle and upper classes, but not the working class. "A workman," Shaw insisted, "ought to have a vulgar prejudice against Oxford. If he goes there, he is likely to be cured of the vulgar prejudice without being taught the enlightened prejudice which led William Morris—an Oxonian likely to be much quoted at Ruskin Hall—to declare that the only money he had ever wasted was the fee he paid for his M.A. degree."[34] Anything that a workman could learn at Oxford could be learned anywhere else, "except the social tone, which will be as detrimental to him as a workman as it is useful to a gentleman." University training of the kind described by Beard in his letter to Shaw would transform the workman into a schoolman. Shaw thought that such a transformation would be deplorable and judged Ruskin Hall to have no chance for long-term success: "Whilst I take this view of the enterprise it is obviously inexpedient that I should accept your invitation to lecture."[35]

In the preface to *The Industrial Revolution*, Powell expressed thanks to "my friend Mr. Beard" for giving him the opportunity to address the working-class readers of this book, "to say here some things to them I have wished to say for some time."[36] Powell, a friend of William Morris whose *News from Nowhere* (1890) took its esthetic principles from *Unto This Last*, echoed Ruskin: "The end of work is to produce useful things, beautiful things, necessary things."[37] As Beard showed in his little book, Powell continued, the Industrial Revolution had resulted in a society almost entirely destitute of Ruskin's esthetic and utilitarian criteria. He had feared that Beard would not like the preface. On January 12, 1901, Powell wrote to him regarding concerns over the bluntness of the warnings in the preface about how democracy might not survive if the people happily adjusted to the level of bovine contentment and stupidity to which their cultural and political leaders had brought them. Powell dreaded preaching, he told Beard, "but this is a time in this country when plain speaking has become a duty one dare not shun at any risk."[38] Powell need not have worried. The preface conformed exactly to Beard's Ruskin-conditioned sentiments about the social and cultural consequences of the Industrial Revolution.

Beard made modest claims for his maiden book. At scarcely one hundred pages, it was only meant "to supply a concise and inexpensive outline of the Industrial Revolution as a guide to students seeking for the first time the historical basis of modern social and economic problems." In his general survey of the Industrial Revolution in England, he assailed the evils of waste and exploitation in the capitalist system, but in the language of *Unto This Last*, certainly not from a Marxist perspective. To make his concluding points about the esthetic and moral failures of a money-obsessed modern English society, he quoted Ruskin: "To be valuable is to avail towards life. A truly valuable thing is that which leads to life with its whole strength. In proportion as it does not lead to life or as its strength is broken, it is less valuable; as it leads away from life, it is invaluable or malignant."[39] He included *Unto This Last* in the short bibliography at the end of his book.

For practical use by a young historian, Ruskin's message had required translation into the idiom of historical scholarship. For this second stage of Beard's intellectual development, his stay in England also figured decisively. He had come to Oxford to study constitutional history with William Stubbs, but this plan had not materialized. Instead, Beard became absorbed in the activities that led to the founding of Ruskin Hall, his researches in the Black Country, and the writing of his first book. Although Beard did not take a degree at Oxford, he did an enormous amount of historical research and reading during this period of his life. Returning to the United States in 1902 because "we 'belonged' at home," he entered the graduate program at Columbia University and took a degree in 1904 with a dissertation begun under Powell on "The Office of the Justice of the Peace in England."[40] Columbia University Press published the dissertation that same year. The research that he had compiled at Oxford as a very part-time graduate student paid off in the end.

The choice of such an anomalously narrow dissertation topic, given Beard's later wide-ranging research and theoretical interests in European and American history, reveals the impact on him at this time of the Oxford School of historians. Led by Bishop Stubbs and Edward Augustus Freeman, who considered history to be the scientific study of political institutions and practices, the Oxford School also included Powell as a distinctly minor and maverick personage.[41] From these figures, Beard would have gained no deep insight into the economic dimension of history and certainly no methodology for writing about it as the force that ultimately controls politics. Beard's social activism, which had thrown him into the company of radicals and socialists in Manchester, made the discipline of history seem to him a thing apart from the actual world of the moment. He was then leading two lives, as a scholar and a reformer. History as practiced at Oxford University did not offer him a way to unify his existence.

Beard evidently had left England just in time before some perhaps irreversible changes to his personality and character. His daughter, Miriam, recalled the reaction of a boyhood friend upon seeing Beard newly returned from England. She remembered that the friend had written in a letter how "Beard came back from England wearing 'British tweeds' and talking in an affected accent, all this making him impossible at home." She also pointed out how both her father and mother "sounded quite 'socialistic' to their old friends, who were shocked." Their perceived socialism had serious practical consequences for Beard, according to his daughter. Because of his radical associations in England, "he could not get a position in the mid-west where he wanted to be, and was forced to come to Columbia University, which at first he did not like." She added, "The Ruskin Hall movement decided his life in this country to that extent."[42]

In the year that Beard arrived at Columbia, Edwin R. A. Seligman published his *Economic Interpretation of History*. A professor of political economics at Columbia, Seligman claimed in his book, "The existence of man depends upon his ability to sustain himself; the economic life is therefore the fundamental condition of all life." Acknowledging Marx's brilliance, originality, and importance, he nevertheless found Marxism fatally lacking in scientific rigor because of its philosophical exoticisms and melodramatic political agenda: "Socialism is a theory of what ought to be; historical materialism is a theory of what has been." In opposition to Marx, Seligman thought that without confirming evidence the historical process could never be predicted with scientific exactitude and, in any case, socialism could not be guaranteed, in the Marxist manner, as a superior way of life. In other words, historical materialism and Marxism needed to be separated and seen as distinct philosophies of history. Both upheld the economic interpretation of history, but "Marx's own version of it is exaggerated, if not misleading."[43]

Beard immediately fell under the spell of Seligman's ideas. He and Seligman also held the same progressive political views, which in no way could be confused with Marxism. It is worth noting for what can be deduced about Beard's politics at this time that the radical economist and controversialist Scott Nearing would judge Seligman to be "the shrewdest defender of capitalism with whom I had an opportunity to debate."[44] Other members of the Columbia faculty, most notably political scientist Frank Johnson Goodnow and historian James Harvey Robinson, also promoted Beard as a coming young scholar. The year that Beard took his PhD, he became a lecturer at Columbia, under the supervision of Robinson, with whom he later would collaborate on the publication of European history textbooks. For an understanding of the historical process, however, Seligman exerted a vastly greater influence on Beard than did either Goodnow or Robinson. In her biography of Beard, Ellen Nore stated that he never ventured theoretically beyond Seligman.[45] It would be more accurate, however, to say that Seligman added some important theoretical refinements to Beard's conception of history. Before Seligman, English historians not to be found among the professors of the Oxford School, already had marked the intellectual path that Beard would follow.

In his second American book publication, *An Introduction to the English Historians* (1906), Beard identified himself in the prefatory note as "a teacher of English history."[46] He had envisaged the book as an anthology of readings for each of which a brief essay of his own would serve as an introduction. It is a book of well over six hundred pages consisting of works by the scholarly authorities of England he most admired. He took a topical approach in chronological order, beginning with the Anglo-Saxon conquest down to the Empire in the nineteenth century. Beard indicated in the preface that he also felt intellectually obliged to several teachers of English history, presumably Powell most of all, but, owing to the "experimental character" of the book, he forbore from naming any of them.

Beard's selections constituted for the most part a standard list of great English historians: Frederic William Maitland, William Stubbs, Edward Augustus Freeman, George Macauley Trevelyan, and names of similar scholarly prestige. Maitland, especially, long retained his place in Beard's pantheon of historians. His name appeared as an august authority in many of Beard's books, including *An Economic Interpretation of the Constitution of the United States*, *Economic Origins of Jeffersonian Democracy*, and *The Rise of American Civilization*.

Beard's introductory essays, by and large, consisted of no more than a paragraph or two. For part IV, "The Tudor Age," he supplied unusually long extracts from economic historian Frederic Seebohm's 1867 book *The Oxford Reformers*, including the famous observation by Sir Thomas More: "Thus, after careful reflection, it seems to me, as I hope for mercy, that our modern republics are nothing but a conspiracy of the rich, pursuing their own selfish interests under the name of a republic."[47] More's withering judgment of government, as an intrigue of the rich against the poor, pointed in the direction that Beard would take in his own writing. As Eugene Genovese astutely observed, Beard thought that history turned on "the parasitism and greed of specific economic interests rather than the class exigencies of capitalism as a whole."[48] Such interests strongly tended to have a collusive relationship with government, which they effectively controlled for the purpose of devising policies both domestic and foreign. Beard from very early in his life had the idea that throughout history all elites and all governments, whatever their professed ideology, behaved essentially in the same way: they ultimately controlled the levers of power against disorganized majorities. Revolutions could create momentary exceptions, but time generally restored the rule.

Of all the English historians in the Beard anthology, John Atkinson Hobson influenced his intellectual biography the most. While living in Manchester, Beard had met Hobson. His daughter, Miriam, identified Hobson, along with the socialist Charles Rowley, as two of the most important individuals to cross Beard's path at this time.[49] Hobson and Rowley would have been particularly interesting to Beard because of their immense admiration for many of Ruskin's ideas. Indeed, in 1898 Hobson had written *John Ruskin, Social Reformer*, which had received an enthusiastic notice in *Young Oxford*.[50] Beard certainly read this book, and, based on his subsequent view of Ruskin, he read it very closely.

Hobson began by explaining why the most successful art historian in the world had decided to become a social critic. *Modern Painters* (5 vols., 1843–1860), the first volume of which he published at age twenty-three, made him famous throughout the world. *The Seven Lamps of Architecture* (1849) and *The Stones of Venice* (3 vols., 1851–1853) added to his fame. He ardently supported the Pre-Raphaelite artists, who in turn found in his books the ideas that animated and justified their mid-nineteenth-century movement. In all his work as an art historian and critic, he held that art without morality and a concern for truth had no value whatsoever. Any artistic movement boasting as its chief or sole accomplishment an innovation in technique incited his disdain. Summing up Ruskin's esthetic philosophy, Hobson had him standing for the principle that "art is the representation of true and worthy ideas seen in nature by the penetrative and constructive power of imagination." Ultimately, great art can arise only from the love of God—hence Ruskin's trademark glorification of Giotto and other medieval painters over the later Renaissance art, spawned by, in his words, "a state of concealed national infidelity and of domestic corruption."[51] The technical sophistication of Raphael and the other Renaissance masters could not compensate for the loss of a pristine faith. With the notable exceptions of the British Romantic landscape painter Joseph Turner and a few others, Western art had been in decline ever since. Convinced that the modern industrial order posed the greatest threat of all time to human creativity and intelligence, Ruskin turned his attention in the 1850s increasingly to social criticism.

With Hobson's celebration of Ruskin's genius as a social critic, Beard certainly would have been in complete agreement. "Mr. Ruskin will rank as the greatest social teacher of his age," Hobson insisted, for he had done more than anyone else to bring before the public the social problems created by modern capitalism.[52] Hobson echoed the consensus about Ruskin's literary genius, but added the much less widely shared view that he also deserved to be regarded as a better economist than most of the academically trained professionals who generally ridiculed him. In his memoirs, *Confessions of an Economic Heretic*, Hobson identified Ruskin as the prime mover of his education in economics: "From him I drew the basic thought for my subsequent economic writings, viz, the necessity of going behind the current monetary estimates of wealth, cost, and utility, to reach the body of human benefits and satisfactions which gave them real meaning."[53] An outsider himself as an economist in the tradition of the mid-nineteenth-century radical Richard Cobden, Hobson faulted the economics profession for its protective devotion to a capitalist system said by its proponents to be free, but in fact under constant manipulation by economic elites.[54] Throughout his long career, Hobson would seek to expose the capitalist status quo as the paramount hindrance to a genuinely democratic society.[55]

Ruskin, too, had thought of most economists as spokesmen on retainer for the controlling interests. Amidst their disputes over this or that policy, the real job of the economists consisted of their solemn responsibility to maintain the fiction that no other system but the one happily in place for the rich ever could be devised. Ruskin could not imagine a worse system than free market capitalism. It had replaced the aristocracy of the Old Regime with an economic aristocracy whose wealth and power over the lives of ordinary people made the elites of medieval Europe look like a collective apostolate devoted to social democracy. Hobson agreed and then added that to bring about a modern democratic industrial order, the free market nurturing system for millionaires and billionaires would have to be overturned in favor of a societal commitment to the general good. Without economic democracy, political democracy would always be controlled and deformed by the chief funders of the parties installed to run the machinery of government and to formulate its domestic and foreign policies.

Ruskin manifestly had not derived his insights about capitalism from the radical tradition that had inspired Hobson. From whence did he derive them? Hobson placed him in a direct line of intellectual descent from Thomas Carlyle, along with Edmund Burke one of the iconic figures in the history of cultural conservatism. Ruskin felt "a passionate storm of sympathy" for Carlyle and particularly for his 1843 book, *Past and Present*.[56] *Unto This Last* took its bearings from Carlyle's fierce polemic against the modern world. The same must be said, if at the one remove provided by Ruskin's pen, of the young Charles Beard's earliest writings.

No less enamored of *Past and Present* was Friedrich Engels, then working on *The Condition of the Working Class in England*, a foundational book in left-wing social criticism that appeared in 1845. Carlyle's true-to-life portrayal of English misery under capitalism moved Engels, and he recommended the book to his future collaborator Karl Marx. Engels praised Carlyle for understanding the economic root of the ruinous living and working conditions that oppressed the English proletariat. Carlyle thundered against the uneven distribution of the nation's wealth: "There is idle luxury alternating with mean scarcity and inability." Marx would have found himself in agreement with Carlyle's contention that the wealth of modern capitalist society results in alienation for everybody, rich and poor. In the *Economic and Philosophic Manuscripts of 1844*, which would not be published until the 1930s, Marx was formulating his ideas about alienation under capitalism. He also would have agreed with Carlyle's depiction of the workers "in utmost paroxysm of desperate protest against their lot."[57]

The workers, of course, suffered the most, but under capitalism, Carlyle and Marx both believed, society generally had fallen victim to the businessmen and their financiers. In a world where the cash nexus determined everything in the lives of men and women, culture began to take on unnatural and even grotesque characteristics. Dupes, flunkies, and quacks would abound in such a time and place. A conservative and a communist might agree on some of the problems created by capitalism, but not on the solutions for them. For

Carlyle—and for Ruskin—only a return to God, to a faith of medieval intensity, could save the world from the approaching nihilism, whereas for the atheist Marx the workingmen of the world under the leadership of the Communist Party would do the saving.

In a line that addressed Ruskin's deepest concerns, Carlyle identified appalling ignorance as one of the chief characteristics of modern industrial society. People did not know anything of genuine importance anymore and, therefore, were unable to produce true art or beauty of any kind. The modern world, chaotic and formless, would "perish in frantic suicidal dissolution." Nothing, least of all efficacious institutional reform, could be expected from the by now totally immoral political system, which had degenerated into a tragic farce of "irremediable bribery." The physical world itself had come under a pitiless assault from the mammon worshippers. Carlyle raged against "the dark poison lanes" that disfigured the natural landscape of England, all in the name of profits.[58] Ruskin would elaborate on all of Carlyle's criticisms, in *Unto This Last* and the great canonical works that followed: *Sesame and Lilies* (1865), *Fors Clavigera: Letters to the Workmen and Labourers of Great Britain* (1871–1884), *Munera Pulveris: Six Essays on the Elements of Political Economy* (1872), and *The Storm Cloud of the Nineteenth Century* (1884).

For the intellectual formation of Charles Beard, Hobson's two greatest achievements in *John Ruskin, Social Reformer* concerned his criticisms of Carlyle and Ruskin. His deep immersion in British working-class politics in any case would have kept him from becoming a species of conservative Pre-Raphaelite esthete ever pining for the vanished certainties of medieval Christendom, but it was the social democratic Hobson who in his mixed review of Ruskin's work gave Beard the pointers he needed to salvage the principles of *Unto This Last* for progressive politics. William Appleman Williams's brilliant intuition about Beard in calling him "the intellectual as Tory Radical," without ever commenting on the origins of his thought in the ideas of Carlyle and Ruskin, was accurate up to the moment of the young man's encounter with Hobson.[59]

The first half of *John Ruskin, Social Reformer* proceeds as a celebration of the master's brilliance and originality, but then, suddenly, the book turns into an indictment of him or, rather, of certain ideas that Hobson thought stand in a perverse relationship with Ruskin's overall philosophy. In a jarring note for the reader, who by this point in the book would have become accustomed to Hobson's unstinting praise, Ruskin's medieval politics received a thrashing. He blamed Carlyle for this atrocious defect in Ruskin's thinking. Carlyle and Ruskin both opposed the principle of human equality, thinking that the accomplishment of servile work required "the continuance of a class of men who shall in all essential facts, though not in name, be slaves." Fortunately for the better people, "there are base mechanic natures intended for such work." Hobson had no patience at all for this "tempered feudalism" in which hereditary elites would keep order among their inferiors. He reduced Ruskin's politics to their underlying principle: "All social order is built upon authority of superiors which imposes upon inferiors an absolute, unquestioning obedience." Such a benighted Carlyle-induced hero-worshipping principle led him into a host of mortifying misjudgments, not the least of which was his extravagant praise for the French emperor Louis Napoleon, "this mountebank monarch" in Hobson's estimation of him.[60]

Beard found a sternly worded political lesson from Hobson in *John Ruskin, Social Reformer*. He admired *Unto This Last* for its social criticism scarcely less than Beard did. Yet this book contained the gateway error that led Ruskin utterly astray as a political thinker. Hobson quoted this passage: "If we once can get a sufficient quantity of honesty in our captains the organisation of labour is easy." The captains, Hobson countered, believed that they already possessed this sufficiency: "At present, the vast majority of them are satisfied that, in taking all the rent, profits, and other emoluments they can get, and in spending them for their private purposes, they are strictly 'within their rights.'" Elites always acted this way. The current crop would be no different; they would not change of their own accord. "Social evils required social remedies," Hobson argued. The general will would have to be engaged, and this meant government intervention in the economy "to break down the evil power which competitive industry for profit places in the hands of the least scrupulous competitors."[61]

Beard found in Hobson's critique of Ruskin's politics the main ideas that would define his own progressivism. First, the government must be wrested from the lobbies that currently control it and transformed into an instrument for public well-being. The lobbies defiled democracy and made a mockery of it. Ruskin, too, mocked democracy as a utopian undertaking, at odds with what we knew to be true about the eternal inequalities of human nature. Hobson acknowledged that men will never be equal in their capacities, but democracy did not stand for absolute equality. Instead it served as "a dramatic protest against inequalities bred not of nature but of human oppression." All citizens had equal value, and a democratic government of the people concerned itself with their true interests in health, work, peace, and war. Pressure groups always sought to substitute their own interests for the general interest. Abuses of power historically had attended the kind of class government advocated by Ruskin. Ironically, the organic conception of society that he advocated required self-government by the people, "a demand which is entirely inconsistent with the dumb submission which his ideal government would seem to impose upon the masses." The whole national organism had to be involved in the work of government, not merely, in Ruskin's fond imagining, a hereditary caste. Naturally, society always would need leaders, and for this part of his democratic philosophy Hobson turned to Giuseppe Mazzini's principle: "The progress of all through all, under the leadership of the best and wisest."[62]

On yet two additional subjects Hobson found Ruskin especially wanting in sound judgment: women and war. In keeping with his opposition to democracy, Ruskin detested the women's liberation movement. Feminist doctrines he found pernicious in the extreme. Homemaking and children should require the full attention of women, as Ruskin saw their mission in society. It certainly would not have required the intervention of Hobson to assist the Beards in their understanding of women's issues. Both had been exposed to the ideas of British suffragette leader Emmeline Pankhurst and saw, unaided by Hobson, the hopeless irrelevance of Ruskin's ideas about women. Yet they certainly would have agreed with Hobson about the democratic right of women "to bear their proper part in the evolution of a sound industrial society."[63]

Ruskin's paeans to war as the health of the race disgusted Hobson. To glorify the predacious culture of militarism required the most serious defects of mind and heart. To explain their presence in a mind as capacious and perceptive as Ruskin's he resorted to psychological speculation. Such foolish ideas were found "rather in physically weak, sensitive men than in robust ones, arising from the idealization of a quality by those who possess it not."[64] Literary men who had seen war, such as Tolstoy and Mazzini, did not describe it as the holiday for heroes that Ruskin made it out to be.

Hobson thought Ruskin profoundly wrong in his views on the subjects of war and imperialism: "The sanction and incitement given by Mr. Ruskin to the English nation 'to undertake aggressive war, according to their force, wherever they are, assured that their authority would be helpful and protective,' however laudable as a theory of national conduct, is one of the most dangerous pieces of advice that could be tendered to a people always able to persuade themselves that their interference is helpful and protective, when it extends the influence of England over a new area of the world." Ruskin's fervent claims about the ennobling effects of war he based on the romance of literature, not authentic accounts from battle fields. "The obtuseness of such a judgment" angered Hobson, as it did the Ruskin College editors of *Young Oxford*.[65] Indeed, in a September 1900 editorial they echoed Hobson's sentiments and very nearly in his language, holding that *The Crown of the Wild Olive*—the book in which his views on war are most fully developed—was "the Ruskin book with which his admirers can have the least sympathy."[66] Ruskin's ideas about the altruistic character of British imperialism, however, took a while longer to be dropped from the pages of *Young Oxford*.

Beard's admiration for Hobson took a pronounced form in *An Introduction to the English Historians*. He introduced Hobson in the section of the book that considered the origins of European colonization and the spread of imperialism. For his own introductory essay he presented a strictly economic argument: "The international politics of Europe for the last three centuries can be understood solely in the light of the economic interests engendered in the race for markets and territorial dominion."[67] For British imperialism in the modern era, Beard relied mainly on Hobson's *Imperialism: A Study*, which had appeared only four years before, in 1902, a few months after the publication of Beard's semi-Kiplingesque "Living Empire" articles in *Young Oxford*.

Hobson's book of revelations about imperialism caused Beard to forget Kipling altogether. He also rejected Ruskin's infatuated thoughts on the subject, along with those of Beard's tutor at Oxford, Frederick York Powell, who gloried in the advance of the British Empire and defended the government's policies in the Boer War of 1899–1902. Powell followed a Ruskin line of argument in praising war and imperialism: "If we mean to secure for our race the high and worthy future we have dreamed of, nay, if we would secure the useful and honourable position we now hold in the world, we must set our house in order while there is yet time to do so." Powell viewed the empire as "the goodly heritage our forefathers' blood has bought for us."[68] Contemporary Britons had to prove themselves worthy of those who had come before, and the only way to do so was to fight for the country. Beard obviously found in Ruskin and Powell the inspiration for the pro-imperialist ideas that he expressed in his "Living Empire" articles.

What a difference a few months and the reading of one book can make. Hobson transformed Beard and set him on the path that he would take as a critical historian. Beard rated Hobson as the master historian of imperialism for his thorough understanding of the ways in which the British possessing classes had imposed their will on the government. The vast sums required to secure an empire never could be recovered from the income that the colonies might return to the mother country. It cost more to raise and provision the army and navy and then to provide for administration and infrastructure than these places on the whole were worth, to say nothing of mounting risks of war between imperialist powers in inveterate competition with each other for exploitable territories. Why embark on a course of empire then, if the policy involved unrecoverable costly outlays and risked pitting the European powers, who were each other's best customers, in a fratricidal war? Because, Hobson answered, the policy worked beautifully for the economic elites, who profited from it at the nation's expense.

Beard took care to include in his anthology Hobson's thesis about American imperialism, a phenomenon that had assumed its fully fledged modern form in the Spanish-American War of 1898. "The driving force of the economic factor" had been the same for the United States as for Britain.[69] The notion of American politicians serving as front men for the power brokers of Wall Street, as in the case of Theodore Roosevelt for Rockefeller, Morgan, and Hanna, conformed exactly to Beard's new understanding of the relationship between politics and foreign policy in the United States. Their officially unspoken but ever-renewing mutual support system, as described by Hobson, eventually would give Beard his starting point for understanding all American wars. Nothing that he found in the archives ever would cause him to lose faith in the fundamental and abiding validity of Hobson's thesis, to which American history in no way constituted an exception. Beard also would agree with the foreign policy implications of Hobson's book, which he quoted in his own anthology: "It is not inherent in the nature of things that we should spend our natural resources on militarism, war, and risky, unscrupulous diplomacy, in order to find markets for our goods and surplus capital."[70]

In Beard's 1936 memoir article about his time in Oxford, he linked Ruskin and Hobson: "Ruskin's spirit lives—in his own works, in the lives of those ancients who knew him in the flesh, in countless books, including John A. Hobson's, and in the thought of British statesmen."[71] The mature Beard echoed his younger self in claiming that the West had arrived at the point of decay foretold by Ruskin. No one more than Hobson, perhaps other than Beard himself, could be said to have carried forward into the twentieth century the essential spirit of Ruskin's indictment against the amoral and materialist basis of the modern world. An intellectual ferment that had begun in Beard's mind while he was still a college student, by reading *Unto This Last*, vigorously continued during his Oxford years, as amended by Hobson's critique of Ruskin. His life experiences outside of the Oxford University classrooms—in the Black Country and at Ruskin Hall—fueled skepticism about the pretensions of the capitalist status quo that propelled him along the path he took as a writer. In the work of English historians, above all Hobson, Beard found the scholarly examples that he needed for a career in his chosen profession. A Hobson-like sensibility stemming originally from Ruskin's *Unto This Last* would animate Beard's analysis of United States history, which he synthesized in the classic *Rise of American Civilization* as "the American acquisitive process."[72] He had left England with a cause, and it would keep him going at his writing desk for a lifetime.

CHAPTER 2

Two Contrasting Progressive Views of the Great War

During the Progressive period in American history, Robert La Follette and Charles Beard held the national stage as two of the movement's leading figures. Some major conflicts between them, however, raise important historical questions about the meaning of Progressivism. Around the time that Beard published his most famous book, *An Economic Interpretation of the Constitution of the United States*, he and La Follette engaged in a spirited correspondence. An analysis of their letters and other documents of the period reveals that the greatest of the Progressive historians and the movement's most iconic political figure entertained sharply different ideas about American economic and political history, as well as where the country might be headed. The contrasts between Beard and La Follette help to explain why the movement failed to speak with one voice on the great issues of the day in American politics and foreign policy: the election of 1912, the Federal Reserve System in 1913, intervention in 1917 in the European war, and the Treaty of Versailles in 1919, to name only the most salient.

The relationship between the two men began in mutual admiration. Some twenty years younger than La Follette, Beard praised him as one of the country's foremost political leaders. On January 11, 1911, the thirty-six-year-old professor invited La Follette to come to Columbia University "to debate with some leading socialist here the issue between Progressive Republicanism and Socialism."[1] Beard continued, "You could make it a memorable occasion, if you thought it desirable to undertake this." He could think of no better representative of the progressive viewpoint to place before the students than La Follette, then at the peak of his power and influence over that still-unified movement. La Follette, however, was forced to decline this invitation: "Under the urgent advice of my doctors I am not taking on anything in the way of platform work at this time."[2] He recently had undergone an operation and still had not recovered from it.

Beard pursued La Follette with another invitation for a later time. La Follette's secretary, John J. Hannan, responded on January 27, 1911, "As you know, the Senator would be pleased to aid the work of your league, but I know how crowded he is and I fear he will not be able to carve out the time necessary to comply with your request."[3] The league to which Hannan referred was Beard's Intercollegiate Civic League, which staged debates on public issues of the day. The main issue that the secretary had in mind as a drain on La Follette's free time in 1911—apart from his health problems, the normal demands of life as a U.S. senator, and editing his own political magazine— concerned the launching of the National Progressive Republican League, the organization that would spearhead the senator's campaign for the 1912 Republican presidential nomination against President Taft. This campaign floundered when former president Theodore Roosevelt entered the field. After ousting La Follette as the favorite of progressive Republicans, Roosevelt eventually established a breakaway progressive party against Taft, but only succeeded during the 1912 election in handing the victory to Woodrow Wilson, the Democratic candidate.

The following year, Beard published An Economic Interpretation of the Constitution of the United States, which La Follette, licking his political wounds in Washington, eagerly anticipated reading. La Follette's wife remembered his excitement upon its publication and how he took care to order the book in advance of its appearance in the bookstores.[4] With obvious reference to Beard, he declared in La Follette's Weekly Magazine that "the federal constitution has been found ill-adapted to the complexity of modern society and to ever-changing social and industrial conditions."[5] He added that the instruments of government should be shaped for the purpose of effectively serving the will of the people. His son-in-law, the dramatist and literary editor of La Follette's Weekly Magazine, George Middleton, wrote a short, but glowing, review of Beard's book and approvingly noted that its thesis "will do much to remove the halo that has surrounded the Constitution."[6]

La Follette published three additional articles about An Economic Interpretation of the Constitution of the United States, all by Charles Zueblin, a former professor of sociology at the University of Chicago, then editor of the

Twentieth-Century Magazine and described by La Follette as "one of the most brilliant radical publicists in America."[7] According to Zueblin, the book demonstrated that the United States had "a constitution devised to avoid the excessive democracy of the colonial governments—a constitution which not only tolerated but supported slavery, and which today is the chief opiate to make statesmanship somnolent."[8] As Beard argued, Zueblin continued, Alexander Hamilton had wanted to make the propertied classes supreme in American politics and had succeeded brilliantly. Thinking the people too unintelligent to choose their president, Hamilton had devised the Electoral College, which he had envisaged as an assembly of elites with the money, social standing, and culture necessary for wise and prudent political judgment. In this way "the power of money began to overshadow the government of the people."[9]

An Economic Interpretation of the Constitution of the United States confirmed but did not create La Follette's convictions about the overmastering role of financial elites in American politics. Beard purported to show how the fifty-five delegates at the Constitutional Convention in Philadelphia sought to replace the weak Articles of Confederation with a strong national government that would create a secure and lucrative environment for the investing classes, as well as to lead the way with an enhanced military establishment in conquering western lands from the Indians. With his matter-of-fact assertions about Founding Fathers held to be godlike by the American people, Beard claimed to be saying nothing new: *"The Federalist* . . . presents in a relatively brief and systematic form an economic interpretation of the Constitution by the men best fitted, through an intimate knowledge of the ideals of the framers, to expound the political science of the new government."[10] Every appeal made by Hamilton, Madison, and Jay in their classic defense of the Constitution reflected some substantial material interest. The most cogent of their arguments concerned the dangers of leveling democracy from which the Constitution would offer a safe refuge: "Property interests may through their superior weight in power and intelligence, secure advantageous legislation wherever necessary, and they may at the same time obtain immunity from control by parliamentary majorities."[11] Beard always would claim to be surprised by the fierce reaction against *An Economic Interpretation.* "It is curious," he wrote two years later, "that this volume raised such a storm of criticism in certain quarters when the leading ideas set forth in it had long been accepted by students of the economic aspects of American history."[12]

In the introduction to the 1935 edition, Beard expressly rejected the claim made by many of his critics that the book owed its methodology and viewpoint to Marxist theory.[13] He countered that the idea of class and group conflict could be traced back to Aristotle. Numerous historians and philosophers since ancient times had commented on the economic dimension of history. Indeed, Beard could have added to his long list of names that of the founding father of humanist historiography, Leonardo Bruni, who based his classic *History of the Florentine People* (1442) on the theme of the "ancient and even primeval struggle between the nobility and the common people," what he called the *popolo grasso* and the *popolo minuto*.[14] Marx himself fully understood how little he had written that was truly new about an understanding of the class struggle's economic character. The economic interpretation of history long had been known to historians, he conceded in a March 5, 1852, letter to his friend Joseph Weydemeyer. Marx's contribution concerned how "the class struggle necessarily leads to the dictatorship of the proletariat" and all that this historical outcome meant for mankind.[15] Beard professed to have become interested in Marx only when "I discovered in his works the ideas which had been cogently expressed by outstanding thinkers and statesmen in preceding centuries."[16] La Follette also thought that the best elements in Marxism were to be found scattered in the public domain of Western intellectual history. Beard's reduction of Marx's overall significance essentially would have conformed to La Follette's ideological views.

In his autobiography, first published in serial form in the fall of 1911, La Follette had made his differences with the socialists plain. For example, they wanted government ownership of the railroads, whereas he thought that government regulation of them would be the best way to achieve the national interest. Although his adversaries in both parties denounced him as an extremist bent on subverting American liberties, he denied any such intention. "I call it common sense," he declared in summing up his railroad policy. He did not want to smash the corporations, but to drive them out of politics. "Equality under the law was our guiding star," he averred. In the Marxist lexicon, La Follette would have qualified as a bourgeois moderate, a full step down in terms of ideological worth from the despised reform socialists. His idea of challenging the capitalist status quo involved little more than strict enforcement of the Sherman Anti-Trust Act, which forbade business combinations to suppress competition or to create a monopoly. He ended his autobiography as he had begun it, with a warning about the great struggle in American politics: "The supreme issue, involving all the others, is *the encroachment of the powerful few upon the rights of the many*." Both parties had fallen victim to financial malefactors, but he thought possible a return to the American golden age of fair competition and honest business practices, which is how he characterized the pre–Civil War era. This earlier form of capitalism, not socialism, appealed to him: "I recognize the rights of capital and the service which capital can render to a great producing nation such as ours."[17]

La Follette expected Beard to agree with him on the crucial political issues of the day. On May 10, 1913, La Follette wrote to him: "I have been very much interested in the work you have been engaged in, and have looked forward eagerly to the appearance of your book." In addition to the short notice written by his son-in-law, La Follette wanted the book to be reviewed prominently in the magazine, perhaps by Gilbert Roe, his best friend and a prominent New York City lawyer, "unless you have someone else in mind."[18] Beard replied four days later to thank La Follette for sending him a copy of the autobiography, by then available as a book, "which I have read again with deep interest, although I knew it very well in its serial form."[19]

Beard had been reading the autobiography of Massachusetts senator and former president of the American Historical Association George Frisbie Hoar, a relentless critic of American imperialism in the Philippines. Beard thought La Follette's memoir vastly superior to that of Hoar: "I shall certainly make my students in Politics read it next year, for in it they will find the inner history of the rise of the progressive movement." Beard especially appreciated La Follette's devastating portrait of Roosevelt. "Your analysis of Roosevelt, I believe, is true to the last degree and confirms the opinion I have always had concerning that shifty gentleman." In exchange, he sent La Follette "a copy of my new book on the Constitution."[20]

Amidst much praise and many expressions of esteem for La Follette, Beard nevertheless raised two points on which they strongly differed. The differences on matters of fundamental, almost existential, importance to La Follette would prove to be insusceptible to compromise. Beard criticized as unfounded the way that La Follette understood pre–Civil War American history. He wrote, "I do not think that it is a question of 'restoring' the government to the people; it is a question of getting possession of it to them for the first time." The country never had been a democracy, Beard insisted. By design, the United States Constitution had prevented such a polity from taking shape. "If you find time to read my book on the Constitution, I think you will see why I believe that we did not have 'a government of the people' to start with," Beard continued. He then added: "Whether the people were ready for self-government then, is another matter." The most essential facts of American history concerned the objectives for which financial elites had set up the system and how their class heirs had kept it in smooth running order ever since. We, therefore, could not go back to an Edenic past. We had not been cast out of a democratic paradise. Our masters never had permitted us to enter such a place—"At least so I read our history," Beard wrote.[21]

On this first point of difference between them, regarding the true character of America's pre–Civil War history, Beard added: "And I may say that my

Republican upbringing was scarcely less thoroughgoing than yours." It took years of historical research for him to discover that the political faith bequeathed to him in the family home corresponded to nothing that he had found in the archives. In the post–Civil War period, the Republican Party had suffered a complete moral eclipse, serving shamelessly as "the advance agent of the plutocracy."[22] Egregious as the party was, however, it differed only in degree, not in kind, from the parties that had come before.

The second disagreement between the two men had to do with the trusts. Beard asserted, "I do not think it is possible or desirable to restore real and effective competition."[23] Here again La Follette seemed to Beard to be mistaking myth for history. The world economic system would not be reverting to an earlier stage of development. Effective reform had to begin with a strong sense of realism. All sentimentality about the past had to be resisted. The existence of corporate power Beard took as a given. The only point in question about this power was how to control it and for which ends. Beard did not push his arguments against La Follette as far as they could go, but the logical thrust of them had to be wounding. Beard told La Follette, not in so many words, but essentially, that he needed to go back to school. He did not know enough about the lessons of the American past. *An Economic Interpretation of the Constitution of the United States* would be a starting point in his reeducation, but then he would have to buckle down and master the whole sordid sequence of events and the ensemble of forces leading to the Civil War and its direful aftermath. No clear-thinking person with a historically informed mind would wish to return to the antebellum era. The Progressive movement had to be looking forward, not backward.

The La Follette archive does not disclose any evidence of further communication between the two men, and the promised Roe review of *An Economic Interpretation of the Constitution of the United States*, or one by a reviewer of Beard's choosing, never appeared. Beard had written in his letter of May 14, 1913, how delighted he would be to have an in-depth review of his book in *La Follette's Weekly Magazine*: "And I should be happy to have Mr. Roe do it. . . . There is no one else who could do the review more effectively than Mr. Roe." Should he be unavailable, Beard added, "I suggest Professor W. E. Dodd, of the University of Chicago, who is keenly interested in the economic interpretation of history."[24] Following the short but positive Middleton review in the May 24, 1913, issue of the magazine, an editorial note read: "This volume will be analyzed in detail later."[25] Charles Zueblin's aforementioned three articles that appeared in October and November 1913 dealt with questions about the Constitution from a pro-Beard viewpoint, but did not constitute a detailed analysis of the book itself.

After La Follette's extravagant effusions of anticipatory delight, his subsequent silence about *An Economic Interpretation of the Constitution of the United States* suggests resistance on his part to the book's core arguments. There can be little question that Beard went much farther in his criticism of the Founding Fathers than La Follette was prepared to go. He, in fact, revered the Constitution. He also possessed a prodigious knowledge of this document and filled his Senate speeches with learned references to the famous precedent cases it had inspired. Its authors he judged to be men of heroic courage and political genius. In La Follette's view, the problems with the Constitution had occurred not in Philadelphia in 1787, but afterward when economic elites gained the upper hand and perverted the system. *An Economic Interpretation of the Constitution of the United States* failed to turn La Follette into a Beardian.

That a friendly relationship continued to exist between La Follette and Beard becomes evident in a January 17, 1914, letter that the senator wrote to Mary Ritter Beard, the historian's politically active wife. After thanking her for information about a strike in Lawrence, Massachusetts, he asked to be remembered to "Mr. Beard and the little Beardies."[26] The senator also wanted her to know that she could call on him if ever he could be of assistance. La Follette, however, continued to praise the Founding Fathers as demigods, in a spirit fundamentally opposed to Beard's thesis about this period in American history as a preamble perfectly in keeping with the corporate takeover of the country. Where La Follette saw a tragic post–Civil War rupture in the continuum of American history, Beard wrote about a genetically ordained perpetuation of the very traits most characteristic of the Founding Fathers and their handiwork in Philadelphia in 1787: a hyper-developed solicitude for the nurturing of business and landed elites. La Follette could not and did not go to school to a historian who appeared to be reducing his exemplars to prototypical politicians essentially in the service of the interests.

For the rest of his life, La Follette continued to think of himself politically as a follower of Lincoln, the American political leader, he believed, closest in spirit to the Founding Fathers. Every February, *La Follette's Weekly Magazine* paid loving tribute to the greatest Republican of them all and a man whose political creed of liberty, freedom, and fairness possessed a universal validity, or so the Lincoln birthday editorials annually declared. The 1850s, the decade of La Follette's birth and that of the Republican Party, remained the paramount object of his nostalgia. He did not really live down to Beard's somewhat caricatured approximation of his views, but anyone reading *La Follette's Weekly Magazine* will notice the nostalgic invocation to the family farms, as well as the small businesses and stores of yesteryear. Beard was wrong to say that La Follette had failed to come to terms with the inevitable corporatization of the

American economy. He did in fact understand that the corporations had come to stay. He argued, though, that in Lincoln's timeless speeches and writings, along with those of Washington and Jefferson, could be found the constituent elements of a genuinely democratic philosophy for our time.

The most profound disagreement of all between La Follette and Beard came over the issue of America's entry into the First World War. They became key figures in the opposing camps over the war. La Follette implacably opposed intervention as a rhetorically camouflaged maneuver to conceal Wall Street's immense financial investment in an Allied victory, whereas Beard criticized President Wilson for taking so long to join the war effort on the side of the Allies. Beard had studied at Oxford University and had helped to found Ruskin College as a progressive institution of higher learning for working-class people. He admired the British and took pride in the Beard family's roots in England. He and Mary seriously had contemplated making their lives in that country. He had begun his career as a historian of England and felt an enormous debt of gratitude to his teachers at Oxford and friends in Manchester, where the young married couple had lived and had brought their first child into the world. Such strong memories and attachments no doubt predisposed him to welcome as true the case that Britain made for its war effort. In *The Rise of American Civilization* (1927), he would explain, with his own case in mind, America's pro-Entente sympathies as a consequence in part of the "large body of Americans of English stock who felt bound to England by ties of blood and affection and who urged upon Wilson a war in the name of kinship."[27] For Beard this was the good-war exception to the general rule of warfare as a reflexive exercise in imperialism, as laid down by John A. Hobson. La Follette, too, had read Hobson appreciatively, but he thought that there were no exceptions to the lessons put forward in *Imperialism: A Study*.[28]

Beard's complicated intellectual itinerary during the war requires here a detailed analysis and is best understood in the context of his final years at Columbia University. As a history and government professor at that institution, Beard had a notorious reputation for being on the left and, particularly among the trustees, for his subversive ideas about the past and present control of politics by money. For these overseers of the university he never had overcome what for them was the disgrace of his scandalous book, *An Economic Interpretation of the Constitution of the United States*. He also had experienced some conflicts with Nicholas Murray Butler, the school's president, over faculty appointments and other campus issues. Butler viewed him as a talented but difficult faculty member for whose economic interpretation of American history he had no sympathy.

The war, however, changed the relationship between Beard and Butler for the better. After hostilities erupted in the summer of 1914, Beard took an immediate stand against German militarism as the cause of the war. Thus, after years of strained relations between him and Columbia—the trustees especially— he suddenly fit right in with the school's pro-war administration, headed by the super-patriotic Butler, who repeatedly would denounce the anti-war La Follette as an arch traitor. With La Follette, Beard, too, lost patience and against him energetically supported the war preparedness movement in America. Despite the many disagreements that Butler and Beard had over American history and campus politics, they both imagined the Allied cause in the war to be a civilization-saving crusade against the unparalleled evil of German militarism. Joseph Freeman, a left-wing radical who studied at Columbia under Beard, remembered, "throughout 1916, Professor Beard urged America's entry into the war. He warned us in class that Germany was a danger to civilization."[29]

With the Wilson campaign running on the slogan "He kept us out of war," Beard and Butler supported Charles Evans Hughes, the Republican candidate in the 1916 presidential race. On November 28, 1916, in the immediate aftermath of the election, Butler responded to Beard's complaints about the victorious Wilson: "I agree with every word in your letter of the 25th. The antics of our government are vexatious in the extreme. Very few people seem to care about efficiency."[30] Earlier that same year, however, Beard had come under fire from the trustees, initially over comments that he had made about the rights of American citizens to speak their minds about the war. He thought that in a free republic no one should have the power to suppress free speech. The New York *Evening Sun* in an April 24 editorial, "Free Speech and Free Treason," criticized Beard by name for that position, and then the trustees initiated an investigation of him.[31]

Forced to appear before a committee of the trustees to explain not only his ideas about freedom of speech in this case but also in general what they characterized as his pernicious example of inculcating disrespect for American institutions, Beard felt outraged by their "inquisition into my views and teachings."[32] Butler stood by silently during Beard's ordeal. It was a silence that Beard could not forgive, their agreement about the need for American intervention in the war notwithstanding. Thereafter, the trustees of the school continued to regard him as a dangerous nonconformist. Partly with him in mind, in March 1917 they established a committee to supervise the curriculum. Beard led the opposition against this naked infringement of academic freedom. He took as the first principle of his professional life that no university could function as a corporation for learning without freedom of speech.

The problem that Columbia had with Beard did not at all concern his attitude toward the war or America's intervention, which occurred in April 1917. No one could better him for pro-war intransigence. In a June 2 letter to the editor of the *New Republic*, he called upon the country to "strain every nerve to the breaking point in the mobilization of our resources." Americans should work for "a smashing victory which will carry the soldiers of the Allies to the streets of Berlin." He echoed the new Wilson line, calling America's intervention a war to make the world safe for democracy. He believed in the new democratic world that the President said was coming, once German militarism had been vanquished. It would be a far better world than ever had been known. For such a glorious outcome in history, Americans had to make certain "that this is not at bottom, or even potentially, a capitalist war for colonies, markets, and concessions." For the Allied victory to be meaningful in the lofty terms expressed by the president in his war declaration speech, the Germans would have to be able to trust the victors to bring them liberty. They could in no way be encouraged to think that the war was about "British and American capitalism bent upon markets, more markets."[33]

The next month, in a *New Republic* review of Salomon Grumbach's *Das annexionistische Deutschland*, Beard continued to contrast German imperialism with the high-mindedness of the American war effort. He quoted Admiral Alfred von Tirpitz, who had said that at war's end Germany must have "a world-spanning horizon." The whole country, Beard contended, had become infected with the diseases of militarism and imperialism, German artists, intellectuals, and clergymen included. Indeed, "all classes of Germany, excepting a few recalcitrant, are won over to the gospel of *Machtpolitik*." The one hope that he could see for the German masses consisted of President Wilson's promise to reintroduce them into the family of nations following the defeat of the Hohenzollerns. German imperialists were telling their people to fight on if they wanted to avoid the economic ruin the Allies had in store for them. Beard, fervent in his faith that Wilson truthfully had defined the Allied war aim as the creation of a just democratic order in the world, viewed the Germans as potential candidates for democratic reeducation, provided that in defeat they were treated generously. Regarding a future postwar settlement, "it must be no trick clumsily designed to deceive the German masses, but a confession of justice and a program that squares with German rights in the earth."[34]

The animosity that had been building in Beard's mind toward the Columbia trustees and president since the spring of 1916 engulfed him completely in October 1917 with the firing of two anti-war professors, James McKeen Cattell and Henry Wadsworth Longfellow Dana. On the second of that month, the *New York Times* announced that the trustees had ousted Dana and Cattell "upon charges that they had disseminated doctrines tending to encourage a spirit of disloyalty to the Government of the United States."[35] With an irony too refined and subtle for common understanding at the time, the fiercely pro-war Beard became the most prominent defender at Columbia of that institution's two leading pacifists.

Dana, an assistant professor of comparative literature with a Harvard PhD who had taught at the Sorbonne in Paris, was the grandson of two giants in American literature. His paternal grandfather, Richard Henry Dana Jr., wrote *Two Years before the Mast* (1840), a classic first-hand account of the miserable conditions suffered by seamen. One of the oldest families in New England, the Danas could boast of the colonial poet Anne Bradstreet among their forebears. His maternal grandfather was the most famous poet in America and the only American poet with a bust in Westminster Abbey—Henry Wadsworth Longfellow, whose translation of Dante's *Divine Comedy* long remained the master version in English. It would not have been possible to find anywhere in America a family tree to match Professor Dana's for prestige and renown. His pedigree and much remarked-upon talent as a lecturer proved unavailing. President Butler and the trustees fired him for bringing shame and disgrace on Columbia by engaging, as reported by the *New York Times* on October 2, in peace activities aimed at "weakening the action of the American Government in its prosecution of the war against Germany."[36] Personal warnings by Butler to desist from these activities had not been heeded.

Butler had issued a general warning to all Columbia faculty members during his commencement address in June. On that occasion he had observed how in times of peace the school had permitted complete freedom of speech. Professors and students could write and say whatever they liked, no matter how foolish and irresponsible they were: "So soon, however, as the nation spoke by the Congress and by the President, declaring that it would volunteer as one man for the protection and defense of civil liberty and self-government, conditions sharply changed." In sum, "what had been tolerated before became intolerable now." He then spoke about what would happen to anti-war faculty members and students: "In your presence, I speak by authority for the whole university—for my colleagues of the Trustees and for my colleagues of the Faculties—when I say, with all possible emphasis, that there is and will be no place in Columbia University, either on the rolls of its Faculties or on the rolls of its students for any person who opposes or who counsels opposition to the effective enforcement of the laws of the United States or who acts, speaks or writes treason." The removal of such persons would be as swift as the discovery of their transgressions. This would be the university's last and only word of warning "to any among us, if such there be, who are not with whole heart and mind and strength committed to fight with us to make the world safe for democracy."[37] He had Dana and Cattell uppermost in mind.[38]

Cattell, much more senior than Dana and by far the more famous of the two fired professors, was a German-trained psychologist and a former president of the American Psychological Association. He long had been a noted figure in the anti-intervention movement. On March 31, 1917, he had written to La Follette, the leader of the anti-intervention members of the Senate, pleading with him: "Please do not permit a Wall Street war." He shared La Follette's conviction that the war concerned nothing but profits for the vested interests of the combatant nations. Unfortunately, the United States had its own vested interests, and their greed would produce the same tragic results that had befallen Europe. "We must not wage war," Cattell continued in his letter to La Follette, "in order that munitions may be transported to Europe and sold to kill, in order that the loans of capitalists may be guaranteed, in order that a militarism administered by the classes may control our country. . . . The European war is a war of the lording classes for power, trade, and territory."[39]

Cattell had appealed to La Follette again on April 12, urging the senator, now that the United States was in the war, to promote the cause of an early and just peace, to oppose conscription, to resist militarism, and to finance the war "by direct taxation falling most heavily on the rich."[40] On August 25, he had praised La Follette for his attempt to mitigate the worst consequences of U.S. intervention in the war. Cattell denounced President Wilson's war measures, especially conscription, as a betrayal of American ideals: "Surely the intent of the Constitution and our consistent national policy should not be reversed without the consent of the people. The President and the Congress were not elected to send conscripts to Europe."[41] Using Columbia University letterhead, he also had urged other political figures in Washington to oppose all conscription measures. Cattell's public opposition to the draft would finally bring down upon him the full wrath of President Butler and the trustees.

Any faculty member's association with La Follette would have antagonized Butler, but the very next month, on September 20, 1917, the senator gave a speech in St. Paul, Minnesota, that caused a national scandal and, in the eyes of pro-war patriots everywhere, blackened his name beyond redemption. La Follette had accepted American intervention as a constitutionally mandated action, but he continued to reserve the right to speak critically about the conduct of the war. In St. Paul, he mockingly derided "the bloated representatives of wealth who are shouting loudest for democracy today."[42] The rich always used the government as a means of increasing their wealth, and never more so than in wartime. Such remarks were nothing out of the ordinary for

La Follette in the period immediately following America's declaration of war, but a journalist misquoted him to say that the United States had no grievances against Germany. In fact, he had said that the United States did have such grievances, though not, in his opinion, of sufficient gravity to warrant a declaration of war. Newspapers all over the country picked up the false report, and for the rest of the war he would be dogged by charges of sedition and subjected to a protracted attempt to expel him from the Senate.

On September 23, La Follette spoke in Toledo, Ohio, under the auspices of "The People's Church," described by the *New York Times* as a union of socialists headed by Scott Nearing.[43] Fired for his radical politics two years earlier from the University of Pennsylvania's Wharton School of Business, Nearing had joined the faculty at the University of Toledo as a professor of political science and dean of the College of Arts and Sciences. With war fever raging across the United States, he lost his position there as well in the summer of 1917. In his autobiography, he noted somberly, "Under intolerable war pressure, American liberals and radicals were bending, conforming, rationalizing, surrendering."[44] The *New York Times* would identify Nearing as "a pacifist and seditionary" and a good example of the wisdom shown by American universities and colleges in getting rid of their radical professors. Academic freedom, the newspaper contended, "cannot protect a professor who counsels resistance to the law and speaks, writes, disseminates treason."[45] The newspaper characterized La Follette and Nearing as birds of a feather.

Though facing death threats in Toledo, La Follette showed no sign of being intimidated when he told the audience that the American war party possessed the same frightening traits of its counterparts in Europe: "It is the party of autocracy. It seeks to dominate absolutely. It is commercial, imperialistic, ruthless." He went further: "The American Jingo is the twin of the German Junker."[46] It seemed to him that the German reputation for militarism had been exaggerated, now that the Americans had shown what they could do in the way of spending money on war. If anything, the Toledo speech of September 23 produced an even greater furor against La Follette than his St. Paul speech had done three days earlier. Former president Theodore Roosevelt commented about La Follette on September 26, declaring him to be "the worst enemy that democracy has now alive."[47] Roosevelt's word carried great weight with Butler, who had been and long would remain an influential figure in Republican Party politics.

The following day, September 27, Butler gave a speech at the Atlantic City, New Jersey, convention of the American Bankers Association and echoed Roosevelt's accusation against La Follette as a traitor who should be immediately expelled from the Senate. La Follette would find a place in history on the same dark page of dishonor reserved for the likes of Benedict Arnold: "Why, you might just as well put poison in the food of every boy that goes to his transport as to permit that man to talk as he does."[48]

All La Follette's efforts for peace and compromise Butler dismissed as an unpatriotic attempt to "stay our hand before the new world of which we are in search has been discovered and organized." La Follette and false leaders like him failed to understand, "Peace is not an ideal. Peace is a state attendant upon the accomplishment of an ideal. The ideal is freedom, liberty to satisfy human wants and aspirations. Give us those and peace is secure." Butler appealed to the senators from New Jersey and New York "to rid the Senate of that man who had betrayed the government of the United States." To leave him in office would mean that the American people had lost "their capacity for corporate indignation." The war had to be fought on two fronts: the battle zone in Europe and the one here at home where "evil-minded sedition, conspiracy, cowardice and treason existed."[49] By demonstrating through his outrageous speeches that the United States did not speak with one patriotic voice in support of the war effort, La Follette deserved to be blamed for the downfall of the Russian military effort on the Eastern Front. Butler's fervently delivered speech received loud applause and cheers from the bankers.

On September 28, Butler called for the dismissal of Cattell and Dana. The trustees proceeded with the firing three days later. Acting on a faculty committee's recommendation, Butler specifically identified Cattell's actions as coming "directly within the scope of my public warnings of June 6 last."[50] Dana, too, had damaged the university's reputation and had caused embarrassment to his colleagues, many of whom had complained bitterly of him to Butler. "He throughout the summer," the president charged, "has been in close public association with individuals and organizations that, under the guise of promoting peace, are in one form or another striving to weaken the national effort and to nullify the national will. These individuals and organizations have included some of the most irresponsible, irrational, and unpatriotic elements of the population."[51] Cattell's usefulness to the institution had come to an end as well. The *New York Times* concurred with the decision for expulsion, warranting that "academic freedom is a pitiful thing by the side of the freedom of United States democracy." The case of Professor Dana seemed particularly shocking, in the newspaper's estimation. Cattell's son Owen also stood charged with sedition. With the Cattells, a disposition toward disloyalty seemed to be a family trait. For a young man with Dana's illustrious family background, however, "the taint of treason should have been impossible."[52]

Beard spent an anguished week before deciding what to do about the firing of Dana and Cattell. He resigned on October 8, and then four days later in a public letter to Butler explained his reasons for doing so. "Having observed closely the inner life at Columbia for many years," he began, "I have been driven to the conclusion that the University is really under the control of a small and active group of trustees who have no standing in the world of education, who are reactionary and visionless in politics, and narrow and medieval in religion." These nullities, as he saw the trustees, had taken it upon themselves to impose their pro-war beliefs on the entire faculty. Beard strongly agreed with the pro-war position and told Butler: "As you are aware, I have, from the beginning, believed that a victory for the German Imperial Government would plunge all of us into the black night of military barbarism. I was among the first to urge a declaration of war by the United States, and I believe that we should now press forward with all our might to a just conclusion."[53]

The ardently pro-war Beard nevertheless insisted on the preservation of his idea of the university. To do their work, faculty members had to enjoy the right of untrammeled intellectual inquiry and expression. There could be no compromise for him on such a fundamental point of scholarly life. Faculty members who opposed the war could not be silenced "by curses or bludgeons." He accused the university trustees of terrorizing young faculty members and reducing all professors to a status "lower than that of the manual laborer, who, through his union, has at least some voice in the terms and conditions of his employment." Professors, on the other hand, could be dismissed without a judgment by their peers or a hearing of any kind. Beard claimed in his resignation letter that he needed to leave Columbia, in order better to serve the war effort as a free man: "I am convinced that while I remain in the pay of the Trustees of Columbia University, I cannot do effectively my humble part in sustaining public opinion in support of the just war on the German Empire or take a position of independence in the days of reconstruction that are to follow." Beard closed his letter to Butler on a grace note, professing undying devotion to Columbia's students, alumni, and faculty: "And to you, sir, I am deeply indebted for the courtesy and thoughtful consideration that I have always received at your hands."[54] The cordiality of this final sentence did not long survive in the aftermath of his resignation. He soon would be denouncing Butler along with the trustees.[55]

Beard's resignation from Columbia took effect on October 9, 1917. His sensational act plunged the university into an institutional crisis, the full force of which newspaper clippings discolored with age in the university's historical and biographical files preserve intact for us today. A star teacher, he had a large and devoted following on campus. The school's archives bulge with testimony about the intellectual excitement and mastery that he brought to the classroom. For instance, Joe A. Jackson, a member of the class of 1916, wrote for the alumni newspaper a vivid account of his teaching style: "When Professor Beard starts to lecture, the students are 'heads up' to watch the pyrotechnics which drop as the gentle bolts from heaven. Whether he be discussing the economic interpretation of the Constitution or the generosity of Mark Hanna there are sure to be sparks." His lecture style strongly tended toward the caustically ironic, Jackson wrote: "One of the most edifying of his performances is to snatch the garment of illusion from the body of history's pets and leave them to shiver, unadorned, before the eyes of some two hundred students." If Beard were to write a book about his teaching methods, Jackson thought that a good title for it would be "Putting Pepper into Prosaic Polemics of Platitudinous Politicians."[56]

Many of Beard's students recorded their highly favorable impressions of him as a teacher. One of them, Arthur Macmahon, from the class of 1912, who went on to become a Department of Public Law professor at Columbia, recalled the electric atmosphere of Beard's pioneering courses on politics and the "sheer vitality" with which he taught them.[57] He described Beard as a beloved faculty member fiercely intent on research, writing, and practical service, but who attracted students, both graduate and undergraduate, and made time for them. He advised the debating team and became associated with the Training School for Public Service. Beard's passionate concern for understanding the realities of government animated his teaching and contributed to the exceptional charisma that he enjoyed on campus. Completely indifferent to academic convention and prestige, as Macmahon remembered him, Beard pursued his work with an energy that never seemed to flag.

Such a commanding figure could not suddenly vanish from the lives of worshipful students and admiring colleagues without incident. Some students threatened to strike over Beard's resignation, and a raging campus battle ensued between his supporters and others who favored the trustees. The *New York Post* described this struggle as "a small civil war at Columbia."[58] The *New York Times*, which never had been well-disposed toward Beard, reported triumphantly how the protesters "were dispersed more or less roughly by a small but vigorous group of patriotic students." When someone tried to make a speech in his favor, "student patriots sounded three cheers for Columbia and the Faculty and gave the radicals what is known among the students as the 'bum's rush.'"[59]

Many faculty members spoke up for Beard. Among the senior professors, James Harvey Robinson and John Dewey were his prominent defenders. Robinson, a professor of history and Beard's longtime collaborator on textbooks, said "I regret exceedingly that Professor Beard has resigned."[60] Philosopher John Dewey lamented "the loss to the university of such a scholarly man and a teacher of such rare power."[61] Carlton J. H. Hayes, a thirty-five-year-old Europeanist colleague of Beard in the history department and much influenced by his economic interpretation of history, spoke for many faculty members in support of him. On October 10, he told his students, "I am afraid I shall not be able to continue this class this afternoon. Professor Beard has been my friend, and I feel so keenly about what has happened that I will have to be excused. This class is dismissed for this afternoon."[62] Robert Livingston Schuyler, another young Columbia professor, just beginning to make his mark in the fields of early American history and British history, celebrated Beard as "a scholar of the highest reputation" and particularly objected to the campaign of the *New York Times* against him.[63]

On that same day, the tenth, the *New York Times* published a scathing denunciation of Beard, "Columbia's Deliverance," in which readers learned that by resigning he "has just rendered the greatest service it was in his power to give." He had been right to call the trustees "visionless," in the sense that "they certainly have no vision of the benefits to come from the overthrow of our institutions and the reorganization of society by the apostles of radicalism." They were "narrow and medieval in religion" for never having imbibed "the blank materialism" of German university training. The *New York Times,* however, gave the trustees credit for knowing, "as every man of sound sense and unclouded vision knows that Columbia University is better for Professor Beard's resignation."[64]

Beard had not been wrong about the war or America's intervention in it, but everything else about him, beginning with his awful book, *An Economic Interpretation of the Constitution of the United States*, displeased the *New York Times*. In that volume, "he sought to show that the founders of this Republic and the authors of its Constitution were a ring of land speculators who bestowed upon the country a body of organic law drawn up chiefly in the interest of their own pockets." The book had done Columbia University much harm, "just as the two professors who were recently dropped for seditious utterances did the university much harm." For the *New York Times*, the book "was the fruit of that school of thought and teaching, again borrowed from Germany, which denies to man in his larger actions the capacity of noble striving and self-sacrifice for ideals, that seeks always as the prompting motive either the animal desire to get more to eat or the hope of filling his pockets."[65]

Reviewers "with due kindness but frankly" had pointed out how bad the book was, but Beard continued to promote his unscientific economic interpretation of American history, creating in the minds of his students a radically false understanding of the country's character and purposes. Such intellectually and morally bankrupt teaching could not be allowed to go unchecked;

otherwise, "we should presently find educated American youth applying the doctrine of economic determinism to everything from the Lord's Prayer to the binomial theorem." The free exercise of doctrines, such as Beard's, that are dangerous to the community and the nation could not be sheltered "behind the shibboleth of academic freedom."[66]

The views expressed in "Columbia's Deliverance" found support in a letter to the New York Times by Annie Nathan Meyer, one of the school's trustees. She wanted to respond to Beard's "passionate diatribe against the Trustees of Columbia in particular and college Trustees in general." The whole idea of professorial academic freedom seemed absurd to her in theory and unworkable in practice. There always would be limitations on free speech, imposed by the boundaries of permissible opinion that were to be found in every age and society, including 1917 America. She derided Beard for complaining that "he is not free to say what he chooses in or out of the classroom, that he is not allowed to shriek sheer treason, that he is not permitted to undermine the holiest relations of life, that he is not given the opportunity to tear and destroy that which civilization must hold fast to or suffer destruction."[67] The conservative men and women who served as university trustees should have the courage to rid their institutions of demagogues like Beard who had disgraced his noble calling as a teacher.

Many people simply did not know what to make of a man who by defending anti-war professors had sacrificed his teaching position, except to conclude that he must have agreed with them. For example, the American Union Against Militarism sent Beard a congratulatory telegram, urging him to join. The New York Times quoted his reply: "My letter of resignation explains my position on the war. Beyond that I have nothing to say."[68] The New York Times continued to portray the Beard case as a contest between "loyal Columbia men" and "radicals."[69] The difficulty with such a portrayal concerned Beard's partisanship for the loyal Columbia men. He opposed the radicals on the war issue. On the issue of academic freedom, he supported them. Loyal patriots of the New York Times breed believed that wartime conditions demanded a 100 percent Americanism, leaving no room for the kind of academic freedom exemption that Beard wanted for university professors. Such a standard for patriotism made Beard a problem, and conservatives generally welcomed his departure.

The New York Times consistently described radical efforts to defend freedom of speech on campus as a cover for the promotion of seditious activities. "Patriotic students, organized like soldiers going into battle," the newspaper exulted, routinely broke up radical protest meetings. Members of the Naval Reserve taking radio and engineering courses at Columbia assisted in such dispersals. "Conservativists among the students" threatened one of the radical leaders with a dunking in the college pond.[70] They sang patriotic songs to drown out radical speakers and chased them with egg barrages. After one such victorious foray at 116th Street and Amsterdam Avenue, loyal students gathered for a patriotic address by C. P. Ivins, the vice-president of the senior class.

On October 28 the Columbia Alumni Association gave its blessing to the actions of President Butler and the trustees in dismissing Cattell and Dana. In its annual report, the association strongly opposed "those that openly breathe treason, sedition or resistance to duly constituted authority." As a place for serious scholarship, the university "is not a public debating forum or marketplace where intellectual novelties may be displayed for the delectation of the young or radical, the emotional, or the undisciplined. It should aim to train scholars, not soap-box orators." It was to be regretted "that a certain element of the student body should attempt to spread propaganda of an anti-war nature." It might be a good idea, the report continued, to restrict the numbers of students to be admitted: "the disadvantages of recent large enrollments" had become plain for all to see. A Columbia education "should not be expended on any but the most worthy and the most promising and the greatest care should be exercised in selecting and determining the student body."[71]

Beard resolved to leave the academic world for good. On December 29, 1917, he published an account in the *New Republic* of the incidents leading up to his resignation. It mattered a great deal to him to set the record straight about his motives, particularly because "it has been insinuated by certain authorities of Columbia University that I resigned in a fit of unjustified petulance." He furnished a detailed catalogue of all his grievances against the university, most of which had been thoroughly reported in newspaper accounts during the fall. The grievance that rankled him the most concerned his interrogation in 1916 by the committee on education of the board of trustees, a proceeding that had begun as an examination of words he had spoken in defense of free speech during wartime, but then had progressed to a condemnation of his understanding of history and politics and of how he taught these subjects to Columbia students. The image of Butler just sitting there without saying a word in Beard's defense still disheartened him with an undiminished implacability. Looking back on the experience more than a year later, Beard reflected, "I realize now that I should have refused to remain in the room, but I was taken unaware and stunned by the procedure."[72]

From then on Beard felt the institution slipping away from him. The trustees and Butler relentlessly had pursued their political agenda of total control over Columbia's response to the war. Any such agenda, Beard thought, "betrays a profound misconception of the true function of the university in the advancement of learning." Scholars of promise and of distinction had been fired or otherwise dropped over differences of opinion about the war. In his article for the *New Republic*, Beard emphasized the vital importance of the much-publicized Dana and Cattell firings, but no less important to him was the relatively unremarked upon treatment of a young politics instructor named Leon Fraser, who had organized courses throughout the country on pacifism and international conciliation. For a critical remark of his about the military training of officers in the so-called Plattsburg Movement, he had been forced to appear before the committee of the trustees and then had been expelled from the university without notice or hearing. In such a viciously politicized and anti-intellectual environment, "the institution was to be reduced below the level of a department store or factory and I therefore tendered my resignation." Beard's last words in the article were for the leader of the school: "These facts I submit to the candid and impartial reader. I believe that they constitute a full and unanswerable indictment of the prevailing methods at Columbia University under the administration of Dr. Nicholas Murray Butler."[73]

Upon leaving Columbia, Beard declared that he now would become a better and freer advocate for the war. Following his resignation, he worked for the Bureau of Municipal Research in New York City as the head of its Training School for Public Service. Later he took over the Bureau itself. All this time, however, he devoted himself to the war effort. He volunteered for service on the Committee on Public Information's Civic and Educational Cooperation Division, headed by the historian Guy Stanton Ford. He also contributed to the *War Cyclopedia*, a patriotic handbook published in 1918 by the Committee on Public Information and co-edited by a pro-war La Follette nemesis at the University of Wisconsin, Frederic L. Paxson, another leading historian of the day.

Reviewing economist Walter Weyl's *The End of the War* for the July 6, 1918, issue of the *New Republic*, Beard expressed in the clearest possible terms the Wilsonian patriotism that continued to motivate him nearly a year after his resignation from Columbia: "Of Germany's conduct in Belgium, of her ravages on the high seas, of her intrigues and indecent conduct in America, of her cold and brutal military calculations, of her power and her determination to use it for economic advantages at any human cost, of her ominous menaces against America's future, of the autocratic character of her political system, of this and more there could be no doubt." Germany's unparalleled criminal record, he reasoned, "is enough to convince all but the unearthly of the justice of the cause for which America took up arms. This is justification enough for America's will to victory." He fervently believed in the purity of American arms and of the country's purposes in the war. As the end of the conflict neared, America would have to take the lead in producing a just peace: "Indeed, the avowed principles on which President Wilson appealed to his countrymen to take up arms against German military power place upon America a peculiar duty of resisting everywhere within the limits of the practicable, imperialistic and selfish pretensions, the realization of which will merely prepare the way for the renewal of the present struggle when the exhaustion of the contestants is repaired." In short, the coming peace congress must not become "the same old trick played all over again."[74]

On December 12, 1918, Beard and University of Wisconsin political scientist Frederic A. Ogg, a classmate of his at DePauw University, wrote in their *National Governments and the World War*, "The late conflict arrayed state against state, people against people; yet it was, at bottom, a struggle between two great schemes of human government—autocracy and democracy. On the field of battle democracy has triumphed." In the sections of the book that Beard wrote, a mentality of unalloyed Wilsonian idealism prevails: "It was against a government conceived in military despotism and dedicated to the proposition that kings can do no wrong, that President Wilson asked his country to take up arms."[75] Beard could find nothing at all wrong with the way Wilson had waged the war. The Selective Service Law and the Espionage Act, which La Follette had fought in the Senate as flagrant abuses of constitutional freedoms, Beard described with perfect equanimity as the unexceptionable means to attain the president's lofty goals in fighting a war to make the world safe for democracy.

La Follette had taken the position after April 6, 1917, that he held an obligation as a senator to support a democratically declared war, to the extent of mitigating as much as possible its effects on American soldiers. He voted for most of the war measures proposed by the administration and eventually, beginning with Wilson's Fourteen Points Address in January 1918, fully supported the war. He was no Eugene V. Debs, who never for a moment doubted the thoroughly imperialistic character of the war and went to prison for his vehement opposition to it. Nevertheless, La Follette continued to speak out forcefully against the draft and war profiteering, as well as for freedom of speech in wartime. The Constitution did not cease to exist when American soldiers, at the behest of their government, went into battle. Therefore, he qualified his support of Wilson and remained, in the view of official Washington, a problematic figure as he continued to undergo a Senate investigation of his allegedly seditious September 20, 1917, speech in St. Paul. Suspicions about him held by the war party behind the president notwithstanding, the editorials that he wrote for *La Follette's Magazine* during the last ten months of the war supported the troops and their mission absolutely. Socialist war protestors he condemned now with an ardor formerly reserved for war profiteers.[76] It would be a good war after all, provided that the victors based the peace on the Fourteen Points, another position that he very belatedly came to share with Beard.

By contrast, Beard had agreed wholeheartedly from the beginning and not only with the president's characterization of America's war aims. As he wrote in *National Governments and the World War*, America had gone to war "to overthrow militarism and imperialism, making way for peace and democratic governments throughout the earth." He could find not a single policy or action by the president to criticize. Wilson's ideas, without any exception that Beard cared to mention, "represent not merely the views of one man, the spokesman of a great nation; they voice the slowly maturing opinion of the great masses of people everywhere in the earth."[77] Far from objecting in the manner of La Follette to the constitutionality or the wisdom of the administration's war measures, Beard marched in perfect cadence with President Wilson. It was the best of all possible wars, he thought, in conception and execution.

CHAPTER 3

Becoming a Revisionist

As a thirty-three-year-old political science professor at Columbia University, Beard had the honor in 1907 of accepting an invitation to join the editorial board of the *Political Science Quarterly* (*PSQ*). To one of its editors, Munro Smith, he wrote on December 2 of that year: "It would give me great pleasure in compliance with your invitation to become associated with the other members of the Faculty of Political Science in the editorial conduct of the Quarterly."[1] Beard would have a major voice on the journal, regularly evaluating manuscripts, as well as writing numerous articles and reviews. His longtime close connection with *PSQ*, among other reasons, makes it certain that he would have read John Atkinson Hobson's "Why the War Came as a Surprise" in the September 1920 issue.

Hobson had influenced the core of Beard's thinking about politics, dating from the time of his Ruskin Hall work in Manchester. Hobson's *Imperialism: A Study* had been a foundational book in Beard's mental development as a historian. The two men, however, had parted ways during the war. A member of the Union of Democratic Control, Hobson had opposed the war, a story he told in *Confessions of an Economic Heretic* (1938). Nothing had fundamentally changed in Hobson's thinking about the relationship between economics and politics since his discovery that interplay between these two fields had produced the Boer War, which he described as "this brutal piece of imperialism." He also had made acerbic comments then about the highly advanced skill of the British war makers in portraying their aggression "in terms of morals and humanity."[2] A pre–World War I lecture tour in the United States, where he met Thorstein Veblen and formed a lifelong attachment with him, helped Hobson to understand that the British did not have a monopoly on the folkways of national self-congratulation. Veblen's *Theory of the Leisure Class* he judged to be the indispensable primer for understanding the American version of imperialist propaganda.

The British response to the Great War Hobson described as "a disturbing revelation." Men of intelligence and learning, even in his left-wing progressive circle, seemed to lose the capacity for critical thought in the atmosphere created by constant indoctrination for war. Hobson, Edmund Dene Morel, Ramsay MacDonald, Norman Angell, and other leading figures in the Union of Democratic Control tried to resist Britain's descent into the organized slaughter of the Western Front, but "The Political and Economic Consequences of the War" chapter in *Confessions of an Economic Heretic* is a record of the group's failure. Hobson concluded that Britain's patriotic reaction to the war "was the first of a series of shocks to my belief that the world was inhabited by a reasonable animal."[3] The real meaning of the war he summarized as the European-wide triumph of perverted nationalism in the service of empire. This perversion had blocked the path of progress and now threatened civilization itself.

"Why the War Came as a Surprise," Hobson's September 1920 article for *PSQ*, revealed the continuities in his thought regarding imperialism as the master variable in modern Europe's wars. Democracy had failed to stop the imperialist war because democracy did not exist anywhere. The countries that called themselves democracies in fact operated under tight oligarchic control. Politics were everywhere the same at the decision-making level, where elites ruled. The issues least susceptible to democratic control were foreign policy and war. "The flaw in the working of the so-called democratic institutions" had been on display in the summer of 1914, when the war began to the amazed surprise of nearly everyone.[4]

Hobson cautioned that imperialism should not be understood as a simple policy with a simple motive. Moreover, many other factors besides imperialist rivalries helped to bring on the war: political ambition, and what he called as a general category of human motivation "the aggrandizing instincts." Specifically, however, "this greed of empire has been the main source of the growing discord in the modern world." All the major powers had pursued empire, and they all bore some responsibility for the outbreak of the war. Empire did not only consist of colonies and coaling stations: "Under the direction of skilled financiers an increasing flow of surplus or savings has gone about the world, knocking at every door of profitable investment and using governmental pressure wherever it was necessary." Politicians had much to do with imperialism as well: "More and more this pressure of financiers for profitable foreign fields has played in with the political ambitions of states-men, to make the inflammatory composition of modern imperialism." He concluded that the Great War had come about not because of German mili-tarism, but because of warped nationalism and capitalist imperialism across Europe. All the capitalist states had "laid the powder train. The dramatic an-tithesis of aggressive autocracies and pacific democracies is false, and the fail-ure to discern this falsehood explains the great surprise."[5]

Hobson's 1920 *PSQ* article belongs to a category of postwar writing that went by the name of revisionism. The individuals participating in this move-ment proposed to revise the official explanation of the victors for their mo-tives and policies in the Great War. Beard would become a revisionist, and in *The Rise of American Civilization* (1927) he would look back to 1920 as the key year in his changing views about the causes and the meaning of the war. In that book, he identified Philip Gibbs's *The Realities of War* as a horrible revelation about the true character of the war. It is impossible to say which publication he read first in 1920, "Why the War Came as a Surprise" or *The Realities of War*, but both men helped to move him into the revisionist camp.

The most famous battlefield journalist of the Great War, Gibbs had been embedded with British troops on the Western Front. In *The Realities of War*, he did not disown the stories that he had written earlier about the conflict. As a war correspondent, he claimed to have been "narrating the facts as I found them, as far as the Censorship would allow."[6] He explained further, in a manner that would reinforce the thesis of Paul Fussell in *The Great War and Modern Memory*, how the sheer ghastliness of the war created a problem of incom-municability for journalists trying to describe it. Fussell explained, "One of the cruxes of the war, of course, is the collision between events and the language available—or thought appropriate—to describe them. To put it more accu-rately, the collision was one between events and the public language used for over a century to celebrate the idea of progress."[7] The existing codes of lan-guage in 1914 did not permit accurate reporting on the war. Throughout the book, Fussell cites Gibbs as a witness of the highest authority.

In *The Realities of War*, Gibbs proposed "to get deeper to the truth of this war and of all war." Looking back on the reasons for the conflict, he dismissed all explanations having to do with German atrocities, which he bluntly asserted had been fabricated by British propaganda agencies to conceal the govern-ment's real reason for fighting Germany: the protection and enhancement of imperial power. Recognizing that it would take a Dante or a Goya to depict the full tragedy of the Western Front, Gibbs nevertheless in *The Realities of War* far surpassed in graphic detail and moral outrage later and more famous novels and memoirs about the fighting, such as Erich Maria Remarque's *All Quiet on the Western Front* and Robert Graves's *Goodbye to All That*. As for the most famous war novel written during the conflict itself, *Under Fire* by Henri Barbusse, Gibbs thought it unrelievedly and excessively bleak, but in a sympathetic manner of basic agreement summed up the Frenchman's interpretation of the war's origins: "The political philosophy on both sides of the Rhine was the same. It was based on military power and rivalry of secret alliances and Imperial ambition."[8]

Look to the secret treaties, Gibbs advised, for an understanding of why the Allies had decided to fight Germany. The close correspondence between the terms of those treaties and the diplomatic outcome at the Paris Peace Conference unmasked the motives for war on the Allied side. Beard claimed to have found Gibbs's argument irresistible. His reading of that book contributed to a process of discovery for him about the war's true origins and meaning. From then on, his wartime image of Woodrow Wilson as a champion of internationalism rapidly faded. In fact, the president had been nothing more than a useful tool for "the Gang," as Gibbs contemptuously referred to Winston Churchill, Georges Clemenceau, and Raymond Poincaré. Beard quoted Gibbs's collective judgment of them: "The old politicians who had played the game of politics before the war, gambling with the lives of men for territories, privileged markets, oil fields, native races, coaling stations, and imperial prestige, grabbed the pool which the German gamblers had lost when their last bluff was called and quarreled over its distribution."[9] The leaders of Germany certainly registered no higher on Gibbs's moral scale, but his argument for an essential equivalence in turpitude between the two sides now seemed incontrovertible to Beard. In addition, the publication of memoirs and documentation, especially from the Russian archives, solidified Beard in his revisionism.

In its July 1920 issue, the *American Historical Review* initiated publication of Sidney Bradshaw Fay's three-part "New Light on the Origins of the World War." These articles would form the basis of his classic *Origins of the World War* (1928). Fay argued that recently released documents from the archives of Austria, Germany, and Russia contradicted the official Allied thesis about the war. Though critical of Germany for its uniquely severe addiction to militarism and of the kaiser for badly mismanaging the diplomatic inheritance of Bismarck, Fay defended the Germans against the main charge laid at their feet by the victors in 1919: "On the whole these new documents from Berlin and Vienna place Austria in a much more unfavorable light than hitherto. They likewise clear the German government of the charge that it deliberately plot-ted or wanted the war."[10] About Chancellor Theobald von Bethmann-Hollweg and the kaiser, Fay explained how they "were not criminals plotting the World War; they were simpletons putting 'a noose about their necks' and handing the other end of the rope to a stupid and clumsy adventurer who now felt free to go as far as he liked."[11]

The adventurer identified by Fay was Austria's foreign minister, Count Leopold von Berchtold, the recipient of the famous "blank check" from his German ally to deal as he saw fit with the Serbian government, accused by him of complicity with the terrorists responsible for the assassination in June of Archduke Franz Ferdinand and his wife. For his recklessness, intransigence, and bellicosity toward Serbia following this assassination, Berchtold deserved the largest share of the blame for the war's outbreak, according to Fay. Russian militarists, working behind the back of the tsar, "peace-loving Nicholas," and undercutting his efforts for peace, also bore a heavy burden of responsibility for the conflict.[12] Militarism in all three countries had to be counted as a propulsive force hurtling Europe toward the abyss. Although Britain and France continued to keep their archives sealed, the imperialist aims of these two countries clearly could be ascertained in the agreements they had made with Russia, now controlled by the Bolsheviks who made a gift to the world of tsarist documents outlining just what the vaunted war of the Allies for civilization meant in practical terms. For Beard, Fay's articles successfully challenged the conventional picture of France, England, and Russia as purehearted innocents fiendishly set upon by the congenitally sinister Germans, as the Treaty of Versailles, with excessive compression about the conduct of the victors, presented matters in the clause assigning full and eternal blame to the defeated foe.

Reviews that Beard wrote in the early 1920s confirm the transformative effect that Fay's articles had on his thinking about the war. In a review published on December 22, 1920, in the *New Republic*, he cited "the painstaking and illuminating researches of Professor Sidney B. Fay published in *The American Historical Review* for July and October 1920."[13] On February 22, 1922, a *New Republic* review of his appeared with the title "Light on the Franco-Russian Alliance," regarding *L'Alliance Franco-Russe* by Henri Welschinger. The book reinforced Fay's thesis in his "New Light on the Origins of the World War" series for the *American Historical Review*. With the opening of the German, Austrian, and Russian archives, Beard wrote, "Slowly the official myth about the war and its origins is being dissolved by sunlight." Welschinger's research showed that arrangements between the two countries had been made as long ago as the 1880s without anyone outside of official circles knowing anything about what had taken place. Summing up Welschinger's argument, Beard explained that, right up to the war, "the grand alliance remained curtained in

darkness." The French had thought that they lived in a free and open republic, but insofar as foreign policy went their leaders behaved no differently from
the autocratic tsarist government, making military commitments and allocat-
ing immense sums without bothering to inform the allegedly sovereign French
people. Beard could see no difference in intent between the military preparations made by the French and the Russians on the one hand and by the Germans and their allies on the other. By destroying once and for all the myth of
a unique German militarism, a belief system that even Fay had left inviolate,
Welschinger deserved a frank expression of thanks, and Beard concluded his
review with the words, "Merci, M. Welschinger."[14]

Lectures that Beard gave in June 1922 at Amherst College, published later
that year as *Cross Currents in Europe Today*, reflected the reading he had done
the previous two years leading to his postwar disillusionment. In these lectures,
he devoted much attention to John Maynard Keynes's *Economic Consequences
of the Peace* (1919). A member of the British delegation, Keynes had witnessed
the proceedings at close range: "Paris was a nightmare and . . . all the elements
of ancient tragedy were there." He portrayed Wilson as a leader completely
lacking in "a dominating intellectual equipment." He judged the president's
advisers, many of them recruited from top American universities, as helpless neophytes, unable to match wits, historical knowledge, and diplomatic
skill with their European counterparts, who roundly succeeded in their aim of
basing the peace settlement entirely on imperialist greed and ambition. The
Europeans resorted to Wilsonian locutions about democracy and the self-
determination of all peoples as a diversionary tactic to conceal their imperialist ambitions and to humor the American leader, whose idealism they
despised. The Paris Peace Conference thus resulted in a cynical and self-serving
treaty "clotted, for the President's sake, in the august language of freedom and
international equality."[15]

Through an irresponsible reparations system of unprecedented severity,
Keynes insisted, the treaty aimed at the systematic destruction of Germany's
economic capacity: "German democracy is thus annihilated at the very moment when the German people was about to build it up after a severe
struggle—annihilated by the very persons who throughout the war never
tired of maintaining that they sought to bring democracy to us." About the
likely political consequences in Germany of the Versailles Treaty, Keynes observed, "Men will not always die quietly." He ventured to predict that some
would be driven "to the nervous instability of hysteria and to a mad despair."
It would be difficult to find anywhere in the published record a more preco-
cious assessment of the historical origins of the Nazi movement, the ultimate
beneficiary of the Versailles Treaty. The degradation of Germany, he pro-

phetically warned, would give rise to a spirit of revenge and another war. "We are at the dead season of our fortunes," Keynes writing in the autumn of 1919 lamented, "Never in the lifetime of men now living has the universal element in the soul of man burnt so dimly."[16]

Beard judged *The Economic Consequences of the Peace* to be the definitive analysis of the postwar settlement. "The Carthaginian Treaty made at Versailles," he told the Amherst audience, proved that the war had been about the furtherance of militarism and imperialism, not their extinction.[17] Throughout his book, Keynes had called the treaty a Carthaginian peace. The terms of that treaty brought into the open what the actual war aims of the victors had been all along. Aggression and covetousness were by no means confined to the Germans. The publication of the diplomatic correspondence of the defeated powers and, even more, the contents of the Allied secret treaties made public by the Bolsheviks contained the true history of the war's origins and meaning. Hobson, Gibbs, and Fay had enlarged Keynes's revisionist interpretation of the Versailles Treaty to include a wholesale repudiation of the Allied interpretation of the war itself, the learned promotion of which in America Beard had addressed. In a *New Republic* review of the previous year, he surely had his own case in mind as an example of how modern war calls on every member of society to contribute, "even the poor professor, once spurned by all, who is able to do his bit with a pen more deadly than the chemist's test tube."[18]

"For many long years," Beard informed the Amherst audience, "we have lived in the mists of official propaganda." He wanted to measure wartime propaganda against the realities to be found in the archival documentary record of the belligerents. The record disclosed that all these countries, on both sides, had been motivated by the same lust for strategic and economic advantage, with no scruples at all regarding the means to attain them: "Behind closed doors diplomats exchanged pledges and created situations which drove Europe into the abyss." For a defense against the deceptions, lies, and chicanery to which all these governments were shown by the evidence to be addicted in the eternal pursuit of their own advantage and that of the people who controlled them, Beard drew from the experience of his own bamboozlement the lesson that America had need of "an ever growing body of enlightened citizens who do their own thinking and are not deceived by official propaganda."[19]

Although Beard at the outset of his Amherst lectures had promised not to lay blame for the war, he proceeded to do so anyway in a series of indictments against the Allied and Central powers. Nor did America escape his censure. America had not been involved in the origins of the war, but had profited from it. Moreover, in the postwar period "our huge industrial and banking corporations are driving hard in every market." He thought that Washington's domineering policies in Latin America sprang from standard imperialist impulses. With American investors "deeply involved in the fate of governments and enterprises in all parts of the world," Beard predicted that the global application of the country's Latin American policies would be only a matter of time. "Days of greater trouble are ahead," he said. For the great powers, among which the United States enjoyed an unrivaled economic eminence, "foreign affairs relate principally to investments, trade, iron, coal, oil, copper, and rubber, and other raw materials."[20] These same resources had been the real issue in the Great War, as they would be in the wars to come. At most, spreading democracy had an incidental significance in explaining intervention by the United States in the war. Indeed, as Beard had worried in another review of the previous year, American democracy itself now stood at risk: "It requires no very vivid imagination to discover where a series of wars and internal disturbances would lead us."[21]

Yet it cannot be said that Beard's conversion to revisionism was complete even as late as 1923. In that year, he and William C. Bagley wrote the revised edition of their school textbook, *The History of the American People*, originally published in 1918. The authors made many changes in the new edition, but their patriotic interpretation of the Great War remained fundamentally the same. German intrigues and "the Hohenzollerns' Dream of World Dominion" they identified as the fundamental causes of the war.[22] They continued to praise Wilson and his war policies unstintingly. Either Beard deemed American schoolchildren unready for full exposure to revisionism or he still had some doubts about it himself. In either case, there is no hint of revisionism in this textbook.

At the same time, Beard continued to read revisionist literature. In the rapidly accumulating bibliography of postwar revisionism, Edmund Dene Morel's pamphlet, "The Secret History of a Great Betrayal" (1923), ranks in importance with Hobson's "Why the War Came as a Surprise," Gibbs's *Realities of War*, and Fay's articles in the *American Historical Review*. Morel, a British journalist and editor, had been the animating spirit of the Union of Democratic Control, the progressive anti-war organization to which Hobson had belonged. The members believed that secrecy in government had led to the world war. Raymond Beazley, an eminent historian and professor at the University of Birmingham, wrote a preface for this pamphlet, which following its entry into the *Congressional Record* on February 7, 1924, by Oklahoma Democratic senator Robert Latham Owen became in America one of the canonical revisionist texts. In it Beard found confirmation for his bitter skepticism about all official explanations, on both sides of the Atlantic, for why it had been the patriotic duty of ten million young men to die on the battlefields of the war.

As an inveterate reader of the *Congressional Record*, Beard in 1924 would have been alerted in its pages to the existence of "The Secret History of a Great Betrayal," if the pamphlet had not come to his attention even earlier.

Beazley, a historian of the age of exploration until the war redirected his scholarly energies into the field of British foreign policy, thought that Morel had the gift of prophecy: "Long ago he pointed out the direction of those currents of uncontrolled imperialism and boiling Chauvinism which have swept us, and swept civilization, into the whirlpool below the falls." Born in France to a French father and a British Quaker mother, he had been a leader in the prewar pacifist movement and, while actively opposing the horrors of slavery in the Congo, had identified imperialism as the systemic curse of contemporary European civilization and the chief agency of its approaching doom, were the present trends of international relations to continue. The world war had come as the fulfillment of his ignored warnings. He continued to speak out even after the fighting had started. The pro-war press condemned him as an agent of Germany. He was physically attacked as well. In 1917 Morel's anti-war activities landed him in jail, where his health became undermined, leading to his death at the age of fifty-one, a year after the publication of his electrifying pamphlet. For years, Beazley concluded, Morel had tried to warn Europeans about "the military demon" in their midst. They unwisely trusted their leaders, who soothingly reassured them that the government had everything under control: "For in their hands had been the rudder all the time while we drifted to no still waters, no green pastures."[23]

Morel's list of factors responsible for the "immense tragedy" of the war greatly exceeded that of Beazley. Of course, the military and political chiefs deserved to be blamed, but the system they dominated had many other working parts, all of which had functioned harmoniously in pursuing "a policy which imparted to the professional interests of the 'fighting services' and their extensive ramifications in the social, industrial, journalistic, and financial world, the power to form 'atmosphere' and influence events occultly, with ever increasing effect."[24]

Focusing on the British role in causing the war, Morel observed that beginning in 1906 their secret military and naval understandings with the French and later the Russians had contributed, as much as anything the Germans had done, to the European disaster of 1914. A handful of men in the British cabinet with their accessories in the foreign office and embassy officialdom bore the responsibility for these policy initiatives, which, Morel angrily pointed out, would bring grief and desolation to many thousands of British homes. He highly doubted that democracy seriously had anything to do with the way the British were governed on the vital questions of national interest. Though standing on a precipice, they "went about their daily business, in blissful ignorance of everything but the fact that they were in the proud position of enjoying a democratic constitution and, unlike their benighted continental neighbors, were the masters and not the servants of their rulers." Then, "when the time came, the only consideration given to 'public opinion' was how best to throw dust into its eyes." The British parliamentary system, with all its democratic safeguards, failed completely: "The destinies of a people could not have been predetermined more arbitrarily under the most despotic of monarchies." Contrary to the Whiggish pieties about the British political tradition, "we are, in effect, slaves from the cradle, slaves of our war lords and the sinister powers behind them."[25]

Winston Churchill, first lord of the Admiralty from 1911 to 1915, seemed to Morel the incarnation of British truculence in international affairs during these years. Ever engrossed in preparations for war with Germany, Churchill did as much as anyone to impart "additional elements of instability to the rocking and swaying European edifice." Morel's contemptuous critique of Churchill made a permanent impression on Beard, who during another war would find simply incredible the publicity campaign of Washington touting Churchill as America's partner in spreading democracy worldwide. From Morel's savage account, he would have learned that Churchill did not know a thing about democracy, except how to manipulate it for imperialist ends. Sir Edward Grey, foreign secretary from 1905 to 1916, and H. H. Asquith, Liberal prime minister from 1908 to 1916, Morel found guilty of the "secret bartering away of the national independence" and "a crime against the State." Morel used the image of a "Russo-French noose" that duplicitous British leaders were fastening around the necks of their fellow citizens.[26]

Morel thought that all the Great Powers worked in the same militarist way and toward the same imperialist ends. The military preparations on both sides of the European alliance system "were perfectly proper, of course—in the great game of arranging a general international massacre. No one suggests the contrary. But what becomes of the legend that poor France and Russia were unprepared and 'wantonly attacked'?" The Russians almost certainly knew about and encouraged the Serbian terrorist plot to murder Archduke Franz Ferdinand. When Morel referred to "the conspirators in Petrograd, Belgrade, and elsewhere," he intended to include Paris on the list of cities engaged in or tolerant of terrorist plotting because French and Russian military cooperation had become complete long before this time. The British War Office, meanwhile, had become increasingly committed to the military plans of "unprepared France and Russia." The Germans, fully aware of Entente military preparations, responded in kind, which spurred more calls for "defense" in Britain, France, and Russia.[27]

"And so to the end," Morel wrote as he began his summation of what the war cost Britain and the world. The British victory had proved barren. No added parcel of territory or trade advantage could compensate for the appalling expense and loss of 2.5 million British military men killed and wounded. Then there were the odious "peace" treaties to consider: "the Sèvres treaty, with its train of humiliations and disasters; to say nothing of the Versailles treaty and the accessory treaties, which have Balkanized Europe, sowed the seeds of new wars, created a dozen 'Alsace-Lorraines' where one had existed before, and finally led, as they were bound to lead, to an Anglo-French breach." Morel concluded "that war to which all our present national and international troubles are due" should teach the British that the single most pressing political issue in the world concerns the struggle of the people to gain control of their government.[28] The leaders do not have the interests of the people in mind. Economic forces control the government, which has fully exhibited its capacity to deceive, to maim, and to kill its own people by the millions to gain the ends important to the men in possession of it.

Morel's "Secret History of a Great Betrayal" prepared Beard for an important reviewing assignment that the *New Republic* gave him the next year, regarding the memoirs of Sir Edward Grey, *Twenty-Five Years, 1892–1916*. The opening of the secret archives of Germany, Austria, and Russia, Beard began, "let a flood of dazzling light in upon the hidden sources of the great armed conflict." Despite much dispute over the forces and events that had led to the tragic summer of 1914, "all must admit that one thing has been established beyond question, namely, that responsibility for the war must be distributed among all the participants, with Russia and France each bearing a Titan's share."[29]

Turning to Grey's two-volume account of his own role in the war, Beard lamented that he found few revelations in it. Viscount Grey did not descend very far into the particulars of the case and rested content with the official British claims about the war, as a consequence of Germany's menacing military buildup and then its invasion of Belgium. These explanations Morel had ridiculed as the typically sanctimonious propaganda to be expected from officials steeped in the hypocrisies of British imperialism. Occasionally, Grey hinted at a serious historical explanation of the Great War. Beard quoted Grey's words from one of those occasions: "The enormous growth of armaments in Europe, the sense of insecurity and fear caused by them—it was these that made the war inevitable."[30] Almost inadvertently, Grey's story left the impression that all the European powers bore responsibility for the war. The great underreported story about this shared responsibility concerned the Allies. From Welschinger, Beard had learned that France and Russia had spent more on arms than had the Germans and their allies. Morel had added vital information about the British connection to the war plans of France and Russia.

When the Russian documents came out following the Bolshevik takeover, Grey had been accused of lying about the extent of Britain's prewar military relationship with France and Russia. He now had an opportunity to tell his side of the story. On the crucial question of the prewar military commitments that he had made as foreign secretary, his answers failed to satisfy Beard, who complained about the "obscurities of Grey's text." He stuck to "the old thesis": German militarism had brought war to Europe. As for German diplomacy during the war, Beard quoted Grey directly: "German diplomacy was expected to do what it could to make it appear that the war guilt was with someone else." In the spirit of Grey's comment, Beard wondered, "Would it be irrelevant to ask whether English diplomacy or French or Russian diplomacy might have been at least faintly tinged with that desire?"[31]

The most valuable part of Grey's memoirs, for Beard, concerned his comments about Anglo-American relations during the war, particularly regarding Ambassador Walter Hines Page's activities in London. Beard observed, "What Grey says about Page confirms the ambassador's own account of himself as working eagerly, first, to help the British government evade skillfully the demands of the State Department at Washington and, second, to bring the United States into the war on the side of Great Britain."[32] He worked with an unbroken devotion on behalf of the British government in every case involving the infringement at sea of America's rights as a neutral country and then with an equal assiduousness reinforced with his diplomatic reports Wilson's anglophile propensities to enter the war on the Allied side. Grey thought and wrote about Page as an ex officio member of his cabinet.

At least Wilson had made a good-faith effort to end the fighting when in 1916 he proposed through his confidant, Colonel Edward Mandell House, that a peace conference be called. Beard explained why London and Paris showed no interest in the president's initiative: "In view of the Secret Treaties by which the Allies had already divided the spoils in advance, it is not surprising that England and France did not agree to the calling of the conference." Grey's memoirs revealed that the lodestar of British policy during the war concerned the advancement and augmentation of British imperial interests, as prescribed in the secret treaties. The most conspicuous feature of his book was the attention that it called to "the practical indifference shown to anything outside of the British Empire that does not impinge immediately and obviously on British interests."[33]

In his review of the 683-page *Twenty-Five Years, 1892–1916*, Beard observed that the charm of Grey's style could not compensate for his complete lack of awareness regarding the research compiled by Hobson, Fay, Morel, and other writers in the revisionist school. The most important of these other writers were Count Max Montgelas and Harry Elmer Barnes, both mentioned by name in the review. The German edition of the major work by Montgelas, *Leitfaden zur Kriegsschuldfrage*, had appeared in 1923. Alfred A. Knopf published the book in 1925 as *The Case for the Central Powers: An Impeachment of the Versailles Verdict*.

Born in 1860, Montgelas had been a career soldier. At the outbreak of the Great War, he commanded the Fourth Bavarian Infantry Division, but then retired in 1915. Thereafter, in the manner of Thucydides following his removal from the Athenian army during the Peloponnesian War, Montgelas devoted himself to research and writing. The German government made him a member of the commission sent to Versailles to present its case regarding responsibility for the war. That same year a volume he co-edited with Professor Walther Schücking, *Die Deutschen Dokumente zum Kriegsausbruch*, went to press. These were documents collected and assembled by the Socialist leader Karl Kautsky. The collection popularly became known as the "Kautsky Documents," and Oxford University Press brought out the English translation in 1924 under the title *Outbreak of the World War: German Documents Collected by Karl Kautsky*. With publications from two of the most stellar presses in the English-speaking world, Montgelas became one of the core figures of the revisionist movement in which, by this time, Beard had made his way to the front rank, but as a reviewer and lecturer rather than as an archival researcher.

What Beard learned from Montgelas further contributed to his education as a revisionist. *The Case for the Central Powers* brought together and substantiated in persuasive detail the varied elements of the argument against the official Allied explanation for Article 231 of the Versailles Treaty. As Hobson, Fay, Morel, and numerous other authors already had charged, the Allies had lied about their motives, which had come out into the open initially with the publication of the secret treaties and other revelations by the Bolsheviks from the Russian archives. Montgelas began his account by focusing on the historical context of the war's outbreak. To understand the coming of the war, many factors had to be considered: "But its essential cause was the Imperialistic rivalry between the great Colonial Powers, their ambition to bring more and more of the world under their domination, which involved the worst possible crimes against the freedom and independence of the Asiatic and African peoples."[34]

If imperialism had caused the war, then which imperialist power deserved to bear the shame of the Article 231 indictment? No one power deserved to be saddled with it, Montgelas contended. He did not try to overplay his hand

and conceded Germany's share of the blame for the tragedy of the Great War. All the major powers had participated in the deadly game of imperialism. They all deserved varying degrees of censure for the aggression, greed, and cruelty that constituted the essence of imperialism. In surveying the history of the European imperialism that led to the outbreak of the Great War, however, he thought it fair to say that the Germans had played a role of secondary importance, certainly by comparison with the more enterprising French and the vastly more enterprising British, on whose empire the sun never set. To make his case, he thought it sufficient to compare the number of colonial inhabitants controlled in 1914 by Germany, France, and Britain: 12 million, 53 million, and 376 million, respectively. He wanted the reader to think for a moment about this last number. The British had under their direct imperial command one-fifth of the entire human race. Why did so many people fear that Germany wanted to control the world? A much more present concern had to do with the monstrous global presence of British imperialists.

Montgelas did not try to whitewash German imperialism. He admitted its exploitative character and its cruelties, in keeping with the imperialism of all nations. Nevertheless, to acquire an understanding of the decisive role that imperialism played in creating the historical context of the Great War, Germany would not be the first—much less the only—place to look. Article 231 of the Versailles Treaty, fixing all the blame for the war on Germany and her allies, was best understood as a polite fiction used to justify the land grabs, the resource reallocations, and the innovations of colonial control mandated at the Paris Peace Conference. No historian of any competence or integrity could fail to see the fallacious reasoning used by the victors in formulating Article 231, which served as the moral basis for the postwar order.

Among the causes of the Great War, the armaments race had been the subject of the most fantastic legends. Militarism had found a home in Germany, to be sure, but wartime propaganda had conveyed the entirely false impression that the Entente powers, as "democracies," enjoyed an intrinsic exemption from pursuing aggressive policies of military preparedness. On the contrary, Montgelas asserted, "The Triple Entente were not only numerically superior to the opposite side as regards manpower, guns, and ships, but their very precise military agreements gave them a further advantage."[35] Though Germany and Austria had a longstanding alliance, they had not concluded any military convention. The French and the Russians since 1891 and the British since 1905–1906 closely cooperated with each other, including annual meetings of their general staffs, as if diligently preparing for war. Britain and France continued to keep their archives sealed, but the disclosures from Russia exposed the fraudulence of the Entente claims for an exalted degree of democratic moral superiority over the autocratic militarism of Germany.

From the historical context of the Great War, Montgelas moved to a consideration of the political and diplomatic crisis that touched off the conflict in the summer of 1914. The murder by a Serbian terrorist of Archduke Franz Ferdinand, the heir to the Austrian throne, Montgelas described as "the incendiary torch which was hurled into an atmosphere charged with combustible material." No country involved in the aftermath of the assassination emerged from the crisis wholly innocent or error-free, but to buttress his argument for a historically sound apportionment of blame Montgelas shrewdly used the findings of French investigators, chiefly Henri Welschinger, whose L'Alliance Franco-Russe had made such a profound impression on Beard when it appeared in 1922. While a conciliatory Germany was trying to mediate the crisis, France and Russia engaged in bellicose tactics. Their machinations culminated in Russia's mobilization of her armed forces, a move that made war inevitable. Not until the spring of 1922 did the correspondence that passed between Paris and St. Petersburg become published. From those documents it could be seen that Russia, not Austria, had been the first country to mobilize: "This fact was concealed for nine years. For nine whole years the Entente peoples have been led to believe that Austria was the first to order general mobilization."[36] The 1922 revelations also exposed as false the invention of Allied propagandists that Austria had been prepared to yield at the last moment and then had been forced to go to war against her will by the intimidations of Germany. Propaganda, not historical truth, Montgelas concluded, constituted the case in support of Article 231 in the Treaty of Versailles.

Barnes's Genesis of the World War appeared in 1926. A 1918 graduate of Columbia University's history PhD program, Barnes had audited some of Beard's lectures, which had made a highly favorable impression on him for their acute sense of realism about the motivating forces in politics. Nevertheless, Beard had been somewhat peripheral in Barnes's intellectual formation at Columbia. As Barnes would explain many years later, "I did not know Beard at all well personally when a student at Columbia or a teacher at the New School."[37] Their close relationship only began in the late 1930s, when they worked together to keep America out of the Second World War. Even earlier, however, Barnes had been an important figure in Beard's life as a fellow revisionist during the 1920s.

A prolific author and a highly successful teacher at Smith College, Barnes published The Genesis of the World War with the prestigious firm of Alfred A. Knopf. The book would establish his reputation as a leading revisionist historian of the younger generation. Like Beard, Barnes had been an ardent interventionist in 1917 and had supported Wilson throughout the war. He saw no reason to change his views about the war until reading the same authors who had converted Beard to revisionism: Keynes, Fay, Beazley, Morel, and Montgelas. Barnes quickly became a revisionist himself. He did so with some trepidation. Six weeks before the publication of *The Genesis of the World War*, he wrote to his friend Yale law professor Edwin Montefiore Borchard: "The book as a whole may lead to my residence in Patagonia after April 1st, but it will be worth the trip."[38] Thanking Professor Borchard the next week for his critical comments on the manuscript, Barnes noted, "I imagine the book will stir the animals rather badly, and . . . we may have some fun out of the enterprise."[39]

Following in the vein of Fay and Morel though exceeding them in the sweep and vehemence of his indictment of the war guilt clause, Barnes turned the Allied thesis in the Treaty of Versailles inside out. Germany, he claimed, deserved to be exonerated for the war's outbreak. The Treaty's infamous Article 231—the German war guilt clause—should have been aimed at France and Russia primarily, with Austria and England coming in for lesser degrees of censure, and with the Germans least of all. The fighting had culminated in "an unfair and unjust Peace Treaty, which was itself erected upon a most uncritical and complete acceptance of the grossest forms of wartime illusions concerning war guilt."[40] All the Great Powers, Barnes claimed, had participated in the chain of events leading up to the war, but a half-dozen men in Paris and Saint Petersburg bore the principal responsibility for its actual outbreak.

In the book's acknowledgments, Barnes thanked sixteen different historians for their help, but did not refer to Beard, unless he had been the "highly competent critic who prefers not to be mentioned by name."[41] Barnes had asked this individual to read the fourth chapter, which dealt with the Serbian crisis. Ever attentive to European affairs, Beard had closely followed developments in Yugoslavia. In 1927–1928 he would spend four months there with his wife and then write *The Balkan Pivot* (1929). Beard very well could have been Barnes's anonymous consultant. In any case, Barnes referred to Beard in the book, citing his October 7, 1925, *New Republic* review of British foreign minister Edward Grey's memoirs as evidence of naked imperial self-interest in Britain's decision to go to war.[42] Concern for "brave little Belgium," the official explanation for that decision, had been only a pretext. In an appendix concerning "The Literature of War Guilt," Barnes cited *Cross-Currents in Europe Today* (1922), in which Beard had abjured his earlier faith in the war. Barnes added, "Beard's trenchant analysis in his work on post-war Europe has not received one-tenth of the attention it deserves."[43]

Barnes and Beard held identical views about the reasons for America's intervention in the European conflict. In *The Genesis of the World War*, Barnes contended that as early as 1915 the pro-British Wilson had decided to take the United States into the war, only waiting for the right combination of propitious circumstances to do so. His 1916 presidential campaign slogan, "He kept us out of war," was a calculated lie. He also dismissed the president's portrayal of Germany's unique dastardliness in her U-boat attacks: "The German submarine warfare was a legitimate retaliation against the British violations of international law . . . against which Mr. Wilson refused to protest with adequate persistence and firmness."[44] By inclination and political calculation, he had been disposed to respond willingly to the pressures exerted by American financiers and businessmen eager to protect their enormous financial investment in the Allied cause. Wilson had lied systematically to the American people about the true motives in his wartime policies.

Contrary to Wilson's war declaration speech to the joint session of Congress on April 2, 1917, America's intervention had absolutely nothing to do with the president's assurance about how the country would be making the world safe for democracy and everything to do with safeguarding the investments of American bankers and financiers in the Allied cause. Wilson's utter subservience to the British lobby and his fantastic megalomaniacal conceits about himself as the savior of the world also deserved notice by historians who might want to understand the real reasons why America entered the war. Barnes closed the American intervention section of *The Genesis of the World War* with the words of Bruce Bliven, a writer for the *New Republic*: "'We have been played for a bunch of suckers,' used to pull the English and French chestnuts out of the fire."[45] Beard shared unreservedly Barnes's revisionist views of the war's origins and America's involvement in it. Thereafter, they would reinforce each other's arguments about these two subjects.

With the eye of a zealous convert to revisionism, Beard in 1926 read the two volumes of *The Intimate Papers of Colonel House*, hoping to obtain from them a full account of why the United States had entered the Great War in 1917. He reviewed the book that same year for the *New Republic*. He could not have been encouraged upon finding at the front of the book a quotation by Viscount Grey of Fallodon: "House longed to get good accomplished and was content that others should have the credit."[46] Grey had not been forthcoming in his memoirs, Beard had concluded, and he must have feared a similar attempt at evasion by House. In fact, the House book turned out to be somewhat disappointing to Beard, offering "few startling revelations" about American intervention in the war.[47]

Despite finding little new insight about the large question of the government's motives for American intervention, Beard admired the structure of the book. The collection consisted of selected House papers arranged as a narrative by Yale University Sterling Professor of History Charles Seymour. Beard praised the editing work that Seymour had done as skillful, tactful, and discriminating. Moreover, he found House to be an impressive figure, particularly for the exceedingly well-developed sense of realism that he showed in dealing with European leaders, above all the British. Unlike Beard himself, House had not accepted "the mythology of the propagandists put out for the gullible."[48] Beard could not have denied that for gullibility about British wartime propaganda from 1914 to 1918 he had shown a most impressive capacity.

Long before it became generally understood among well-informed people that the British leaders had lied with every utterance they made about the reasons for declaring war on Germany, House had shown "no patience with Britain's Belgium yarn."[49] The German invasion of Belgium, as Montgelas and Morel had shown, counted only as a pretext for the British, who made their moves in the summer of 1914 in fulfillment of the military conventions created to protect and enlarge the Empire. House had found stubbornness, selfishness, and cant in all the European capitals he visited on the president's behalf. He did agree with Wilson about the danger to America that a German victory would produce and thus had lent his support to intervention, but the propaganda of the Allies about their own motives did not deceive him. He knew too much about the European situation to believe that Germany deserved full blame for the war.

Reading *The Intimate Papers of Colonel House* gave Beard additional reasons to detest the American ambassador in London, Walter Hines Page. About House's account of the ambassador's activities, Beard wrote, "The picture of the American ambassador in London condemning his own government and an unofficial special agent negotiating separately with the British ministry is one of the curiosities of intellectual and moral history." Beard admired the perceptiveness of House's judgments about the personalities in the Wilson administration and found in the book a strongly pronounced aversion to the commonplaces of Allied propaganda, a characteristic that made him "one of the biggest men of his time."[50]

House's comments on his boss, President Wilson, fascinated Beard most of all. One of the supremely enigmatic figures in American history, Wilson had started out in life as a conservative. Beard thought that his political record allowed for no debate about Wilson's fundamentally conservative outlook and claimed, "before his translation from Princeton to Trenton" he had shown few signs of discontent with the prevailing governing system in America. He detested socialism, opposed the direct government movement espoused by progressives like Robert La Follette, deemed women's suffrage a stomach-turning development in American life, fought the popular election of United States senators, and showed no sympathy for trade unions. "To make a long story short," Beard summarized, "Woodrow Wilson derived his religion from John Calvin, his economics from Adam Smith, and his politics from Edmund Burke."[51] For most of his life, he considered the left to be enemy territory in American politics and held all forms of radicalism in abhorrence.

The image of Wilson as a progressive politician only began to take form in 1912 during the presidential campaign of that year. Designed to meet the needs of a political situation and not to reflect in an accurate way the personality or the philosophy of the candidate, this image seemed to have come from House, who in that year anonymously had published a political novel, *Philip Dru: Administrator*. The progressivism of Wilson's "New Freedom" campaign, Beard guessed, might well have come from Philip Dru's philosophy. He further speculated in the review, "No doubt these volumes will make a storm in the Wilson camp for in effect they portray House as furnishing the ideas and the drive for his partner's administration." The Wilson described in House's book seemed to Beard fundamentally weak and highly suggestible, in the manner of Keynes's portrait of the president, just the sort of man who would undergo repeated conversions from principle to necessity. The 1916 campaign slogan, "He kept us out of war," did not deter him five months later from issuing a war declaration against Germany. "Open covenants openly arrived at" and the other principles in the January 1918 Fourteen Points Address would be cancelled out the next year at the Paris Peace Conference.[52] For Beard, the chief value of *The Intimate Papers of Colonel House* consisted of its incriminating revelations about Wilson by the man who knew him better than anyone else in the world did.

In a conversion that would be complete and last a lifetime, Hobson, Gibbs, Fay, Keynes, Morel, Montgelas, and Barnes made a revisionist out of Beard, though they did so at a pace much slower than the one he described in *The Rise of American Civilization*. By 1927, when the first two volumes appeared, Beard could only think of the war as a completely useless sacrifice for all the killed and wounded. It was the greatest calamity ever to befall Western civilization. He would spend the rest of his life trying to identify the tragic flaw that had caused Europe's downfall and to understand the American side of this horrific story. In some important respects, he assumed the role of an American Oswald Spengler, whose *The Decline of the West* (1918–1923) he read carefully and admired. *The Rise of American Civilization*, which he co-wrote with his wife, contains his preliminary synthesis about the Great War and America's part in it.

Thus, a storied husband-and-wife collaboration in American letters began. Controversy persists over the extent of Mary's contribution to the work that they published together. Though not trained as a historian, she certainly became one. Mary would publish books of her own, but she is known primarily today as her husband's co-author of *The Rise of American Civilization* series, which eventually would total four volumes. Later in life, she would insist that her role involved more than solely drawing attention to women's issues. Indeed, her wide-ranging interest in politics and foreign policy paralleled his. They worked as a team and tested each other's thinking. The two volumes that came out in 1927 provide the deep historical background, as the Beards saw it, for the American involvement in the war. They also reflect the extent of Charles Beard's revisionist thinking, which Mary shared completely, about the war's causes and true significance as the epitome of imperialist ambitions.

The Beards viewed American history as a series of turning points determined chiefly by economic forces. None of the country's wars could be understood without a careful analysis of the always prominent part taken by commercial and financial interests. Beginning with the colonial wars and continuing with the American Revolution, the Civil War, and the Spanish-American War, the same pattern revealed itself, with economic elites at these key moments seeking to secure their interests through military action. If American history could be said to contain a master variable, this conjunction between military means and imperialist economic ends would be it. The prevalence of economic motives in American history could be traced back to the Pilgrims. It would be wrong to oversimplify the past by explaining it in a mono-causal way. Other motives, not least religious ideas, had a large share in the American experience, but trade and conquest mattered more over the long term. A great economic struggle pitted the North American colonists against the British Empire. Having won their revolution, however, the Americans ironically found themselves in the position of having to create an empire of their own, with headquarters eventually in Washington. About the beginnings of this American state, the Beards wrote, "A new political organism had been called into being, feeble at first, but destined to rule a continent and islands in distant seas." The Constitutional Convention of 1787 decisively conditioned what followed in American history, having created a political system that served an elite class as "an instrument of power in the direction of national economy and in the distribution of wealth."[53]

The major developments in American history leading up to the Civil War were fundamentally economic in character, each one a consequence deeply conditioned by "this titanic conflict over the distribution of wealth." The Beards attached little significance to the issue of slavery as a cause of the Civil

War. To them slavery was only "a minor element in the sweep of political and economic forces that occupied the attention of statesmen throughout the middle period and finally brought on the irrepressible conflict." The two historians focused their attention primarily on the prerogatives of centralizing finance as the driving force of events. The Civil War the Beards described as a second American Revolution and the culmination of "the deep-running transformation that shifted the center of gravity in American society" toward Wall Street.[54]

The second American Revolution assured the triumph of business enterprise, the ruling elements of which turned their attention after the Civil War to the conquest of the continent. The golden age of "the American business peerage" lay at hand. Supreme at home, the barons of capitalist enterprise by the end of the nineteenth century began to look for foreign conquests. The Spanish-American War would make the United States a world power with a foreign empire in the Caribbean and the Pacific. American foreign policy did not proceed in fulfillment of an overall imperialistic design; instead "it slowly broadened out from episode to incident." The Americans shared with their English cousins an Anglo-Saxon version of imperialism in which "a high sense of moral responsibility could accompany security for invested capital."[55]

Beard and his wife spent five years writing their book, from 1922 to 1927, almost exactly the period when he underwent his conversion to revisionism. The revisionist thesis permeated their account of the Great War in *The Rise of American Civilization*. They adopted an openly mocking attitude toward Entente propaganda, which solemnly had maintained that England, France, and Russia "all unsuspecting, had pursued the ways of innocence, had sincerely desired peace, and made no adequate preparations for a great cataclysm." This same propaganda had expressed moral outrage against the Central Powers for leaping "like tigers upon their guileless victims." For such tall tales the Beards now had only words of scorn. The steady diet of German atrocity stories fed to the American people by Allied propagandists they impatiently derided as a "story for babes," which swiftly became an article of faith in the circles of opinion that determined policy: "To question any part of it in those spheres was to set oneself down as a boor and a 'Hun' and, after 1917, as a traitor to America besides."[56]

The Beards stressed the importance of Anglo-French loans and war orders as crucial factors in the fateful policy decisions of 1917, in keeping with the general thesis in *The Rise of American Civilization* regarding the economic determinants of war. About the bankers, financiers, and leaders of the giant corporations, they wrote: "the war dirge raised by these selfish factions was adequately financed, astutely managed, and effectively carried into strange

out-of-the-way places as well as into the main highways." They did not spare
the history profession or, by implication, Beard himself for leading the
people astray with patriotic interpretations of the war that subsequent archival
revelations confirmed to have belonged to the realm of imaginative literature: "To the necessities of this campaign, trained historians bent their supple
discipline while the sciences and arts rendered their full tribute to the cause."
Indeed, the entire school system "was easily brought into line with mechani-
cal precision, subduing the minds of even tender children to the official thesis
concerning the origins and merits of the contest." Looking back on those
terrible war years, the Beards expressed amazement at "how thoroughly,
how irresistibly a modern government could impose its ideas upon the whole
nation and, under a barrage of publicity, stifle dissent with declarations,
assertions, official versions, and reiteration."[57]

The Rise of American Civilization lavishes praise on Senator Robert La Follette for his rear-guard effort to keep America out of the war. The Beards analyzed at length La Follette's anti-war rebuttal in the Senate against Wilson's
war message, pointing out its three core elements: the gross favoritism always
of the United States toward Great Britain, the wholly fictitious character of
the war for democracy, and the opposition of the American people against the
financial elites who wanted the war. To La Follette, America had applied two
sets of standards during the war: a demand for strict accountability following
German outrages against the rights of neutrals; and an entirely different response, characterized by sympathy and forbearance, regarding anything that
the British might do. As for making the world safe for democracy, he held that
to participate in such a lofty enterprise the British would have to contravene
all the laws of their nature as imperialist overlords in Ireland, Egypt, and
India, where the people in those lands would go on being disqualified for
membership in the democracies. On the third point, La Follette had dared the
government to submit the war resolution to a popular referendum, which he
felt certain would fail by a vote of ten to one. La Follette had the high honor of
being "the leading champion of peace in the Congress of the United States."[58]
Tragically, he had gone down to defeat at the hands of an inferior man who
held the highest office in the land. The Beards paid tribute to La Follette in *The
Rise of American Civilization* for having been right when Beard himself and
virtually the entire governing class of the country had been wrong.

Beard despised Bolshevism as a political ideology, but the Bolsheviks, too,
were shown in *The Rise of American Civilization* to have been right about the
thoroughly imperialist character of the war. Moreover, with the secret treaties they had furnished unassailable evidence in support of their thesis: "If the
Bolsheviki had not torn open the secret archives of Petrograd and flung the

documents in the face of mankind in December 1917, these plighted war aims of the Entente Allies would have remained unknown perhaps forever and their official hypothesis would have been questioned only by the cynical at home and abroad." Such shocking documents had compelled the Allies to think quickly about a rebuttal to, or at least a distraction from, their incriminating contents. Only at that moment of awful disclosure had the Allies subscribed to Wilson's Fourteen Points Address strategy in presenting their war aims as the apotheosis of democracy and the rights of man, "privately subject to discreet and appropriate reservations." Accordingly, at the Paris Peace Conference decisions came about based on "the fine old Roman principle of 'Woe to the Vanquished.'" The secret treaties, not the Fourteen Points, won the day at the peace conference. As for Article 231 placing sole blame for the war on Germany and its allies, the Beards called it "a solemn declaration that must have brought an exquisite smile to the lips of Lloyd George and Clemenceau as they thought of the secret archives in London and Paris."[59]

Beard's *New Republic* review of André Siegfried's *America Comes of Age* also appeared in 1927, the same year as *The Rise of American Civilization*. Siegfried's book had met with enormous success in its English translation. In the review, Beard succinctly expressed in the language of revisionism his aversion to the concept of an exceptional American past, echoing a claim more implicitly made in the 1,600-page survey that he wrote with his wife and destined to be at the center of his subsequent writing.

In the review, Beard approached the concept of a sublime American past indirectly at first. Siegfried had contrasted the materialistic culture of the United States with the unique spirituality of French civilization. Beard found such a claim untenable in the light of contemporary history, particularly the Great War and the Paris Peace Conference. He could see very little of the spiritual in the comportment of any combatant nation. He strongly identified with the American people who "have been voraciously reading huge tomes on the war origins, and have been suffering from some resentment over the way in which they were unmercifully gulled by the Entente prophets of the higher morality." He agreed with those Americans who "think that England and France owe this country an apology for the continuous and mendacious propaganda carried on during the early years of the World War."[60] It seemed to Beard that based on the amazingly precise correlation between the wartime secret treaties and the treaties emanating from the Paris Peace Conference all talk of France's unique gifts in the department of spirituality should stop at once. Obviously, greed and egotism knew no boundaries.

America's ideas about its sacred past also could not withstand the scrutiny of seriously informed persons, the category Beard referred to as readers "who have left the abc class." In modern times, the same kinds of elites have run the United States and Europe. The actual power structures, rhetorical and cosmetic distinctions aside, are strikingly similar, he thought. Examining the contemporary moment, he found these similarities of economic aim and political method to be increasingly pronounced. To illustrate his argument, he cited the cases of the United States and France, the comparison that had inspired Siegfried to write his book. Beard had "some difficulty discovering profound spiritual differences between M. Poincaré and Mr. Coolidge, between the use of Annamese troops to preserve French loot in China and the use of American Marines in the interest of law and order in Haiti, between the conduct of French authorities in Asia Minor and American authorities in Santo Domingo, between the Paris bankers and the New York stock brokers, between the editor of *Le Temps* and the editor of the Times, and so on."[61] Imperialism, the defining reality of the twentieth century, did not change from country to country, except in the capacity of some empires to be more successful than others.

The historical lesson that revisionist Beard took away from his study of the Great War concerned the objectives for which the nations had fought: territory, markets, and resources. From that point on in his life, he assumed that modern war, at bottom, could never be about anything else.

CHAPTER 4

Washington and Wall Street Working Together for War

Beard began to sense no later than 1936 that the government of the United States might be vulnerable to involving the country in war again. That was the year in which he wrote *The Devil Theory of War: An Inquiry into the Nature of History and the Possibility of Keeping Out of War*, an early statement of his neutralist viewpoint. Recent revelations by the U.S. Senate Nye Committee Investigation of the Munitions Industry and the financial and banking interests that underlay American involvement in the recent war made a profound impression on him. The committee, chaired by forty-one-year-old Republican senator Gerald P. Nye of North Dakota, had been created in 1934. The Women's International League for Peace and Freedom, a pacifist organization, had conceived the idea for the committee, which soon attracted widespread support and interest.

During the 1920s and early 1930s, dozens of books and articles had appeared about how the munitions industry had influenced American intervention in the war, but the publication in 1934 of *Merchants of Death* by Helmuth Carol Engelbrecht and Frank Cleary Hanighen dramatically augmented the audience for the Nye Committee's work. The book included a foreword by Harry Elmer Barnes, a historian well-known to Beard. Later in the decade the two men would become close friends and like-minded critics of what they saw as the pro-war foreign policy of the FDR administration. Barnes described *Merchants of Death* as "an exposure of the degradation of ethics which has accompanied the efforts of the armament moguls to market their products."[1] He took away from their book the conclusion that among the causes of modern warfare the munitions makers themselves mattered far less than the international bankers who financed the fighting, an idea Beard himself would come to view as the most self-evident of truths about the arms trade.

Well-educated and talented writers, Engelbrecht and Hanighen did try to place the armament business in full social, economic, and cultural context, but also included much commentary on the individual arms merchants themselves. The unsavory image of Andrew Undershaft, George Bernard Shaw's munitions maker character in *Major Barbara* (1905), dominates their book. They identify Shaw's exaggerations and oversimplifications in the play, but, after tracing the history of the munitions business from the Middle Ages to modern times, conclude, "it would seem that Shaw's Undershaft was perhaps not such a gross exaggeration, after all."[2]

Turning to their main theme—the role of armaments dealers in the Great War—Engelbrecht and Hanighen document the profits generated by that conflict. They find it telling that any talk of peace or a negotiated settlement among the combatants invariably depressed the world's stock markets. Wall Street profited most of all. Here they touch directly on the theme that would matter most to the Nye Committee, the extent to which arms dealers and their partners in banking and the brokerage houses might have been responsible for bringing the United States into the war. *Merchants of Death* avoids summary conclusions about the cause or causes of American intervention, but by their use of statistical information the authors convey the distinct impression that they subscribe to an economic interpretation of the country's decision to go to war in 1917.

The chapter dealing with America's intervention, "The World War—Enter Old Glory," begins with a quotation by Frank A. Vanderlip, president of the National City Bank: "As a result of the war, a million new springs of wealth will be created."[3] Indeed, by 1918 the country had 21,000 new millionaires and billionaires. Du Pont stock rose from $20 to $1,000 per share by war's end. Bethlehem Steel and United States Steel, the other two major pillars in the military-industrial complex of the time, similarly gladdened the hearts of their stockholders. The gravy train had left the station in 1915 when the United States entered into financial arrangements with one side in the war, the Allies. War loans made to Britain, France, Italy, and Russia eventually totaled in the billions of dollars, which the Allies used to pay for war materials purchased in the United States. The arrangement could not have been more satisfying to the investors. In more good news for them, the volume of foreign trade, reaching gargantuan proportions under the stimulus of war orders from the desperate Allies, created shortages at home. The ensuing sharp rise in domestic prices created an even bigger windfall for Wall Street than did the war traffic with the Allies.

The continued prowess of the German Army in 1917, however, cast a potentially extinguishing shadow across the happy prospect of a perpetually expanding American economy, which had been rescued from the recession of 1913 by the lucrative convulsions of Europe. Just as the military crises on the western, eastern, and Italian fronts were maturing and putting the loans at risk, the United States entered the conflict. Wilson's political genius lay in his capacity to imbue American intervention with the cosmic significance of a crusade to make the world safe for democracy. Although the president set new standards of uplift for American foreign policy, he did not cause Engelbrecht and Hanighen to lose sight of the more mundane factors involved in the fateful decision to go to war in 1917. As they put it in their deadpan style, "On April 6, 1917, the United States entered the conflict, and the heartbeats of the war traffickers became normal again." More soberly, they added that if the United States did not enter the war solely because of armament makers and their financiers, "American commitments with the Allies were so enormous that only our entry into the war saved the country from a major economic collapse."[4]

Not from the urgings of pure patriotism alone did three hundred stock brokers on a Wall Street aflutter with the red, white, and blue sing "The Star Spangled Banner" upon hearing the news that America would be going to war. Now the Allies had an absolute guarantee from the United States government for their credit. A money-making system that had been hugely remunerative now promised to bring investors into uncharted realms of profit taking. Had it only been a quarter of a century ago, during the administration of Benjamin Harrison, that the United States government had presented its first annual $1 billion budget? Washington's colossal buying spree of 1917 and 1918 totaled $22 billion, and the government gave another $9.5 billion in loans to the Allies. Of course, the whole system came crashing down in recession at war's end, when the orders stopped. Engelbrecht and Hanighen explained the steadily rising American defense budgets after the war, up from $348,032,000 in 1914, to $678,256,000 in 1923, and to $838,547,144 in 1931, as an attempt, in part, to compensate for the abrupt cessation of the war orders.[5] The law of compensation worked imperfectly in this case, however, as no one in Washington had yet hit upon the happy idea of maintaining a perpetual war economy.

Beard's *The Navy: Defense or Portent?* (1932) served Engelbrecht and Hanighen as an important source for *Merchants of Death*. They basically took a

Beardian approach in their book. He thought it a fatal course of action by the United States to pay heed to the "big navy" enthusiasts who wanted a force "big enough to defend commerce against any power or combination of powers anywhere."[6] Germany had been led to defeat and ruin by its embrace of just this kind of argument, which Captain Alfred von Tirpitz had used successfully with Kaiser Wilhelm II. Basing his critique on Eckert Kehr's research in the secret archives of the German government for *Schlachtflottenbau und Parteipolitik 1894–1902* (1930), Beard pointed out that the kaiser and Tirpitz himself had been highly enthusiastic readers of American naval strategist and historian Captain Alfred T. Mahan, whose *Influence of Sea Power on History* was translated into German and became required reading for that country's naval officers. Though in the beginning an intellectual reaction to books and ideas, the program for a big German navy soon acquired a powerful economic dimension as interested ship builders, munitions makers, merchants, and tradesmen of all kinds discovered the enormous profits to be made in building up the fleet. Journalists, publicists, intellectuals, and professors offered their blessings to the enterprise, which the public was led to believe would promote and assure German greatness and safety. The Tirpitz program alarmed Great Britain, and the naval rivalry between these two countries had to be counted as a major factor in the origins of the Great War. Yet, when it came to the fighting, the big German navy proved to be a nonfactor. Rather than investing in great battleships, the Germans would have been much better off strengthening their submarine fleet, which Tirpitz had neglected. His ideas had led Germany to war, defeat, poverty, and ruin.

Beard concluded that the naval experts in the 1930s calling for the enlargement of an already big American navy might also be wrong. He noted a high degree of similarity in the German and American big navy programs. Both had originated in the desires of the naval hierarchies themselves and their respective political institutions, not by order of the big capitalists. Focusing specifically on the economic factors in the American case, Beard observed, "the industry itself was not at first formidable enough to exert any considerable pressure."[7] For some time, the businessmen remained in the background. As the navy grew in the 1880s and 1890s, it attracted the same economic interest groups that would grow along with the German navy. An identical propaganda system took root in both countries. Equally inspired by the work of Mahan, the arguments made by the big-navy men in America and Germany were basically interchangeable. Beard, famous for the emphasis that he placed on economic motives in history, acknowledged their relative insignificance in explaining the origins of the big-navy program in America.

To tell the story of American naval expansion, Beard fell back headlong to the great-man theory of history. The charisma and magnetism of Theodore Roosevelt mattered far more in the creation of a great American navy than did any activities on Wall Street. Indeed, Roosevelt had to educate the captains of industry and their stockbrokers about the need for colonial possessions and the armed forces necessary for their acquisition and defense. After some initial reluctance, however, they soon saw the wisdom of his teaching. Thereafter, and especially during the Great War, naval defense became "organically rooted in the vast network of private interests engaged in building and operating merchant ships."[8]

The year when Beard published *The Navy*, 1932, he would support Franklin Delano Roosevelt in the presidential election, remaining for some years an advocate of the New Deal. Ultimately, he would conclude that in the history of the American people, FDR had played the role of Augustus Caesar in the transformation of the Republic into an empire. In 1932, however, he still retained hope in the capacity of the American capitalist system to reform itself democratically without resorting to a permanent war economy.

Despite Beard's enthusiasm for FDR at this time, he concluded his book with a glowing tribute to President Hoover, then flailing about helplessly in the throes of the Great Depression. He had been unequal to the challenge of this devastating economic crisis, as FDR also would be until 1941, when permanent war for permanent peace, in a memorable phrase associated with Beard's name, would become the American way. Hoover did not yield to this temptation. Had he done so, it might have been possible for him to avoid his crushing defeat at the hands of FDR. Unlike his successor, Hoover sought to keep clear of conflict with the Japanese in the Pacific. Throughout history, war had served to distract public attention from domestic crises, Beard observed. Despite every conceivable setback on the home front that could come to a political leader, Hoover genuinely sought peace. Moreover, he resolutely confronted the Navy League lobby and turned down calls for added naval expenditures: "It is evident, therefore, that President Hoover has contributed powerfully to the clarification of the navy issue by asserting anew the supremacy of the civilian branch of the federal government, by defining in terms of policy the objects and objectives of national defense, by repudiating the gospel of *Welt- und Machtpolitik*, and by bringing the Navy League propagandists to bay."[9]

In the same year that *The Merchants of Death* appeared, 1934, Beard gave an address at the New School for Social Research, "Hitlerism and Our Liberties." Much of the criticism against Beard's foreign policy views of the 1930s would concern his alleged failure to comprehend the true character of the menace posed by Hitler. In fact, he fully realized what the Nazis represented. He saw in their movement "brutal and irresponsible power enthroned and exalted." They had replaced equality before the law with a campaign of degradation aimed at entire races, classes of people, and all women. They had unleashed a reign of terror in the heart of Europe, beating, mutilating, and murdering people. He distilled the essence of Nazism as "government by brute force, by unquestioned and unchallenged berserker rage." It meant "sheer militarism now and war later." It was a "low diabolical philosophy."[10] He applauded the New School for opening its doors to the scholarly refugees who had fled the Nazi scourge. Beard's critique of American foreign policy in the 1930s cannot be explained as a consequence of his alleged ignorance regarding Nazism.

Despite the obvious importance of *Merchants of Death*, to which his ideas had made a signal contribution, Beard thought that the findings from 1934 to 1936 of the Nye Committee overshadowed all other investigations of this kind. For their historical significance he claimed that the Nye Committee testimony and reports deserved to be classed with the diplomatic revelations from the secret archives of Petrograd, Berlin, and Vienna about the true origins of the war. In some ways, the Nye Committee findings surpassed in importance even those European archival documents. About the Nye findings he wrote: "They deliver positive information showing the pressures exerted by economic interests upon the government of the United States which carried the nation into war."[11] Irrefutably, in his opinion, the Nye Committee documented the ignorance masquerading as sagacity in wartime Washington and the complete misrepresentation of the war by the newspapers. The imperialist ambitions of all the Great Powers, not only those of Germany and Austria, caused the war. Both sides fought for gain, as the secret diplomatic correspondence and now the Nye Committee showed in appalling detail.[12]

As a small-town North Dakota newspaper editor before becoming a senator in 1925 at the age of thirty-two, Nye stood politically to the left of New Deal liberalism. He was an agrarian radical in a state wracked by the postwar agricultural depression that coexisted offstage with the Roaring Twenties of urban America. Nye criticized FDR for not going nearly far enough with his reforms. The senator blamed the nation's economic paralysis on the concentration of financial power in the hands of the few. He called for a redistribution of the country's wealth, a consummation to be achieved by simply and justly ending the culture of insider favoritism that informed Wall Street and its wholly immoral relationship with Washington. He believed that the bankers who had looted the country now were setting their sights on the even larger dividends of the global marketplace.

Like Beard, Nye had waved the flag as America had gone to war in 1917, but by 1934 both men reasoned that only the invincibly naïve could place any genuine trust in the word of a government under total oligarchic control, least of all its professions about mankind's need for the liberating prophylaxis of American military power. Neither of them experienced any surprise over the revelations in *Merchants of Death*. The book had reinforced their convictions about the economic motives of the war and of America's postwar foreign policy. Even more than Beard, Nye fiercely had criticized the government in Washington for sending the Marines into Latin America. He bluntly denounced the incursions there of the Coolidge years as nothing but financial imperialism in its most disgusting form.

Beard expressed similar concerns about the potential for militarism in the FDR administration. In January 1934, he wrote to the president protesting an article by Assistant Secretary of War Harry Hines Woodring. The article, "The American Army Stands Ready," had recently appeared in *Liberty* magazine. A worried Beard wondered, ready for what? He complained that the assistant secretary's call for a strong military in peacetime "contains such an outrageous and amazing flouting of the basic principles of American democracy, such an overt threat to the liberties and rights of American citizens, as to awaken in us a profound fear."[13] He declared the abuse of power by the military to be a serious problem for all Americans. Beard advised the president to disavow the article and to fire Woodring. Instead, two years later, Woodring became secretary of war, a position he would hold until 1940, when Henry L. Stimson, a pillar of the Republican party and regarded by Beard as the epitome of American imperialism, took over the department.

An American public still profoundly disillusioned about the Great War wondered what the Nye Committee could add to the findings of Engelbrecht and Hanighen. Four Democrats and three Republicans sat on the committee, which benefited from an advisory council of experts and a team of investigators. The first set of hearings began on September 4, 1934, and lasted through September 21. Witnesses spoke of bribery, corruption, rake-offs, and other crimes as the common practice of the munitions business. Worldwide headlines blared the committee's preliminary findings. After the first set of hearings, Nye himself went on a national speaking tour to denounce war profits as a standing menace to the peace of the world.

The Nye Committee's public hearings resumed on December 4, 1934, and continued regularly for the next five months. After adjourning in late April 1935, the committee held no more hearings until January 7, 1936. Its last witness appeared on February 20, 1936, a year and a half after the first hearing. In all, two hundred witnesses testified. Their testimony and exhibits would fill

39 volumes, totaling 13,750 pages. The committee submitted a preliminary report and two major reports in the spring and summer of 1935. Five more major reports would be released before the end of June 1936.

In his biography of Nye, Wayne S. Cole emphasizes the importance of a fundamental change that the hearings caused in the senator's thinking about the relationship between Wall Street and Washington. In good agrarian radical style, he had assumed that Washington played the role of adjutant to the masters on Wall Street. The hearings had disabused him of that simplistic view. He had set out on a mission to expose the corporations and the bankers as the paramount villains responsible for America's disastrous economic inequalities and evil wars. Indeed, the committee had found an enormous amount of evidence to support just such an indictment of the economic elites. The question of supremacy in the cast of villains, however, turned out to be much more complicated than Nye had anticipated. His big shock on the committee resulted from the revelations about the role of the federal government as a protagonist in munitions traffic and, particularly, the machinations of the Wilson administration in dragging the United States into the war.[14]

Writing in *The Devil Theory of War* about the Nye Committee, Beard attached the greatest significance to its culminating revelations of January–February 1936, concerning the economic motives for American intervention in the war. Testifying in the closing months of the committee's deliberations were J. P. Morgan and two of his partners, Thomas W. Lamont and George Whitney, along with National City Bank president Frank A. Vanderlip. Their testimony and the exhibits connected with it filled several volumes and more than four thousand pages of the Committee's findings. For Beard, it amounted to a book of revelations about how the real mechanisms of American economic and political power functioned in generating the country's foreign policy and wars.

Though formally cordial toward each other at the outset of the January–February 1936 hearings in the caucus room of the Senate Office Building, the committee members and the witnesses soon formed battle lines. On January 8, Lamont complained, "Heretofore members of this committee have stated again and again that it was the bankers and industrialists who got the country into the war. Believing that is entirely incorrect, we want to take every opportunity that we can to controvert that belief while we are on the stand and show what we think the causes of the war were."[15] When on the next day the discussion turned to the war loans policy of the J. P. Morgan Company, he rejected the committee's line of inquiry about profit as a motive: "You talk like businessmen in America and others were greedy enough to have the war continue. . . . Nobody wanted to get into the war just because he had good business."[16] The bankers, Lamont continued, had acted within the law to assist the Allied cause for which all the witnesses professed personal sympathy, and, by facilitating war orders, to ease the country out of the economic slowdown of 1913–1914.

Nye certainly had made the kind of statements attributed by Lamont to the committee generally. The senator well understood that Lamont had him chiefly in mind as an anti-bank voice on the committee. He spoke directly to Lamont on that same January 9: "I want to ask Mr. Lamont if he believes that it is possible for a nation, our nation in particular, to remain strictly neutral while profiting from wars that are being fought elsewhere in the world."[17] The loans to the Allies clearly had embroiled the country in the European war. Lamont and the other witnesses speaking to the committee flatly rejected Nye's thesis, arguing instead that German outrages on the high seas had brought the United States into the war. For its honor and self-respect, the country could not tolerate the casualties and destruction of property resulting from Germany's unrestricted submarine warfare campaign, which had resumed in February 1917, two months before President Wilson's call for a declaration of war. Germany, not the Wall Street bankers, caused American intervention in the World War. The Nye-Lamont confrontation underscored and synthesized the main difference of opinion between the witnesses and the committee, at least its most active members—Nye along with Bennett Champ Clark of Missouri and Arthur H. Vandenberg of Michigan.

Many such exchanges took place. For example, also on January 9, the committee presented documentation that showed how bankers had pressured the government to rescind its prohibition of loans and credits to belligerent nations. Why, Senator Clark asked, would the government have reversed itself by opening the door and saying, "All right, boys, go ahead and float all the loans and get all the credits you can."[18] Clearly, a powerful political force had been exerted to produce such a drastic change in government policy. Lamont again took the lead in defending the bankers against the inference of Senator Clark's line of questioning. "You speak of leverage brought on the Secretary of the Treasury and on the Department of State. According to my experience, bankers do not bring leverage on governmental Departments over here, and if they attempted to do it they would be very badly rebuffed."[19] The next day, Morgan plaintively echoed Lamont: "I want to deny in the most clear manner that I can that such a thing was ever thought of by us or done by us at any time in any way. That is one of the discreditable actions which is foreign to our history, and it is foreign to our traditions, and we never did such a thing in our lives."[20]

In a rejoinder that would make absolute sense to Beard, Senator Clark pointed to the documentary evidence, which revealed the truth about "all these machinations" to bring about a change of policy regarding war loans.[21] Only a few months before, on April 29, 1935, a Beard statement about corrupt practices by the Morgan bank had been entered into the *Congressional Record* by Senator Burton K. Wheeler, the chairman of the Senate Committee on Interstate Commerce, who was then trying to gain support for railroad reform. Beard identified how the Van Sweringen railroad empire and the banking syndicate behind it "are in a position to descend upon Washington and on the Government agencies that have anything to do with the railroads, to descend upon Washington in full force, and both in Washington and throughout the country to press the views and requirements of J. P. Morgan & Company and its affiliated banking houses and institutions with the utmost astuteness and power. In brief, the bankers for the Van Sweringen empire have such potent charms that most doors open readily to them."[22]

The same charms had been employed twenty years earlier, and Senator Clark described them at the January 10, 1936, meeting of the Nye Committee. To finance the war orders then pouring into the United States from the Allies, who already, in 1915, were complaining about their straightened economic circumstances, Washington had to permit American banks and financial houses to float loans. No other source of money existed, the Allies had protested. These transactions eventually totaled in the billions of dollars and, as a practical business matter, tied the United States to the Allied cause, becoming a major factor in the country's involvement in the war. Clark very much doubted that after only one year of war the bountifully endowed British Empire had come to the end of its resources: "The fact of the matter was that they wanted to use our money instead of their own."[23] Worse, they would not pay back most of it. In other words, not only had the loans led to American involvement in the war; they had the long-term effect of damaging the American economy, with direct responsibility as a factor in the Depression of the 1930s. Through their loan policies and their lobbying in Washington to make them the real law of the land, the bankers had undermined the country's neutrality in the war and had produced results that had failed every standard for the common good.

Morgan once again sought to defend his profession: "In certain speeches by several members of the committee there have been direct accusations against the New York bankers having brought on the war, and that is one of the things with which I have not been particularly pleased, and one of the things which is not borne out."[24] Morgan's response to Senator Clark brought Senator Nye into the exchange: "I want to deny as one member of the committee, that you are right in concluding that the charge [against the bankers] has been as direct as that. . . . I am more convinced this morning than I have ever been at any stage heretofore, that it was the commercial activity as a whole, in which the bankers had a hand, which did finally break down completely our neutrality."[25] The bankers had acted only as one element in a large economic context, which consisted of a constantly expanding segment of the society, until the kinetic energy for intervention had become unstoppable. Without the loans, Nye concluded, "the problem of staying out would not have been what it was."[26] Later that same day, Senator Vandenberg observed, "Does it not become impossible, under the play of these forces, both financial and industrial, for the country to escape the flow which carries it straight on into the war?"[27] He continued, "The constant trend was to bring the United States into line with the investment."[28] It was impossible for him to see how a country engaged in war investments and war trade at the same time could be neutral in any meaningful sense.

Not that the committee itself enjoyed unanimity in its frequently adversarial relationship with the witnesses. A fierce debate among the committee members erupted on January 16 over the role of Woodrow Wilson and his administration in bringing about American intervention in the war. On this date, Democratic senator James P. Pope of Idaho declared that although he had up till then supported most of the committee's work, "it appears now, however, that the investigation has degenerated into an attack upon our wartime President, Woodrow Wilson, and his Secretary of State, Robert Lansing." He then offered a robust defense of Wilson and added, "we must express our resentment at any effort to impugn the motives of Woodrow Wilson and to discredit his great character."[29] He had been particularly upset by statements in the press attributed to Nye, to the effect that Wilson and Lansing "were falsifiers." The purpose of the investigation had been lost sight of and had descended to the level of partisan in-fighting. Another Democratic member of the Committee, Walter F. George of Georgia, signed Pope's statement.

Senator Nye retorted, "No man can read the record that has been made respecting history, actual history of those days, and ignore the fact that both Secretary Lansing and President Wilson had departed from the facts when they pleaded that they had no knowledge of these secret treaties. . . . [T]hose who were leading our American cause did have knowledge, and that direct, that secret treaties had been entered into."[30] Nye here referred to a two-day-long presentation by Senator Clark, begun on January 14, during which he had argued how President Wilson knew full well about secret treaties among the Allies as their intended basis for the peace at war's end. According to evidence compiled by the committee's research staff members, the president had claimed falsely that he first had learned about these treaties at the 1919 Paris Peace Conference.

Senator Clark argued that President Wilson could protest no more effectively against the secret treaties than he did when Britain repeatedly violated American neutrality. A low point in relations between the two countries had been reached in the summer of 1916 when British censorship of United States mail outraged American public opinion. At the same time, as part of the effort to strengthen its blockade of Germany, the government of Britain had created a black list of eighty-five American companies, a measure that had infuriated Wilson himself. This also was the summer when Britain's savage treatment of Irish rebels, following the Easter Rebellion, further had eroded good will in America toward Britain. Almost simultaneously Germany issued the Sussex Pledge and discontinued the strategy of unrestricted submarine warfare, thus inaugurating a brief period of relatively good relations between Berlin and Washington.

Yet, Senator Clark contended in his presentation to the committee, no outrage by the British or concession by the Germans could overcome the fundamental American commitment to the Allied cause. To be understood fully, the commitment had to be seen from two different but ultimately connected ideological and economic standpoints. The first one concerned the world view of the American leaders. From the very first, a pro-British bias completely dominated thinking in Washington: "President Wilson, Colonel House, and Secretary Lansing, apparently from the outset of the war, were convinced that in the interests of the United States in particular, and of civilization in general, a German victory could not be permitted." Convinced that a triumphant Germany would be a menace to America and the world, the Wilson administration adopted policies that during the first two years of the war were "almost never neutral in spirit."[31]

By the summer of 1916, however, an accumulation of American grievances toward Britain raised the strong possibility of a change in Wilson's policies toward the belligerent nations. Though contemplating drastic measures toward Britain over that country's lack of respect for American rights, the president ultimately did nothing. Senator Clark explained why, in the end, the special relationship between the United States and England held. Wilson, he said, "discovered that the tremendous commercial and financial involvements of this country in the Allied cause rendered drastic action against the Allies impossible, rendered him powerless to effect any change, fundamentally, in the policy which for reasons of sentiment, tradition, and a belief in Allied ideals, he had pursued during the first two years of our so-called neutrality."[32] Taking these vital economic truths into careful consideration, the United States decided "it was better to suffer British violations and Allied violations of our asserted neutral rights than run any risk of the loss of trade by asserting them and maintaining them by retaliatory measures." Retaliation would endanger "this huge, abnormal war-time trade in the face of the great vested interest in war traffic which had grown up in the United States by that time."[33] It became politically impossible for Wilson to disturb commercial relations between the United States and Britain.

In a famous book published the year before and cited by Senator Clark, *The Road to War*, journalist Walter Millis made an identical argument. Millis considered the Anglo-French loan of 1915 to have been decisive in the events leading to America's intervention in the European war. Thereafter, "the two economies were for the purposes of the war made one; each was entangled irrevocably in the fate of the other."[34] In his presentation to the committee, Senator Clark distilled the essence of the Millis argument.

Senator Clark's most sensational remarks and the fundamental cause of Senator Pope's outburst of indignation concerned President Wilson's alleged lies about when he had learned of the secret treaties, which, in flat contradiction of the Fourteen Points, turned out to be the actual basis of the 1919 peace treaty. He quoted phrases from the president's April 2, 1917, war declaration speech to Congress about fighting to make the world safe for democracy, to vindicate the principles of peace and justice. Such lofty sentiments thrilled the nation and the world, but "President Wilson knew when he uttered them that the Allies were parties to a series of secret agreements which divided up the spoils of war in a manner far removed from the principles of peace and justice."[35] Clark reasoned that Wilson's confidant, Colonel House, knew all about the secret treaties, which he deplored as a guarantee for a second world war, and, therefore, Wilson assuredly would have known about them. He cited Lansing's *War Memoirs* as the best source for discovering the truth about the president's knowledge of the Allied war aims and of the secret arrangements that they had made among themselves. Wilson had been told about the existence of the treaties. The British even offered to furnish copies of these documents, which would have made the full truth of Allied war aims completely clear to Wilson, but he "did not desire to have it told him."[36] He wanted no details that would conflict with the sales pitch being readied for public consumption. To the truth about a war planned, begun, and fought for economic gain and strategic advantage, he preferred his own fantasy about a crusade to make the world safe for democracy.

In his devastating analysis of Wilson's evasion of the real character of the war that he had committed the American people to fight, Clark portrayed the president as a leader in the grip of yet another fantasy. He sincerely believed that the secret treaties, whatever provisions they might contain, would not matter in the long run. Senator Clark read an excerpt from a July 21, 1917, letter written by Wilson to House. Differences between the Allies and the United States over their war aims did not concern him: "When the war is over we can force them to our way of thinking, because by that time they will, among other things, be financially in our hands." The whole business of war aims could safely be dropped for the time being, "except for an appeal to general principle."[37]

Yet, at the Peace Conference, the financial club to which the president referred scarcely mattered at all in the treaty that the victors fashioned. About the handiwork of the peacemakers, Senator Clark observed, "with a very few minor exceptions, the Allies did precisely as they pleased and as they had planned before our entry into the war."[38] The Allies, in short, succeeded in their design to make Germany and the United States pay: the first for starting the war, and the second for not having come in sooner. The unpaid war loans were part of the American debt to the Allies, which already in 1919, Senator Clark complained, were spending money on armaments and the imperialist consolidation of newly won territories instead of squaring accounts with their American creditors. The Americans had lost all around, except on the battlefield. As Stephen Raushenbush, the son of Protestant theologian Walter Rauschenbusch, and secretary of the Nye Committee, later would observe, military victory by itself does not mean much: "You may have crushed Germany and Hitler may crop up, and your war, if you have won it, is very briefly won."[39] Senator Vandenberg went further in his criticism of American intervention, which he characterized as a total loss for the United States, "unless we can learn something advantageous from it."[40]

With the Nye Committee hearings entering their climactic phase in January 1936, Beard wrote to his close friend Oswald Garrison Villard. On the twenty-sixth of that month, he told the longtime editor and owner of *The Nation* magazine that the facts now known about the secret treaties clinched the case against the Wilson administration. About the president's claim that he knew nothing of the treaties until his arrival in Paris for the Peace Conference, Beard acidly commented: "Either Wilson knew and lied, or he and the State Department were ignorant of matters known to men in the streets (thanks to your labors). I believe that I should rather be known as a plain liar, at least for strategic reasons, than as a dangerous ignoramus."[41] Three days earlier, Villard had informed him that as of 1917 the administration had full access to the texts of the secret treaties: "The whole bunch lied outrageously about the matter. But they were too stupid to realize the significance of these treaties." Villard himself had published information about them. Yet, "nobody, not Lansing, nor anybody else in the State Department took them seriously or went to work on them, and I have never come across anything to show that the Lippmann-House aggregation of experts knew of them when they went abroad."[42] Villard's low opinion of the Inquiry, the body of experts directed by Colonel House accompanying President Wilson to the Paris Peace Conference, equaled that of John Maynard Keynes, who in *The Economic Consequences of the Peace* ranked the American advisers as woefully deficient in the knowledge and expertise they would have needed to contend successfully with their European counterparts.

Writing in the *Washington Daily News* on February 6, 1936, Beard subscribed to Villard's damning assessment of the Wilson administration: "We were confronting the alternatives of a domestic crash and a foreign war when we entered the war."[43] Decisions made by Wilson and his Cabinet had brought the United States to that tragic confrontation. War became inevitable because no one in Washington cared to contemplate a crash that might destroy the entire economic system. The prospect of a cataclysmic depression had been raised in 1915 when the bankers had presented to the officers of the United States government "a proposition in the nature of an ultimatum": either grant loans to the Allies or prepare the American people for their economic ruin. Beard observed, "Like all governments threatened by domestic crisis, the Government of the United States sought an escape by yielding." Of course, the Allies could have their loans as an investment product exclusively reserved for the American market. Two years later, when the president issued his war declaration to a joint session of Congress, the stakes had risen. America's dependence on the war orders had become absolute, following "the expansion of productive activities" to meet the voracious needs of the Allied war machines. Beard worried that "the outbreak of another war in Europe will bring about conditions similar to those prevailing in 1914–17, if bankers, industrialists, and farmers insist upon 'making a profit' and the Government of the United States pursues the same policy."[44]

In *The Devil Theory of War*, Beard summarized what he had learned from the Nye Committee's January–February 1936 sessions, which, to his complete satisfaction, destroyed the government's case about why in 1917 it had led the country into war. He understood well the complexity of causation in history and conceded that for an event as vast and multifarious as the Great War it would be impossible to speak with absolute precision about the individuals and entities responsible for it. Nevertheless, evidence unearthed by the Nye Committee made it possible for historians to identify "the leading persons who took action verging in the direction of war."[45] There now could be no question about the important role played by American bankers who successfully had lobbied Wilson to lift an earlier ban on loans to the Allied belligerents. In the typical manner of American politics, the government had yielded to the pressure of ruling class interests. In a political atmosphere thoroughly conditioned by the economic slowdown of 1913 and widespread unemployment, the temptation of the war orders and the need to protect the huge American financial investment in the Allied cause proved to be irresistible.

Yet Beard could draw on his own personal experience as an ardent enthusiast for American intervention in the war as a way of illustrating the futility of any simplistic conspiracy theory about iniquitous bankers and munitions makers as a sufficient explanation of why an American army took the field against the Germans in 1917. The Nye Committee documentation contained the proof for the necessary role that President Wilson, J. P. Morgan, the Du Pont family, and many other political, financial, and business figures played in the tragedy of American intervention. Beard, however, identified himself as one in the great multitude of American citizens' groups and individuals who honestly believed in the Allied cause and lobbied the government for intervention in the conflict, "to save civilization."[46] Any true history of America's involvement in the Great War would be obliged to give credit for our intervening to the American people themselves. They did not have a merely passive part to play, but instead had to be viewed as willing and even eager accomplices of the bankers and politicians.

Their complicity did not result solely from the educational disadvantages at the lower end of the country's class system. A person could have an Ivy League PhD with a long résumé of book publications, as Beard did, and still not really comprehend as a practical matter how the country's political system worked. Beard, of course, had understood it. That a scholar of his caliber suddenly could have become a pathetic victim of historical amnesia, as he certainly did for about five years, from 1914 to 1919, makes it easier to understand how the average person, without Beard's expensive education and hardwon insights from the archives about the real workings of politics, could have been swept into the pro-war mainstream. *The Devil Theory of War* is one of Beard's most confessional books.

If *The Devil Theory of War* has a hero, it is William Jennings Bryan, who, as Wilson's secretary of state from 1913 to 1915 understood exactly what American war loans to the Allies meant and where such transactions inevitably would lead. He respected and admired Wilson, but thought the president's PhD education at Johns Hopkins University singularly deficient, in that he had not learned there the correct definition of the word "neutrality." Evidently, a person could become a famous Princeton University professor and even the president of the school without learning what this simple English word meant.

By the lights of Bryan's humble state college education, neutrality in wartime meant even-handed treatment of the belligerents. He did not at all understand how America could profess to be neutral in the European war while funding and taking on a very special relationship with one side in the struggle. It had to be counted as a vital life sign for American culture that the country still could place such an independent-minded man in a position of high government authority. The vastly more powerful economic and political forces arrayed against Bryan, however, swept him out of their way as they energetically got on with the business of increasing the country's war-dependent profit cycle.

Reading the letters unearthed by the Nye Committee, Beard had the same sensation that he had experienced while doing the research for *An Economic Interpretation of the Constitution of the United States*. Just as Madison and Hamilton had explained in painstaking detail exactly which political and economic objectives they had hoped to achieve at the Constitutional Convention of 1787, so the bankers presented a wholly unobstructed view of what they expected to obtain from the government's approval of the war-loan policy. The bankers made a simple and straightforward proposition to Secretary of State Robert Lansing and Secretary of the Treasury William Gibbs McAdoo: by assisting our customers to buy from us, the loans would finance American prosperity. The alternative to the war-loan policy, as McAdoo warned the president, was economic stagnation and perhaps collapse. It would be un-American to stand in the way of the country's prosperity by remaining at peace.

As usual in his writing, Beard followed an essentially Hobson-like line in *The Devil Theory of War*. To protect wartime profits totaling approximately seven billion dollars, "participation in the World War cost the people of the United States, besides death and suffering, at least one hundred billion dollars, counting outlays to come for pensions, bonuses, and other war charges." He added, "It does not seem to have been in the long run a 'paying' proposition, considered in the terms used by the bankers and politicians between October 1914 and April 1917."[47] According to the documentary evidence, not much had been said in those years about democracy and civilization as the motives for the policies proposed by the bankers and implemented by the government. The granting of credits and loans to the Allies would be profitable for business, but society generally came out of the war deeply in debt and with an artificially stimulated war economy roaring in reverse. It was the usual outcome in principle, although this time with some monstrous features attributable to the unprecedented scale of the war's costs, that Hobson had declared to be the law of modern warfare.

Writing in 1936, Beard worried that yet another economic crisis even worse than the 1913 recession might turn out to be an irresistible inducement for

Washington once again to go to war as a solution for the failures of the capi-talist system. "Have economic activities and interests changed since 1914?" he asked.[48] The heart of the American dilemma over war and peace, to him, lay in the failure of Americans to make the domestic changes necessary to keep the country out of war and at peace.

If only the tragedy of American foreign policy could be blamed solely on the leaders, one could always place hope in a new administration. Alas, the problems went far deeper than this or that president or secretary of state. An-other obstacle in the way of a legitimately democratic and peaceful foreign policy concerned the political system itself, which had been designed to do what it always did: advance the policy initiatives, domestic and foreign, of eco-nomic elites. Beard always could be counted on to emphasize economic in-terest as a key factor in understanding how politics worked. Other factors could be important, too, in given historical circumstances—personal ambition, ide-ological fervor, stupidity—but as a general way of thinking about history the economic interpretation possessed the greatest explanatory power. If the Nye Committee proved anything, it was that the political system responded to the needs of its top investors. Beard also saw Nye's point about the parity of the political and economic elites. They all tended to come from the same class and to represent the same world view, which the Beards had denomi-nated in *The Rise of American Civilization* as the American acquisitive system.

The American people themselves formed the stoutest line of defense for the status quo that ruled them. Beard's direst concern for the future arose from the weaknesses and immaturity of his fellow citizens. Americans, he lamented, still tended to think in the extremely simple-minded moralistic terms of 1917 about the outside world. Their condition, while not congenital, appeared now to be permanent. The situation in 1936 Europe seemed to him a particularly vivid example of the problem that the world would have in an American-centric order. Yes, the Italians, Germans, and Japanese were doing some ter-rible things, but did their guilt mean, as our leaders and their media seemed to be proposing, that the enormities of British and French imperialism had to be overlooked or misrepresented as relatively charming eccentricities of brother democracies? He answered, "My trouble lies in the fact, that greed, lust, and ambition in Europe and Asia do not seem confined to Italy, Germany, and Japan; nor does good seem to be monopolized by Great Britain, France, and Russia."[49]

The American people had been badly rebuffed in their 1917–1918 crusade to bring democracy to the world, which did not want it—or whatever the system was that Wilson proposed to give them. They would be thwarted again, if another such attempt were to be undertaken. *The Devil Theory of*

War ends with Beard appealing to his countrymen to busy themselves with the conversion of the United States from oligarchy to democracy. They did not have a decently serviceable political product to offer anybody. When more seasonably than in the greatest depression the country ever had known could the obviously failed American system be replaced by something better? Taking a page from Voltaire's *Candide*, Beard called upon Americans to cultivate their own garden: "It is a big garden and a good garden, though horribly managed and trampled by our greedy folly. Tilling it properly doubtless involves many drastic changes in capitalism as historically practiced." Difficult and controversial though his reform program might be, "I should certainly prefer any changes that might be required in it to the frightful prospects of American participation in a war in Europe or Asia."[50]

No socialist and utterly removed from the mental universe of Marxist theory, Beard proposed an "open door" system for the American people. Here he summed up the points made in his *Open Door at Home: A Trial Philosophy of National Interest*, published in 1934. By the 1930s Beard had come to regard the unequal distribution of wealth as the country's fundamental problem and the ultimate cause of its foreign policy misadventures. The economy needed to be planned and managed in a way that would permit the country to use at home its enormous industrial and agricultural surpluses. The general well-being of the populace, not the dividend statements of the investor class, had to be the objective of domestic and foreign policy. He called on American leaders to augment the buying and consuming capacity of their own people, to sell agricultural and industrial surpluses at home as a way of relieving the shameful poverty and want there. Such a plan, he claimed, drastically would reduce the foreign policy commitments arising from the quest for private profit abroad. The United States should have a fully engaged economic relationship with the world, but 1917 had revealed what an abnormal reliance on overseas trade would entail: war without end. "Till our own garden," Beard repeated, and set a noteworthy example for mankind by creating a society devoted to the mental and physical well-being of the American people.[51]

The Ruskin of *Unto This Last*, as modified by the social democratic political philosophy of Hobson, deeply influenced Beard's thinking about his "open-door" program. Ruskin's name appears repeatedly in *The Open Door at Home*, and Beard specifically cited *Unto This Last* as his primer on economic theory conceived mainly as a problem in ethics and esthetics, not profits. Summing up the master's thought, Beard observed, "As Ruskin phrased the issue, life without industry is guilt, and industry without art is brutality—and brutality cannot make an enduring civilization."[52] A brutal civilization could not long remain at peace. Ruskin and Carlyle, his foremost teachers among

the social critics of the nineteenth century, had been dismissed as sentimen-
talists by mainstream economists, whose ideas about applying English classical
economics on a world scale had gained acceptance. Their wholly unmerited
triumph had created the imperialist order from which the Great War and the
Depression stemmed.

The vagueness of Beard's replacement proposals for American capitalism
provoked strong criticisms, even from readers who held him in high regard.
For example, a student named Sidney L. Jackson wrote "An Open Letter to
Dr. Charles A. Beard," which appeared in the May 4, 1935, issue of the *Social
Frontier*, a journal of social and educational commentary edited by the historian's friend and collaborator George S. Counts in Columbia's Teachers College. Articles by Beard had appeared in that journal. Jackson claimed to be
looking for guidance from Beard on the great economic and political questions of the day, but after reading *The Open Door at Home* and other books by
him he could not see anything of practical value in his thinking. What would
replace the institutions of private property and private profit? Jackson charged,
"You have accepted a place in the ranks of leadership. You therefore have a
grave responsibility to those who trust your learning and experience. Dr. Beard,
where do you stand?"[53]

Beard never fleshed out his proposals for social change. He has not gone
down in history as an original social or moral philosopher. He thought that
all the fundamental philosophical points about the good society already had
been made by Ruskin. Beard's work concerned the historical analysis of capitalism's all-too-numerous failures in providing basic sustenance and opportunity for enlightened living to human beings trapped in an imperialist world
system that already had plunged mankind into one world war with an even
worse conflict in the offing.

Having summarized in *The Devil Theory of War* his open-door-at-home
ideas, Beard asserted that a good first dividend of the program would come
from cuts in the defense budget. Americans could reduce the size of their
navy and keep it at home. Defense would consist, as it properly should for a
democratic people, in protecting the United States from actual invasion,
which, Beard had learned from no less an authority than Marine Corps Major
General Smedley Darlington Butler, did not exist as a credible military possibility.[54] To repel this repeatedly invoked phantom threat, a bloated military
establishment had been created. Reference to Butler's *War Is a Racket* (1935)
appears in the section of *The Devil Theory of War* that deals with Beard's open-
door economic plan for America. He heartily agreed with Butler's characterization of the actual American foreign policy as essentially a master plan to
drum up and then to protect business for Wall Street. Borrowing language

from Butler, Beard described American imperialism of the John Hay–Theodore Roosevelt–Alfred Thayer Mahan type as a "plain capitalist racket."[55]

In the same year when his pamphlet had appeared, Butler had published an article in *Common Sense*, "America's Armed Forces 2 'In Time of Peace': The Army," summing up the true purposes of his deployments as a Marine Corps officer. He had spent most of his time in the military serving as "a high-class muscle-man for Big Business, for Wall Street, and for the bankers. In short, I was a racketeer, a gangster for capitalism."[56] His orders had taken him to Mexico, Haiti, Cuba, Nicaragua, the Dominican Republic, China, and other exotic ports of call. His main job in these places had to do with furthering the national interest not of the American people, but of the oil companies, the sugar monopolies, and the banks. Butler likened his actions in uniform to those of a rapist; only he had received decorations, medals, and promotions for his rapes of republics and whole peoples. Butler could give a few tips to Al Capone: "The best he could do was to operate his racket in three city districts. We Marines operated on three *continents*." All of their depredations came under the heading of national "defense," according to the deranged fantasies of the War Department, "that military sap factory," from whence a flood tide of imperialist propaganda never ceased to flow. In American military parlance, defense "means, of course, vast schemes for foreign invasion and offensive war," the cost of which would end up killing the country.[57]

Beard once had thought of the military as a school for the inculcation of high civic ideals where the defects of American materialism and acquisitiveness would undergo the correctives of a morally superior culture. Reviewing in 1918 Thorstein Veblen's *Higher Learning in America*, Beard sought to comfort "those who looked with distress upon the uniformity of American interest in measurable vendibility." They could take heart "in the thought that concern with the glories, honors, and sacrifices of war may act as a salutary check upon the drift toward the 'mechanistically matter of fact.'" American colleges and universities, he thought, would gain from their wartime association with the military and overcome their drift, much lamented by Veblen in his book, toward "the exigencies of advertising." Far from sharing Veblen's despair about the future of higher education in America, Beard thought that the sky over American campuses had never looked more perfectly blue. A great renewal, prompted by the code of the soldier, was under way: "To be plain, military standards may supplant those of the business college."[58]

If any Ruskin-like regard for military values had survived in Beard's thinking as late as 1935, his reading of Butler's *War Is a Racket* would have put an end to it. In *The History of Italy*, Francesco Guicciardini had observed that men go to war because they think that they are going to win and to gain from it.

Minus the sonorous cadences of Guicciardini's high Renaissance style, Butler made the same point plainly with regard to American warfare. Citing as evidence the 21,000 new American millionaires and billionaires produced by the World War, he asserted, "Out of war a few people make huge fortunes."[59] Another war is coming, Butler thought. It, too, would pay high dividends, but only to the corporations and the financial sector behind them that ruled the country.

Like Beard, Butler attentively had followed the deliberations of the Nye Committee. He welcomed its probe of the munitions industry. Despite the Committee's sensational disclosures, however, he thought that it hardly had made a start in understanding the military-industrial problem in America. Boondoggles and fraud at the taxpayers' expense characterized the purchasing system of every item in the military budget, from boots and uniforms to weapons and ships. If only money had been at stake, perhaps matters could be left to sort out themselves over time, but the racket destroyed lives and, far from protecting Americans, it threatened their collective existence. The Republic itself stood in mortal danger because it had embraced militarism. Relentless propaganda for the military had begun during the World War and had never stopped. What Beard in 1918 had celebrated as a magnificently martial uplifting of an American people in arms, Butler, who had been in the war, denounced as a very thorough campaign to brainwash them. He had especially bitter words for the clergymen of all denominations who had blessed the cannons and had found scriptural texts to justify the absolute waste of the slaughter as something sublime, which, every appearance to the contrary, not only could be reconciled with the Sermon on the Mount but had to be seen as the apotheosis of Christianity's deepest meaning.

Butler's predictions in War Is a Racket, about some of the likely consequences of American militarism, touched on one issue in particular that would dominate Beard's thinking about American foreign policy. Severely critical of the naval and military expansion that accompanied the New Deal, Butler worried in 1935 about America's naval maneuvers in the Pacific. He wrote, "The Japanese, a proud people, of course will be pleased beyond expression to see the United States fleet so close to Nippon's shores. Even as pleased as would be the residents of California were they dimly to discern, through the morning mist, the Japanese playing war games off Los Angeles."[60] One way to cut down on the chances of pitching the United States into war would be to keep the navy from venturing farther than two hundred miles from our coastline. The army, he thought, never should go beyond the territorial limits of the United States. The American military had no function outside the country except to serve the needs of big business. In an objective homage to Guicciardini, Butler concluded his pamphlet with a simple injunction: take the money out of war, and war would stop. Money is the answer to the question of why America went to war in 1917 and why it would do so again. Butler had reinforced in Beard's thinking the neutralist lessons of the Nye Committee.

CHAPTER 5

Isolationism versus Internationalism

It would be difficult to think of a historical movement that has fallen more deeply into disgrace and general desuetude than isolationism, the cause of slavery possibly excepted. The isolationists sought to prevent America from entering the Second World War, not recognizing, as history textbooks soon would proclaim, that this conflict was unlike all the others. It was the good war against known perverts and freaks of inhumanity. Victory in 1945 inaugurated the American Century. Those Americans who had failed to understand the need for our intervention in the war against Nazism and Fascism stood condemned by every rule of history as men and women without sense or feeling. The worst of them persisted in their errors even after Pearl Harbor. Most of the isolationists had quickly adjusted their thinking to the necessity of intervention once much of the Pacific Fleet had been destroyed, but a handful of the old believers never did see the light. Among these benighted, Beard took his place.

In a manner reflecting the American consensus today about the isolationists, the novelist Philip Roth told their story in *The Plot Against America* (2004).[1] He imagined what would have happened had the isolationists prevailed. Their paladin, the world-famous aviator Charles A. Lindbergh, becomes president in 1941, having defeated FDR in his bid for an unprecedented third term. For Roth, Lindbergh's Nazi sympathies define the foreign policy that he adopts for the United States. He and Hitler are bound together by "the Iceland

Understanding," an agreement that parallels the Roosevelt-Churchill Atlantic Charter of history. The new president and his even more despicable vice-president, Montana isolationist Senator Burton K. Wheeler, see the eternal Jew as the fundamental cause of the country's woes. Montana comes under consideration as the site for the concentration camps that will be needed as part of an American Final Solution. For the Lindbergh administration, which includes the notoriously anti-Semitic Henry Ford as secretary of the interior, the Jews are the leading warmongers. The war that they want would be, at bottom, a Jewish war. The one difference between Hitler and Lindbergh concerns the Nazi conviction that by the taint of their blood the Jews are responsible for what is wrong with the world. Roth's Lindbergh thinks that some of them at least, through his Office of American Absorption, can be assimilated into the American mainstream and made into decent citizens, a kind of thought that never would have sullied the fervidly anti-Semitic imagination of Hitler.

A partly autobiographical novel, *The Plot Against America* includes the story of the Roth family and the travails they would have undergone under an anti-Semitic Lindbergh administration. The family mistakenly thinks, midway through the novel, that their deliverance from the bigot president is at hand when at a Madison Square Garden rally a politically resurfacing FDR declares, "The only thing we have to fear . . . is the obsequious yielding to his Nazi friends by Charles A. Lindbergh, the shameless courting by the president of the world's greatest democracy of a despot responsible for innumerable criminal deeds and acts of savagery, a cruel and barbaric tyrant unparalleled in the chronicle of man's misdeeds."[2] In real life as of 1941, however, Stalin far surpassed Hitler in the criminal misdeeds department. Yet the historical alliance that FDR forged with the greatest mass murderer in history received no comment from Roth, either in the novel or in its historical postscript.

Jewish radio personality and relentless Lindbergh critic Walter Winchell runs for president, touching off an American pogrom in which Roth gives "Hitlerite America Firsters" a shameful role to play, alongside their natural political allies, the Jew-hating Christian Front of "Radio Priest" Father Charles E. Coughlin, "the dean of anti-Semitism" Reverend Gerald L. K. Smith, the American Nazi Party, the Ku Klux Klan, and all the other anti-Semites abounding at that time, especially in Irish, Italian, Slavic, and German working-class neighborhoods. Even the upper-class Jews hated Winchell, fearing that he might be endangering their place in the American establishment. Following the assassination of Winchell and the mysterious disappearance of Lindbergh, all comes out right in the end when FDR is returned to power, the attack on Pearl Harbor occurs about a year later than the real one, and America finally goes to war against the Axis powers. America and its Jews are saved.

In a bibliographical note at the end of his novel, Roth cited Wayne S. Cole's *America First: The Battle Against Intervention 1940–1941*, a scholarly account of the leading non-interventionist pressure group in the year or so preceding Pearl Harbor. The America First Committee (AFC) had 450 chapters and subchapters with a national membership of between 800,000 and 850,000. Liberals and conservatives belonged to it, although most of its funding came from conservative businessmen. Cole argued that the AFC had a weak hand to play against the interventionist-minded FDR. He defeated them repeatedly on the key foreign policy issues and by November 1941 had the authority to aid Britain in every way except for sending U.S. forces directly into battle. Pearl Harbor cut out all political ground from under the AFC, which then disbanded itself. Most of its leading members thereafter sought to accommodate themselves to the new realities created by the Japanese attack.

Roth appeared, however, to have learned nothing at all from Cole, who about the motives of the non-interventionists wrote, "A very small percentage of the American people took this position because of their pro-Nazi and pro-fascist views."[3] Most people joined because of their disillusionment with World War I and desire to avoid another useless slaughter. In a chapter titled "Anti-Semitism and America First," Cole directly took up the theme developed by Roth in his novel. AFC leaders actively sought to distance the organization from any anti-Semitic elements that might be drawn to it. They left a long paper trail, exhaustively traced by Cole, attesting to the genuineness of their aversion to anti-Semitism. They invited all patriotic Americans, regardless of race or religion, to join the group and actively sought to recruit prominent Jews to occupy leadership positions, succeeding in some cases. Anti-Semitism did exist in the organization, but more as a consequence of general cultural attitudes in America at the time, and not at all because of the philosophy and practice of the America First Committee.

When Lindbergh gave a notorious address at Des Moines, Iowa, on September 11, 1941, in which he identified powerful Jewish elements in the media and government as a propelling force behind the interventionist movement, the AFC faced renewed and dramatically augmented charges of anti-Semitism. In defending itself, the organization pointed out that its critics had overlooked Lindbergh's denunciation in the speech of the Nazis for their cruel treatment of the Jews in Germany. He had not criticized Jews for anti-Semitic reasons, on the basis of their race or religion, but for the political choices some particular Jewish individuals and groups had made. Jews could not be placed on a pedestal beyond the reach of historical criticism. No group could, without turning history into some kind of a fable for the perpetual enchantment of a race of heroes. Although Cole judged the speech to have been a political disaster for the AFC by furnishing interventionists with their best opportunity to discredit the organization, he gave no credence to the charge of anti-Semitism leveled against Lindbergh.[4] His monograph was an anticipatory rebuttal of Roth's accusations against the AFC and an invitation for Americans today at least to consider the possibility of reevaluating the last serious foreign policy debate held in the United States prior to the bipartisan internationalist consensus. It had been all war all the time ever since the America First Committee went down to its final defeat on December 7, 1941.

An excellent example of Cole's argument about the AFC was the chairman of the organization's 200,000-strong New York City chapter, John T. Flynn.[5] A liberal journalist and longtime columnist for the *New Republic*, he energetically resisted the efforts of Father Coughlin and other anti-Semites to infiltrate the AFC. Flynn also spurned the blandishments of the German government, avowing that he detested the Nazis and everything they represented. He personally shut down subchapters suspected of anti-Semitism. He could not guard the organization against every extremist or the agents provocateurs planted in its ranks by pro-interventionist forces. Nevertheless, there could be no doubt about his commitment and that of the AFC generally to a peaceful and wholly democratic foreign policy agenda for the United States. Despite such facts and the prominent role that Jews played in the New York City chapter, interventionists assailed the AFC as the "Hitler First Committee" and the "Nazi Transmission Belt." In the public mind, their accusations prevailed over the truth.

Cole also made it clear why Beard had no role to play in *The Plot Against America*. Roth included many historical figures in his cast of characters and provided detailed accounts of some of them in the appendix to the novel. No one at all resembling Beard played a part in the story. He barely appeared in Cole's book. The key moments in his relationship with the America First Committee came when the organization twice asked him to join its national committee, but he declined each time. Beard clearly saw the chasm between his politics and those of the AFC. The most surprising aspect of their relationship is that the AFC approached him at all. Beard's views about turning the United States into a workers' republic were well to the left of the New Deal and contrasted even more sharply with the laissez-faire economics espoused by the conservative businessmen who bankrolled the AFC. On foreign policy generally, though, Beard had much in common with the AFC, and about the war in Europe they agreed completely on the need to keep the country neutral. He did publicly endorse the organization but followed his own path.

Kingman Brewster Jr., a future president of Yale University and at the time a student leader there of the AFC, had initially hoped to bring Beard into the organization. In a July 1940 letter to fellow Yale student and the founder of the

AFC, R. Douglas Stuart Jr., Brewster explained that Beard "appears very willing to give us personal advice and support." Yet he foresaw difficulties with Beard's inclusion in the organization. Other members had expressed reservations about Beard, and Brewster himself thought, "He's so doctrinaire on the subject [of non-intervention] that his strength is well located by everyone anyway." A. Whitney Griswold, an assistant professor of government and political science at Yale, and another future president of the institution, had the same America First concerns about Beard. Brewster reported in his July 1940 letter to Stuart that Professor Griswold worried about Beard's "name value to us anyway."[6]

His growing disillusionment with the president on foreign policy matters notwithstanding, Beard had continued to defend him on other issues. For example, he had taken the president's side publicly in the acrimonious controversy over the court-packing plan of 1937, to increase the number of Supreme Court justices as a means of gaining support on the bench for New Deal measures. He had declared in a March 29, 1937, radio address, "The President's plan laid before Congress is a constitutional plan. It squares with the letter of the Constitution."[7] In another instance, after expressing doubt about FDR's intentions to keep the United States at peace, Beard acknowledged the president's uniqueness in American history: "Whatever else may happen it seems safe to say that President Roosevelt has made a more profound impression upon the political, social, and economic thought of America than any or all of his predecessors."[8] Yet despite all the president's nostrums, the country's economic system continued to fail.

Beard's unrelenting hostility toward Wall Street defined his politics in the late 1930s. He fully revealed his state of mind in the thousand-page *America in Midpassage* (1939), which became the third volume in *The Rise of American Civilization* series written in collaboration with his wife. Before coming to their main subject, the supreme disaster of the Depression and its ramifications for American politics, culture, and foreign policy, they first described the ballyhoo of American capitalism's golden age in the 1920s. As long as the wonder-working ways of "the National Shrine in Wall Street" continued in prodigious evidence, few Americans thought to question the economic system under which they lived.[9] The stock market crash in October 1929, however, raised unfriendly questions of unprecedented severity about the true character of American capitalism, particularly regarding its capacity to meet consistently the basic needs of the population.

"The Lords of Creation," the pet term of the Beards, along with "Pillars of Society" and "Peers of Respectability," in describing the big money men on Wall Street, need not have worried. Even the catastrophe of the Great Depression failed to result in a serious challenge to the status quo. On FDR's New Deal, supposedly a drastic overhaul of American capitalism, they wrote, "On the assumption that minor modifications and the elimination of 'abuses' would make the system run better, if not well, the Roosevelt administration . . . made many experiments not contemplated by classical theory, without departing essentially from its presuppositions and predilections."[10] As for the prospect of a revolutionary challenge to the system, political support for the socialists and communists sharply declined between 1932 and 1936.

Foreign policy during the 1930s, always an extension of domestic policy for the Beards, followed a path well-worn in American annals. They paused to praise President Hoover as an admirable anomaly in American diplomacy. In retrospect, he held the distinction, the two historians argued, of having served as the last of the country's stay-at-home presidents. He had turned down the big-navy proponents, whose funding desires FDR delighted in gratifying. Hoover remained confined in the logic of Washington's Farewell Address and thought that American resources should be employed at home, a position that should have won him the support of the Beards. They did admire Hoover's foreign policy views, but in 1932 they had immersed themselves in the popular tide that swept FDR into the White House. He appeared to have answers for the Depression nowhere to be found in the mental universe of Hoover. Along with most other American voters, the Beards felt entranced by FDR's personal magnetism, charm, and energy.

Despite FDR's New Deal, the Depression continued to ravage the land. In the context of that overwhelming economic disaster, the Beards analyzed the Roosevelt administration's foreign policy. In their estimation, FDR essentially represented a full reversion, after the Hoover deviation, to the standard American line after 1898 about the country's purpose in the world. The Beards explained this national purpose as a work in progress with a central core that never changed: the doctrine of empire and intervention as bequeathed by Alfred T. Mahan, Theodore Roosevelt, John Hay, and Henry Cabot Lodge and then repackaged by master foreign policy rhetorician Woodrow Wilson as a sacred American covenant to make the world safe for democracy. FDR, first tentatively, in recognition of the power still wielded by the isolationists, and then with increasing determination and sureness of touch, fully restored the Wilson legacy, eventually adding to it his own trademark rhetorical flourishes. "Endowed with a positive genius for the opalescent phrase, clever in forming rounded sentences, agile in springing the trap of logic, proficient in insinuation,"[11] FDR began as the student of Wilson, but ended as a past master of internationalist dialectics in his own right.

Of course, FDR's foreign policy involved more than rhetoric. *America in Midpassage* would not have been a Beardian book without sustained reference to what the authors liked to call "the forces of economic gravitation." They had no interest in the Marxist theory of dialectical materialism about how at all times and in all places economic substructures dominated political and cultural superstructures. Instead, they modestly put forward an empirically based methodology for their work: "Cautiously applied, with a sense of its limitations, the economic interpretation merely meant the persistent association of ideas and personalities in historical writing with the relevant economic interests in which they were entangled in history as actuality."[12] They thought that the findings of the Nye Committee convincingly illustrated the way economics influenced political policy, domestic and foreign.

For insight into the economic system that gave life and force to American militarism and imperialism, the Beards looked primarily to the analysis of Thorstein Veblen. They praised him for his brilliant uncovering of "economics in its social affiliations as a phase of culture, rather than as a hypothetical mechanism."[13] Regarding these connections among money, war, and culture, they saw him as the heir, not of Marx, with whom he obviously had some intellectual relationship, but, to a much greater degree, of Thomas Carlyle in *Past and Present* and, most directly, of John Ruskin in *Unto This Last*. Here Beard traced his own intellectual pedigree as well. Veblen's idea that the enterprise of business elites in America, the country's ruling stratum, had to do with pecuniary as opposed to productive activity, seemed to Beard the American variation of the social criticism handed down by the two great Victorian-era cultural conservatives. Their legacy had undergone the progressive modifications imposed on it by John Atkinson Hobson in *John Ruskin Social Reformer* and then in *Imperialism: A Study*, a book that particularly impressed Veblen and deepened his understanding of the economics of foreign policy and war.[14] Veblen's early ideas about imperialism revealed their derivation from Hobson. He had Hobson's sense of the hyper-imperialist future that history was preparing for mankind. The Beards explained, "Veblen thought in 1904 that the immediate future was more likely to comprise war, a growth of military force in society, the recrudescence of arbitrary discipline, the decline of laissez-faire and civil liberties."[15]

Beard himself had made the same intellectual itinerary and recognized in Veblen a kindred spirit. The two Americans had similar effects on their respective fields. What Beard wrote about Veblen in economics could have been applied just as easily to him in the history profession: "Veblen resorted to emphasis rather than to the measurement of exact proportions, but even a mere recognition of the facts seemed to the orthodox almost like a wanton riot in a Sunday school." Out of the military activity required by the imposition of economic imperialism would arise "a growing power of the State over business."[16] In broad outlines, American foreign policy had followed the course that Veblen had said it would and was still following it now.

In September 1939, Beard published an article in *Harper's Magazine*, derived from a theme that he and his wife raised in *America in Midpassage*: government employment of foreign policy as a diversion away from domestic crises. The article also appeared as a short book that same year, *Giddy Minds and Foreign Quarrels: An Estimate of American Foreign Policy*. One of Beard's most trenchant anti-interventionist polemics of the period, this book borrowed its title from a scene in one of Shakespeare's history plays. In the fourth act of *Henry IV, Part Two*, the dying king beckons his son:

Come hither, Harry, sit thou by my bed
And hear, I think, the very latest counsel
That I shall ever breathe.

He reflects on the "by-paths and indirect crook'd ways / I met this crown." Once on the throne, he worried incessantly about the men,

By whose fell working I was first advanced
And by whose power I well might lodge a fear
To be again displaced: which to avoid,
I cut them off; and had a purpose now
To lead out many to the Holy Land,
Lest rest and lying still might make them look
Too near unto my state.

There is nothing like a good crusade to keep domestic politics safe from prying eyes and hands.

. . . Therefore, my Harry
Be it thy course to busy giddy minds
With foreign quarrels. . . .

Prince Henry responds:

My gracious liege,
You won it, wore it, kept it, and gave it me
Then plain and right must my possession be:
Which I with more than with a common pain
'Gainst all the world will rightfully maintain.[17]

Beard thought that this exchange between the two Plantagenets, father and son, caught the true spirit of American foreign policy in the FDR era. For sheer deviousness, American leaders belonged in the same class with Henry IV. Ever since the Spanish-American War, the United States had been inserting itself ever deeper into world affairs. The Depression, however, had forced the country to concentrate on its economic problems at home. As the grim decade wore on, the Depression did not relax its hold. Beard thought that the president had steadily shifted his attention to world affairs for the same reason that Henry IV had fomented a crusade, as a diversionary tactic. Whenever FDR made his internationalist foreign policy moves too suddenly or sharply, the powerful neutralist and isolationist forces in the country blocked him. As Justus D. Doenecke explained in his history of the opposition to FDR's foreign policy on the eve of America's intervention in the Second World War, "obviously the house of anti-intervention contained many mansions."[18] He meant that a vigorous opposition to FDR existed at this time across a broad spectrum of opinion, left and right, in American politics, journalism, and intellectual life.

For Beard, a speech that FDR gave in Chicago on October 5, 1937, marked a fateful turning point in American foreign policy. The president called on all the democracies to quarantine the aggressor states of Germany, Italy, and Japan. Beard noted in *Giddy Minds and Foreign Quarrels* that "the significance of this address was grasped immediately." All the forces devoted to the neutrality legislation of the mid-1930s reacted vigorously in a counterblast of criticism. Ever the tactically astute leader, FDR wisely retreated, but the following January called upon Congress to vote for an enormous increase in naval outlays, ostensibly to protect world peace and security. Beard thought that in this address to Congress, the president all but proclaimed his "resolve to act as a kind of arbiter in world affairs." He hardly could play such a role without a convincing display of military power as a necessary corroboration of his speeches. The January 1939 address that he made to Congress, full of grave warnings about crises and tumults abroad, recalled to Beard's mind the "latest counsel" of Henry IV to Prince Henry. He said of the president's message, "Evidently, he was clearing a way to make the next war a real holy war."[19] The administration thereafter, in opposition to the findings of the Nye Committee, set itself the task of breaking down the embargo on munitions in the event of foreign war.

Beard faulted American policymakers most of all for their ignorance. They did not know enough about the history of Europe or Asia to come to intelligent and realistic conclusions about what to do, much less how to lead, in those places. About America's internationalist foreign policy, Beard criticized, "it assumes that somebody in the White House or State Department can calculate the consequences likely to come out of the explosive forces which are hidden in the civilization of those immense areas." He doubted that the leaders in Washington had the kind of historical education that would enable them to understand the deeper realities behind the headlines. The economic, political, and cultural forces churning the world would not be a factor in their plans for peace and security, the usual American oversight, which Beard identified as the reason why the previous war to make the world safe for democracy had produced the present world crisis. He concluded, "Hence, in my judgment it is folly for the people of the United States to embark on a vast and risky program of world pacification."[20]

In its internationalist enthusiasms, the Roosevelt administration had failed to take another vital matter into account, Beard continued. They had assumed that the economy and democracy of the United States were secure, but he wondered, "Is the management of our own affairs so efficient and so evidently successful that we may take up the role of showing other countries just how to manage their internal economies?"[21] He thought that George Washington's advice in his Farewell Address contained more wisdom than all of the foreign policy state papers of the past forty years, going back to the Spanish-American War. The president had spoken of American foreign policy as a natural tributary of the country's mainstream domestic policy, which for him had as its paramount aim the steady uplifting of the American people in peace and freedom. One of Washington's warnings seemed especially prophetic to Beard, to "avoid the necessity of those overgrown military establishments which, under any form of government, are inauspicious to liberty and which are to be regarded as particularly hostile to republican liberty."[22]

Reasons of state, Beard believed, made it unlikely that the American people would hear FDR or his lieutenants cite passages from Washington's Farewell Address. It was far too subversive a document, expressly contradicting as it did every principle of the internationalist foreign policy. Beard thought the address "a precious heritage." The logic of it led inexorably to the conclusion that for legitimate defense needs modest military and naval establishments would be adequate. As for the savings made possible by reduced defense budgets, we then would have the wherewithal to meet social problems at home: "We need to put our national life, our democracy, on a foundation of internal security, which will relax the present tensions and hatreds." Presently, too much of our national wealth went to the military, he warned. We should not be creating a military juggernaut for the purpose of increasing America's global presence when the home front itself stood in peril and need, its condition further weakened by the withdrawal of tax money and human energy for redeployment abroad: "A lust for unattainable preponderance and a lack of sense of the limitations of power have probably done more damage to nations and the world than any other psychological force in history."[23]

The fundamental question facing the American people in 1939, Beard observed in *Giddy Minds and Foreign Quarrels*, concerned their core values. The administration's internationalist rhetoric about America's role as the essential preserver of world peace and security Beard thought needed to be translated into Standard English. The president spoke euphemistically about the duties of keeping the peace and security of the world. Such an arduous task historically meant that the peace-keeper and the security guard had required supreme power in the world. In all recorded history no people ever had known for long how to use such power without becoming a moral desperado among nations and hated, with just cause, universally. Did we really want to become the new Rome, as the conqueror, ruler, and robber of the world, "and then crumble in ruins?"[24]

The model of the British Empire Beard found even more unattractive, because at least the Romans had the integrity to admit what they were doing and even to glory in it. The British, on the other hand, possessed a peculiar quality of mind that allowed national self-indulgence and a kind of moral vanity about their empire to assume some truly weird forms. They imagined themselves not as the oppressive and exploitative colonial masters that they were, but as bearers of civilization bringing soap and long pants to "fluttered folk and wild," in the image of Rudyard Kipling. The bard of British imperialism had reassured his countrymen that the British Empire existed as a moral obligation and as a confirmation of their superior humanity. Beard, as an Oxford student and under the influence—for both good and ill—of John Ruskin, had gone through an imperialist phase during which the strains of "Rule Britannia!" stirred profound emotions in him. Then, with one glaring lapse during World War I, he had recovered his senses as a critical historian. In *Giddy Minds and Foreign Quarrels*, he wrote, "the jig is up for British imperial dictatorship in the old style."[25]

Beard hoped that the United States would not be taken in again by the British, as in the Great War, to think that an American alliance meant anything to them but reinforcement for their empire. Americans by and large, and certainly at the level of the power elite, had an extremely romantic conception of the British, a view not shared by the Irish, the Indians, the Egyptians, the blacks of Rhodesia, and any other people actually under their rule. Britain welcomed the participation of the United States in maintaining "security and order," the better to facilitate full access to the resources and markets of the world. Access was another word in the imperialist lexicon that required decoding. Beard implored his readers to resist the imperialist temptation. The coming war, for which FDR already assiduously had begun to prepare America's participation, at bottom would be, like the last war, about the imperial control of the world. All of the other issues, some of them truly important and moral, stood in a subaltern relationship to the one that mattered most of all. The people mistakenly called isolationists "do not propose to withdraw from the world, but they propose to deal with the world as it is and not as romantic propagandists picture it."[26]

Beard's article for *Harper's Magazine* appeared during the same month as the Second World War's outbreak. He certainly held the Hitler regime in abhorrence. Beard consistently had condemned the Nazi ideology as nothing but a repulsive accumulation of right-wing totalitarian delusions. Yet, with the isolationists, whose most important organization, the America First Committee, would be launched on September 5, 1940, he did not suspend critical judgment about the imperialist motives of Great Britain in the war. Nor did he stand idly by as FDR sought to repeal the existing arms embargo and other neutrality legislation. On January 18, 1939, Beard had written an article for the *New Republic*, "Neutrality: Shall We Have Revision?—The President's Policy and the People's." As a consequence of the proposed revision, he contended, the power to declare war would be transferred from Congress, where the Constitution plainly stipulated that such authority should reside, to the executive branch. The president then would be free "to use the economic power of the United States against any belligerent that he may designate."[27]

The following month, Beard wrote in the magazine *Common Sense*, "it is my firm conviction that the United States should stay out of the next war in Europe and all the wars that will follow the next war." The United States, he thought, lacked the capacity to settle European affairs, to "make the peoples of Europe prosperous, happy, and good, make human nature in Europe anything else than it is and will be, and close the long and bloody history of Europe by the beatitudes."[28] By getting into the next war we would inflict incalculable material, intellectual, and moral damage on the country. We would do well to have smaller ambitions.

In the April 1939 issue of the *American Mercury* magazine, Beard strongly had criticized the recent conduct of the German, Italian, and Japanese governments: "It has been, in most respects, barbaric, indecent, cruel, and inhuman. What I do say is that the underlying issues accompanying their conduct cannot be reduced to a single issue—democracy against despotism, humanity against inhumanity." He meant that the tragic blindness of the Versailles Peace Treaty had to be taken into account as the prime cause of the evils now besetting the world. Italian fascism, German Nazism, and Japanese militarism could not be understood outside the historical context that actually had produced them. Neither could current British and French actions, which Beard believed had their ultimate rationale in the preservation of the imperialist gains that those two countries had made at Versailles. Somehow the agenda of British and French imperialists had escaped the notice of our leaders, who wanted the American people to believe, against all evidence, that the only issue at stake in current events concerned the conflict between freedom and its opponents. The United States, according to Beard, "should not dabble in quarrels and squabbles in Europe or in Asia, about the origins and intentions of which it knows little or nothing."[29] He feared, though, that American politicians would not be able to resist the temptation of war as a way out of the impasse in the country's economic life.

Five months later, in his "Giddy Minds and Foreign Quarrels" article for *Harper's Magazine*, Beard identified partisan aid to Britain as a likely cause of America's eventual intervention in any future European war and as a reinforcement of the British Empire. He judged the president's appeals for the support of Britain in the name of democracy and freedom to be nothing but the recycled propaganda of Woodrow Wilson from the last war. To Beard, the conflict that broke out on September 1, 1939, was another war between imperialist thieves. At this point, well before the Holocaust and the other horrors for which the Nazis would become branded as moral lepers in the pages of history, the fundamental difference that he saw between the two sides had to do with territory: Britain already had lebensraum to spare and Germany wanted some. This war, too, he believed, was about the economic control of the world.

Just as Germany's blitzkrieg campaign was overrunning Western Europe in the spring of 1940, Beard published *A Foreign Policy for America*, a short book that drew freely on his writings about the open door at home, as well as *The Idea of National Interest* and *America in Midpassage*. Lack of wisdom in foreign affairs, he wrote, may bring down upon a country "domestic tyranny, debts, economic destruction, war, death, and consequences far more revolutionary than popular agitations and disturbances." He had uppermost in mind the consequences of World War I, soon to be repeated, he feared, in another imperialist conflict. At bottom, America's participation in the First World War involved our cooperating with British and French imperialism "in the war of European powers for world hegemony." Beard dryly observed how at the Paris Peace Conference the United States had helped Britain and France obtain their imperialist spoils of war "after the war for democracy had come to a close." Since 1898, the American people had become entangled in the quarrels and crises of Europe and Asia, so much so that "it was but a step to President Wilson's scheme for permanent and open participation in European and Asian affairs in the alleged interest of universal peace and general welfare."[30]

American foreign policy from 1917 to 1940 had to be understood as a consequence of its two driving forces, imperialism and internationalism. Summing up American imperialism, Beard made obvious his continuing reliance on Hobson's thesis in *Imperialism: A Study*. Such a large number of winsome claims had been made about the windfall sure to ensue from the acquisition of the Philippines, yet "carefully drawn balance sheets of the Philippine adventure showed specific gains to specific American interests, but a general loss to the country, entirely apart from increased naval expenditures." Instead of positive advantages, imperialism had brought dangerous commitments in the Far East. Hobson's point about the exorbitant cost to the taxpayer for an empire-winning effort applied to the American case. The navy's budget, "already many times the total annual profit of all Asiatic trade," had first tripled and then quadrupled. Beard kept coming back to the Philippines as his foremost example of the Hobson thesis about how imperialism does not pay, "despite the profits made by a few traders."[31]

Internationalism Beard defined as the foreign policy "which sets *world* peace as the fundamental objective for the Government in the conduct of relations with other countries." In theory, an internationalist foreign policy called upon the United States to cooperate with like-minded countries in establishing a just and stable world order. Unfortunately for the theory, the like-minded countries chosen by Wilson for this crusade, Britain and France, had been "feverishly engaged in the secret negotiations, conversations, and combinations which were soon to eventuate in the greatest slaughter and destruction that the world had ever witnessed."[32] Not justice and stability, but the intensified imperialist exploitation of the non-Western world Beard reckoned as the chief result of internationalism. In practical terms, internationalism had developed as a new and improved marketing strategy for imperialism.

The repudiation of Wilson in the congressional election of 1918, the rejection of the Versailles Treaty in 1919, and the defeat of the internationalist-minded Democratic Party in the presidential election of 1920 cumulatively appeared to have checkmated the American jihad for world peace. Beard, however, pointed to the continuing vitality of "the international faith" in American colleges and universities where isolationists precariously survived as an embattled minority.[33] Based on the way that policy elites were taught in the schools, the future would belong to the international program, he lamented. The high-minded vocabulary of the internationalists exerted a powerful appeal, but Beard doubted that peace and prosperity for a democratic world figured in the thinking of the men who held power, except as a verbal flourish in directing attention away from their real agenda.

The Kellogg-Briand Treaty of 1928 outlawing war and signed by most of the world's nations seemed to Beard a perfect illustration of the distinction between the appearances and realities of internationalist foreign policy. For piety of purpose the treaty, which epitomized the internationalist ethos, could not be bettered. Who could be opposed to peace for all mankind? Looking a little deeper into the matter, Beard observed how "Great Britain excluded from the operation of the document her own special interests, which were indeed rather wide." Not to be outdone, the United States insisted on the right to enforce the Monroe Doctrine in its sphere of influence. Marine Corps forays, such as the ones led by Smedley Butler into Nicaragua, Haiti, Dominican Republic, and elsewhere in Latin America, would go on as before. Most revealing for Beard, the United States continued to enlarge its navy, adding billions to the national debt. Wars for "defense" of course would still be allowed, but Beard wondered, "defense for what?"[34] By 1940, when he was writing *A Foreign Policy for America*, the Kellogg-Briand Treaty had become a byword for utopian thinking in foreign policy. Internationalism, he argued, always projected a utopian image of itself, but its underlying program had an imperialist core. Pieties about human rights made a perfect semantic cover for the rich who through their banks and armies lorded over the poor.

As a proponent of an internationalist foreign policy, Franklin Delano Roosevelt appeared to Beard as a double Wilson. With the Depression withstanding FDR's program, the stage was set, Beard worried, for a reenactment of a classic political drama endlessly repeated throughout history: "The unrest might increase in intensity and encourage politicians to take refuge in another foreign adventure of some kind." Busying giddy minds with foreign quarrels might become an irresistible temptation in the face of the administration's failure to cope with the crisis at home. Speaking about American politicians, Beard added: "In an hour of sheer desperation they might resort to the last expedient of bewildered and frustrated minds." Roosevelt and his entourage would not be the first "restless élite engaged in planning a new outburst to release stifled energies or escape from domestic troubles."[35] Such a resort to force Beard believed to be the most likely response by the president to the worsening dilemmas that he faced. A coalition of navy bureaucrats, imperialists, and internationalists behind the president would constitute an irresistible force in American politics.

Beard recognized the moral failures of Germany, Italy, and Japan, although his censure of the Nazi regime later would seem grievously understated. In 1940, however, with the Holocaust still in the future and general knowledge of it even more so, critics concerned about mass murder would have been much more justified in censuring Stalin, who already had murdered millions, than Hitler. In any case, Beard focused his attention in this book on mistakes that America might make in response to a world situation that the country did not understand. A preliminary problem for the Americans resulted from their lack of self-knowledge. They had forgotten their own history. Their genocidal wars against the native inhabitants of the country counted for nothing on the American conscience. They had no knowledge to speak of about their own wars of expansion and imperialism against Mexico, Spain, and the Philippines. What was Hitler doing in 1939, if not following the American example of extending the sphere, only in the German case for lebensraum instead of an empire of liberty? Yes, the Germans were acting atrociously in 1939 and 1940, but in some of the same ways done earlier by the Americans.

Referring to the impact on the American consciousness of Germany's march through Europe Beard wrote "to a tender hearted people, with a tendency to forgetfulness, this was indeed shocking."[36] Yet how familiar and close to home these enormities would seem to Americans seriously informed about the history of their own land. The war being fought now, regardless of what our internationalist leaders were saying about democratic freedoms, would end as all wars had been settled in the past, by an arrangement reflecting the dominant military and economic power of the victors. Beard reacted skeptically to the president's claims about the moral superiority of democracy. As he would observe some years later to Merle Curti, the historical record furnished very little evidence in support of FDR's description of the United States as "our peace-loving democracy."[37] Beard identified the cause of democracy as the one reason, most certainly, for which this war, much like its predecessor in 1914–1918, could not be said to be fought. More plausible reasons had to do with the old standbys—domination and empire.

Against the empire, which Beard thought would kill American civilization, he held up the republic as an existential ideal for the country's authentic patriots. The foreign market outlet doctrines of imperialists and the world peace phantasms of internationalists had deceived the country and had turned it away from its true traditions. Americans need not go abroad, either as imperialist exploiters or as world-saving internationalists. Imperialism bankrupted every country that ever embraced it. America would not be the living exception in the graveyard of ruined empires.

As for saving the world, we did not know enough to undertake such a task, Beard contended in *A Foreign Policy for America*. We could not save ourselves. Our own country suffered from dire internal economic and social threats, with no sign of a civilization-saving renaissance. Touting a political philosophy of "continentalism," he called for Americans to apply their energy at home: "all about us, right here, lay the materials for a magnificent civilization." By focusing on our own problems, we would not become a hermit nation, as the internationalists said: "Continentalism merely meant a recognition of the limited nature of American powers to relieve, restore, and maintain life beyond its own sphere of interest and control." We simply did not have the power or the resources to force peace on the world or to assure the establishment of democratic governments everywhere, or to provide the wherewithal for social and economic nation building. Along the internationalist path, sure to involve an overextension of the country's resources and capabilities, lay the abyss. We lacked the capability to create an empire and to protect our own republic or to develop it democratically to the full extent of its potential. The republic had to be protected "against misadventures headed in the direction of disaster," which is how Beard thought about the international foreign policy of the Roosevelt administration. He felt certain that the president's "vain and verbose dissertations on the manners and morals of other countries" served no purpose, except to exacerbate the crises engulfing the Western world.[38]

A Foreign Policy for America became a much-debated book in the United States. It found a warmly approving reception in anti-interventionist circles.[39] The America First Committee placed the book prominently on its recommended reading list for members, noting "the distinguished historian submits a foreign policy designed to meet challenging world conditions and at the same time to realize the democratic 'aims' of America."[40] West Point graduate General Hugh S. Johnson, formerly a key figure in the New Deal but by 1940 a supporter of the isolationist AFC, praised the book and called Beard "as seasoned a student, teacher, and expounder of American history as we have." Johnson had found "considerable aid and comfort in this scholarly analysis," which had exposed the FDR administration's delusive internationalist foreign policy.[41]

In the United States Senate, Gerald P. Nye called to the attention of his colleagues "a very splendid work recently done by that most eminent historian of our time, Charles A. Beard, entitled 'A Foreign Policy for America.'" He began, "Mr. President, I am going to say this afternoon things that I have hesitated for a long time to say; but they are things that had better be said now, lest we surprisingly reach the hour when it is not going to be the smart thing to say even things approximately what ought to be said now."[42] In short, Beard had shown how the United States already had abandoned the noninterventionist law of the land and, in a foreshadowing of the country's political future, how the office of the presidency had substituted its own will for that of the people. For citizens determined to keep the country out of foreign wars, Beard enjoyed an unrivaled prestige among American historians.

The book also brought down on Beard criticisms reflecting the scholarly consensus already beginning to form around FDR's internationalist foreign policy. Beard had received many critical drubbings for his books over the years. In the eyes of conservatives, *An Economic Interpretation of the Constitution of the United States* had made him a marked man for life. He would not have been surprised by the attack of Columbia University's Allan Nevins, who in the same year that *A Foreign Policy for America* appeared would publish *John D. Rockefeller: The Heroic Age of American Enterprise*, one of his many tributes to the corporation chiefs Beard continued to condemn as robber barons who had despoiled the American people of their national patrimony. About Beard's book, Nevins wrote, "it is not necessary to say much." To the study of American foreign policy Beard had applied his "usual smart, hard materialism," without, however, taking into account "that the Western world is being shaken today by the mightiest conflict of moral forces in centuries; that democracy is struggling for its life against fascism, liberalism against brute intolerance, freedom against tyranny." Nevins condemned him for "this frigid indifference to moral considerations."[43] Beard, he criticized, simply did not appreciate America's passion for freedom and noble desire to safeguard it against the forces of oppression.

For his part, Beard professed to believe that the deepest issue in American foreign policy should concern the country's cardinal values, a theme he developed in a 1941 book, *Public Policy and the General Welfare*. He once again proclaimed his own personal faith in Ruskin, still for him the most profound social critic of modern times. Applying Ruskin's principles to the major extant ideological traditions—liberalism, conservatism, socialism, and fascism—Beard found all four wanting. Their limitations, in his view, constituted the crisis of Western thought. Fascism hardly appeared to be a system at all. He found in it little more than "a combination of personal tyranny, state socialism, great capitalism, militarism, and war." Socialists had fallen out among themselves and could provide no coherent leadership on the great political questions of the day. Indeed, "Marxists are utterly bewildered in the presence of practical issues—tactics; and they are questioning the validity of a system of thought that cannot give them unequivocal directions for correct actions." Yet the other two systems were badly riven and in disarray as well, because of their failure to meet Ruskin's criteria for a true politics, as outlined in *Unto This Last*, which Beard mentioned by name. He found all four great ideological systems to be "alike in resting their structures on material interests and in either rejecting or minimizing ethical and aesthetic considerations—of the Ruskinian type, for example."[44] Other examples furnished by Beard came principally from Ruskin's great precursor in cultural conservatism, Thomas Carlyle.

The language and values of *Unto This Last* still permeated Beard's thought in 1941, nearly fifty years after his initial reading of Ruskin's great book. Early in *Public Policy and the General Welfare*, he asks, "And where shall the statesman find guidance or a firm center of reference for the determination of policy concerned as the good life for the nation?" This had been Ruskin's question. He had answered it in the manner of Carlyle by saying that it was not enough for public policy to produce wealth for the possessing classes. Such a system would not last and would not deserve to last. Beard had exactly this idea about the liberal tradition and its very close relative in the family of ideological traditions, conservatism. Much of the argument in *Public Policy and the General Welfare* consists of a Beardian diatribe against the structurally toothless agenda of laissez-faire economics and its two principal political support systems, liberalism and conservatism. America had become "the new Leviathan of capitalism," and this was the country's misfortune.[45] Neither liberals nor conservatives had demonstrated the slightest capacity for managing the relentlessly aggressive and socially destructive energies of capitalism.

Obviously, the conservative Republican Party existed for no other reason than to minister to the political needs of economic elites. Nothing else needed to be said about Republicans, according to Beard. Although the liberal Democrats enjoyed a reputation for progressive legislation, their political role varied but slightly, and only at a rhetorical level from that of the Republicans. Beard cited Woodrow Wilson, thought to be a paragon of progressive reformism, as an example of his thesis about American liberals. Wilson had been an exponent of laissez-faire capitalism for most of his life. The progressive reforms that he implemented as president came nowhere close to touching the fundamentals of America's exploitative economic system. Laissez-faire American style, in either its liberal or its conservative variant, amounted to a shameful fraud perpetrated against poor people. Of course, the American government zealously intervened in the economy on behalf of railroad barons, industrialists, and financiers. The American system of government derived its policy bearings from the lobbies that worked on behalf of the rich. Pressure group politics explained the history of land giveaways to railroad corporations, tariff legislation favorable to businessmen, and the creation of a financial system utterly shorn of a concern for the general welfare. The motto of American elites came from the old adage: "Anarchy for ourselves, propriety for others."[46]

Despite the fractious din in American politics over Roosevelt, the New Deal seemed to Beard only a mildly augmented version of Wilson's "new freedom." Nothing in Roosevelt's program threatened the fundamentals of the capitalist system or even modified it in a way that might lead to a genuinely democratic society with anything like so much as an aspiration toward economic equality. He listed the salient features of the New Deal programs, but all of the decade-long legislative activity in Washington had not restored the economy to health, "until the armament boom of 1941 gave it a temporary lift."[47] Here Beard referred to the economic consequences of the increasing support, against its own neutrality laws, that the United States then was giving to Britain in the country's struggle against Nazi Germany. Beard had long been on record in opposition to the administration's pro-interventionist policies, but he did not understand the true character of the adversary that he faced in this conflict. He thought that the issue of American intervention in World War II would turn on public policy arguments, such as the one he made in *Public Policy and the General Welfare*. The publication in 1999 of Thomas E. Mahl's *Desperate Deception: British Covert Operations in the United States, 1939–1944* revealed in unexampled detail the intelligence history behind the event that led to the American Century and the consummation of Beard's worst fears for the country.

Mahl documented the massive secret political campaign in the United States begun in 1939 by the British to undermine the isolationist movement and to bring the country into the war. He described a textbook case of the role played by covert intelligence in bending American policy to the will of a foreign power. In his preface, he cited Beard as a precursor who had understood that American foreign policy in those five years had been shaped by a strategic and economic agenda essentially having nothing to do with the official reasons stated by the government. Mahl praised Beard's 1948 study of American foreign policy on the eve of the country's intervention in World War II, *President Roosevelt and the Coming of the War, 1941*. He wrote that Beard had written "the only book similar to this one." Beard, however, lacked access to the documents that buttressed Mahl's book and did not know the details of the covert activities undertaken by the British to achieve their goals in Washington. For his pioneering effort to acquaint the American people with the truth of why their country had intervened in the war, he "became an object lesson used to train young historians," the moral equivalent for them, in other words, of Brutus, Cassius, and Judas Iscariot who are horribly, but justly, chewed and ground up for all eternity by the three-mouthed Satan in the frozen lake of Cocytus imagined by Dante in *The Divine Comedy*.[48]

Mahl acknowledged the importance of one other precursor, Harford Montgomery Hyde, a British intelligence officer engaged in counter-espionage work in the United States. In 1962, Hyde published *The Quiet Canadian*, in which he recounted the activities of the British intelligence office in New York City under the direction of Sir William Stephenson, "the quiet Canadian." The book came out the following year in an American edition under the title *Room 3603*. Mahl pays tribute to Hyde: "Despite successful sales, few in journalism or academia realized this book's importance."[49] As a primary source of the highest value, it gave an eyewitness account of Stephenson's schemes to draw America into the war. For all his major disclosures, however, Hyde had not told the whole story. This is the task that Mahl sets for himself.

The comprehensiveness and sheer artistry of the British campaign to make their war America's war won Mahl's grudging admiration. "The genius of British intelligence in the United States during World War II" was the masterpiece of the trade, to which all subsequent efforts to bring American policy into line with the aims of foreign powers owed a debt.[50] The isolationists had to face not only their internationalist adversaries in the Roosevelt administration, but also thousands of British spies and propagandists. The British Security Operation, run by Stephenson and headquartered in Rockefeller Center, conducted relentless political warfare against the isolationists.

Mahl's cast of pro-British American sympathizers extended far beyond the WASP elite that continued to rule the country and included "available, willing, and powerful agents, subagents, and collaborators at the very nerve centers of American politics, news, and entertainment."[51] Journalists and radio commentators, such as Walter Winchell, the hero of Philip Roth's *The Plot Against America*, had close ties to British intelligence. Publishers Arthur Hays Sulzberger of the *New York Times* and Henry Luce of *Time, Fortune, LIFE*, and many other magazines had the same affiliations. Hollywood directors, with Winston Churchill's good friend Alexander Korda in the lead, helped to make the movies a powerful pro-British instrument for educating the public about foreign policy. Gore Vidal in his William E. Massey Sr. Lectures on the History of American Civilization, which he gave at Harvard University in 1991, described the enormous impact of pro-British propaganda movies in the lead-up to the Second World War: "On both sides of the Atlantic the movies were preparing us for a wartime marriage with our English and French cousins against our Italian and German cousins."[52] By his count, a hundred such movies appeared during the years 1937 and 1941, with *Fire over England* (1937) and *That Hamilton Woman* (1941) the bookends and the consummate products of the genre.

Of the same class of interventionist Anglophiles was the playwright and screen writer Robert Emmet Sherwood, who wrote speeches in the British Security Operation manner for FDR. The Committee to Defend Democracy by Aiding the Allies, headed by the iconic Midwestern progressive journalist William Allen White, had a national presence in the country and sought to counter the influence of the America First Committee. According to Mahl, British agents, informers, collaborators, and sympathizers moved unimpeded to involve the United States in the Second World War. German propaganda activities met with constant harassment in the United States, those of the British never.[53] Any public figure showing sympathy toward Germany, such as Minnesota's Farmer-Labor senator Ernest Lundeen, acquired an FBI file. When he died in a plane crash on August 31, 1940, two agents, along with everyone else on board, went down with him. Speculation about possible foul play in his death continues to this day.[54]

The presidential campaign of 1940 starkly revealed the political weakness of isolationism, despite that movement's broad popular appeal. FDR, by then an open adversary of the isolationists, had no serious competition for the Democratic nomination, the anti-third-term tradition notwithstanding. Republican isolationists went to their convention in Philadelphia confident that one of their own would be nominated, but instead a candidate whose foreign policy views were indistinguishable from those of FDR easily won.

The victor, Wendell Willkie, had mounted one of the strangest candidacies in American political history. To begin with, most people never had heard of him, even by the time of the convention. Mahl presented the Willkie campaign as a red-letter example of his thesis in *Desperate Deception*. He identified the British ambassador, Lord Lothian (Philip Kerr), as a prime mover behind the Willkie candidacy. A man without experience in political office and a registered Democrat as of 1939, Willkie nevertheless overcame the candidacies of far more experienced and established officeholders—District Attorney of Manhattan Thomas E. Dewey, Senator Robert A. Taft of Ohio, Senator Arthur H. Vandenberg of Michigan, and former president Herbert Hoover.[55] The isolationists would have taken any one of these four over Willkie, whose appeal for the British consisted of his complete agreement with FDR on the need for the United States to furnish unstinting support for the British war effort.

From a wholeheartedly pro-interventionist viewpoint, Susan Dunn in *1940: FDR, Willkie, Lindbergh, Hitler—the Election amid the Storm* documented the pleased British reaction to the Willkie nomination. With the Battle of Britain raging and victorious Nazi armies on the march across the European continent, both Willkie and FDR deserved credit for their "lucid understanding of the grave crisis abroad." The real campaign in 1940 "was not between the two candidates, but between them and the extreme isolationists."[56] The interventionists controlled the political process completely, for Dunn a sign of the vitality of American democracy and a life preserver for the world.

The Japanese attack on Pearl Harbor suddenly in the most dramatic way ended the debate over American intervention in the Second World War. The America First Committee quickly dissolved itself and, as Mahl observed, "the very word 'isolationist' became a scandalous epithet, to be hurled at one's enemies."[57] The isolationist cause went down to an obliterating defeat, to be followed by the bipartisan internationalist foreign policy with which the country has engaged the world ever since.[58] The main question for Beard at that point concerned how best to resist an internationalist fate for the American people. Still the country's most influential and best-selling historian, he would be heard from in opposition to the good war.

CHAPTER 6

A Wartime Trilogy

Between 1942 and 1944 Beard published three of his most commercially successful books: *The American Spirit*, *The Republic*, and *A Basic History of the United States*. He collaborated with his wife, Mary, on two of them. About the much-debated character of their collaboration, she explained to their mutual friend and fellow historian Merle Curti, "In fact I try to help CAB escape the burden of carrying me for he is so much a personality alone. I would not allow my name to be placed on our co-authorship if I could prevent it because the major contribution is his."[1] Nearly ten years later, she returned to the question of their collaboration, with a distinct change of emphasis: "It is commonly assumed that I injected women into the thought of history and just that. Let it all ride."[2] They were a team, and no one can say where her powerful influence left off in his thinking or writing. It certainly went very far in both activities, but her description of him as "so much a personality alone," which she often repeated in many variations, has the ring of overriding truth.

All three of these books contain wartime commentary on the foreign policy of FDR and thus constitute a trilogy of primary-source Beard works about the Second World War. *The American Spirit: The Idea of Civilization in the United States*, appearing in 1942, revealed the extent of their fears about the incompatibility of FDR's internationalist foreign policy and the continued existence of the American Republic. The Beards thought of this volume as part of their

Rise of American Civilization series. Volume 1 they had called *The Agricultural Era*, volume 2 *The Industrial Era*, and volume 3 *America in Midpassage*. The fourth volume they would devote to "the intellectual and moral qualities that Americans have deemed necessary to civilization in the United States."[3]

The Beards relied on *The History of Western Civilization* (1935) by their friend and like-minded FDR critic Harry Elmer Barnes as a general study that "enables the reader more intelligently to understand the present and more rationally to work for a better future." With the historical context provided by Barnes and others, they established a comparative framework for the study of civilization, a term they defined as a general world view of politics, culture, and morality. They divided the world views of history into two broad categories: pessimistic and optimistic. Pessimistic world views, such as the one espoused by Friedrich Nietzsche and selectively adapted to Hitlerism, held humanity in low esteem and gloried in the predatory values of power "at any cost in terms of human suffering."[4] Life-affirming optimistic philosophies taught men the lessons of human equality and the value of struggling against suffering and evil. For Western peoples, Christianity and the Enlightenment contained the greatest treasures of moral and intellectual optimism. American civilization derived its strength and vitality from both these sources. Though not committing themselves to support the war, the Beards made it clear that they took the side of Western democratic values over the totalitarian world view of Nazism.

The primary question that the Beards set for themselves in *The American Spirit* concerned the solidity of the connections between the war policy of the Roosevelt administration and the wellsprings of American civilization. In other words, did American actions from 1939 to 1942 keep or break faith with the country's core values? The authors made no attempt to hide their negative views of FDR. The comments that they made about the president's "mandates for civilization" and his concept of the United States as "the guardian of the world heritage of liberty" echoed the polemical tones of their anti-interventionist writings.[5] Most of the book, though, dealt with the ideals and values that constituted the lineaments of American civilization from the founders to the present.

The country's annals contained a rich assortment of morally and intellectually commanding figures, but one man held special significance for the Beards in their description of the essential elements in a distinctive American civilization as an ideal. They found meaning of exceptional importance in the political philosophy of John Quincy Adams, who devoted much thought to "the problem of administering the nation's magnificent endowment of natural resources for the advancement of civilization in the United States." American resources, he urged, should be developed in the interest of the people. The historian Brooks Adams interpreted his grandfather's legacy as a plea for Americans to recognize that all their problems as a people had an umbilical relationship with a single question. How should the fabulous bounty of American land be distributed? Speaking of the American people, the younger Adams wrote, "The only serious problem for them to solve, therefore, was how to develop this gift in a collective, and not on a competitive or selfish basis." For dominant private interests to be turned loose on the patrimony of the American people would introduce permanent distortions in society. Such views had not endeared the sixth president of the United States to his constituents in the aborning get-rich-quick culture of Jacksonian America, and the voters excused him from office after one term. The Beards lamented, "The natural resources of the nation which he would have dedicated to the improvement of the condition of the people were handed over to exploitation by private interests."[6]

The judgments of John Quincy Adams seemed to the Beards prophetic of subsequent American history down to their own time. More than any other single event, the defeat of his national government idea cleared the way for a buccaneering form of capitalism that then would define the American way of life. The country's salvation and the triumph of the best features in American civilization depended on the full recovery and advancement of Adams's idea about a collective administration of America's resources, for the benefit of the people as a whole. Every spark of sense and humanity in American politics had come from an Adams-like recognition of the country's need for a grander civilization than anything that might come from a relentlessly greed-driven exploitation of the American continent. The driving force of a high civilization could not consist of the energy derived from the activity of great money makers ceaselessly concerned about adding to their personal wealth. The manipulators of finance capitalism threatened the destruction of American civilization. The Beards called these individuals burglars and barbarians wielding an indescribably vast and wholly destructive power. Fresh batches of slaves, tied to the establishment by a golden ball and chain, annually reported for duty from the nation's best universities and law schools. Nearly everything in capitalist America passed under the control of the money power.

America, however, to its everlasting honor, possessed a magnificent dissident culture. The paragons of American civilization all had struggled, in one way or another, to turn the country from a society of acquisitive individualists into a true social commonwealth. The heroes of the American spirit came from Enlightenment and Christian traditions. They included Ralph Waldo Emerson, Margaret Fuller, Walt Whitman, Mark Twain, Henry George, Simon

Patten, Thorstein Veblen, Edward Bellamy, Henry Demarest Lloyd, George D. Herron, Vida Scudder, Jane Addams, Walter Rauschenbusch, and Henry Adams. Beard regarded Henry Adams, another grandson of the sixth president, as a historian of genius. His historical writings held a place of unparalleled distinction in the field of American masterpieces. In writing about him, Beard made a most revealing comment about his own attitude toward the university world: "Possessor of an inherited fortune, he was able to withdraw from the drudgery of teaching, enjoy complete freedom from the strictures of academic endowments and management, and give all his intellectual energies to his quest for the meaning or sense of history."[7]

Commenting on the destiny of American civilization as a growth separate from Europe, the Beards came to the main political points of *The American Spirit*. Americans had to concentrate "on tasks clearly within the scope of American capacities and opportunities, clearly delineated by the necessities of American life." They had to avoid "romantic enthusiasm for designs remote and obscure." For the Beards, the creed of internationalism belonged in the category of remote and obscure designs. Internationalists contended that American policymakers should be concerned primarily about world order. From the internationalist perspective, policies devoted to the diversification of the American economy, to the protection of American labor against competition from nations with low living standards, and to a provision for the internal security of the United States minus a global presence of American soldiers could be dispensed with in favor of the world order security plan. Internationalists held that the national interest best could be served by American involvements worldwide. American energies would be submerged in the promotion of world civilization. Reading the August 1941 Atlantic Charter agreement between FDR and Winston Churchill, the Beards surmised that the current war had one supreme aim, the creation of "a world order with free trade throughout the earth."[8]

The seemingly irenic phrase, free trade, did not do full intellectual justice to the actual content of the internationalist agenda. Freedom here meant the control through powerful Western military and financial institutions of the world's resources. Such had been the reason for the First World War as well. Then America's military alliance with Great Britain had involved many goals, but the primary one for the British had to do with protecting and augmenting their empire. At Versailles, the real significance of that conflict became clear when the British Empire, more than all the others on the winning side, grew to fantastic proportions. The Beards could not bring themselves to believe that anything about Britain's imperial economic and strategic aims had changed since the last war. As before under Wilson, Americans now under FDR knew how to apply the right verbal gloss for the public presentation of Allied war aims.

The Beards revealed in *The American Spirit* how they personally had been affected by the national debate over America's intervention in the Second World War. They criticized "the world planners" who had proposed "to fix up a warring world by means of American energies, treasures, and blood at the same time that they added to national bewilderment by pouring odium on other Americans who questioned the validity, utility, and advantage of such expeditions." The two authors warned that under "the supranational class" now in power, America would no longer be the country that George Washington wanted.[9] Internationalism, in its current usage, denoted the advancement of foreign interests as the best means of securing the national interest, the special relationship with Great Britain being the foremost example. The Beards thought that America's global leadership responsibilities would involve a string of special relationships in the country's future, as world conditions evolved, in flat repudiation of the counsel given in Washington's Farewell Address.

An American foreign policy calling for the extension of freedom everywhere when it had not yet been extended fully to the American people seemed to the Beards like a severe case of misplaced priorities. The government in Washington would serve the American people better by first freeing them from want. The two historians identified *The American Century*, written by the magazine magnate Henry R. Luce, as a most illuminating document for what internationalists intended to do with their power. They attached enormous importance to *The American Century* and judged it to constitute a far more sincere compilation of American motives in the Second World War than any statement ever issued by the government or found in the great majority of history books written on the subject. The essential points of the Luce book could be found in an editorial that he had written for the February 17, 1941, issue of *LIFE* magazine.

Nearly ten months before Pearl Harbor, Luce declared that the American people, without understanding why, already were in the war. A Republican antagonist of FDR, Luce complained about the confusion and deceit in Washington regarding the nature of American foreign policy after September 1, 1939. Of course, the United States had to get into the war right away and did, though without admitting it or explaining why. Luce did not think to mention any moral reasons why the United States should have felt obliged to fight Hitler. There was nothing in the editorial about the unparalleled evil of Nazism or the criminal madness of Hitler. Luce expressed himself in sober strategic terms about the necessity for American participation in the conflict.

He began by offering a vocabulary lesson: "To the average American the plain meaning of the word defense is defense of American territory." In anticipation of George Orwell's 1984, that was "Oldspeak." Luce provided a "Newspeak" translation for the word "defense" by way of explaining what America should be doing in its foreign policy and why: "We are *not* in a war to defend American territory. We are in a war to defend and even to promote, encourage and incite so-called democratic principles throughout the world."[10]

The American people, Luce observed, now stood face-to-face with a historical opportunity to become the leading nation on earth. Objectively they could be said to occupy this position of primacy already, but thus far had failed to rise to the challenge of exercising their power: "In the field of national policy, the fundamental trouble with America has been, and is, that whereas their nation became in the twentieth Century the most powerful and vital nation in the world, nevertheless Americans were unable to accommodate themselves spiritually and practically to that fact." The failure of Americans to play their proper part as the leader of the free world had had disastrous consequences for all mankind. To atone for our negligence, we would have "to accept wholeheartedly our duty and our opportunity as the most powerful and vital nation in the world and in consequence to exert upon the world the full impact of our influence, for such purposes as we see fit and by such means as we see fit."[11] America itself could not be free and prosperous without a world environment hospitable to the country's values.

Luce identified isolationism as the grand illusion of American politics and lamented that an element of the Republican Party had become captivated by it. FDR, he thought, had adopted isolationist policies during the first seven years of his presidency, although now he had the right idea about helping Britain against Nazi Germany and Fascist Italy: "Under him and with his leadership we can make isolationism as dead an issue as slavery and we can make a truly *American* internationalism something as natural to us in our time as the airplane or the radio." The United States had to retrace its steps back to the tragic days of 1919, when we had disobeyed the command of Providence to assume leadership of a war-torn world: "Roosevelt must succeed where Wilson failed." The tyrannies and dictatorships now on the march would fall when democracy "is the faith of a huge majority of people in the world."[12] Only in an American Century could that democratic revolution happen.

The first requirement for an American Century "must be a sharing with all peoples of our Bill of Rights, our Declaration of Independence, our Constitution, our magnificent industrial products, our technical skills. It must be an internationalism of the people, by the people and for the people." American popular culture and entertainment would continue to be instrumental in spreading the gospel of democratic freedom. The American people needed a revitalized faith in their own creed: "As America enters dynamically upon the world scene, we need most of all to seek and to bring forth a vision of America as a world power which is authentically American and which can inspire us to live and work and fight with vigor and enthusiasm."[13]

Economics would be the first area of life in which the American Century vision might be realized: "It is for America and for America alone to determine whether a system of free economic enterprise—an economic order compatible with freedom and progress—shall or shall not prevail in this century." Free economic enterprise would fail if the system remained confined to the United States. Hence, for its own survival, capitalist America required the living space afforded by like-minded political and economic institutions throughout the world: "The vision of America as the principal guarantor of the freedom of the seas, the vision of America as the dynamic leader of world trade, has within it the possibilities of such enormous human progress as to stagger the imagination."[14]

The image in Luce's "The American Century" of America as "the Good Samaritan of the entire world" intrigued the Beards. What might such a role entail? To Luce it meant that American plenty "should forthwith be dispatched to the four quarters of the globe as a free gift, administered by a humanitarian army of Americans to every man, woman and child on this earth who is really hungry." It would be the realization of a great principle in Western civilization: the ideal of charity. Thus, "it now becomes our time to be the powerhouse from which the ideals spread throughout the world and do their mysterious work of lifting the life of mankind from the level of the beasts to what the Psalmist called a little lower than the angels." American enterprise and humanitarianism would save the world as nothing else could. In the spirit of freedom's cause, we are called "to create the first great American Century."[15]

The Beards placed Luce's argument in the context of the country's history and found that *The American Century* fit naturally into the general run of imperialist statements since the time of Mahan, Roosevelt, Beveridge, and the updating of them by the hitherto incomparable Wilson. The word "hitherto" became necessary because subsequently FDR had shown a genius of his own for inventiveness in devising fresh images and original locutions in discussing America's tasks as a Good Samaritan for all humanity. The Beards continued to think that the American government could play such a part more convincingly, arousing fewer suspicions in the world about its real designs, with a better record to show for its attentiveness to the still desperate plight of the American people.

From within the deepest intellectual and moral reserves of American civilization had emerged a noble antagonism to the false counsel of the country's imperialists. In his 1936 acceptance speech at the Democratic Convention, FDR had proclaimed, "This generation of Americans has a rendezvous with destiny." At the January 20, 1937, inaugural ceremony, he clarified what this American destiny would involve on the international stage: "We are fashioning an instrument of unimagined power for the establishment of a morally better world."[16] For the Beards, such universal aspirations would always seem unattainable so long as the historic capitalism that had produced the Depression continued in existence. That FDR had no intention of replacing or meaningfully altering the country's economic institutions made it unlikely that the current war would lead to the creation of a better world. The world would remain what it always had been: prey to the exploitation of economic power elites.

The next year, 1943, Beard published one of his most peculiar books, *The Republic: Conversations on Fundamentals.* As with everything that he wrote, this book sold extremely well and came out in a sixth printing in February of 1945. Modeled on Plato's *Republic*, the book consisted of a series of dialogues between Beard, in the role of Socrates, and two fictional characters—Dr. Robert Smyth and his wife, Susan. Other fictional characters participated as well in what Beard called "this discussion course," which he conceived as a vehicle for analyzing the efficacy of historical knowledge as a means of testing the truth of government propaganda.[17]

The most important theme in American history, Beard began, concerned what he called constitutionalism, "the civilian way of living together in the Republic, the way of preserving our liberties and the decencies of social intercourse against the frenzies of the despotic and violent temper." He thought it worthy of notice that nothing could be found in the U.S. Constitution about an international agenda for the government. The country's founders had focused their attention entirely on achieving a more perfect union. Susan Smyth observed, "but internationalists tell us that this very unionism, this thing called nationalism, fostered by the Constitution, is positively vicious, is a source of wars among nations and must now be abandoned or severely modified in the interest of a new world order."[18] With nothing in the Constitution about the responsibility of Americans for regulating the affairs of the world, the question arose in Beard's mind about what would take the place of this document as the fundamental law of the land. We clearly and for some time, going back to the McKinley administration's policy for the Philippines, had left the U.S. Constitution behind. Wilson, by calling on Americans to fight a war to make the world safe for democracy, had distanced the country even farther from the Constitution. The problem of constitutionality now had grown larger still in the wake of FDR's plans to commit Americans to the cause of spreading freedom around the globe.

The founders of the country had feared large military and naval establishments, but the internationalist agenda would make such forces a permanent part of American life, thus magnifying a weakness in the Constitution that Beard described as "the unexplored and dark continent of American government": the virtually unlimited war powers of the president.[19] When it came to war, the protections of the Constitution always became weaker. That problem had grown more severe in the twentieth century. Beard noted that Lincoln's critics during the Civil War had enjoyed a degree of freedom made impossible by the Alien and Sedition Acts of the First World War. An eternal struggle between liberty and authority had continued throughout human history. America had not been an exception to this rule of life. Beard thought that the Alien Registration Act of 1940, passed in anticipation of America's going to war again, constituted a new Sedition Act. The future of freedom in the United States ultimately would depend on the character of the American people and their intellectual and moral leaders. In any case, the cause of freedom could not be guaranteed in the very country now arrogating to itself the responsibility for its introduction and preservation throughout the world. Moral leadership would matter the most in the long run. Beard in Socratic character identified his three moral exemplars as Thomas Jefferson, Abraham Lincoln, and John Ruskin. Pictures of all three of them he said adorned his walls.

Beard thought that FDR had become the protagonist in the unfolding drama of the American Republic. Dr. Smyth asked Beard to tell him in simple words just what the president of the United States was. In crisis periods, he replied, the power of the president is as great as he can make it. The president is not omnipotent, as the case of Wilson in 1919 exemplifies. He overestimated his power and went down to defeat, but, according to the Constitution, the president as a wartime leader has few legal restraints. On the other hand, the president's vulnerabilities attracted the notice of Alexander Hamilton, in *The Federalist* No. 75. He expressed concern about guarding "against improper foreign influences in the executive department."[20] The president might come under foreign control and betray the country. The founders had expressed viewpoints of exceptional acuity on every political question that they raised, and never more so than on the dangers of both strength and weakness in the office of the presidency.

The dialogue in Beard's *The Republic* concludes with some mystical observations by him on the role of fate in history, a concept that would have been thrust upon his attention by the extensive reading that he did in the history of ancient Greece and Rome. Following the logic of Niccolò Machiavelli in *The Prince*, Beard claimed that human actions fell into two categories: those we can control by *virtù* or skill and those we cannot because of *fortuna* or luck. As a Renaissance humanist steeped in the masterwork of classical historiography, Machiavelli perforce thought that we had ample reason to study and to reflect on human experience for the insight that these activities would give us in influencing to our advantage the part of life susceptible to human control. In the lives of individuals and the history of peoples, however, the role of fate could not be resisted. Beard took a distinctly Machiavellian view of fate as the part of life and history "beyond the power of individuals and parties to control."[21] For example, he thought that over and above the particular factors in the historical process, the inexorability of fate had brought on the Civil War. No political party had presented abolition to the voters in 1860, but abolition came from some deep veracity in American life. Economics, as always, mattered, but the Greeks, from whom Machiavelli had derived his understanding of fate, remained our foremost teachers in the writing of history.

From the vantage point of 1943, Beard looked ahead and wondered about "the fate hidden in our time which will be revealed in the coming years." What would FDR's internationalist foreign policy bring the country? He professed to be dubious about the president's promises for a new world order. He wanted there to be no confusion about his stand on the war itself: "Personally, I am in favor of pushing the war against Germany, Japan, and Italy to a successful conclusion."[22] His unambiguous statement of support here for the American war effort constituted a dramatic departure from his previously unalloyed opposition to intervention. At first glance, it would appear to have come as a La Follette moment. The Wisconsin senator had opposed American intervention in the Great War and continued to believe it mistaken long after the declaration of hostilities by Congress on April 6, 1917. He thereafter justified his support of military measures on the grounds of democratic process, not because he believed the war itself to be just. The war had been declared by Congress according to the rules set down in the Constitution. Only after January 1918, however, under the spell of President Wilson's idealistic Fourteen Points Address, did La Follette change his mind and enthusiastically support the war. What was the comparable turning point for Beard in World War II?

Based on the extant record, Beard, though changing his mind about the Second World War, did not go through a clear and definite conversion experience, in the manner of La Follette twenty-five years earlier. The weight of the argument made the previous year in *The American Spirit*, regarding the odious character of the Nazi and Fascist ideologies, disposed him to want those forces defeated and eradicated from the world. Yet at no time did he think of the war as a clash of civilizations between democracy and totalitarianism. The inclusion of the Stalinist Soviet Union, still the bloodiest of all totalitarian regimes, on the Allied side ruled out such a neat pairing of antinomies. With the nation completing the second year of its war against the Axis dictatorships and his son, William, in the armed services, he evidently concluded that the Allied campaign against Hitler, Mussolini, and Tojo could be justified. It was the positive part of this campaign regarding what the Allies hoped to gain from the war that continued to trouble Beard, in a way that La Follette throughout 1918 did not experience.

The slogan, endlessly repeated by FDR and Churchill, about all nations at war's end having equal access to the world's raw materials did not seem to Beard, as it did to these two world leaders, a preventive for future wars. He thought that just the opposite was true. Rich men in the victorious nations would be conniving to exploit those resources for themselves and would continue to do so until the vanquished nations or some new combination of forces had gained enough power to mount a challenge to the status quo. Then another war would break out, or perhaps wars would become a permanent feature of the contemporary world, each of them with an ostensible issue, but all of them fundamentally about the same thing: the control of the poor and their resources by the rich.

In the last chapter, "The Fate and Fortunes of Our Republic," Beard reflected on the parallel between the fate of the American Republic and the transformation of the ancient Roman Republic into a militaristic empire. He could not say for sure what the outcome for the American Republic would be: "many contingencies and great events now unforeseen will occur in this unfolding future."[23] There could be shifts in the two coalitions now engaged in war, he prophetically forecast.

Dr. Smyth, one of his two original students in the dialogue, asked Beard to apply Oswald Spengler's *The Decline of the West* thesis to America. What could we expect in the United States if Spengler was right and Western civilization was now fated to expire? The doctor wanted to know if America of necessity would go down to obliterating defeat as well. To begin with, Beard replied, nothing conceptually new could be found in *The Decline of the West*. Versions of his cyclical theory of history had appeared in the writing of Aristotle, Giambattista Vico, and Brooks Adams. On the question of fate, however, Beard remained adamantly a follower of Machiavelli. He observed, "We cannot master our fate. What is fated is fated and is beyond our power of control." He nevertheless believed that essential features of America would survive. As an ideal, American civilization embodied fundamental Christian and Enlightenment values that certainly deserved to survive. However great the changes that Americans might have to undergo after the war, the country "will long endure; forever, I hope."[24]

Beard concluded on a note of optimism. He thought the analogy of ancient Rome, in one crucial respect, inapplicable to the United States. Rome had not been a nation, but an ensemble of nations ruled by Roman officials and headed by an emperor. America was a nation and still struggling to define itself. There was fate, to be sure, "but according to my world view, our universe is not all fate; we have some freedom in it." We still had the resource of creative intelligence at our disposal. America suffered from many problems. Nevertheless, the country had experienced nothing like the eclipse of Rome in the fifth century. "Calamities may come upon America or be brought upon the country by demagogic leadership," but he judged American resilience to be great still. His benediction for the dialogue took the form of a prediction couched in hope: "Surely the unresting spirit of Americans will endlessly strive to carry on the values in their heritage, to improve upon them, to create new arts and sciences of living, to sustain and make better the Republic."[25]

The Republic prompted an unlikely association between Beard and *LIFE* magazine owner and editor Henry R. Luce. Active in the publicity campaign for naval aid to England and a leading interventionist under the spell of such grand strategy thinkers as Walter Lippmann, Luce should have viewed Beard as an isolationist adversary.[26] In *The American Spirit*, the historian had been withering in his opposition to the messianic globalism of Luce's "American Century." Earlier he had attacked one of Luce's pet pro-intervention ventures, *The Ramparts We Watch*. Following a private screening in the White House that Luce attended, this Time Inc. film came to theaters nationwide. The film glorified the American war effort of 1917–1918 and praised both FDR and his Republican opponent in the 1940 presidential campaign, Wendell Willkie, for uniting the nation against the threat of Hitler. It also warned against a fifth-column of isolationists undermining the national resolve to resist tyranny and aggression. Beard had criticized *The Ramparts We Watch* for its historical inaccuracies and bias. His authority had heartened isolationists in their campaign against the film, which in the still strongly isolationist atmosphere of the time did not do well at the box office.[27]

Despite his long-standing opposition to Luce's foreign policy ideas, Beard appeared on the January 17, 1944, *LIFE* cover with the caption "Charles Beard and 'The Republic.'" In the photograph, Beard is shown elegantly attired and gazing out over the Blue Ridge Mountains of North Carolina where he and Mary wintered. The editors gave him the full *LIFE* treatment: "Charles A. Beard has the profile of a Roman senator and the well-stocked mind of a classical philosopher."[28] The magazine announced that it would be reprinting a condensed section of Beard's new book every week for its twenty-two million readers. The editors praised the book for its timeliness and wisdom: "It is important because it is written, not for the ages, but for us—for living Americans who believe in their form of government, who are fighting for it and yet are troubled by the great problem of its continuance in the modern world." They hoped that *LIFE*'s readers "will, perhaps, want to do more than just listen to Beard and his friends; they may wish, on Friday nights this winter, to hold their own serious discussions of the subjects covered by 'The Republic.'"[29]

The magazine ran ten *The Republic* installments in 1944, from January 17 to March 20, each lavishly illustrated with photographs and artwork. A different photograph of Beard at his winter residence in Tryon, North Carolina, or rambling about in the community appeared in every issue. Letters to the editor about the series began appearing on February 7 and uniformly struck a positive note. Readers said that they appreciated Beard's learned love of country. One man in uniform congratulated the magazine for the Beard series because through it "you will help the people to comprehend the ideas for which we are at war."[30] A junior high school principal in Gorham, Maine, announced that at his school students would recite the dialogues, which then would be broadcast to homerooms "with discussion to follow in social studies classes."[31] A refugee from Nazi Germany who had just passed his citizenship examination wanted to thank the editors for acquainting him with Beard's extremely useful book: "The knowledge it conveys to us will help us to be good citizens of the United States."[32]

Beard himself wrote a letter to the editors at *LIFE* on March 6, in response to several letters that he had received from the magazine's readers concerning his statements about women. He had asserted, "women now vote, hold office and, as persons and/or citizens are entitled to all the rights, privileges and immunities conferred on persons and/or citizens by the Federal Constitution." Several people had written to tell him that such a characterization bore little resemblance to the reality of women's lives in America. Numerous discriminations against women continued to exist throughout the land, they had told him. Though claiming to be factually right about his assertions regarding women, Beard conceded the larger point made by his critics and concluded, "In any case, rights are not self-enforcing and women will have to keep battling for them, as men do, in legislative committees, legislatures, and courts of law, to make real in life any rights proclaimed on paper."[33] As an ardent proponent of women's rights himself, Beard held to a conciliatory line in this exchange, which was the only outward sign in the magazine from readers of any opposition to what he had written in the ten-part series.

A *LIFE* editorial accompanied the final installment of the magazine's series on *The Republic*. The tone and content of the editorial do not approach the euphoria of what the magazine had to say about Beard at the start of the series, when only images of classical Rome would do for the introduction of "this great American historian." The editors figuratively had put him in a toga holding scrolls of parchment in each hand, as if he were Seneca or Tacitus descending the Palatine for daily observations of the Roman Forum. The close-out editorial, on the other hand, made only modest claims about what had been achieved in the series. The articles had created general interest, and many readers had written to say that they liked them. Others, however, "have said that they were hard to read, or 'too academic.'" What did people expect, the editors queried. The articles were not intended to be "easy reading." And, yes, they were academic. "Beard himself admits that." The way the editors put their point about the academic character of the articles, it was as if Beard had admitted to having committed an indiscretion. At the very least, the editors continued, "to some this kind of approach may appear remote and unrealistic."[34]

The editors wondered about the foreign policy implications of Beard's *The Republic* series. A bold internationalist American foreign policy obsessed Luce, as he famously had revealed in his "American Century" editorial of three years earlier. Beard's articles served as a reminder that the U.S. Constitution leaves an enormous amount of room for interpretation about foreign affairs. Although the document sets definite limits on the president's sphere of action, the editors ill-humoredly noted that "our foreign policy is now being handled exclusively by Franklin Roosevelt as President and commander in chief." Yet, according to the Constitution, the document so ably analyzed and placed in historical context by Beard, the president has no exclusive power, by law, to make foreign policy, "or even to commit the United States to any policy whatever." The editors observed that by law the president should be working with Congress on matters of foreign policy, a point that Beard would make most fully and to the scandal of many in his two post–World War II books on FDR. They concluded, "If the President is going to work with Congress, then the fact to remember is that Congress and the people must be told clearly what the President's proposals are in order that they may pass intelligent and honest judgment thereon." It seemed obvious to them that "if the President tries to act without a full understanding of his purposes by Congress and the people then he is bound to fail—unless the people really want a dictatorship."[35] In a democracy, if the president concealed or lied about his actual policies, the whole edifice of a people's government collapsed.

Despite their misgivings about Beard's "textbook language with a vengeance," the editors relished the substance of the series. The peroration in the tenth and final installment they singled out for special praise: "I believe that there will always be an America, an America with unique characteristics, however great the changes to come."[36] *LIFE* magazine took its stand with Beard in celebrating the genius of the American Republic and the promise it held for the whole world.

For World War I, Beard had been a true believer in the Allied cause and in American intervention. By the mid-1920s, however, he had become a deeply embittered revisionist, consumed by a loathing for what he passionately condemned as the lies and deceptions of the warmongers on both sides of the Atlantic. For World War II, was he now reversing that earlier process, and retreating from revisionism into a loving embrace of the patriotic editors at *LIFE*? To reach the conclusions that they did about *The Republic*, the editors would have had to read the book selectively, ignoring the critical comments about and aspersions on FDR's internationalism, an agenda that bore such a striking resemblance to the "American Century" views of the magazine's owner.

It is not a simple matter explaining the relationship between Beard and Luce. Perhaps the best explanation is the one offered by John K. Jessup, the chief editorial writer at *LIFE* from 1944 to 1948. According to him, the claims in *The Republic* about the beauty, strength, and permanent worth of American civilization reminded Luce of *The Federalist Papers*, his favorite work of political thought: "When Charles Beard wrote *The Republic* expounding such a view in 1943, Luce decreed that *LIFE* run a condensed version of the book in no less than ten installments."[37] Beard's argument, which was not out of character for him but expressed in *The Republic* with unusual warmth and fervor, would have washed away a multitude of sins and must have had a transfixing effect on Luce. For his part, Beard fully cooperated with *LIFE* in promoting the book. He certainly would have been aware of the irony involved in his relationship with a magazine bent on making the world safe for democracy, but a subscribers' list of 22 million might have had a transfixing effect on him.

One week after publishing the final installment of Beard's *The Republic*, a *LIFE* editorial on American foreign policy appeared. The magazine complained, "In the Spring of 1944 the standout fact about American Foreign Policy is that America hasn't got one. Or if it has one, it is so obscure that hardly two members of the President's cabinet can agree on what it is." Foreign policy developed organically from domestic policy, the editors reasoned. America's domestic policy consisted of two foundational elements: constitutional government in politics and free enterprise in economics. Without these two starting points, "the American experiment, the greatest ever made, would make no sense."[38] The cardinal aim of American foreign policy, therefore, should be the preservation through external action of political and economic freedom in the country.

Prevailing conditions in the world mandated an internationalist foreign policy for the United States: "Because all the members of the human family have now become so highly interdependent, the chances of maintaining American freedom bear a close relation to the maintenance and spread of freedom elsewhere." We should not impose freedom on others: "But we would have it understood that we are sympathetic to political freedom and unsympathetic to political tyranny wherever we find it. And that we shall act accordingly." To accomplish its aims, the United States would need a powerful military establishment after the war. Through its membership in a world organization, the country would have to help develop legal and economic codes capable of fostering a global environment hospitable to American conceptions of freedom. To be safe under our own freedoms, we would have to extend them to the whole world: "We cannot live with reasonable safety under our own laws in a lawless world." Postwar Europe would be a proving ground for the kind of American foreign policy that *LIFE* envisaged. A breeding ground for global conflicts, the Old World would continue to be a menace to peace until it achieved some internal stability "based on the application of the Federal Principle to the States of Europe."[39] For its own safety and economic well-being, the United States should be in the business of promoting American-style political and economic arrangements wherever possible.

Beard thought such plans moonstruck and the very essence of everything that he opposed for American foreign policy. He interpreted internationalism as the equivalent of calling upon Americans to fight for the preservation of world capitalism, with the United States functioning as the general manager of the postwar status quo. We know what his thoughts were about such matters from his other books, but also from a telling March 27, 1944, letter to the *LIFE* editors from Black Mountain, North Carolina. The letter writer enclosed a photograph of Beard, taken during a recent visit that he had made to Black Mountain College. While at the college Beard had raised an issue unmentioned in the *LIFE* articles. Describing the photograph, the letter reads in part: "He is here warning the group of students and faculty against the use of state secrets for private profit."[40] This was the old Beard who spoke of how the economic "lords of the universe" stood to gain the most from the war, a theme that he would develop in his next book.

In 1944, the Beards published *A Basic History of the United States*, which they presented as their final attempt "to interpret the long course of American history." They wished to assure readers that this new book stood on its own as an original publication. They had not rested content with a mere summary or digest of their previous books: "On the contrary it is newly designed and newly written to express the historical judgment which we have reached after more than forty years devoted to the study of documents and observations of life first-hand in all parts of the United States, rural and urban, and in parts of the Old World and the Orient." In the last chapter, "Global War and Home Front," they continued their wartime commentary on the foreign policy of FDR.[41]

In their analysis, the Beards continued a line of argument familiar to readers of *The American Spirit* and *The Republic*. Once again, they emphatically stated their support of the war against the aggressor nations of Germany, Japan, and Italy. Wherever they exercised power, the leaders of these three countries had suppressed civil liberties and freedom of any kind. The vile ideas and horrendous practices of the Axis dictatorships had condemned those systems of government for all time. Hitler was the worst of the Axis dictators for having "started a more than savage persecution of Jews, Social Democrats, Communists, and Liberals."[42]

On the Allied side, however, the coming of the war and the fighting of it had involved policies and actions that contradicted the official pronouncements emanating from Moscow, London, and Washington. Reconciling the cause of freedom with the enormities of the Soviet past and present could not be accomplished by the standard methods of truth telling. To present Joseph Stalin as a champion of freedom, some prodigious feats of historical engineering had to be undertaken. From the major premise, as the Beards phrased it, that "the government of Soviet Russia was frankly an unlimited dictatorship," no minor premise could lead to a conclusion involving freedom in any meaningful sense of the term.[43] Nor in many parts of the world, least of all in Ireland and India, could the British Empire credibly be advertised as an agency committed to a new birth of freedom. Allied mission statements ran counter to historical experience, leaving critically minded people to suspect the real intentions of the leaders espousing freedom as a way of life.

American leaders fell under the same suspicion. Whatever the objective case against the Axis countries might have been, FDR had deceived the American people about the purposes of his foreign policy, which after the October 5, 1937, quarantine speech, at the latest, had been devoted to internationalism. While claiming to be steadfast in his support of the country's neutrality legislation, he had worked assiduously to undermine it. The transformation of America's foreign policy followed the specifications of the president's designs, a process that called into serious question the political structure of American democracy. For an American president to deceive the citizenry, as FDR manifestly had done, raised a host of complex issues about the actual process of how political power functioned in an allegedly democratic society. Intimately acquainted as they were with the founding documents of American history, the Beards naturally would have thought about the great debates over the Constitution and, specifically, about the fears of the anti-Federalists concerning the presidency as an office designed for the abuse of executive power. This anti-Federalist criticism had turned out to be prophetic.

Much fighting remained when early in 1944 the Beards sent their manuscript to the press, but already it certainly could be said that the global war had changed America forever. By comparison, the regimenting and disruptive effects of World War I had been negligible. Now government controls had been expanded to regulate all facets of American life. The regimentation that served military purposes had a corrosive effect on the stability of society. By 1944 nearly nine million men had been enlisted in the armed forces. Their absence had a profound impact on family life, but the involvement on a mammoth scale of women in war work created an unprecedented disruption in the raising of children. The Beards dwelled on the significance of skyrocketing juvenile delinquency and promiscuity rates as an ominous portent of America's postwar future. Education and culture also had to be listed as casualties of the global war. From primary school to university, education had deteriorated into preparation for military service. The Beards predicted that education for humane letters and life would not survive in the world produced by the global war. As for culture, if the propaganda movies mass-produced by Hollywood signaled the coming trends, a new era of thought control had opened for the American people.

As historians both celebrated and reviled for their economic interpretation of American history, the Beards could be expected to comment on the expense of the war. Only fifty years earlier the first annual national budget of one billion dollars had created a sensation in the press, as if the leaders in Washington had wildly mismanaged the nation's affairs. Expenditures for the Second World War would run to three hundred times that amount. With 70 percent of war production in the hands of the one hundred biggest business establishments, the long-term trend toward the concentration of economic power in the corporate sector continued inexorably.

According to the Beards' reading of history, it was almost as if the Second World War had resulted in a Third American Revolution, following the one in 1775–1783 and the other in 1861–1865. As the authors had shown in *The*

Rise of American Civilization, both of those earlier revolutions had transformed American society and its power structure, the first by creating a new status quo of native commercial and agrarian elites in place of the British imperial order, and the second by excising the Southern planter class and turning all power over to Northern businessmen and bankers. The years from 1941 to 1944 seemed no less momentous to the Beards. Without any real historical precedent to go by, the government had revealed a stupendous capacity for the exercise of military and economic power. They likened government administrative activity in World War I to a mere episode foreshadowing the managerial revolution that had taken place during World War II. Bureaucracies being what they are, it could be safely assumed that Washington would not relinquish the control that it had acquired during wartime.

With Fascist Italy now out of the war and Nazi armies falling back, the Beards turned their attention to questions about how the United States government would use its immense and unrivaled power in the postwar period. They did not derive any reassurance from what FDR continued to say, in "the most general language," about American war aims as a ceaseless and noble quest for the worldwide enshrinement of freedom. American freedom, still imperfectly realized, should be guaranteed first, the Beards continued to think. They suspected fraud in the government's advocacy of freedom on a global scale, when in the United States the president's partisans during the 1942 congressional elections had demanded "a wholesale repudiation of citizens who had formerly opposed getting into the war."[44] Then on July 25, 1943, Vice-President Henry A. Wallace attacked isolationists by lumping them in with reactionaries and American fascists. The government, insofar as the home front went, did not in the least seem to be concerned about freedom of expression or thought. Any comment not directly in line with the government's foreign policy views was cause for official concern. One might be called a fascist and subjected to all the implications such a label might entail for begging to differ with the leaders. Such freedom as this would have to be understood in a carefully circumscribed way, according to the new American style.

A Basic History of the United States closed with some reflections on the worldwide goal of freedom from want. In his January 6, 1941, State of the Union address, FDR spoke of the Four Freedoms. He listed them in the following order: first, speech and expression; second, worship of God; third, economic security; and, fourth, arms reduction. According to the Beards, the first, the second, and the fourth freedoms depended for their viability on the third, which the president had described as freedom from want everywhere in the world. Without a secure economic foundation, the other freedoms could not survive.

Trouble lay ahead for the world's economy in a postwar era dominated by the United States, the two historians predicted. In the first place, the American record in dealing with its own economy aroused serious concerns. As an economic program, the New Deal had failed to end the Depression. Wartime spending, not the New Deal, had revived the American economy. FDR's reform policies had left the corporate capitalist structure intact and primed to take advantage of the fabulous economic opportunities of the global war. The Republicans had no economic ideas of their own, except for a wistful yearning to return to the laissez-faire status quo that had produced the Depression. Neither liberals nor conservatives knew how to solve the problems arising from the boom-and-bust economic cycles of capitalism—apart from the solution offered by war spending. The Beards observed, "Everybody presumably knew that the war boom, like the New Deal spending before it, had not permanently solved the problem of depression and poverty."[45] Whatever the outcome of the global war, the old conflicts of interest would persist at home. In the postwar period, moreover, Americans would face not only daunting domestic problems, but also the additional burden of enforcing the Four Freedoms throughout the world. Such a foreign policy would have the United States on permanent military alert in defense of the postwar status quo.

To Merle Curti, Beard reported feeling elated by the public response to his new book. "Americans," he proclaimed, "are interested as never before in history—especially their history," and then added: "Confidentially to you, 545,000 copies of the *Basic History* have been printed and nearly all of them sold."[46] It would be his last runaway best-seller success. He savored the praise of friends like Edwin Montefiore Borchard, who upon reading the book told him: "It is good and I admire your restraint. You could have said much more and been right," particularly about Wilson and FDR, whose legacies had left the country "more bewildered than ever."[47]

Richard Hofstadter, one of the foremost historians of the postwar generation, judged *The Republic* and *A Basic History of the United States* to be tantamount to a concession speech by Beard about how he earlier had misunderstood American history. As a young scholar, Hofstadter had come under the influence of Beardianism and Marxism, but then had broken with the left and had gone on as a protagonist of the consensus school of history to write books famous for their brilliant style and spirited challenges to economic interpretations of history.[48] Consensus historians found more unity than conflict in American history. The change in his thinking can be seen in *The American Political Tradition and the Men Who Made It* (1948). The country's politics, he claimed, had been framed by a general acceptance of capitalism, resulting in "a democracy in cupidity rather than a democracy in fraternity." Thus, "above and beyond temporary and local conflicts there has been a common ground, a unity of cultural and political tradition upon which American civilization has stood."[49] Historians had misinterpreted the country's past by emphasizing conflict over consensus. The historian chiefly responsible for this misinterpretation was Beard.

In *The Progressive Historians: Turner, Beard, and Parrington*, Hofstadter would remember Beard with considerable respect. He had read *The Rise of American Civilization* in 1934, "when all American history seemed to dance to Beard's tune." That book had made Hofstadter a historian. By 1968, however, when he wrote *The Progressive Historians*, Beard's economic arguments seemed to him misleading. In that book, he likened the postwar decline of Beard's reputation to "an imposing ruin in the landscape of American historiography." Speaking for a post-Beard generation, Hofstadter continued with his architectural metaphor about the demise of Beardianism: "What was once the grandest home in the province is now a ravaged survival."[50]

In the essay that he wrote for Howard K. Beale's anthology, *Charles A. Beard: An Appraisal* (1954), Hofstadter identified *The Republic* as the beginning of a momentous turning point in Beard's thinking about the Constitution and, consequently, about the whole course of American history. That book, Hofstadter thought, reflected Beard's "essential satisfaction with the American form of constitutionalism, which he attractively defined as 'the civilian way of living together in the Republic.'"[51] Gone from this 1943 book was the iconoclastic spirit of *An Economic Interpretation of the Constitution of the United States*. Compared with the military dictatorship that the country easily might have become following the Revolution, the handiwork of the proceedings at Philadelphia in 1787 deserved to be viewed as a monumental triumph for the American people.

In *A Basic History of the United States*, Hofstadter found what he considered decisive evidence that Beard essentially had abandoned his economic interpretation of history or at least had modified or supplemented it greatly. Comparing that book with the earlier *The Rise of American Civilization*, Hofstadter underlined "the entirely different verbal formulations" about the Constitution.[52] By the time of *A Basic History of the United States*, Beard no longer believed in his classic theory about the Constitution as a conspiracy against democracy. Instead, Beard displayed an almost religious reverence for the Constitution as an enshrinement of American political ideals. The class character of the struggle over the Constitution, once the defining element of the Beard thesis, lost its primacy and imperceptibly blended in with cultural, intellectual, and political factors. Next to the Fascist and Nazi dictatorships, the American political system seemed to Beard a paragon of wisdom no longer deserving of prosecution by disparaging comments and pejorative inferences.

Hofstadter's comparison of *A Basic History of the United States* with *The Rise of American Civilization* touched mainly on Beard's changing views of the Constitution. True, Beard was not the same historian in 1944 that he had been in 1913 or 1927. The question that Hofstadter's comparison raises concerns the nature of the changes in Beard's thinking, whether they were organic or refutative. Even for Beard's interpretation of the Constitution, Hofstadter conceded that over the years much had not changed. What stayed the same was Beard's recognition that wealth always left its superincumbent imprint on politics. Other forces in history—ideas, culture, and personality—affected politics as well, but Beard never lost sight of what he had learned from Hobson about the eternal contradictions between elite prerogatives and the general good.

In a speech that Beard had given on January 13, 1936, under the auspices of the Independent Legislative Bureau at a gathering of public officials, educators, social scientists, and farm and labor leaders, he spoke about the Constitution. It was like the Bible, he said: "Everybody has heard of it and feels competent to discourse on the subject. Yet it is safe to say that 99 percent of those who speak of the Constitution in tones of awe or disrespect could not pass a high-school examination on its phrases, principles, and applications. Fewer still could write a correct 50-word account of how it was framed and adopted."[53] Good reason existed for the public's lack of acquaintance with the fundamental law of the land. The Constitution did not encourage light reading. For example, "nearly all the important provisions of the Constitution dealing with the powers and limitations of the government are open to diverse interpretations, and the guess of one season is often not the rule of the next."[54] The political process by which this intricately worded and oracular document had first materialized in Philadelphia and then had gained acceptance nationally could not fail to inspire diverse historical interpretations as well. For Beard, however, any such interpretation that presumed to ignore the decisive role in that political process of the country's economic power structure would come dressed in the swaddling clothes of intellectual infantilism.

Hofstadter's good friend Irving Howe agreed with Beard. In a private evaluation of *The Progressive Historians* that this eminent writer and public intellectual gave to Hofstadter before publication, he thought that the material on Beard fell far short of an obituary for the economic interpretation of history: "I didn't feel that even when you were cutting him up in *re*: the Constitution. The reason is, I think, this: you implicitly and explicitly make clear that no matter how wrong he was in detail, no matter how vulgar in application, *that* had its revolutionary implication." The socioeconomic approach to constitution making and to the historical process generally still held the place of crucial importance that Beard had given it. Moreover, Howe added in defense of Beard, "I think he can be charged with crudity only if he says people acted as they did out of direct economic motives or intent. But to show that 'economic interest' is present does not seem to me necessarily crude."[55]

Louis Hartz, the author of *The Liberal Tradition in America: An Interpretation of American Political Thought Since the Revolution* (1955) and a leading figure in the consensus school, made a related point: "But after all is said and done Beard somehow stays alive, and the reason for this is that, as in the case of Marx, you merely demonstrate your subservience to a thinker when you spend your time attempting to disprove him." Hartz added that the way to refute a man is to ignore him and then "to substitute new fundamental categories . . . so that you are simply pursuing a different path."[56]

Hofstadter himself came to realize that such a substitution of "fundamental categories" never had been made by Beard's critics. An honest evaluation of the historical record foreclosed the possibility of dispensing with conflict analysis.[57] In correspondence with the historian Arthur M. Schlesinger Jr., he said as much in distancing himself from the consensus school of history: "I think it had a certain value as a corrective of some of the Progressive simplifications, but it does appear to me now that we have to go back to conflict as the center of our story."[58] He retreated still further from the position that an American uniqueness had been achieved through equality of condition in a distinctively democratic society: "I do heartily agree with you that the consensus idea is a poor guide to the writing of American history, and that it hardly has the status of an adequate 'theory' of American history."[59] Evidently, the violent eruptions at Columbia in the late 1960s over student protests involving the Vietnam War and the civil rights movement disabused Hofstadter of his assumptions about a common climate of opinion in America. The radical violence had horrified him. Hofstadter continued to love Columbia University, but speaking about himself and his family in a letter to the historian Dumas Malone, he could not say amidst so much mayhem "whether it will be possible for us to like New York any longer."[60]

In *The Progressive Historians*, a valedictory book for Hofstadter, he contended that shared American values and beliefs united Americans more than historians like Beard had allowed. Nevertheless, the forms of economic conflict that Beard had written about, even if flawed on the levels of detail and methodology, had shaped American history in its major key. Beard had succeeded in the way that all great historians do, by setting the terms of fundamental debates about the past. He also managed to hold his own in many of these debates, and particularly in the one concerning the way that the country had been set up to work. Writing about the adoption of the Constitution, Hofstadter conceded, "one aspect of the period on which Beard's view seems sound, even if drawn out of perspective: the ruling elites . . . still had matters in hand."[61] This was the essential principle to get right, and Beard applied it consistently to the whole American record down to his own time. Both ruefully and admiringly, Hofstadter acknowledged in *The Progressive Historians* that no other principle of historical analysis had taken its place. The consensus school only had succeeded in chipping away at the Progressive tradition—by which he meant essentially Beardianism—but not in replacing it. By far the longest essay in *The Progressive Historians* is devoted to Beard, as it should have been.

CHAPTER 7

Waging War for the Four Freedoms

In a September 2, 1943, letter to Harry Elmer Barnes, by then one of his closest friends and political allies, Beard described the disappointment that he felt over the virtual transformation of American journalism into a wartime propaganda machine. Only one journal seemed to him worth reading any more: *The Progressive*, the descendant of Robert M. La Follette's old magazine. He explained further to Barnes: "We are regular subscribers to *The Progressive* and agree with you that it is about the only civilized sheet in the country. I hope it has increasing circulation. Sometime, I'll try my hand for it."[1] Indeed, he would do so, and the magazine became an important channel for his articles during the war years. It also served as a kind of schoolroom for him. The major anti-war and anti-FDR publication of the day, *The Progressive* specialized in uncovering corruption and mismanagement in the war effort. The journalists who wrote for the magazine, Barnes most of all, expressed a persistent skepticism about the sincerity of America's war aims. All of them took their foreign policy bearings from Beard. *The Progressive* story is a vital component in Beard's intellectual biography.

Beard's relationship with the La Follette family went back many years and now centered on Robert M. La Follette Jr., who, following his father's death in 1925, had replaced him in the Senate. He also took over as the editor of *La Follette's Magazine*, which for a few years would continue to be a family-run business. The magazine perpetuated its founder's anti-imperialist foreign policy views. The foreign policy editorials by Robert Jr. echoed his own speeches in the Senate against America's Coolidge-era economic imperialism in Nicaragua and Mexico. The magazine published like-minded foreign policy articles by such leading progressives as George W. Norris, Burton K. Wheeler, and Gerald P. Nye.

The magazine acquired a new name in 1929, *The Progressive* and became a weekly instead of a monthly. Senator La Follette ceased to be the editor of the magazine. The new editor, William T. Evjue, had founded in 1917 the *Capital Times*, a progressive pro–La Follette newspaper in Madison. Senator La Follette would go on contributing editorials to the magazine, but no longer had a direct role in its operations. *The Progressive* continued to promote the political careers of the La Follette brothers, Robert Jr. in the Senate and Philip in the governor's mansion. The magazine also supported FDR and the New Deal, as Beard himself did in the beginning.

Young Bob, as he always would be known, lacked his father's magnetism as a speaker, but he quickly emerged as a leader of the Republican Party's progressive wing and naturally gravitated into the orbit of FDR. When the La Follettes re-launched the Progressive Party in 1934, they did so in support of the New Deal. The extensive correspondence between Senator La Follette and FDR amply reflects the affectionate regard in which they held each other. In effusive "Dear Bob" letters redolent of the president's legendary charm, he had repeated occasion to thank La Follette for defending and advancing New Deal legislation. Despite being well disposed in general toward FDR, he did venture some criticisms of the New Deal from the left for its inconsistent approach to the Depression. About Senator La Follette's criticisms of the New Dealers, however, his biographer, Patrick J. Maney, observed, "Like them, he offered no fundamental challenge to the basic structure of capitalism."[2] Though an active promoter of labor reform legislation, he did not have an alternative economic system in mind. He followed the progressive political lead of his father, and, like him, rejected socialism and communism as hopelessly unsuited to the American temper.

The thorough coverage by *The Progressive* of the Nye Committee hearings reflected Beard's own estimate of that investigating body's importance and would have been another reason for him to look with favor on the magazine. Echoing the committee's recommendations, the magazine enthusiastically promoted the Neutrality Act of 1935 and rejoiced in its passage: "The enactment of this legislation is a step forward of tremendous importance for the cause of peace. It is hoped that the next congress will reinforce its provisions and make its mandatory provisions permanent."[3] The measure called for a six-month embargo on the shipment of munitions and war supplies to belligerents.

In addition, it authorized the president to forbid America's ships from carrying arms and war materials to belligerent nations, to keep the submarines of warring nations out of American ports, and to warn American citizens to stay off ships in war zones. Had such rules and guidelines been in place during the Great War, the United States could well have stayed out of it, the magazine reasoned.

Contemporaneous with its coverage of the Nye Committee hearings, *The Progressive* published a series of blistering anti-war articles by General Smedley D. Butler, the nation's most outspoken anti-militarist, much favored by Beard. Butler had responded to the Neutrality Act with nothing like the enthusiasm of *The Progressive*: "The United States looks grotesque waving its drooping olive branch toward Europe. We are really waving a lighted cigar over the international powder keg."[4] The drooping olive branch was the neutrality legislation, "forced down the throat of a reluctant president and a Wall Street-dominated state department." The lighted cigar was his image for "our arrogant and irresponsible armed forces." For him, the new highs in war spending undermined all the optimistic interpretations of the Neutrality Act as the harbinger of peace for the American people. "Our financial muscle-men are already figuring prospective war profits," he observed. Economic forces in complete control of the political process had turned the United States into a nation of saber rattlers: "We are astride the tiger of war preparations, and we dare not dismount."[5]

The vicious cycle of endlessly mounting military expenditures, Butler continued, could not be stopped short of a revolution, which would entail, to begin with, abolishing West Point and uprooting the clique that controlled the American military machine. Then the big business and banking cartels would have to be smashed. The world would never have peace so long as the financial elites dominated the American people. Everything Butler said Beard was thinking and, in a higher register of English, was already beginning to write at this time. He certainly welcomed the barrage of publicity that *The Progressive* gave Butler.

Like Beard, *The Progressive* thought that the revelations of the Nye hearings deserved comparison for their historical importance with those furnished by the secret treaties that had explained in unexampled detail the real motives on the Allied side for the First World War. These treaties had exposed government justifications for the war as ridiculous propaganda confections. In light of the documents, no intelligent person could believe a single word of what the Allies had said about their motives for the fighting. The government spokesmen had lied or had deceived themselves about the facts of the case. What the secret treaties did to the reputation of European war mongers, the hearings of the Nye Committee, especially the last batch of them in January and February 1936, did to the Wilson legacy, or what remained of it.

Front-page stories about the Nye hearings appeared in *The Progressive* during January and February 1936, beginning with accounts of how in abandoning U.S. neutrality during the war Wilson had submitted to the relentless pressure of the country's financial leaders. While publicly committed to neutrality, he "personally turned on the spigot that poured American dollars into France, Russia, and England."[6] The bankers invested billions in the Allied cause while the government in Washington maintained the fiction of American neutrality, but the economics of the situation made intervention a necessity. As Smedley Butler would observe, "Our entry into the war with the Allies was on the theory of the department stores—'Our customer is always right.'"[7]

On January 25, 1936, *The Progressive* published a story about Charles Beard. They did not mention him in the context of the Nye probe, which he had been following with the same avidity shown by *The Progressive*. The article dealt with an appearance that Beard, along with United Mine Workers president John L. Lewis, had made before the Independent Legislative Bureau in Washington, D.C. Both men had criticized the Supreme Court and Congress for failing to promote the general interests of the American people, an argument in keeping with the editorial line of *The Progressive* at that time. The magazine expressed admiration for Beard, whose *Economic Interpretation of the Constitution of the United States* it described as "a classic among students of government."[8] Beard would return the compliment in his correspondence with Harry Elmer Barnes. Beginning with their shared assessment of the Nye Committee hearings as an incomparable exposé of the government's inner workings, the historian and the magazine formed a relationship that grew in importance for both.

Although not a conspicuous participant in the Senate battle over the Nye hearings, Senator Robert La Follette Jr. took a firm stand in favor of American neutrality legislation. In a February 15, 1936, editorial for *The Progressive*, he supported Senator Nye's proposal for a stronger neutrality law than the temporary one currently in effect. Citing the work of the Nye Committee, he argued: "We should have learned a lesson from our ghastly experience in the last war."[9] To avoid another catastrophic war, the American people needed comprehensive and mandatory neutrality legislation. He called upon the president to support the neutrality law proposed by Senator Nye. The subsequent reinforcement of the neutrality law he welcomed as a clear victory for the cause of peace.

Senator La Follette and Beard essentially would follow the same path in their mounting criticism of FDR. Completely absorbed in the fight for New

Deal legislation, the president gave little attention to foreign policy issues during his first term. La Follette's serious problems with FDR began with the president's shift away in 1937 and 1938 from domestic politics to foreign affairs. He consistently opposed FDR's attempts to weaken the Neutrality Act of 1935, which authorized the president to prohibit all arms shipments to warring nations and to forbid U.S. citizens from traveling on belligerent vessels. In 1936 the Neutrality Act was extended to May 1, 1937, and adjusted to include a ban on loans or credits to belligerents. In response to the Spanish Civil War, which had broken out in 1936, a January 6, 1937, joint resolution of Congress forbade the export of munitions to either side in the conflict. Five months later, another piece of neutrality legislation became law, authorizing the sale of commodities other than munitions, to be paid for on delivery. The Neutrality Act of 1937 also made travel on belligerent vessels unlawful. La Follette supported the series of neutrality acts passed by Congress from 1935 to 1937, while resisting all efforts to grant the president discretion in their application and administration.[10]

Five weeks after the outbreak of the Second World War, La Follette spoke in the Senate against a proposed revision of the U.S. arms embargo called for in the Neutrality Act of 1935 and subsequently renewed. He made a Beardian argument against the measure: "There is a great temptation for people weary of the struggle against the domestic economic crisis to find escape in the war crisis in Europe."[11] In the Beardian manner, too, he attributed the Depression to "our last mad adventure in Europe and the distortion of our entire economic life produced by the World War." He quoted from "Giddy Minds and Foreign Quarrels," Beard's September 1939 article in *Harper's Magazine*: "'From the point of view of the interest of the United States as a continental nation in this hemisphere, the Roosevelt policy is, in my opinion, quixotic and dangerous.'"[12] La Follette also quoted a passage from the eighth edition of Beard's *American Government and Politics*, regarding the almost unlimited authority that President Wilson had exercised over manpower, economic resources, and expression of opinion. In the next war, Beard had predicted, "'Congress would probably confer upon the President practically unconditional power over all citizens and their property and the right to use them at his will and pleasure as long as the emergency lasted.'"[13]

Another issue of mutual interest to La Follette and Beard rang out in the senator's October 12, 1939, speech. He could understand and completely agree with the condemnation in America of Germany's invasion of Poland the previous month, but where was the outrage over Soviet Russia's invasion of that country? He judged this silence to be most revealing about the real foreign policy agenda of the forces in America pushing for our intervention in the war, the clear long-term aim of the arms embargo revision proposal. He noted Britain's current trade deal and rapprochement with the Russian government, "which gobbled up as large a slice of Poland as Germany ever did, or a larger slice." It seemed to him, as it did to Beard, that the United States found itself mixed up in the vagaries of British foreign policy. "Is it so necessary for us to have the British Empire preserved that we should, and must, be willing to defend it whenever and on whatever terms it chooses to fight?"[14]

La Follette echoed Beard as well in casting suspicion on the integrity of British and French war aims. The senator doubted very much that these two imperialist nations would be "trustworthy partners for us either in our own national defense or in any grandiose schemes which may later develop for reforming the world."[15] They had too much blood on their hands from time immemorial. Ever true to form, with their cruel and vindictive policies after World War I they together had helped to undermine German democracy and had furnished the most effective assistance in bringing Hitler to power. Having done after the last war what they always did, playing "their own game of power politics," they now had to face a situation of their own making. Many things would be at stake in the current war, but democracy would not be one of them. La Follette ridiculed as an absurd falsehood the argument of his Senate opponents, that democracy was a reason in the fighting then taking place in Europe. Wherever they had ruled, Britain and France never had shown "the slightest interest in carrying out the tenets of democracy." All he could see resulting from the administration's desire to put an effective end to the nation's neutrality legislation was another "dangerous war boom."[16] The misnamed Neutrality Act of 1939 passed the Senate 63–30 on October 17, and the House 243–181 on November 2. The president signed it into law on November 4.

La Follette soon became involved in America First activities. He would take *The Progressive* with him. As editor Evjue had become increasingly enamored of the president's foreign policy, Senator La Follette had grown disenchanted with it. A break became unavoidable. In his unpublished PhD dissertation, *"The Progressive's* Views on Foreign Affairs, 1909–1941," John Alan Ziegler sums up what happened: "The editor's strong, uncompromising support of Roosevelt's foreign policy and his outspoken denunciation of Hitler's aggression in Europe during the first half of 1940 finally led to Evjue's departure in June."[17] The June 28 headline read, "New, Militant Progressive Takes the Field."[18]

The replacement editor, twenty-eight-year-old Morris H. Rubin, had been a longtime La Follette operative. From 1938 to 1940, he worked as an administrative assistant for Governor Phil La Follette. He wrote speeches for both La Follette brothers and had contributed articles on Wisconsin politics to *The*

Progressive. On foreign policy, he fully subscribed to the anti-interventionist viewpoint of the La Follettes, claiming in his own editorials that the Second World War, like the first one, concerned rival imperialist systems, not rival ideologies. It was an editorial line fully consonant with the declarations of the America First Committee and to which Beard gave thankful assent.

On September 21, 1940, *The Progressive* published the following article: "Charles Beard Urges U.S. Stay out of Europe." Described in the article as the "dean of American historians," Beard had sent a message to the America First Committee, supporting its call for the United States to avoid involvement in the European war. About the AFC, he was quoted in the article as saying: "It believes that the foreign policy of the United States should be directed to the preservation of the peace and security of this nation in its continental zone of interests, that the United States should not resort to any more measures verging in the direction of war outside its continental zone of interest."[19] Beard and the magazine continued to view foreign policy questions from the same non-interventionist perspective.

Three days later, R. Douglas Stuart Jr., the director of the America First Committee, wrote to La Follette about a recent radio broadcast: "We have been swamped with requests for copies of your speech from all parts of the country. We are still receiving on an average of two hundred requests a day."[20] Stuart hoped that he might consent to participate in a short America First film that would also include appearances by Senators Arthur Capper of Kansas, Henry Cabot Lodge Jr. of Massachusetts, and Burton K. Wheeler of Montana. Citing in his speech the lessons of the last war, Senator La Follette fought for the retention of the strictures that remained in America's neutrality legislation. Like Beard, he viewed the period immediately following the outbreak of the Second World War as a repetition of what had happened from 1914 to 1917. He feared that once again Americans would be deceived by their leaders and stampeded into war. La Follette, who, also like Beard, saw both wars as struggles for imperialist spoils, now repeated his father's anti-interventionist arguments from 1917. The fundamental issues in American political life had not changed since then. Unsolved domestic problems posed a bigger threat to the United States than Germany did, then as now.

Beard took the side of the America First Committee in an American Political Science Association (APSA) battle that erupted over this scholarly organization's decision to grant exhibit space at its December 1940 convention to the interventionist Chicago chapter of the Committee to Defend America by Aiding the Allies. On January 1, 1941, he wrote to his old friend and one-time collaborator Frederic Austin Ogg, then the president of the APSA, protesting the use of the Association "for any propaganda whatsoever." He declared, "If we start on the propaganda line, we are ruined, for it will introduce ideological fights without end. If our association is a political propaganda organization, it should disband and hoist the skull and crossbones over a new craft."[21] When informed that APSA officers, concerned about rising convention costs, had decided in 1940 to begin accepting advertisements and rental fees from outside organizations, Beard replied, "I don't want to be cantankerous about the business, but I do regard the concession to propaganda organizations as dangerous to the peace and the resolution impossible to administer without stirring up ill-feeling and, sometimes, scandals."[22]

Soon after defeating Wendell Willkie in the election of 1940, FDR took another long step in the direction of war by recommending to Congress a lend-lease program for the Allies, enabling them to receive arms and other war materiel. As a witness before the Senate's Committee on Foreign Relations, Beard spoke against the bill. On February 13, 1941, Senator Burton K. Wheeler of Montana asked to have Beard's entire statement printed in the *Congressional Record*, saying, "It is, I believe, a very clear analysis of the bill."[23]

About America's pro-British sentiments in this war, Beard told the Committee that he shared them. The shocking fall of France in June 1940 had created apprehension in the minds of the American people. Hitler's victorious march through Europe dismayed them, and no right-thinking person could view the European situation with anything but alarm, Beard acknowledged. Yet, the language of this bill seemed to aim at something greater than a mere aid package to beleaguered Britain, fraught with risk to the American people as even the ostensible purpose of lend-lease would be. Beard warned, "under the loose, indeed limitless phrase 'national defense'" no bounds would be placed on the president's powers to employ the nation's resources and productive capacity as he saw fit. Only the words of Milton seemed adequate to describe the power that lend-lease would give the president: "Without dimension, where length, breadth, / and height, / And time and place are lost."[24]

Indeed, if words meant anything, the bill authorized the president "to wage undeclared war for anybody, anywhere in the world, until the affairs of the world are ordered to suit his policies." Ordering the affairs of the American people had far overtaxed their leaders, who without the requisite credibility had now presented themselves as guides for all humanity. Beard asked, "Can they, by any means at their disposal, make over Europe and Asia, provide democracy, a bill of rights, and economic security for everybody, everywhere in the world?"[25] The rhetoric of the administration sounded thoroughly familiar to him, as a warmed over and even more rhetorically inflated version of what Woodrow Wilson had said a generation earlier. After Wilson's deceptions and failures, the American people would do well to be skeptical about any promises emanating from Washington.

The coming and the conclusion of the First World War contained the fundamental lessons needed to understand the current conflict. For the Committee, Beard distilled the essence of the lessons that he had learned from studying the documents found in the archives of Russia, Germany, and Austria: "I have spent many weary months studying these documents, and I will say, gentlemen of the committee, that these documents do not show that the European conflict was, in the aims of the great powers, a war for democracy, or for the defense of the United States, or had anything to do with protecting the interests of the United States." The FDR administration had spoken nonsense in claiming that by fighting for democracy Britain was waging America's battle. Britain then and now had its own imperialist agenda. Beard then posed the crucial question facing Congress in the debate over lend-lease: "Does Congress intend to guarantee the present extent, economic resources, and economic methods of the British Empire forever to the Government of Great Britain by placing the unlimited resources of the United States at the disposal of the British Government, however constituted?"[26]

A related question concerned defeated France. Beard wanted to know if we would be supplying money, ships, and commodities of war until the restoration of the French Republic and "until the integrity of its empire is assured." He had a similar question about Japan: Would we be pouring out American wealth until Japanese forces were expelled from China? Beard counseled the Committee to reject the lend-lease measure, above all because it asked Congress to suspend the Constitution by conferring dictatorial powers on the president. The war-making powers should be kept in the hands of Congress. Legal means might be employed to aid Britain, "without erecting a bureaucratic monstrosity."[27]

In his Senate speech against lend-lease eleven days later, on February 22, 1941, Senator Arthur Capper of Topeka, Kansas, also praised Beard for his testimony before the Senate Committee on Foreign Relations. "Mr. President," Senator Capper said, "I assert those words of Dr. Beard are words of wisdom, patriotism, and plain common sense, and I would to God this Congress would adopt that kind of program." Senator Capper lauded Beard for echoing the warnings of George Washington's Farewell Address and then made a prophecy about what he called our next world-saving effort: "We shall have a government debt that in all probability will run into the hundreds of billions. We shall have an economy geared to war production, probably to war-making."[28] Despite Beard's testimony and the impassioned speeches of Wheeler and Capper, the lend-lease measure passed the Senate

60–31 on March 8 and the House 317–71 on March 11. The president signed it immediately.

La Follette, too, had voted against the lend-lease bill. He agreed with Wheeler and Capper that the measure constituted a flagrant violation of American neutrality certain to lead to war, a view that won him Beard's warm support. The alarm over the unique evil of Hitler had been mischaracterized because Stalin, soon-to-be a beneficiary of the Lend-Lease Act, was worse. Certainly, as of 1941 Stalin had killed far more innocent people than had Hitler, and yet, for reasons never clearly spelled out, only the Nazis appeared in the popular media as unparalleled monsters of human depravity. La Follette continued to believe that something very odd about American foreign policy could be detected in the silence of Washington over Stalin's treacherous collusion with Hitler. There had been no mention of a "stab in the back" that time, as in the case of FDR's response on June 10, 1940, to Italy's declaration of war against France a few days ahead of Germany's occupation of Paris.

One week before passage of the lend-lease bill, Beard had written an article for *The Progressive* in opposition to the measure. He began with a statement that had appeared in his testimony earlier that year before the Senate Committee on Foreign Relations: "I have devoted fifty years to the study of history, here in my own country and abroad, in Europe and Asia; but the older I grow the more I am convinced that the wisest amongst us knows little about the great history which we now are writing." He then summarized his chief arguments against lend-lease, drawing particular attention to it as "a bill for waging an undeclared war." To the individuals who argued, as the president had, that lend-lease would keep the United States out of the war, he declared, "I confess to an utter inability to understand the reasoning and morals of those who use this formula." If, as the president had said, the British were fighting a war for democracy, we should be fighting it, not "buying peace with gold."[29] He did not think, however, that the war had anything to do with democracy, any more than the last war did.

Beard had a message for the American leadership class, whose deadly combination of pride, arrogance, and ignorance would prevent them from receiving it, but he felt obliged to try. The United States lacked the knowledge and the power to transform the cultures of Europe and Asia. We did not know what we were dealing with in these places, and we lacked the patience to learn. That was why we wanted everyone to look like us. It would make the world a happier and more harmonious place if the American way became the way for all peoples. He concluded, no matter what you hear from Washington, we cannot "provide democracy, a bill of rights, and economic security for everybody, everywhere in the world." Only people who did not know anything about history or how civilizations work could believe such fatuities. The Bolsheviks, much despised by Beard, had believed their own fairy tales about "the gospel of one model for the whole world."[30] Beard did not say what the likely outcome of Russia's historical process would be for the Bolsheviks, but he had a dread certainty that the interventionist exuberance would bring disaster to the United States.

In April the Progressive Publishing Company launched a four-week antiwar radio series, which was broadcast nationally. All through the spring the magazine ran "Keep America Out of Europe's Blood Bath" advertisements. On June 21, it published Frank Lloyd Wright's "America! Wake Up!" The architect worried, "Our danger lies not so much in far-reaching German Geopolitik as in the fact that the judgment of our leader nods, taxed beyond human endurance." He criticized FDR's decision to run for a third term, saying that the president had lost touch with common sense and seriously took as fact his own propaganda, which had flooded the United States in the form of endless lies to the American people by newsreel and radio. The truth about the administration's desire for war did not conform to FDR's platitudinous ejaculations about freedom and democracy. "Going to war is the natural basis of Empire," Wright insisted, "and off we go again on the well-worn path to Nowhere and Never. Forever."[31]

No less emphatic in denouncing FDR's interventionist policy was Oswald Garrison Villard, a founder of the Anti-Imperialist League in opposition to the annexation of the Philippines following the Spanish-American War, a pioneering civil rights leader, and a former owner and editor of *The Nation* magazine. The tragic flaw in American foreign policy, he lamented, lay in the country's delusions about itself, "as if America were God" and charged with putting the world in order. He wondered where such a stupid and ignorant presumption originated. The United States had been a sensible country once, prone in the natural scheme of human fallibility to mistakes and crimes, but not pathologically disturbed to the point of megalomania, with all its weird insecurities and constant need for reassurance about its special place in the world. "We have broken utterly with the American principle of minding our own business and letting other people attend to theirs," he rued. Washington and Lincoln would be horrified by our global foreign policy today: "This is the most monstrous and unparalleled revolution that has ever occurred in our history." The cult of "the American Century" and "God's chosen people" did not become a nation fitted to lead the world in anything worth doing.[32] Indeed, with such flimsy ideas in their heads, the Americans seemed to him every bit as much a menace to mankind as Germany, Russia, and Japan.

In the company of the likes of the La Follette brothers, Wright, and Villard, Beard felt himself to be in his natural element as a critic of American foreign policy. He and Robert La Follette Jr. enjoyed an especially close political rapport at this time. Senator La Follette had supported FDR for reelection in 1940, but as the country moved toward war in 1941 he distanced himself from the administration. On August 15, the senator's secretary, Norman M. Clapp, released a statement about his position on the war in Europe. He did not assume that the current fighting simply was a repetition of the last war, "but there remain certain fundamental similarities which also must be acknowledged." In 1918, the American people had been told that with the kaiser bent on world domination, Americans, armed with the Fourteen Points, would have to save democratic civilization: "With this cunning combination of fear and idealism the American people were stampeded to the slaughter."[33] There followed an infamous peace from which a second world war sprang. Now, with Hitler alleged to be threatening our shores, the Four Freedoms were said to be at stake.

La Follette disputed the claim that the Allies were fighting to uphold the Four Freedoms. The British Empire had very questionable credentials as a source of freedom for the peoples it exploited worldwide, and the Soviet Union, Britain's ally in the struggle against Nazi Germany, had no credentials at all as a bringer of liberation. He could not tell the difference between Nazi Germany and the Soviet Union, a point that Beard would be making as well. With Britain's fervor for democracy much exaggerated by the administration, the war had to be about something other than the Four Freedoms. It would be advantageous for the American people to discover the war's true purposes before entering it.

On August 23, 1941, Philip La Follette offered his explanation of the war's meaning. Unlike his brother, he saw a precise parallel between Wilson and FDR: "Having failed to defeat the enemies of democracy in America, each undertook to do in the world what they could not achieve at home."[34] He was making a complex argument here. The domestic enemies of American democracy were the oligarchs. Neither Wilson nor FDR had been able to win a decisive success against them. The tepid reforms in Wilson's "new freedom" had failed to rid American capitalism of its oligarchic character and ruinous panics. Philip thought that FDR had abandoned the New Deal "as a dead cat" by 1938. His reform program, too, had failed. In the manner described by Beard in *Giddy Minds and Foreign Quarrels*, both presidents had looked abroad for the success that had eluded them at home.

Conservative former president Herbert Hoover used the pages of *The Progressive* to criticize the warmongering foreign policy of FDR. He, too, judged

Nazism and Communism to be abominable in the same degree: "I abhor any American compromise or alliance with either of them."[35] Our de facto alliance with Stalinist Russia created some serious problems for the propagandists in Washington then attempting to present the war as a crusade for human rights and the protection of weak, vulnerable peoples. Stalin's blood-curdling résumé condemned such a sales pitch, on its face, as a farrago of distortions and outright lies. Hoover could find nothing sensible in FDR's rationale for violating the spirit of the Neutrality Act. Contrary to the stream of alarmist communications emanating from Washington, the United States had absolutely nothing to fear from an invasion by Germany. The Germans had no desire for war with the United States and, in any case, had their hands full with the British and the Russians. Moreover, FDR's plan for America to build a democratic world had been tried by Wilson, with results that did not warrant a second attempt. The former president concluded: "We can do our greatest service to civilization by strengthening here in the Western Hemisphere free institutions and free men and women. That is not isolation. It is service to all mankind."[36]

For Beard, one of the most appealing features of *The Progressive* concerned the regular column that Harry Elmer Barnes wrote for the magazine. In a series of three articles written in November and early December 1941, Barnes offered his opinions on the causes of World War II and America's role in it. The war, he thought, was not fundamentally about Britain's holding on "to their ancient ill-gotten gains or of the upstart Nazi militarists to overrun Western Europe."[37] World War II had become necessary for the victors to retain the spoils of World War I, but to understand fully the events of 1939 we would have to dig deeper "than the diplomatic stupidity of the democracies or the bellicosity of the dictators."[38] Amidst much speculation about a general trend in the world toward collectivism, Barnes concretely identified the disruption of Western progressive movements by World War I as the fundamental cause of World War II. The social revolutions that began during World War I and continued until 1933 had kept the war system in constant stimulation. Hitler was best understood as a product of World War I rather than as a cause of World War II, which had many causes, not least the Western foreign policies that "were directed by the desire to protect the financial interests of a wealthy and effete minority."[39]

In the last of the three articles, published the day before Pearl Harbor, Barnes asked, "can anything we might gain out of a war with Japan in any way equal what it would cost us to defeat the Japanese?" He had in mind something other than financial costs, staggering as those surely would be. His main concern had to do with the regimentation that the war would introduce into American life. Far from saving democracy, the war would put it at greater risk than ever before. We would be going to war "to bail out the British, French, and Dutch Empires in the Far East." Our own motives in that region could not bear scrutiny either. The open-door philosophy of American Far East diplomacy he denounced as "a sordid instrument of western imperialism in the Far East." The doctrine merely meant "the declaration of open season on China for all imperialistic thieves. All are to have the opportunity to steal from China on equal terms." He feared that the upshot of America's foreign policy initiatives against the Japanese would be war, an outcome that would be "nothing short of sheer national idiocy."[40]

The first post–Pearl Harbor issue of *The Progressive* carried the following headline: "Nation United Against Aggression." On the front page a story announced that Robert La Follette had joined his Senate colleagues in an 82–0 vote supporting the declaration of war against Japan. In the House of Representatives, only Jeannette Rankin of Montana had opposed the measure, taking the same anti-war stand that she had in 1917. *The Progressive* announced that the America First Committee supported the war, as did Charles Lindbergh, Burton K. Wheeler, Herbert Hoover, and all the other famous Americans who up until December 7, 1941, had opposed FDR's foreign policy. The magazine declared its unqualified support for the war, but added how it would be working in the tradition of the magazine's founder, Robert La Follette Sr. to defend democracy during wartime: "We propose to say a great deal about the conduct of the war, and just as important, we intend to say a great deal about the peace to come."[41] Editor Morris H. Rubin further specified that he and his writers would expose war profiteering, defend the Bill of Rights, promote labor, and call for democratic postwar planning.[42]

During the war *The Progressive* indeed did follow an editorial line that conferred upon it a quasi-dissident character, much to Beard's satisfaction. He and Senator La Follette exchanged mutually admiring letters. On January 11, 1942, Beard wrote to him from Aiken, South Carolina, where he and Mary had gone for the winter. He asked the Senator for help in rounding up research materials regarding the immigration bill of 1924, a subject treated in *The Republic*, which he would publish in 1943. "We often think of you these days and are grateful that you are young and still with us in this vale of tears," he told Senator La Follette, who sent the requested materials, along with his own expressions of esteem.[43] On January 27, Beard praised him for insisting that a thorough investigation of the Pearl Harbor disaster had to be undertaken. Beard noted in his letter that the fundamental responsibility for America's lack of preparedness at Pearl Harbor fell on the FDR administration and members of Congress, especially the chairmen of military affairs and naval affairs committees in the two houses of Congress: "Even the *New York Times*, which has been a war-mongering sheet for years, has honesty enough to say this morning that part of the blame also rests on men higher up."[44] The senator replied on February 4 that he, too, hoped the investigation into the Pearl Harbor attack "will provoke a more thoughtful consideration of certain current affairs."[45]

FDR worried about La Follette's inclination to raise awkward issues over the alliance with Britain. In a "Dear Bob" letter of February 20, 1942, the president told him, "I am really concerned by a report that you are planning to make some kind of speech asking that we withhold Lend-Lease aid from the British until they grant India independence." Such a speech would do incalculable harm to the cause of freedom, the president insisted, and "as an old friend, I am asking you not to do this."[46] La Follette complied with the president's request, but in a letter written the same day expressed his "grave concern over the failure of the British government to make it clear that it is *not* fighting to maintain its colonial empire and extraterritorial rights in China and elsewhere." As his father had before him during the First World War, he wanted the government to be clear about its war aims and what the United States would be prepared to countenance in the postwar peace settlement: "the failure of the British government or our own to make it clear that we are not sacrificing American lives and treasure for the maintenance of the British colonial empire or its extraterritorial rights, as well as our own, will, I fear, have a very adverse effect on the morale of our people." Yet he maintained a deferential tone toward the president: "Naturally a request from you at any time could never fail to receive my most sympathetic consideration. At a time like this, it carries even more weight."[47]

Articles in *The Progressive* sounded a much less deferential note. Hardly had the shooting begun when Barnes asked how Japan had gotten its start as an imperialist power. The Japanese had gone to school to the paragons of imperialism and diplomatic duplicity, Great Britain and the United States. Barnes's characterization of the Japanese as "the smartest pupils of western land-grabbers" did not at all fit the story line, dramatically amplified by the war movies of Hollywood, about the unique dastardliness of the enemy.[48] So long as the Japanese cooperated with the British and American empires in the Pacific, our relations with them had been as collegial as any association of robber barons can be.[49] The trouble began when, calculating that their cut was too small, it occurred to them that they could do better on their own. He wrote in this sardonic vein throughout the war.

Barnes persistently ridiculed the American case for intervening in the war. On March 28, 1942, he wrote, "We are now committed to a planetary war to bring the blessings of democracy to the whole world."[50] But why, he asked, would other peoples want a system that does not work very well in the United States, except for the economic elites who control it. Americans, Barnes contended, had no conception about the country's actual political life. On April 4 he described American politics as being so complicated "that to ask people to vote on them intelligently is about like asking them to decide the validity of Dr. Einstein's theory of relativity."[51] All the government talk about a war for democracy he thought completely insincere. The leaders knew better about what they were doing.

In a letter written some months later to Yale University law professor Edwin Montefiore Borchard, Barnes would enclose one of his articles on the conflict with Japan and comment, "If my article does not get me hung during the war it should get me on the grave digging squad after the war."[52] Borchard then replied with a tribute to Barnes's perspicacity. His predictions about the real meaning and consequences of the war had been amply verified, and worse was to come. Here Borchard, at this time also in steady correspondence with Beard, ventured a prediction of his own regarding the foreign policy precedent set by the FDR administration. There would be no terminus for the United States in its role as the world's guardian of democracy: "We can keep at the game of suppressing evil doers indefinitely, or as long as the American public will stand for it."[53] He presumed that the United States would be called upon to guarantee the world's peace after the war, a task that would have Americans permanently on the march from one end of the world to the other. Keeping the peace, he told Barnes, as a rule in history meant "permitting no changes in the status quo anywhere."[54] Did we really want to bear the responsibility of keeping a lid on the cauldron of the world's dissidences and disaffections?

Barnes was not an isolated critical voice on *The Progressive*. Editor Rubin, in a May 2, 1942, column, made clear the magazine's skeptical position on the war policy of the United States. The Allies had presented themselves in the Atlantic Charter, the proffered basis of their war effort, as champions of freedom for all peoples. The document, however, candidly revealed its practical limitations: "Its promise of a better post-war world under Allied auspices is drastically circumscribed by a neat little imperial clause that such changes as are promised will be made 'with due respect for existing obligations."[55] The extant empires, including their economic lineaments, would be maintained after the war. Rubin thought it a reasonable assumption, based on the obedience shown by the governments of the democracies to economic elites, how the war might have as its deepest cause the protection and promotion of the international cartel arrangements in which American corporations were deeply involved. He did not think that the British or the Americans had a credible answer to Japan's claim regarding its war in Asia against Western imperialism. He conceded that the Japanese were thieves, too, but, realistically, the war boiled down to a gangland eruption over market share.[56]

The editorial line marked out by Rubin and illustrated prominently by Barnes guided *The Progressive* throughout the war. It would be an error to assume that the magazine's skepticism about the American war effort can be dismissed as an unimportant exception to the general rule of patriotic enthusiasm regarding a crusade for the Four Freedoms. For example, Senator Robert A. Taft of Ohio, very nearly the Republican Party's presidential nominee in 1940, made kindred comments in some of his wartime speeches, deriding the declared motives of U.S. foreign policy as a tissue of deceptions and worrying about the potential for a victorious America to turn itself into an imperial overlord.[57] There never had been in all of diplomatic history an agreement of such large-souled imperialist aspiration as the Atlantic Charter, which only needed Stalin's signature to actuate fully its satirical potential, Taft objected. The communist dictator he denounced as the worst tyrant in the world and a suitable ally for an imperialist government, but not a democratic one.[58] Taft and La Follette had supported each other through the fight in the Senate against America's intervention in the war, becoming good friends despite their sharp differences on domestic issues. After December 7, 1941, their mistrust of FDR steadily deepened into a reflex antagonism toward what they perceived to be his pretensions as a paladin of human rights. Both senators saw empire as the real endgame of the war, a viewpoint that Rubin made the mainstay of *The Progressive*. The magazine's reporting gave Beard a deep insight into the war's causes and likely consequences.

The correspondence that Senator La Follette had begun receiving from John Williams on March 16, 1942, following a Washington meeting between the two men, had a direct bearing on the editorial line of *The Progressive* about the economic nature of the war. A veteran freelance Pacific correspondent, Williams had spent fifteen years before Pearl Harbor investigating Pacific-Asiatic issues. He became an expert on British-controlled Burma and reported on the colony's turbulent politics leading up to the war. His interviews of U Saw, the prime minister of British Burma and a nationalist leader, helped to shape his view of the Empire as an extortion mechanism, an image in keeping with the first-hand reporting of George Orwell in his novel *Burmese Days* (1934). Williams obtained eyewitness impressions of the Burma situation from American, British, and Japanese experts who worked on the Burma Road, the artery used by the British to supply Chinese forces after the outbreak, in 1937, of the

Second Sino-Japanese War. He furnished several confidential reports to the United States government about conditions in Asia and witnessed the attack on Pearl Harbor, which he had predicted a year earlier. It seemed obvious to him that the Second World War had begun not at Pearl Harbor but with the Japanese invasion of China in 1937. Everybody wanted Chinese resources and markets.[59] China was the apple of discord thrown into the feast of the imperialists causing the events that led to Pearl Harbor.

With characteristic immodesty, Williams had presented himself to La Follette as "the best-informed man on the whole Pacific in a practical war-waging sense."[60] He had been supplying the Senate's Truman Committee, then investigating inefficiency and corruption in the American war effort, with information regarding defense contract scandals in Hawaii. A frequent visitor to Washington and always searching for a government job, Williams met on several occasions with La Follette in late 1942.

On January 19, 1943, Williams wrote to Senator La Follette about his "Jap files" concerning conspiracies during the 1930s between companies such as Alcoa and Bethlehem Steel and the Japanese.[61] A week later, Williams informed the senator about what he had found in his investigation of "the scandal behind the Grumman aircraft plant" involving dud shells sold to the Navy.[62] La Follette responded, "It looks as if you had struck indications that there might be a lot of pay dirt in the vein you are working on," adding that he looked forward to seeing Williams again.[63] "We sure have hit some pay dirt," Williams acknowledged, especially regarding efforts by American companies to circumvent Washington's embargo of Japan before the war.[64] Five days later, he evoked, once again, the pay dirt metaphor: "The mining project we are on here is still shocking the pants off everybody. Some of the biggest names are involved."[65] La Follette continued to express his appreciation to Williams, and on March 6 wrote, "Hope your work is going well."[66]

Two months later, Williams dwelled upon a theme only touched upon in his previous correspondence with La Follette: the economic motives of the war. "I have a private hunch," he wrote, "that the British and Dutch are determined to maintain their rubber-tin-oil cartel based in Malaya and the East Indies." Postwar planning had already begun. For Churchill, Williams had no respect at all and called him "a glib phony." A completely unreconstructed imperialist, Churchill aspired only to maintain the status quo of Britain's colonial rule. His signature on the Atlantic Charter had turned that document into a farce for anyone knowledgeable about Britain's history and current affairs. The British did not care about a better world: "So long as they can trade and remain the dominant traders, they don't worry at all about international underdogs. But when other traders get above them (notably the Germans and the Japs), then we have a 'world' war."[67] La Follette laconically replied, "I agree pretty generally with your analysis of the situation."[68]

Late that summer, Williams sent La Follette a summary of remarks made by Brendan Bracken, the British minister of information, at a private cocktail party for British Empire reporters held in New York City's St. Regis Hotel. An Australian editor sent Williams an account of the minister's officially off-the-record comments. His basic message concerned Britain's refusal to surrender its grip on Asia from India to Hong Kong. Japan had interfered with British imperial interests in the Pacific. For that reason, Bracken explained to the reporters, Britain intended to dispose of its Japan problem by calling in strategic bombing expert Ted Harris: "Japan has always talked about population problems, etc., and Ted Harris will take care of that." Bracken called the Harris solution much better than "the American plan of sending star-gazing missionaries."[69] The Americans had a strategic bombing specialist of their own, Curtis "Bombs Away" LeMay, who would make a pair with Harris in the mass murder of civilians.[70]

America's isolationists, Bracken continued, always would prevent the country from playing a large role in world affairs. Thus, "The British intend to dominate the whole Allied strategy in Asia so that by the time Singapore and the Dutch Indies are re-taken the British and Dutch interests, which are interlocked, will be dominant in the plan for re-occupation." The British thought of the Americans as children with no understanding of Asia whatsoever. All their preachments for political and social freedom in India would make no difference in the end: "As Mr. Churchill has said, we are going to keep the British Empire intact."[71] Humoring their American cousins should not be difficult. Both Anglo-Saxon peoples would agree on the nobility of their shared idealism and recognize the necessity of deferring its implementation until a more seasonable time. They understood each other and the respective parts that each had to perform in the Four Freedoms morality play, which, from the beginning with the Atlantic Charter agreement Churchill and FDR anticipated would not disturb the fundamentals of the world situation.

Williams began to write for *The Progressive* in late 1943. Ill health brought on by overwork and stress had begun to dog him by then, and his contributions to the magazine would be limited to only four reviews and one article, all dealing with the war in the Pacific. He had a low opinion of the conventional wisdom on the Pacific war. He explained in a letter dated "day after Thanksgiving 1943" to Julia Emory, the secretary for senator La Follette, himself then seriously ill: the literature on the war, corrupted by "a whole lot of pageantry baloney, sidesteps vital fax like a post mortem on the quinine, rubber, oil, opium etc. cartels which rode high, wide, and handsome in the Indies prior to the war." A severely underreported story in all of this sentimental government propaganda concerned "how the big monopolies in the USA have used the war to crush or absorb small concerns."[72] The only change in the network of imperialist exploitation covering the Pacific would be the elimination of the Japanese from the controlling power structure, which in the postwar era would be run by the British and the Americans, with assistance from the French and Dutch. It is as if Williams's reporting from the Pacific serves as prologue for C. Wright Mills's contention in *The Power Elite*: "In capitalistic economies wars have led to many opportunities for the private appropriation of fortune and power. But the complex facts of World War II make previous appropriations seem puny indeed."[73]

The only article that Williams wrote for *The Progressive*, "America Is Britain's Rubber Stamp," appeared on July 2, 1945. He meant by this title that American lives and money had been spent to restore British imperialism, which would be "doing business at the same stand." The promises of the Atlantic Charter had all been forgotten, as the peoples of Asia were being subjugated to new masters or reacquainted with old ones. He had in mind particularly the people of Burma, whose vast national resources had long been exploited by the British. Washington had made possible Britain's reoccupation of Burma. The Americans were underwriting British imperialism in the Pacific and preparing to augment their own: "These actions speak louder to Asiatics than the double-talk of our propaganda transmitters."[74]

Three days later, Williams wrote to La Follette about how within the past year his health had "rapidly disintegrated."[75] He hoped that they could continue to work together, but a few months later worriedly observed, "I have a feeling—and hope I am wrong—that someone has made derogatory statements about me to you. I can assure you that they are wrong."[76] La Follette did not reply to this letter. Williams wrote twice more in 1945 to Julia Emory, usually a sign that the senator was indisposed because of illness, and then the record of their correspondence and all sign of further activity, literary or otherwise, by John Williams ceased.

Nevertheless, La Follette's own editorials for *The Progressive* reveal the influence of Williams on his thinking about the war. In a typical editorial of his that appeared on May 22, 1944, he described how "powerful forces at home and abroad are striving to bring about the strengthening of the cartels' stranglehold on international trade." He decried the enormous power of "domestic monopoly corporations with international cartel relationships," such as DuPont, Alcoa, and Standard Oil. Many cartel arrangements had been disrupted during the war, but soon would be resumed and enlarged: "Already plans are being advanced for even more sweeping and more complete domination of world markets in the postwar world than before."[77] Like Williams, he thought that international monopolies bred wars.

Many other contributors to *The Progressive* wrote in a similar vein about the economic origins and consequences of the war. Frank Hanighen, coauthor with H. C. Engelbrecht of *Merchants of Death* and a regular columnist for *The Progressive*, specialized in writing articles for the magazine about the conflict between the stated war aims of the Allies as found in the Atlantic Charter and the realities of their continued colonial occupation of subject peoples. For instance, he wondered how the Atlantic Charter would be applied in French North Africa. From what he could find out about Tunisia, Algeria, and Morocco, the peoples in those lands had very little reason to suppose that the Four Freedoms would be extended to them. Hanighen suggested that it would be well for the American people to learn about "the oppression of colonial peoples by the French and British as well as the crimes of Nazidom." Newspapers had shown admirable concern about the treatment of Jews by Nazi Germany, but French oppression and exploitation of their North African populations had merited no coverage at all. The American media seemed to be concerned only about "good strong stuff about the Nazis." Hanighen dryly offered that instead of going to war to free Poland and Czechoslovakia, democratic France might have attempted the much easier job of freeing North Africa. Evidently, "the fight for freedom was like an exclusive club—some oppressed people could join, others could not even get on the waiting list."[78] De Gaulle did not want to preside over the liquidation of the French Empire any more than Churchill could countenance the same fate for Britain's.[79]

Hanighen's columns in *The Progressive* acquire a particular significance for our purposes because of the high tribute that he paid Beard as the paramount intellectual guide for those looking to find the deep underlying causes of this war and all wars: "I've been raised in the texts of Professor Charles Beard who depicted the U.S. going to war in 1917 to 'run away' from the problems of populism and the New Freedom. And I recall the father of all our living historians warning us in 1939 of the danger of running away from the failures of the New Deal." The rule of history discovered by Beard could be formulated as follows: "When a nation evades its domestic problems by escape into foreign adventure, it puts off the day of internal reckoning."[80] Postponement, however, does not mean cancellation. Nemesis, the remorseless goddess of retribution in history against the sin of pride and arrogance, in the end claims her due.

The Progressive editor Rubin also hailed Beard as the country's leading historian and featured his work as an inspiration for the magazine.[81] Beard's *Amer-*

ican Spirit, The Republic: Conversations on Fundamentals, and *A Basic History of the United States* all received prominently placed and glowing reviews in *The Progressive.*[82] On September 2, 1943, Beard had communicated to Barnes his interest in writing for the magazine. The issue for the following February excitedly announced: *"Coming soon. . . .* Dr. Charles Beard (Dean of American Historians) on 'Irresponsible Government.'" The article would be exclusive to *The Progressive.*

Beard's article appeared as a front-page editorial in the March 6, 1944, issue. It took the form of a *j'accuse* denunciation of the United States government for its dereliction of duty to the American people: "an air of irresponsibility seems to hang thickly over the Capitol Hill as well as the White House."[83] It seemed to him that constitutional government had disappeared from American life. The manifold activities of the federal government, extending far beyond anything conceived in the minds of the Founding Fathers, now eluded the comprehension of the American people. He wondered if anyone apart from a tiny circle of elites had any effective say about the policies pursued by Washington. To illustrate his point, he cited the complete confusion and lack of transparency about what the government was doing during the war in Latin America. Despite his best efforts, he could not obtain clear answers either about U.S. policies in Latin America or the resources being employed to implement them. He thought the case of Latin America representative of American foreign policy generally. The American people had lost control of their government and its policies. He concluded: "I submit to candid readers the proposition that the methods and machinery of the legislative and executive departments at Washington need a drastic overhauling in the interest of safety for constitutional government."[84]

In its advertising, *The Progressive* celebrated the magazine's association with Beard. Editor Rubin wanted the world to know that the publication enjoyed Beard's esteem and favor. He was one of them. Full-scale publicity barrages preceded his interventions in the magazine. Moreover, Rubin repeatedly used Beard's name as a way of authenticating the magazine's intellectual seriousness.

On September 3, 1945, another article by Beard appeared in *The Progressive*, "Pearl Harbor: Challenge to the Republic." Once again, his chief concern had to do with the "issues of government by constitutional means, conduct of foreign affairs, realizing ideals of democracy."[85] The most serious problems facing the American people came from their own government. The lack of credible answers by Washington to questions about the American catastrophe at Pearl Harbor seemed to him one more instance of the government's failure to abide by its constitutional obligations. The Constitution called for the government to keep the American people honestly informed about its conduct. Yet, instead of acknowledging government responsibilities and failures at the highest level for December 7, 1941, the FDR administration had sought to blame isolationists for America's lack of preparedness. Government responsibility, the American people had been told, went no higher than the failures of the commanding military and naval officers in Hawaii. By this time, Beard was getting ready to publish the scalding *American Foreign Policy in the Making, 1932–1940*, a book for which his association with *The Progressive* had imparted a vital preliminary impulse.

CHAPTER 8

Beard Finds an Ally in Herbert Hoover

As Beard's disenchantment with FDR became acute and finally complete, he began to think about Herbert Hoover in more positive terms. He had long admired Hoover's genuinely neutral foreign policy, but had judged him to be a failed president because of his poor record in dealing with the Depression. A clearly identifiable turning point in his overall thinking about Hoover occurred in 1944, immediately following the publication of *A Basic History of the United States*. This change can be dated from August 30 of that year, when in a letter from Ray Lyman Wilbur, the chancellor of Stanford University, he received a mixed review of the book.

A former president of Stanford and the secretary of the interior in Herbert Hoover's administration, Wilbur professed admiration for Beard's scholarship, except for his account of the years 1929 to 1933. He had enjoyed a close relationship with Hoover for fifty years: "Knowing him, his views, and his work as I do, I feel that your presentation needs extensive revision." In comprehensive detail, he presented a critique of Beard's standard progressive liberal interpretation of the Hoover years as a classic example of orthodox Republican politics with no chance of coping effectively with the Depression. In fact, Wilbur countered, Hoover "was a far greater force in bringing the Republican Party to a progressive point of view than was Theodore Roosevelt or any of his predecessors. He made more practical although less theatrical revolution in that party to a social point of view than any President up to that time."[1]

Wilbur thought that many injustices had been done to Hoover through a smear campaign designed to celebrate FDR as the stainless champion of redemption for the American people. These two myths, about a feckless Hoover and a heroic Roosevelt, had become intertwined in the national mythology about the Depression.

Wilbur implored Beard to rise above the level of myth in his account: "I am sure, if you will now take the time to study his actions, his addresses, and his writings, that you will place them in a far different relation to progress and a great President than now appears in your otherwise admirable book."[2] Beard wrote back to him on October 3, 1944, and made it clear that he did intend to reconsider what he had said about Hoover. Lyman replied, "I am much pleased to note that if there is occasion to revise your history you plan to reconsider some of the points about which I wrote to you."[3] Indeed, Lyman's respectful remonstrance regarding *A Basic History of the United States* inaugurated for Beard a wholesale reevaluation of the former president. Republican domestic policies of any kind, including Hoover's, held no appeal for Beard. In any comparison with FDR, however, Beard now thought that Hoover came out ahead. With a frightening clarity, he saw that FDR's transfiguration of the American Empire into a hegemon of global aspirations posed an existential threat to the country and the world. Beard and Hoover soon would become allied in the revisionist campaign to expose FDR as an imperialist warmonger.

In 1945, Beard exchanged letters with former president Hoover, who had begun to consider writing a book about the origins of the Second World War. Before contacting Beard, Hoover wrote to Truman Smith, a U.S. Army infantry officer and well-regarded authority on Germany. Hoover had asked Smith, who had been a vehement critic of FDR's foreign policy, to assist him with the book project that he had in mind. Smith wanted to think about the offer and, in the meantime, to find out what other writers were doing on this subject: "I know of two persons working on similar books from our point of view: Charles Beard and Harry Elmer Barnes."[4] He would be having lunch with Beard and Charles A. Lindbergh the following week and would seek "to draw him out, without however disclosing your plans." Hoover thanked Smith and told him to take his time, "as I don't propose publication for some years, when many hidden things can be proved." Regarding Beard and Barnes, the former president noted, "If you find these gentlemen are of my mind on the history of the last seven years, I would like it very much if you could suggest they call on me some time. They were both New Dealers and severe critics of mine in years gone by—but we might be united on this issue."[5]

Smith gave Hoover a detailed report about his lunch in New Milford with Beard and Lindbergh. He had a message from Beard for the former president:

"He told me that he was most anxious to talk with you and that he would write you at once and ask for an appointment." Beard had shocked Smith with a comment about Pearl Harbor: "He made the astounding statement to me that he had seen a Navy message indicating that the Navy Department knew the location of the Japanese carrier fleet on the day before Pearl Harbour." Smith averred that Beard probably had received this intelligence from Admiral Husband Kimmel himself and then added, "If this statement of Dr. Beard is correct, I shall have to revise all previous ideas on this catastrophe. I have never heard in all my career in the War Department any fact anywhere so sensational as this." About Beard's current book project, which would be published the next year with the title *American Foreign Policy in the Making, 1932–1940: A Study in Responsibilities*, Smith reported, "He has done an immense amount of work," having studied every speech and note concerning FDR's policies toward the outside world. Barnes too, he learned from Beard, had compiled much research on the causes of the war, but from the angle of European diplomatic history: "I rather gather that he and Dr. Beard have an informal agreement to confine their research to separate fields."[6] There certainly would be ample room for the book that Hoover, from his uniquely privileged position as a former president, hoped to write, Smith encouragingly concluded.

When Hoover answered Smith two days later, he could report on a lunch of his own with Beard. "He is doing a good job," Hoover told Smith. Despite their past political disagreements, they had come to identical conclusions about the Ahab-like madness fueling American foreign policy under FDR and Truman. The country could not survive the ideas of these two leaders. Smith had been right to see no conflict between Hoover's projected book and those of Beard and Barnes. Their two books would be out within a year, whereas Hoover had "no intention of publication for five or ten years, as I want to get many disclosures of truth which will be slow."[7]

Hoover followed up his lunch with Beard by sending him some confidential memoranda: "For obvious reasons I ask you to keep my memoranda confidential until I am dead or until I sooner release them. They may serve someday as reminders of the blundering in our foreign roles."[8] Beard for his part had thoroughly enjoyed their lunch together, and he thanked Hoover profusely for the documents: "I have read with excited interest the memoranda which you were good enough to send to me." Of course he would keep the trust that Hoover had vested in him: "They are not only powerful documents. They were when drafted prophetic in a measure seldom encountered in history, at least the history of great and complicated public affairs." Beard added, "they are among the judgments of our time most worthy of standing among the permanent memorials of the Republic."[9]

Hoover had sent Beard five memoranda, the first addressed to unnamed cabinet members dated May 15, 1945, and the other four, dated May 30, 1945, to Truman himself in response to a request from the president. Like Beard, Hoover thought that the war had ended in a terrible disaster, not only for Europe and Japan, but in some crucial respects also for the United States. The former president said as much in his memorandum to the cabinet. He tallied the gains and losses in Europe for both sides in that conflict. Crushing the Axis Powers had come at an appalling cost in millions of deaths, physical destruction unparalleled in European history, and the economic ruin of victors and vanquished alike. The war had been Europe's greatest tragedy. On the plus side, a minor advantage had accrued to the non-communist Allied nations: "The British, French, Belgian, and Dutch Empires are safe for a while."[10] To judge from the dark book about the war that Hoover already had begun to write, it is difficult to believe that he composed these words about the preservation of the victorious empires in anything but an ironic vein.

Then, with a complete lack of irony, Hoover went on to observe in his memo to the cabinet that the Soviet Union now enjoyed the lushest fruits of victory. Stalin had added fifteen countries and two hundred million people to the Soviet empire. From the American perspective there might be reason to question just what kind of victory our leaders had fashioned for us, particularly in view of the economic consequences that Hoover foresaw. There would be no opportunity in Russia's socialist sphere of gigantic state monopolies for American free enterprise. Moreover, "those monopolies will compete with us in other markets."[11] Strategically, the war had resulted in the replacement of Nazi Germany's capitalist monopoly state by the communist monopoly state of the Soviet Union. Strictly as a business proposition the change did not turn out to be a positive development for American interests. It is easy to see why Beard greeted Hoover's memorandum to members of Truman's cabinet in words that came close to echoing the laudation he usually reserved for *The Federalist Papers*.

Hoover's messages to Truman contained many additional points to which Beard gave his vigorous assent. A fifty-five-minute meeting between Hoover and Truman had preceded the writing of the memoranda. Edgar Rickard, a mining engineer who in the First World War had assisted Hoover in his heroic relief work for the people of Belgium, wrote in his diary about the former president's low expectations for this meeting. Rickard, recalling Hoover's description of his conversation with the president, noted "that his invitation from Truman was strictly political, that Truman was strictly partisan and that he had no intention of asking any Republican to participate in his Administration." The invitation had been extended only to give "public impression that the (Truman) administration was broadminded and above party politics and animosity."[12] Yet Hoover had welcomed the opportunity to present his views about the war. In a May 30, 1945, cover letter to Truman, he listed the titles of the four memoranda: the European Food Organization, the Domestic Food Organization, the creation of a War Economic Council, and the Japanese Situation. He concluded the letter, "I am indeed indebted for your consideration and I trust you will command me in any further service."[13]

The memorandum of greatest interest to Beard concerned the Japanese situation. Hoover began by enumerating the essential American objectives in the Pacific War: restoring Manchuria to China, turning over all Japanese government property in China to the Chinese, unconditional surrender of the Japanese military, disarmament by Japan for at least a generation, fair trials for war criminals, and ceding certain Japanese islands to the Allies. "Beyond this point," he counseled President Truman, "there can be no American objectives that are worth the expenditure of 500,000 to 1,000,000 American lives."[14]

Insofar as possible, Hoover continued, the Japanese should be given opportunity to save face, and this best could be done by reassuring them "that the Allies have no desire to destroy either the Japanese people or their government or to interfere in the Japanese way of life; that it is our desire that the Japanese build up their prosperity and their contributions to the civilized world." There should be no thought of reparations and indemnities. As a means of inducing the Japanese to accept the postwar order, he even recommended that they be allowed to "retain Formosa and Korea as trustees under the world trustee system." The Japanese, Hoover made bold to say, are capable administrators, and the picture of Asia completely devoid of Japanese power and skill would not come into focus for him. Once the fighting had ended—and he thought that in view of their desperate military situation reasonable peace terms would be sufficient inducement for the Japanese to lay down their arms—we would want to cooperate with them in managing the affairs of Asia. By such an outcome, Hoover concluded, "we will save ourselves the impossible task of setting up a military or civil government in Japan with all its dangers of revolution and conflicts with our Allies."[15]

Truman thanked Hoover for his suggestions and promptly sent the memorandum on the Japanese situation to Joseph Grew, acting secretary of state in place of Edward R. Stettinius, who was in San Francisco chairing the U.S. delegation at the United Nations Conference on International Organization. Few people in America knew Japan as well as Grew did. Appointed by Hoover in 1932 as U.S. ambassador to Japan, he had served in Tokyo until the attack on Pearl Harbor. His influential memoir, *Ten Years in Japan*, had appeared in 1944. Grew was part of a committee, appointed by the president, seeking an alternative to using the atomic bomb as a means of ending the war in the Pacific. Could a way be found to end that war without sacrificing the million American lives that an invasion of the home islands could be expected to claim? He, therefore, read Hoover's memorandum with close attention and produced a detailed response to it.

Ever respectful toward the man who had appointed him to his diplomatic post in Japan, Grew praised Hoover's general assessment of the situation in the Pacific. He began, "Mr. Hoover's conception of American objectives in relation to the war with Japan . . . falls substantially within the framework of policies with regard to the post-defeat treatment of Japan that are now being formulated by the Department of State in connection with other interested departments." Regarding the removal of the Japanese military caste, he emphatically agreed with the former president, and then added, "there must be also a program of intelligent reeducation." Grew agreed that American peace terms should be presented in a way that would enable the Japanese to save face, particularly on "the non-molestation of the person of the present emperor and the preservation of the institution of the throne."[16] He claimed that any effort to try the emperor as a war criminal or to abolish his office would enrage the Japanese.

Grew found one major mistake in the Hoover memorandum: "Mr. Hoover has assumed that the task of setting up a military government in Japan would be 'an impossible one.'" Speaking for the State Department, Grew countered, "We conceive of the war against Japan as having two components, the military war and the intellectual war." He meant that after winning the war on the battlefield, America "must pursue the victory into the field of ideas." The second victory would constitute the real one with the creation "on the part of the Japanese of a progressive and cooperative attitude." The desired outcome could be achieved only through a military occupation and a military government. Grew came back to the word "cooperative" in his closing statement. He described the main aim of America's postwar policy as the promotion of "democratic tendencies within Japan and cooperative attitudes in Japan's relations with the rest of the world."[17]

In reading Hoover's memorandum on Japan, Beard found it to be especially powerful and prophetic because of its minimalism regarding the American postwar role in that country. Hoover had wanted America to return as quickly as possible, once the military caste had been neutralized, to a collaborative relationship with Japan. Washington, he said in the memorandum, should "demonstrate that America is not in the war for any purpose but to establish order in the world."[18] It should not be an American order. An order emanating from Washington would produce the kind of problems that in one combination or another had destroyed every empire known to history. Military occupation and military government suggested to Hoover, as it did to Beard, an imperialist agenda.

The other three memoranda that Hoover had written to Truman on May 30, 1945, and then six months later had sent to Beard, dealt mainly with famine relief. They, too, possessed very high historical importance. The war had produced conditions threatening the extinction of entire populations. Current efforts to relieve these conditions Hoover judged to be the work of amateurs with no understanding of the problems they were facing. Based on his varied experiences as the organizer of humanitarian food relief at the time of the First World War, Hoover did have a robust understanding of what needed to be done in the famine-stricken Europe of 1945. He lamented, "When the War Food organization was set up in 1941–42 the experience of every nation in the last war was discarded or ignored."[19] Moreover, in a typical denigration of FDR's New Deal liberalism, he complained how the whole system of famine relief had been undermined by the fatal economic principles of costly bureaucratic inefficiency. Hoover advised Truman that "the food muddle" could be overcome only by creating a War Economic Council made up of the president, key cabinet officers, and—most important—three members without portfolio. About these last three, Hoover recommended, they "should be men of public experience who would devote their entire time to consideration of economic policies and the methods of their execution."[20]

In addition to the precious memoranda that Hoover had sent to Beard, the former president also put him in touch with diverse individuals whom he knew would be of assistance in his research on *American Foreign Policy in the Making, 1932–1940*. Potentially the most helpful of them would be William R. Castle Jr., a Japan expert who had served Hoover as his undersecretary of state and later had become a member of the National Committee of America First. On January 3, 1946, Hoover had a portion of a letter by Castle sent to Beard: "Of course, anything I can tell Mr. Beard I shall be delighted to let him have. . . . I think from the questions you say Mr. Beard has in mind that I might be able really to be of use."[21] Castle's personal archive contained a huge store of documents. In the immediate aftermath of Pearl Harbor, Hoover had asked him to preserve every record pertaining to the background of the war with Japan. He also had kept a detailed diary during this period.

Castle would be an invaluable contact for Beard, who especially would want to learn from him how he viewed Henry L. Stimson, his immediate superior in the State Department during the Hoover years. Beard viewed Stimson with profound distaste as a classic Washington operator with no loyalty to anyone but himself. In his November 17, 1945, letter to Hoover, Beard declared that he had discovered "a fundamental distinction between your own position and that of Mr. Stimson."[22] The part of the world where this distinction mattered the most was in the Pacific, where Stimson's grandiose schemes for American domination would find their ideal patron in FDR.

On the very day when Hoover first communicated with Beard, he was working on his so-called war book, identified also by him and his staff as the "magnum opus." About the draft of that book dated November 15, 1945, his biographer, George H. Nash noted, "Hoover wrote scathingly of the contrast between President Roosevelt's idealistic 'Four Freedoms' proclamation of 1941 and the actual condition of the postwar world."[23] He wondered now how anyone ever could have believed a word of such transparent nonsense. Hoover had been writing in this vein throughout the war, and not only for the war book. His address at the 1944 Republican convention had inspired an admirer, James A. Healy, to exclaim, "It was a grand exposition of things as they are with our beloved country today after eleven years on a dead-end street at whose end the ever-disregarded stop sign read 'WAR.'"[24]

Hoover's speech had reminded Healy of a 1935 book by former *Nation* magazine journalist Mauritz A. Hallgren, *The Gay Reformer: Profits Before Plenty Under Franklin D. Roosevelt*. Hallgren had charged that FDR's foreign policy consisted essentially of a program to guard the capitalist state and its worldwide interests. This foreign policy served a second purpose, as a diversion from the increasingly evident failure of the New Deal to solve the problems of the Depression. Hallgren's second point anticipated, according to Healy, Beard's critique in 1939 of FDR in *Giddy Minds and Foreign Quarrels*. Beard had made the clearest and sharpest case yet about the ulterior motives of the foreign policy that had led to America's tragic intervention in the Second World War. Healy cited other writings by Beard that had exposed the truth of what FDR had been doing in contradiction to his administration's gauzy rhetoric about keeping American boys safe at home by a professedly wholehearted and loftily patriotic adherence to the country's neutrality legislation.

Replying to Healy from Stanford University, where he had established the Hoover Institution on War, Revolution, and Peace, the former president gratefully thanked him and added a note regarding the recent Republican gathering in Chicago: "The outcome of the convention with [Thomas E.] Dewey and [John W.] Bricker should give confidence of victory. But it will be a stiff fight in which we all need to do everything we possibly can for we have a country to save."[25] It was in this spirit of extreme anxiousness for America over the threatening consequences of the war that he had begun to write the magnum opus. This book would not be published until 2011. Nash recounts the book's tortuous path to completion and publication in his 105-page-long editor's introduction, including its 432 footnotes, to *Freedom Betrayed*.

It is a simple matter to understand Hoover's keen interest in Beard, really their interest in each other, at the war's end. They shared radically revisionist conceptions regarding that conflict's origin and outcome. With the publication of *Freedom Betrayed* Hoover belatedly took his place as the most thoroughgoing of all the revisionist historians, including Beard. Certainly, this book consisted of the most voluminously detailed denunciation of the real motives behind American intervention in the Second World War. It looms over the landscape of World War II historiography as an epic account of FDR's mendacities and deceptions in leading the United States into the war, in some respects surpassing in depth even Beard's attacks, while at the same time remaining in essential harmony with them and their most important conclusions. Hoover in 1945 had sent Beard his memoranda as a sign of trust and faith in the most famous historian publicly identified, by *Giddy Minds and Foreign Quarrels* and numerous other writings, with the anti-interventionist position. The next year, with the publication of *American Foreign Policy in the Making, 1932–1940*, Beard would dramatically enlarge his reputation as the paramount voice of World War II revisionism. Hoover, on the other hand, held back his book, for reasons carefully documented and explained by Nash in his mammoth editor's introduction to *Freedom Betrayed*.

Hoover had begun to write the war book as a memoir, a genre that permitted him to be completely open about his true opinion concerning the causes and the perpetrators of the 1939–1945 conflict. He would publish several other memoirs about the varied aspects of his career, but the war book had a special purpose: to expose the misconduct of FDR and how "the Japanese war was deliberately provoked."[26] The book started out as a prosecutor's brief against FDR and also, with equal implacability, Churchill. Such was the book's character at the time Hoover made his overture to Beard, who in his subsequent discussion with the former president no doubt felt thrilled to find a revisionist ally so prestigious and well placed. At some point after Beard's death in 1948, however, Hoover decided to turn the book into a memoir/history, a change that thrust upon him the responsibility, he believed, for greater scholarly exactitude and objectivity. Nash explained what then happened to the war book: "Bit by bit it took on the appearance of a doctoral dissertation."[27] He nevertheless contended that even in the finished draft Hoover never denied the book's underlying revisionist point of view.

One of the many virtues of Nash's achievement as the editor of *Freedom Betrayed* was his decision to include in the appendix of the book some specimens of its earlier versions when the "good work" of Beard, as Hoover himself had put it, had an important claim on him. Hoover cited Beard in "A Note on Current Historians of This Period." He divided these scholars into two categories: apologists and revisionists. "The apologies," he wrote, "are mostly from civilians who participated in these policies or from professional historians either associated with the Roosevelt and Truman administrations, or . . . later were supplied with records in support of the two regimes."[28] The intellectual dishonesty of such historians would inevitably be exposed in the winnowing process of time, he predicted. Among the revisionists, Beard held a place of primacy. Hoover listed books of his own in this category as well: *Addresses on the American Road* (1933–1953, seven volumes) and *Memoirs* (1952, volume three).

In the earlier versions of *Freedom Betrayed*, Hoover had attacked Churchill and FDR without quarter. Beard's influence had given color and character to some of his historical judgments. In the Beardian manner, he expressed a low opinion of Churchill as a leader. Hoover had become acquainted with Churchill at Versailles after the First World War. "Intellectual integrity," he wrote sometime around 1950, "was not Churchill's strong point."[29] He portrayed the British leader as an utterly ruthless man and a genius-caliber demagogue, far inferior in human qualities to the two British political figures with whom he was favorably compared by a generation still marinated in Allied wartime propaganda: Stanley Baldwin and one of the most unfairly maligned men of the twentieth century, Neville Chamberlain. In Hoover's opinion, the endlessly denounced Munich agreement of 1938, the arch symbol in conventional thinking of Britain's appeasement of Hitler, had to be understood not as the result of Chamberlain's dithering and cowardice, but as a compromise made necessary by the criminal follies of the Versailles Peace Treaty. Most of all, Hoover faulted Churchill's assumption that Hitler alone posed a mortal threat to democracy when, in fact, "Stalin's Red Imperialism represented an equally dynamic aggressive force."[30]

As a historian, Churchill had to be granted all praise for style and force of language, Hoover conceded. He had read *The Gathering Storm*, the first volume in Churchill's history of the Second World War, and had found it to be a brilliantly written work: "But his personal prejudices, his constant rationalization after the events with persistent evasion of facts and realities are much short of objective truth."[31] Churchill had filled the book, Hoover added, with grotesque misrepresentations of his own positions and those of his adversaries at home and abroad. The fire and drama of his presentation could not compensate for the flaws that made *The Gathering Storm* almost wholly unreliable as a work of history. To Hoover, it would later seem like a travesty for this self-serving book and its sequels to be counted as a justification for Churchill's

Nobel Prize for Literature in 1953. Oft-told myths continued to eclipse the real history of the Second World War, Hoover complained. As Beard had, he wondered if the American people would ever be permitted to acquire an adult understanding of what truly had happened in "the good war."

Nash repeatedly underscored the Hoover vendetta against FDR. About the 1947 draft, the editor exclaimed, "Once again one notices the polemical fury of the early versions of the Magnum Opus."[32] Referring to yet another passage on FDR in an early draft of *Freedom Betrayed*, Nash pointed out "Hoover's relentless, prosecutorial fervor."[33] About still another passage, he noted how "Hoover summed up, with remarkable candor and intensity, his revisionist indictment of the Roosevelt-Truman foreign policy record."[34] These are perfectly apt descriptions of Hoover's vitriolic style in dealing with FDR. In the version of the manuscript published as *Freedom Betrayed*, he would tone down his language. Castigation without remedy would become relatively mild reproof amidst the clutter of scholarly footnotes.

Prominent traces from the meeting of minds that he had with Beard in the mid-1940s, however, can be seen in the book's early versions, where with words not very different from those used by the poet Robinson Jeffers in his still shocking work, *The Double Axe* (1948), Hoover damned FDR as a monstrous villain. *The Double Axe*, a poetic invocation of the heated anti-FDR arguments that Hoover was making, revealed a similar degree of Beardian influence. Indeed, Beard had provided the main historical arguments for all revisionist interpretations of the Second World War. The critical fate of Jeffers's brutally revisionist poetry may have given Hoover pause about setting his similarly minded book before the public.

A world-renowned writer at the peak of his fame when *The Double Axe* appeared, Jeffers in this book angrily defended the isolationist cause, with historical references that echoed to the last detail Beard's core contentions on the subject. He certainly admired Beard and in 1946 voted to elect him to the American Academy of Arts and Letters.[35] Although there is no record of any personal contact between them, they knew of each other's work. In *America in Midpassage* (1939), the Beards cited Jeffers as one of the important poets of the 1930s. The personal library of Jeffers included at least one Beard book, the 1923 edition of *The History of the American People*, a textbook written with William C. Bagley.[36] Beard's withering castigation of FDR, *President Roosevelt and the Coming of the War: A Study in Appearances and Realities*, came out in February of 1948, and Jeffers's *Double Axe* in July of that year. It is highly probable that Jeffers, a voracious reader, would have been familiar with a work by the most famous historian in America about the identical subject of his own book of anti-war poetry.

The Double Axe is one of the angriest books ever written. In the long narrative title poem he imagines a dead American soldier, killed in the Pacific campaign, coming back to life and seeking revenge for his unnecessary death and all the other soldiers destroyed by the war: "it is the lies, it is the lies, it is the dirty / lies, / War-peddlers lies and the people's imbecility / That raked me out of the grave."[37] He wants to see hanged in a public execution all those, such as his father, who had justified the war: "You'll be there, old man, right along with the President / And his paid mouths; and the radio-shouters, the writers / the world planners, the heavy bishops / The England-lovers, the little poets and college profes- /sors, / The seducers of boys, the pimps of death, the pimps."[38] The soldier condemns American involvement in both world wars: "—twice now we've taken / An ordinary European kennel-quarrel / And blown it into a world-war, and swollen our fate / Fat with dropsical victories."[39] The story ends in madness and violence, with the soldier killing his father and the young lover of his mother, who then kills herself.

In the collection's other poems, Jeffers continued to advance a Beardian isolationist message, as in "Teheran" where he asks about the leaders meeting at the Allied conference of 1943, "—but who are these little smiling attendants / On a world's agony, meeting in Teheran to plot against / whom what future?"[40] He observes in that same poem, "How rapidly civilization coarsens and decays; its better / qualities, foresight, humaneness, disinterested / Respect for truth, die first; its worst will be the last." In "Historical Choice," written in 1943, he lamented the way in which the American people had been deceived "By fraud and fear, by our public fools and a loved leader's / ambition, / To meddle in the fever dreams of decaying Europe." Within two years, Jeffers predicted, Americans would have "to take up the corrupting burden and curse of / victory. We shall have to hold half the earth; we shall be sick with / self-disgust, / And hated by friend and foe, and hold half the earth—/ or let it go, and go down with it." Such a burden Americans had not been fitted by nature or history to shoulder: "We are not like Romans and Britons—/ natural world-rulers, / Bullies by instinct—but we have to bear it. Who has kissed / Fate on the mouth, and blown out the lamp—must / lie with her."[41]

Beard might have been able to identify with the image Jeffers fashioned for himself in "So Many Blood Lakes." Jeffers lamented his power to foresee the consequences of America's victories in the world wars. We had vanquished Europe and reduced it to dependence on us. Now would follow the realization of America's fondest hopes: "We have enjoyed fine dreams; we have dreamed of unify- / ing the world; we are unifying it—against us."[42] Well should we be invulnerably armed forever more: "Now guard the beaches, / watch the north, trust not the dawns. Probe every / cloud. / Build power. Fortress America may yet for a long time / stand, between the east and the west, like By- / zantium." Sure that his judgments and predictions would be proved right, Jeffers nevertheless agreed with a hypothetical critic: "—As for me: laugh at me. I agree with you. It is a foolish / business to see the future and screech at it. One should watch and not speak." In the book's preface, he recognized that his political cause had been lost in advance. Isolationism deserved an encore, "But it is futile at present to argue these matters."[43]

The Double Axe had other aims as well, philosophical and artistic, but the entirety of it met with obliterating critical disaster. Jeffers's book offended nearly everyone who wrote about it. A premier writer with Random House, Jeffers had published with that company for more than fifteen years. On this occasion, however, his publisher declared in a prefatory note: "In all fairness to that constantly interdependent relationship and in complete candor, Random House feels compelled to go on record with its disagreement over some of the political views pronounced by the poet in this volume."[44] Reviewers found *The Double Axe* to be distasteful, unpatriotic, and defamatory. Twenty-five years later, during the national crisis generated by the Vietnam War, *The Double Axe* was reissued with an introduction celebrating the author's strengths as a poet, but still lamenting his rhetorical excesses that earlier had incensed readers. Noting that *The Double Axe* had been published at the peak of America's self-esteem following World War II, William Everson observed in his foreword to the 1977 edition, "Into this bland, complacent atmosphere Jeffers' book dropped like a bomb (a stink bomb, many thought)."[45]

It would be interesting to know if Hoover had read *The Double Axe*. It stands to reason that he at least knew about Jeffers. They had mutual friends. Foremost among them was Charlotte Kellogg. A prominent writer and social activist at the center of the Jeffers' social circle in Carmel, California, she held his poetry in the highest regard and thought of him as a mentor for her own writing. She had participated in Hoover's relief work during the First World War. Her husband, the Stanford University zoologist Vernon Kellogg, had been Hoover's chief assistant in Belgium. After the Nazi and Soviet invasion of Poland, Hoover helped to establish the Commission for Polish Relief, where Charlotte Kellogg served on the organization's board of directors and worked as a tireless fundraiser. She would have been a likely link between Hoover and Jeffers.[46]

Another mutual friend, the financier Eugene Meyer, had been a key member of the Hoover administration. Hoover had made him the chairman of the board of governors of the Federal Reserve System, and then the chief of the Reconstruction Finance Corporation, a government lending agency created as part of the president's economic recovery program. Meyer later bought the

Washington Post and adopted a strong anti–New Deal editorial line. He and Hoover remained close friends. Meyer and his wife, Agnes, also befriended Jeffers. On a poetry reading tour in 1941, Jeffers and his wife, Una, stayed with the Meyers as their guests when they came to Washington. Following a reading that Jeffers gave at the Library of Congress, Meyer held a reception at his home attended by numerous dignitaries. A *Washington Post* headline the next day announced the brilliant success of the reading.[47] Hoover and Jeffers also would have been united in their opposition to FDR's interventionist foreign policy. In any case, the Beardian pessimism of Jeffers's poem runs like a swift-moving current throughout the early drafts of *Freedom Betrayed*, carrying the narrative to its despairing conclusions about the overarching tragedy of the Second World War.

Hoover's portrait of FDR, his bête noire, bears a strong likeness to the image of the President in *The Double Axe*. Who else could be blamed for the 385,575 dead and missing or the 225,000 permanently incapacitated American victims of this treacherously confected war?[48] On none of the revisionist accusations made by Hoult Gore, the dead soldier who's come back to life in "The Double Axe," would Hoover in the late 1940s and early 1950s have voiced any opposition whatsoever, nor would Beard have found anything wrong with the poem's political analysis.

Roosevelt wanted the war, Hoover believed. Stimulating hate, raising fears, and smearing opponents of the war, he bore personal responsibility for America's intervention in 1941. He could have avoided the war: "Neither Hitler, Mussolini, nor Tojo wanted war with the United States or to invade the Western Hemisphere; they tried to evade war with us, even with the great provocation of undeclared war from Roosevelt."[49] Not even the most remote possibility existed for these powers to invade the United States. The strongest of them, Nazi Germany, had failed to invade Britain across the twenty-five-mile-wide English Channel. What prospect of success was there for Hitler's forces to come four thousand miles across the Atlantic Ocean to lay siege to New York City, or for Tojo's to come six thousand miles in the Pacific for an attack on Los Angeles? The Japanese had not followed up their hit-and-run raid on Pearl Harbor with an attack on the West Coast because they never had any intention of doing so. Yet between 1939 and 1941 the Roosevelt administration and its servants in the media relentlessly conjured up fantastic stories about nefarious Axis plots to bring down the Republic, when nothing of the kind existed, or could exist, in objective reality. Hoover lamented that modern governments possessed the power to make their peoples believe anything, no matter how ludicrous.

FDR's provocative acts against Japan led directly to America's involvement in the war. For his Asia policy, he would have much to answer for, Hoover felt certain, before the bar of history. It was not necessary for him in July of 1941 to impose the economic sanctions on Japan that meant war in every way "except the shooting." Hoover asserted, "no nation of dignity would submit to such a provocation—least of all, a nation in which hari-kiri in presence of failure was a part of its religion." FDR could have made peace in September by accepting Prime Minister Fumimaro Konoye's offers of concessions. Both the British and the American ambassadors to Japan had urged FDR to respond in good faith to that initiative, but he chose to ignore it. Hoover could only conclude, "Any objective review of the years 1938 to 1941, with the cold light of history even so far exposed, will demonstrate clearly that it was Mr. Roosevelt who got the United States into the war. He deliberately provoked war upon us by the Japanese."[50]

The only question in Hoover's mind about FDR concerned his real motives. Why did he want war? To answer this question, Hoover began by repeating the argument that Beard had advanced in *Giddy Minds and Foreign Quarrels*. FDR had begun to emphasize foreign affairs as a way of covering up the failure of the New Deal to restore the economic health of the nation: "for that purpose he entangled himself in world power politics as a diversion of public mind." Other factors motivated him as well: "he led a people into an unnecessary and monstrous catastrophe by consuming egotism, by evil intrigues, by intellectual dishonesty, by lies and by violations of the Constitution." FDR's dishonesty could be documented in "his scores of assurances over the years to the American people that he would never send her sons to war while he was driving to that end."[51]

The president's arrogance figured in Hoover's tally of the reasons why America went to war in 1941. Following the Nazi invasion of the Soviet Union in June of that year, the United States had become a de facto ally of Stalin, one of the most dreadful dictators in all human history. Hoover judged Stalin and Hitler to be equally depraved as human beings. Both of their political systems lacked a moral basis to the same degree of zero. FDR, by his alliance with Stalin, had touched pitch. Hoover declared, "It is to be supposed that a statesman of status capable of leading the American people would inform himself of the history, the beliefs, the policies, and the character of leaders with whom he chose to make partners." As for Stalin's character, its manifest deformities had been paraded "in headlines over years recounting the thousands of even his own colleagues whom he had put to death in order to further his own ambitions."[52] A war said to be for freedom could not be fought shoulder-to-shoulder with Stalin. For people prepared to take in evidence, FDR's obscene embrace of the Soviet dictator destroyed completely the official rationale for America's entry into the war.

Arrogance in the Oval Office led to many other disasters as well. FDR gave himself credit for possessing the capacity to control and, for the purposes of advancing a global democratic agenda, to domesticate Stalin. Stalin had much greater success domesticating FDR as a means of advancing the Soviet agenda. FDR's defenders had put forward the thesis that "had he lived he could have beguiled Stalin into the ways of rectitude. But beguilement had already failed at Teheran and Yalta," where the Soviet Union had secured agreements guaranteeing the communist enslavement of millions of people. Hoover thought that FDR's ego had driven him to fantasize about presiding as a "war president."[53] All the great presidents had waged wars, and FDR wanted one. In the grip of his egotistical day dreams, he had lost his faculty to apprehend reality or to follow the dictates of prudence, most conspicuously in his thoroughly botched relations with Stalin.

In confronting such "malignant and malign figures" as Stalin and Hitler, the president should have had the wisdom to let the two maniacs fight it out among themselves to exhaustion.[54] That is what Hoover would have done and kept America out of the European madness. FDR could have done the same: "No greater opportunity for lasting peace ever came to a President, and he muffed it." He wondered what had been accomplished by American intervention, other than replacing German power with Soviet power. "Amidst words of freedom and democracy," the Baltic states and Eastern Europe had been sacrificed to Stalin.[55] The Allies had puffed themselves up with pride over their firm resolve to avoid the mistakes made by Chamberlain at Munich. They had learned their lesson and never would practice anything as craven as appeasement. Hoover, however, thought that the Allies in their dealings with Stalin had done something far worse. Chamberlain had presided over the partition of one country, Czechoslovakia, but the Allies, as Hoover had noted in one of the memoranda that he had shared with Beard, had sold into the icy darkness of communist slavery all of fifteen countries with their two hundred million citizens.

Hoover asserted that the moral costs of the Second World War, on the Allied side, had been severely underreported. In the triumphalist glow of the postwar period, comparatively little was heard about the ways in which the American people had been brutalized and their sensibility as a nation coarsened. "Who would have believed," he asked in 1947, "America without public protest, would drop an atomic bomb on helpless civilians whose government had already offered surrender?"[56] In subsequent versions of *Freedom Betrayed*, he continued to express moral revulsion about Hiroshima and Nagasaki. In 1953, he wrote that one of the most appalling crimes of American statesmanship during the war was "Truman's immoral decision to drop the atomic bomb on the Japanese. Not only had Japan been repeatedly suing for peace but it was the act of unparalleled brutality in all American history. It will forever weigh heavily on the American conscience."[57]

It was as if, with the decision to drop the bomb, a deadly poison had been injected into America's bloodstream. In the same passages where Hoover discussed his shock and horror over Hiroshima and Nagasaki, he cited statistical evidence for rising rates of crime, divorce, illegitimacy, teenage delinquency and imprisonment, government corruption, black market activity, gambling, and the general extravagance and decadence of American society. All these woes had a prime mover: "The first of the moral costs of the war," Hoover affirmed, "was the total failure of our second crusade for independence of nations and freedom of men."[58] The dolorous chain of events had originated in FDR's initial lie about the war's purpose as a quest for independence and freedom. The military skill and valor of American soldiers and sailors had won a magnificent victory, but its fruits would be of wax. Lies beget more lies, and so on until the end.

Hoover could not say which national disgrace bothered him more: the government's methodical lying and inability to tell the truth except very occasionally and only for an evil end, or the eager gullibility of the American people in uncritically believing their leaders. Hoover effused that he had grown up in a wonderful country, but something terrible had happened to it. Perhaps the tragedy for America had begun even before the First World War, but Washington's intervention in that conflict marked a definite moral decline for the nation. He often described America's interventions in the two world wars as a twin catastrophe, reserving for Hiroshima and Nagasaki, however, the crucial place, in the early drafts of *Freedom Betrayed*, for his reflections on how a nation takes its life in its hands by transgressing moral laws.

Even in the book's final version, Hoover could think of nothing worse in the Second World War than Hiroshima and Nagasaki. Although at various times he had expressed outrage over Nazi attacks on Jews, the Holocaust did not come up for discussion in *Freedom Betrayed*. In chapter 83, "Aftermath of Dropping the Atomic Bomb on Japan," he began, "The use of the atomic bomb on Japan has continued to stir the American conscience as well as the conscience of thinking people elsewhere in the world."[59] He then quoted from statements by Major General Curtis LeMay, Admiral Chester Nimitz, and Admiral William D. Leahy to the effect that there had been no military necessity for using the atomic bombs. He cited a comment by Maurice Hankey, a baron who had served in the British war cabinet: "If the enemy had solved the atomic problem and used the bomb first, its employment would have been included in the allied list of war crimes, and those who took the decision or who prepared and used the bomb would have been condemned and hanged."[60] Hoover obviously agreed with Hankey, but in the discreet mood of his last years refrained from using his own words to make the point.

Even with the rhetorical tamping down in the final draft, Hoover could not let the book go. He died in 1964 without ever seeing it in print. In his editor's introduction, Nash asked why Hoover had held back. Recruiting a staff of secretarial assistants, a full-time research assistant, and expert readers, Hoover had devoted more than twenty years to this project. He also had spent an enormous amount of money on research and page proofs for the manuscript's various editions in the years before the introduction of photocopying. The book had become his obsession. Yet the space reserved for it alongside Hoover's other publications would not be filled in his lifetime.

In speculating about Hoover's hesitancy to present *Freedom Betrayed* to the world, Nash mentioned the former president's complicated relationship with the revisionist movement. Intellectually, he remained a revisionist to the last. Nash accurately described the final and published version of the book as "an unabashed, revisionist reexamination of the entire war—and a sweeping indictment of the 'lost statesmanship' of Franklin Roosevelt." Politically, however, Hoover's aims had changed over the years. As a result, the tenor of the book became more modulated. Moreover, his literary advisers counseled him to strive for objectivity and restraint. Many good reasons existed for his taking their advice, such as the need to consider the constantly expanding literature on the war and to write with as much accuracy as possible before going to print. Nash, though, identified the most compelling reason of all for Hoover's inveterate delaying when he wrote, "his very title, *Freedom Betrayed*, hinted at gross misjudgments, even perfidy, in high places." He was, after all, "writing a relentlessly revisionist history of Franklin Roosevelt's foreign policy and . . . he could expect to be attacked by the targets of his criticism." To a man "yearning for esteem in the eyes of the American people" and looking "to enhance his growing prestige as an avuncular elder statesman," it would have been counterproductive to burst onto the scene with a book so discordantly at odds with the zeitgeist of Eisenhower's America.[61]

The risks of revisionist publishing in these years have been set forth in a minor classic, James J. Martin's *Revisionist Viewpoints: Essays in a Dissident Historical Tradition*. A rapt admirer of Beard and admired in turn by William Appleman Williams, Martin led a precarious existence as an academic and publisher of his own books.[62] He dedicated this one to Harry Elmer Barnes, his mentor in World War II revisionism, but the chief inspiration for the book came from Jonathan Swift's treatise, "The Art of Political Lying."[63] Swift defined political lying as "the art of convincing the people of salutary falsehoods for some good end." Wars in particular require artists of this kind, but all politics, he satirically observed, consisted of such activity in varying degrees of professional skill. No government could survive for a day without lying. All political parties would go out of existence the second that they started telling the unvarnished truth. Mixed lies are best, the ones with just enough factual content to confuse and to mislead their intended victims, the people. All in all, Swift concluded, the best political weapon against a lie is another lie. Happy are the party and the land, "having regulated their affairs upon lies of their own invention."[64]

Martin took wing from the perch provided by Swift and observed that some governments possess an unusual competence, approaching the level of genius, for artistic political lying. The United States, he so much as suggested, deserves its own national gallery just for the major masterpieces of its greatest political liars. It would take more than an alcove and possibly as much as the space afforded by several floors in a major building to display the artwork of FDR in this category. Martin would have enjoyed *Freedom Betrayed*, particularly its appendices, if he had lived long enough to read it.

In a chapter called "Revisionism and the Cold War, 1946–1966: Some Comments on Its Origins and Consequences," Martin explained what happened to historians in the grip of Hoover-like ideas about the Second World War. He began by pointing out that at war's end "the world was on the verge of the next stage in what Charles A. Beard was to describe as 'perpetual war for perpetual peace.'" Imperceptibly, Allied propaganda about the war's origins and aims became a vulgate version of these events and the unchallengeable basis for nearly all historical interpretations of them. A handful of revisionists, inspired chiefly by Beard, begged to differ. Martin explained the continuities between the revisionists of World War I and World War II: they "sought to balance the propaganda accounts of the coming of these conflicts, by demonstrating through emphasis on the part left off the record by all the belligerents, the mixed nature of the problem and the universal fact of responsibility on the part of victors and defeated alike."[65] Revisionists in both wars had sought to counter the salutary falsehoods that the wartime leaders, in the pursuit of their good ends, had professed as truth.

Conditions following the First World War had favored revisionism. In the early 1920s the revisionist interpretation of that war won widespread acceptance and held the field throughout the interwar period. Martin argued that the Second World War produced an almost entirely different reaction among the historians, mainly because of the immediately following Cold War. Truth becomes the first casualty in every war. This is how he put the dilemma of post–World War II revisionism: "Coming on the scene after the successful had already written the first version, revisionists undertook their work with such a hazard as one of the expectable risks of their literary occupation." There would be no welcome for revisionists this time. Indeed, as Martin attested, partly based on his own personal experience, "revisionism enjoyed a maximum lack of welcome everywhere. It undermined the entire fabric of postwar politics."[66]

Hoover evidently wanted to trim back his revisionism to a point where the risks of such an unpopular viewpoint would be checked as much as possible, but never succeeded in finding a golden mean between the truth and a palatable truth. His frustration over this failure must have caused him intense suffering. Beard, on the other hand, went ahead with the work that he and Hoover had talked about over lunch in November of 1945. Beard's final two books would be an inspiration to all revisionists, but they also touched off the most furious critical and personal assault ever unleashed against an American historian.

CHAPTER 9

Attacking "the Saint"

Throughout the war, Beard painstakingly collected documents for a book that would be published in 1946 under the title *American Foreign Policy in the Making, 1932–1940: A Study in Responsibilities*. He would need research help to complete it. Complaining of weakness, he asked his friend Edwin Montefiore Borchard to find a research assistant for him. Borchard recruited two Yale graduate students, noting with more than a whiff of condescension, "They are both women, but seem to be strong-minded and competent."[1] The two students were Suzanna Small and Louise Powellson. Beard found their assistance invaluable and repeatedly informed Borchard of his complete satisfaction with their work.

Borchard also made his personal newspaper clipping file available to Beard, and then, after reviewing the book manuscript, negotiated a publishing contract for him with Yale University Press. To Borchard, Beard communicated the reason why he felt called to pour the last bit of his health and strength into this project: "But your ancient friend up here in the eternal hills is still foolish enough to believe that it is worthwhile to search for the utmost truth about great matters and set down the findings, come what may."[2] Trying to figure out Roosevelt also kept him at his task: "The more I read over his reiterated pledges up to the last bitter day, I wonder and wonder what kind of man FD was, above all why he was not ready at Pearl Harbor. He baffles me more than any character I have met in history."³ Beard's search for the key to the president's character would consume the rest of his life.

With his health failing, Beard complained to Harry Elmer Barnes on September 2, 1945, about a dwindling capacity for work. He had much work to do, "but my strength is limited and ebbs." He continued to make progress on his book about U.S. foreign policy for the years 1932 to 1940, but would have to restrict himself to the American side of the story, leaving Barnes and others the larger task of telling how European events and diplomacy affected Washington. Essentially, he would be relating a tale of FDR's duplicity, "how the peace psychology was built up while other things were being done by the administration." By "other things" Beard meant that in public FDR spoke as if he wanted peace while relentlessly working to involve the country in war. In Beard's estimation, the war had not turned out as expected, and its unlooked-for consequences would keep the country in permanent crisis. There would be much digging for historians to do to find out "how we got this way."⁴

Two weeks later, Beard repeated to Barnes the concerns he had about his health: "At seventy-one I must work against time and hence try to limit my scope to things I can manage, for which I have materials, leaving the larger problems to others like yourself."⁵ More than ever, he needed to conserve his energies for writing about the subject that interested him most: "the *way in which foreign affairs have been conducted* for more than ten years, for that has a bearing on what is now ahead of us in this respect." Beard would not be covering Pearl Harbor in this book. Nevertheless, Pearl Harbor was on his mind in the September 15, 1945, letter that he wrote to Barnes. About the December 7, 1941, Japanese attack, Beard explained, "I do not claim to know the secret of the mystery, but I do not think that F.D. was surprised."⁶ Whether the president had precise foreknowledge of this attack or had set forces in motion that would make it inevitable, Beard did not say, but it was one or the other and most likely both. To Barnes he wrote again, on September 26: "The Army and Navy reports on Pearl Harbor, which I have read and re-read are astounding documents. Whitewashing is now out of the question."⁷

Beard worked relentlessly in late 1945 and early 1946 to finish *American Foreign Policy in the Making, 1932–1940*. He continued to complain about his lack of stamina. In a letter to Barnes on December 13,1945, he wrote, "Damn it at seventy-one I have to whip up my old body every morning to get started and there is no telling how long I can do that, for how long will the 'I' have will power left?" Beard would have to submit final copy by February 1. He then explained to Barnes his objectives in the book: "In this volume, I am reviewing only foreign policy as announced by President Roosevelt to the American people from year to year. I am not going into foreign affairs, what he did and what he said privately and secretly to his officials and other governments."[8] In short, Beard would be confining himself to the president's public pronouncements about foreign policy. He hoped that Barnes and other scholars would fill in the larger picture.

Others noticed Beard's waning energies at this time. Kenneth Colegrove, his longtime colleague in the American Political Science Association, commented on December 29, 1945, in response to a query about Beard's suitability as a convocation speaker, "He used to be one of our most remarkable speakers before academic audiences. But in later years he is not as effective as formerly. And I would have some doubts regarding his effectiveness before an audience of several thousand."[9] The person making the query directly had asked about Beard's physical condition. Colegrove thought it best, in view of Beard's sharp decline, to look elsewhere for a suitable speaker.

On February 9, 1946, Beard excitedly wrote in reply to a letter that his friend Oswald Garrison Villard had sent him three days earlier. Villard's long letter had included a lapidating judgment of President Truman: "Such incredible ignorance of what is happening is really beyond belief. The truth is, we have a highly militaristic, lower middle-class, back-slapping American legionnaire in the White House who has given free rein to the militarists, and we are being made over under our eyes into a tremendous military and imperialistic Power—exactly what we went to war with Germany to prevent their becoming!" He had lamented, "It is very hard, dear friend, to keep one's spirit up in the face of all this utter destruction of the finest American traditions and ideals."[10] Very much on the bright side, Villard eagerly anticipated the publication of Beard's new book. He had heard about it in a conversation with Hoover, who also greatly looked forward to Beard's revelations.

Beard, in his reply to Villard, came right to his main point: "I suppose you have seen the Welles diary. It is an atom bomb."[11] Sumner Welles, a career diplomat with the same Groton-Harvard academic pedigree possessed by FDR, had served as the undersecretary of state from 1937 to 1943. What Beard found particularly fascinating about Welles he had explained in an earlier letter to Borchard: "The Welles diary on the Atlantic Conference is the most amazing document yet. How the mighty one bamboozled the dear public in his press conferences: 'No commitments'—just a military alliance with Churchill to 'police the world' for years—FDR's own words."[12]

Welles had told this story in a book that appeared in 1944, *The Time for Decision*. A passionate advocate of FDR's internationalist program and one of its key architects, Welles used this book as a weapon against isolationists. While German Nazis, Italian Fascists, and Japanese militarists stood poised to wage a war against civilization, "Senate committees were indulging in long-drawn-out sessions to prove that the country had been plunged into the first [*sic*] World War solely because of the Machiavellian machinations of the arms manufacturers and of the international bankers." When Welles wrote about the country's neutrality laws, he put the adjective in quotation marks, sorrowfully pronouncing, "This legislation was a humiliating admission of the extent of America's delusion."[13] With what supernal fortitude and sagacity had the president overcome isolationist foes, who, no less than the Japanese for Pearl Harbor, would live in infamy for their obstructionism in preventing the United States from ensuring its own military security and playing its proper role in the world as a champion of democracy.

In Beard's letters to Villard and Borchard, he expressed the most interest in what Welles had to say about the Atlantic Charter. He repeatedly in his letters and books would come back to this document as an unequaled source of insight into the real purpose of the Second World War on the Allied side. A joint pronouncement by the governments of Britain and the United States, the Atlantic Charter would serve as the moral foundation of the war effort, which FDR and Churchill obviously were planning at their August 1941 meeting, nearly four months before Pearl Harbor. Welles wrote the draft text of the document and participated in the discussions about it. The president had told him of "the need for a general agreement between the two governments, while the United States was still at peace and the European war was still in its earliest stages, covering the major bases upon which a new world structure should be set up when peace finally came."[14] Welles encouraged his readers to suppose that the promises in the Atlantic Charter would be honored and transformed into real policies and practices, but Beard could not free himself from the suspicion that an imperialist future awaited the postwar world, no matter which side won.

Even before the publication of *American Foreign Policy in the Making, 1932–1940*, Beard knew that by putting FDR in the dock for his lies and deceptions he would be exposing himself to public execration. On February 18, 1946, he wrote to Barnes: "I fear that I couldn't be elected dogcatcher at the New Milford town meeting." Unlike most of the isolationists who from 1939 to 1941 had shared his view of the Second World War as, at bottom, an imperialist undertaking by both sides, Beard did not change his mind after Pearl Harbor, nor would he ever. To him the incipient Cold War between the United States and the Soviet Union also derived its deepest meaning, in keeping with all wars, from the basic struggle to control territories, markets, and resources. The immiscible coalition between the United States and the Soviet Union could not be understood in terms of shared values or ideals, but it did make sense as a means for thwarting the imperialist ambitions of Germany and Japan. Beard doubted very much that promotion of democracy and freedom had anything to do with the real objectives of the United States during the Second World War or the Cold War, except as a rhetorical device for concealing the real intentions of the Roosevelt and Truman administrations. Commenting on the deteriorating relations between the United States and the Soviet Union, he signed off his February 18, 1946, letter to Barnes by coupling the Cold War with the struggle against Nazi Germany and Imperial Japan: "The grand farce roars ahead to its thunderous dénouement."[15]

Carolyn Woods Eisenberg's brilliant analysis of U.S. postwar policy, *Drawing the Line: The American Decision to Divide Germany, 1944–1949*, confirmed the intuitions of Beard about the fundamental aims of American leaders in these years. She observed, "State Department planners brought to their work a perspective akin to that of the industrialists, bankers, and Wall Street lawyers who had flooded into the Roosevelt administration when the war began." Their planning "presumed a global economic system conducive to corporate expansion," an ambition Beard would have learned from the reporting of *The Progressive* had been uppermost in the minds of American leaders throughout the war. Because the German economy would be vital to the renewal of European capitalism, conservative American business leaders figured prominently in the military government imposed on postwar Germany. The sedulous promotion of the free enterprise system completely overshadowed the de-Nazification program, said in the beginning by American leaders to be their supreme aim. Throughout Germany's integration into the American-dominated system of international capitalism, the national security bureaucracies retained the upper hand in guiding the process and continued "in their own closed system of thought, immune from criticism and barely accountable to the American public." National security in their parlance meant obeisance to "the aspirations of the large internationally oriented corporations and banks."[16] Beard filled his postwar correspondence with just this kind of argumentation about the economic motives of American leaders.

American Foreign Policy in the Making, 1932–1940 appeared in the summer of 1946. Beard began with a critique of Thomas A. Bailey's *Woodrow Wilson and the Great Betrayal* (1945), which had exalted the president as the incarnation of democratic idealism and had condemned his adversaries in the Senate who had opposed the Versailles Treaty and the League of Nations, thus making another war inevitable. Evil isolationist senators bore the ultimate responsibility for the sequence of tragic events that led to the Second World War. Beard dismissed Bailey's thesis as a total perversion of what had happened between the two wars. As for the First World War, the publication of the secret treaties destroyed the Allied arguments about why they had fought. In these documents they never thought to mention any fine phrases about the blessings of democracy or peace or disarmament, but it did occur to them to stake out imperialist claims, the most important of which Wilson at Versailles took care to leave undisturbed. The president thereby made the most eloquent of all possible pronouncements about his devotion to the sanctity of the British Empire. Not the "treason" of the United States Senate, but the iniquities and crimes committed at the Paris Peace Conference accounted for the international tensions that in turn produced the Second World War.

FDR first appears in Beard's book in his role as James Cox's running mate in the 1920 presidential campaign. An ardent Wilsonian, he spoke fervently in that campaign for the League of Nations. Beard had no doubt that in thus speaking he had revealed his true convictions. Crushed in 1920 and then again in 1924, the Democrats thereafter abandoned their internationalism. Al Smith barely mentioned foreign relations in 1928. Beard interpreted the change as a return to pre-Wilson Democratic politics, when the party "had fiercely opposed Republican imperialism as an insidious betrayal of the American Republic, rejected 'the white man's burden' as hypocritical cant, denounced 'the greedy commercialism' of the Republican policy, and spurned the idea that the United States must resort to imperialism in order to demonstrate its 'maturity,' its 'responsibility to the world,' or its superior virtues as a nation." Imperialism he defined as the "employment of the engines of government and diplomacy to acquire territories, protectorates, and/or spheres of influence occupied usually by other races or peoples, and to promote industrial, trade, and investment opportunities in competition with other imperialist powers or on occasion in collaboration with them when there is mutuality of interests or perils."[17]

Running for the presidency in 1932, FDR showed every sign of having had a change of heart and during that campaign spoke as an isolationist. He repudiated the League of Nations that year, and with the nation tormented by the Great Depression focused his campaign entirely on domestic issues. After winning forty-two of forty-eight states in the election, he adhered to an isolationist policy throughout his first administration, even exhibiting, according to Beard, hostility to the Wilsonian internationalist thesis. Instead he sought to advance a program of economic nationalism while proclaiming a foreign policy of strict neutrality, disinterestedness, impartiality, and nonparticipation in European and Asian quarrels. He continued the foreign policy of Herbert Hoover, who had opposed economic sanctions against Japan for its aggressive actions in Manchuria and China. Hoover reasoned that, reprehensible as the Japanese incursions were, they did not imperil the freedom and well-being of the American people, the only guideline that seemed to him truly essential for the country's foreign policy. Beard, now a strong admirer of Hoover, wrote: "If he was tempted, amid the tightening coils of the depression to free himself from their iron grip by resorting to a war and bringing on the inevitable economic boom that would have made brighter his prospects for re-election, Mr. Hoover made not even an open gesture in that direction."[18]

Beard thought that in his foreign policy FDR had played a double game with the American people before his first administration. To illustrate his contention about Roosevelt's true purposes, Beard cited a five-hour January 9, 1933, meeting between the president-elect and longtime Republican insider Henry L. Stimson, who had served as Hoover's secretary of state. Beard viewed him as an imperialist of the Theodore Roosevelt–Henry Cabot Lodge–Alfred Mahan–Albert Beveridge type. The president-elect and Stimson had discussed the Far Eastern situation. Stimson, who had been restrained by Hoover, long had advocated a policy of U.S. opposition to Japanese expansion in Asia, in complete opposition to the traditional American foreign policy principles of noninterference that had held the field until the Spanish-American War of 1898 and the even greater innovations of Wilson in 1917. In a letter written to Hoover on November 17, 1945, Beard bluntly had asserted: "I also have evidence, convincing to me, that Mr. Stimson was playing his own game behind your back."[19] Beard concluded in *American Foreign Policy in the Making*, "the Stimson Doctrine meant in 1933 precisely what it proved to be when tried out in 1941."[20] By then, in an appointment that for Beard all but formally announced the administration's hostility toward American neutrality, Stimson had joined FDR's cabinet as secretary of war.

Later developments confirmed for Beard that the seed of the Stimson Doctrine had been planted in FDR's mind even before he had taken office. Political exigencies stemming from the disillusionment of the American people with Wilsonian idealism and their passionate devotion to neutrality made it necessary for Roosevelt to conceal his real aims, but the Second World War inevitably followed from the implementation of the Stimson Doctrine. Postwar disillusionment had given the isolationists, or the traditionalists, as Beard insisted on calling them, their opportunity for a comeback, which Pearl Harbor thwarted, seemingly for all time. For Beard, Stimson embodied the enormous staying power of the internationalist thesis in American foreign policy, which called for the country to become involved in every issue affecting the national interest.

Beard wondered what people meant by the term "national interest." In 1934 he had written *The Idea of National Interest: An Analytical Study in American Foreign Policy*. Though often marked down as one of Beard's most turgid books, it comprises the summa of his philosophical inquiries into the assumptions of American foreign policy.[21] This brilliantly prophetic book also serves as a primer for understanding the deep historical background of the revisionist movement as a whole and Beard's two great postwar critiques of FDR's foreign policy, *American Foreign Policy in the Making, 1932–1940* and *President Roosevelt and the Coming of the War, 1941*.

In *The Idea of National Interest* Beard had explained how with regard to policies adopted and wars fought the national interest always had to do with the requirements of economic elites. There could be no serious debate over the question, "For whose benefit is diplomacy carried on and whose will is to determine the policy and exercise the greatest control."[22] From the inception of the Industrial Revolution in the eighteenth century, the competition between capitalist countries for raw materials and markets more and more had become the motor force behind diplomacy, foreign policy, and war. American history perfectly illustrated the connections between economics and international relations. The United States Constitution had come into being at the behest of powerful economic groups whose aggressive energies fueled the country's westward expansion for the first hundred years of its history and thereafter its acquisition of overseas empire in the Pacific and the Caribbean. In making such pronouncements, he did no more than advance an interpretation of historical events familiar to students of the Beard canon. To safeguard the American stake abroad, the full power of the national government, including its military interventions, had been employed throughout American history.

To a degree not found in his earlier books, Beard stressed the independent role that government could play in national and international affairs. The immense federal bureaucracies did not simply obey orders from Wall Street, although its concerns always had to be taken with the utmost seriousness and sympathy in Washington as the ineluctable consequence of an economically conditioned political process made to seem more natural than nature itself through long and uncontested usage. The economics of political campaigns in America conferred upon the financial elite privileges of access and influence enjoyed by no other constituency in like degree. Yet Beard saw the government as "an interpreter of national interest on its own account as well as the promoter and executor of interpretations provided by private parties." Though divided and disjointed, the government did become a unitary body in time of war, when the office of the presidency assumed supreme power. Beard claimed as well that the navy, an immense economic interest with its own prerogatives and skilled in attaching itself to other dominant interests, exerted "a powerful independent influence on opinions and decisions pertaining to the interpretation of national interest."[23]

Bringing *The Idea of National Interest* up to the year of its publication, Beard could not find in 1934 any fundamental foreign policy change made by FDR. "The formula," as Beard called it, remained in effect: using foreign policy as a means of protecting and advancing elite economic interests. The Wall Street crash of 1929 and the subsequent depression, however, had called into question the entire economic and foreign policy status quo. Beard himself found wanting even on the level of technical competence, let alone that of social justice, the wisdom of the bankers and financiers whose instruments of capital exports and foreign lending had produced the most ruinous depression in the history of economic crises.

With astonishing foresight, Beard understood how the financial people would ultimately and best benefit from investing abroad. They would receive bribes in the form of huge commissions to export American industries abroad. He did not comprehend how the American people collectively would prosper from such exports. Building up with American resources great industries abroad to compete with American industries and workers seemed like a poor proposition, unless the goal of such transactions had nothing to do with national well-being and everything to do with the engorgement of the bankers and financiers and their various satellites in politics and the media. From what could be determined about the patterns of high finance in the 1920s and 1930s, he could see nothing to stop the eventual outsourcing of as much of the American economy as the tycoons might require for the satisfaction of their epic lust for profit. The peace and stability of the world counted for nothing next to the manifold exigencies of the acquisition process. Turgidly written, as Beard's critics like to say, the book may have been, but it deserves to be placed alongside *The German Ideology* of Karl Marx and Friedrich Engels as a forecast of disaster for the globalized economy under capitalism. Beard's contribution to this literature took the form of a warning about what globalization would mean to American workers.

The United States continued to embrace an imperialist foreign policy because to do so served the purposes of the elites who ran the country. Beard argued in the conclusion of *The Idea of National Interest* that the failure of this foreign policy should lead Americans to reconsider the question of empire. The profits derived from American investments abroad never got much farther than Wall Street. American farmers and workers did not see any of these revenues and, in fact, suffered economically from them as their jobs and livelihoods began to disappear. Beard hoped that FDR would adhere to the campaign promise he had made about the need to focus on the plight of the depression-ridden American people. To make good on such a promise the president would have to abandon the imperialism "which supports outward thrusts of American economic power and sustains them by diplomacy and arms." Even in 1934, though, Beard worried about FDR's program for naval construction. His endlessly repeated concerns about domestic recovery through economic action at home had not "suppressed or even curtailed the particular interests that throve by the pursuit of *Machtpolitik*."[24] Beard feared that a response in kind from Japanese imperialists would be the prelude to a new world conflagration.

Twelve years later, Beard presented *American Foreign Policy in the Making, 1932–1940* as an illustration of his thesis in *The Idea of National Interest*. Only an economic interpretation could explain FDR's foreign policy in those years. The president had employed elaborate rhetorical deceptions to conceal his true purposes, which always concerned his support for and collusion with the British Empire as the best means of securing a global market for American commerce and finance. Beard condemned the Roosevelt administration for its deceit. It had lied to the American people, pretending to be neutral while taking sides in the worsening quarrels of Asia and Europe. By his actual policies Roosevelt had made war inevitable for the United States.

At a moment in history when FDR's popularity, one year after his death, stood at an all-time high, Beard had him play the role of a villain, with a script appropriated from Machiavelli and Shakespeare. Secretive, scheming, and contemptuous of an American people too stupid or ignorant to know what was good for them, the president gave a brilliant performance as the faithful executor of their will to preserve the peace. Beard put the performance in the context of the president's earlier career. He observed, "Mr. Roosevelt was not unacquainted with imperialism and its works." He had served as the assistant secretary to the navy from 1913 to 1920 and helped to supervise military operations against Mexico, Dominican Republic, and Haiti in what Beard called "the classical imperialist style."[25] He had a long record of achievements in extending U.S. power in the Caribbean. Moreover, he had been a true believer in Wilson's crusade to make the world safe for democracy, a term synonymous in the Wilsonian lexicon with global capitalism. For a man of FDR's stamp there always would be something forced, unnatural, and temporary about a neutralist American foreign policy committing the nation to minding its own affairs at home.

Through the first Roosevelt administration and into his second, foreign affairs received little attention from him as the Depression raged. When the president did speak about the outside world, he took care to express himself in the popular language of strict neutrality. The United States, he said, had learned the lesson that George Washington had tried to teach about the dan-

gers of entangling alliances and the need for Americans to focus on the culti-
vation of republican virtue in their own country. No more was heard from
him about the League of Nations, except to lament its tragic flaws and those
of the Versailles Treaty. He continued to hew to the isolationist line throughout 1934, 1935, and 1936. The president supported and adhered to the country's neutrality laws. Self-defense literally meant self-defense, not some
metaphorical code phrase for planetary guard duty.

Roosevelt's isolationist mask slipped out of place in 1937. On October 5 of
that year in Chicago he gave what became known as his "quarantine" speech,
"in which he discarded the doctrine of neutrality for the United States and espoused the idea of collective security."[26] Beard interpreted this speech as a
reflection of the president's true mind. It was his road-to-war speech. While
still claiming to be neutral, he sought to align the United States with nations
alleged to be peace loving—first and foremost that paragon of peaceful coex-
istence and democratic self-determination for all peoples, the British Empire.
Beard wondered how FDR could claim to be neutral and at the same time join
with one group of nations against another group. Egregious as the actions of
Germany, Italy, and Japan might be, the only question for a foreign policy based
on neutrality should concern the actual threat they posed to the United States.
Beard declared that these three countries did not threaten the United States
at all in 1937. Yet after the quarantine speech, American foreign policy ceased
to be neutral and despite the president's claims to the contrary became overtly
partisan. Beard estimated that in addition to the large anti-war bloc in Congress, fully three-quarters of the American people—convinced of the folly of
U.S. intervention in the Great War—supported the neutrality legislation that
had been adopted during the mid-1930s.

The raucous reaction in Washington and nationally to the quarantine
speech alerted Roosevelt to the need for a cautious strategy, which he implemented with eloquent obfuscations about how his every move sprang from a
devotion to neutrality and lessened the likelihood of war. On January 28, 1938,
FDR called for an increase in naval armaments, a move that "was taken by watch-
ful critics to be an indication of a purpose to underwrite or implement the
quarantine principle, by augmenting the navy and making provisions for an
immense army."[27] Critics of the president asked why world peace and security
had become such a concern in Washington when nothing at all in the U.S. Constitution could be found to justify it. In that document, only American peace
and security mattered. Beard agreed with the critics, that the naval appropriations of 1938 had as their aim the pursuit of power politics in Asia. In his opinion, Roosevelt's rearmament policy would have the same effect as Wilson's
preparedness program twenty years earlier and lead the country into war.

In a January 4, 1939, address to Congress, the president claimed that no break had occurred in American foreign policy. He attacked his opponents as uninformed malcontents pedaling "bunk" about him. True, he wanted to adjust the neutrality laws in ways that would facilitate resistance to those wanton nations intent upon aggression, but only to preserve peace and stability. The isolationists for whom Beard spoke countered that they had heard this argument twenty years earlier. Wilson had made similar professions just before calling the nation to arms in 1917: "the isolationists felt certain that Executive manipulation of foreign relations, coupled with the munitions traffic, was mainly responsible for getting the United States into the World War in 1917."[28] To dilute the neutrality laws in any way, despite the arguments made by the proponents of change, would signal a retracing of the steps that led to American intervention in 1917, precisely what the war profiteers and international bankers again wanted. The Senate proved obdurate, and in the summer of 1939 voted down the reform legislation. The munitions embargo remained in force. When war broke out that September, FDR proclaimed America's neutrality and his desire to keep American soldiers out of the conflict.

Three weeks later, however, the president asked Congress to repeal the embargo on munitions. He presented his proposal as a measure that would protect neutrality and improve the country's chances of staying out of the war. As Beard had done in magazine articles and in testimony before Congress, he ridiculed the president's logic as transparent nonsense and quoted with approval the many rejoinders to him made by isolationist senators. Perhaps he relished most of all the criticisms of North Dakota's Gerald P. Nye, who implored his colleagues not to make America "the silent partner of the British Empire."[29] An American president once more was talking about making the world safe for democracy against lawless aggression, but Nye predicted that Roosevelt's crusade would have the same result as Wilson's. Hiram Johnson of California argued that with arms embargo repeal, the United States would be half-in and half-out of the war. It would only be a matter of time before we were in all the way.

FDR intervened in the debate on arms embargo repeal. In an October 26, 1939, radio broadcast, he repeated his resolve to keep American boys out of European wars. To say otherwise would be "a shameless and dishonest fake." He held American neutrality as a sacred trust and had no intention of involving the country in war. This time he prevailed. Congress voted for the repeal of the arms embargo, and FDR signed the measure on November 4, 1939. The new neutrality law permitted sale of munitions and put the full economic, agricultural, and industrial resources of the United States at the disposal of the Allies. Thus, Beard observed, had the history of 1914–1917 been repeated in a drastically foreshortened form. All through the presidential campaign of 1940, FDR continued to preach the virtues of neutrality and peace. Yet the military budget kept climbing. "Our defenses must be invulnerable, our security absolute," the president said.[30]

The appointment, in June, of Stimson to be secretary of war and Frank Knox secretary of the navy—two orthodox Republicans known to be in favor of aiding the Allies—set the stage for the final act of the tragedy, as the isolationists viewed the national scene. The Republican candidate for president in 1940, Wendell Willkie, did not differ with Roosevelt on foreign policy issues. During the campaign, both candidates defended the measure to exchange overage American destroyers for British bases in the Western Hemisphere. Beard wrote that the transfer of war craft to a belligerent nation constituted an act of war, making the kind of argument that FDR in the campaign disparaged as a "deliberate or unwitting falsification of fact." The president said that he had no secret treaty or obligation of any kind. "Your boys are not going to be sent into any foreign wars," he promised.[31] The sole purpose of our policy involved shielding the United States from war, and he boasted in the campaign about having kept the United States at peace for nearly eight years. On the other hand, as he mentioned on December 29 in a fireside chat following his victory, our own future security depended on the outcome of the fight between Britain and Germany.

Beard prepared himself for the attacks that he knew would be coming in response to *American Foreign Policy in the Making, 1932–1940*. In thanking Barnes for his praise of the book, he wrote, "Your letter cheers me up and braces me for the coming work of the hatchet men."[32] The following week he responded to Borchard's praise for the book and hopes that it would make a great hit: "No such luck. I am the one likely to be hit good and hard by the hatchet men."[33] Even readers not necessarily disposed to criticize him on political grounds had expressed disappointment with the book over his refusal to provide any conclusions. To Barnes he defended himself against this charge: "In fact, given the record, conclusions may well be left to the readers—so I think at least, and you seem to agree heartily."[34] As he would write in a letter some months later to Barnes, "Maybe you and I are all alone and just plain nuts."[35]

The book did receive rough handling by some reviewers, but to Beard's surprise not sensationally so. Moreover, it garnered some very good reviews, such as Oswald Garrison Villard's for *The Progressive*. Villard had written to him on August 14: "I am reading your book with unadulterated joy."[36] His review appeared that October. The former editor of *The Nation* and now regular columnist for *The Progressive* thought, "The evidence here is overwhelming and cannot be denied." He noted how Beard's critics were faulting him for ignoring the significance of Hitler's rise and the threatening global context in which FDR had been forced to act. To such critics Villard replied, "These are specious pleas in avoidance of the fundamental truth." The fundamental truth was the one illuminated in Beard's book: FDR had lied, the members of his administration had lied, the government from top to bottom had lied. Washington was a city of liars. The American people could not trust what their leaders told them. Villard concluded, "As long as the history of these years is honestly written, Dr. Beard's book will be foremost among the authorities of this period. It is a great and patriotic achievement which adds no little to the luster that his pen has already earned."[37] That same month, Villard wrote to Beard to praise "the tremendous cumulative effect" of his book, particularly regarding "the overwhelming proof you have brought out that Roosevelt was playing the no-war game right up to Pearl Harbor. I shall look with eagerness to your next volume when you really will blow him to pieces."[38]

Beard fully understood the risks he was taking in *American Foreign Policy in the Making, 1932–1940*. He informed Villard on January 24, 1947: "Touch the hem of the sacred garment, and you are condemned to perdition with lightning speed." It pleased him, though, to observe how "the present guardians of the garment are tearing one another's hair out over who's to divide it, and keep the fragments." Some very revealing memoirs by administration officials were then appearing in print: "A few more of the kind and only madmen will insist on this case of immaculate conception." Far from being immaculately conceived and implemented, FDR's foreign policy failed to rise to the level of even ordinary political morality: "The professors who tore me to shreds took the only line: 'Of course he lied to the dumb American people, but it was for the glory of God and the salvation of souls.'"[39] On April 15, he repeated to Villard: "the President was definitely seeking a war (an attack) in the Atlantic."[40] When that failed, he went fishing in the Pacific and came home with his objective achieved.

Despite the hostile treatment that *American Foreign Policy in the Making, 1932–1940* had received in some quarters, Beard wanted to caution Barnes about exaggerating the vendetta against the book. Barnes had written a manifesto on the blackout in the historical profession in which he claimed how revisionist historians, like Beard, no longer could find higher-end commercial presses to publish their work. Beard thought such a claim much too extreme, at least in his own case. He had been given "a brush off" by the *American Political Science Review* and could cite other instances of dismissive or hostile treatment, but this was not even close to the whole story about the critical fortunes of his work. Moreover, it could not be said as a historical fact that the better commercial publishers actively had sought to censor Beard. He wrote to

Barnes on May 23, 1947: "I suspect you are right—but *I do not know that none* of my old commercial publishers would take my book." At the time that Beard had thought about sending out *American Foreign Policy in the Making, 1932–1940*, he continued, "I knew better than to waste time with them and went direct to the Yale Press, on good advice." He judged Barnes to be correct in principle "in thinking that no big New York publisher will touch anything that does not laud the Saint."[41] Still, one had to keep well within the facts of the case.

The facts would be enough to expose Saint Roosevelt, Beard believed. The Roosevelt priesthood of historians led by Samuel Eliot Morison, Thomas Bailey, and Arthur M. Schlesinger Jr. would not be able to protect his reputation from the crushing evidence against him. The justifications for the war had been either lies or deceptions consisting of expatiations on, at most, secondary considerations in the thinking of the war party. To the category of outright lies he consigned the old favorite in Washington, the struggle for democracy. No one in a position of decisive power there knew the first thing about democracy or wanted to, designed and committed as the system had been from birth to the eternal renewal of oligarchy.

The deceptions rivaled for imaginativeness and appeal those perpetrated by Woodrow Wilson, who, unlike Roosevelt, had the misfortune to live too long for the good of his historical reputation. FDR had passed from the scene at a moment most propitious for his elevation to sainthood, before any of the consequences of his lies and deceptions had materialized. The American fight in the Second World War had been presented by Washington as a struggle for freedom and against tyranny, but this description did not meet the test of truth in advertising. Beyond the stated goals the real one beckoned. According to Beard, the Roosevelt administration only had one ultimate rationale: "to deceive the idiots in order to save their souls and prepare the new heavenly world order for them."[42] The new-world order was in truth the old-world order with some streamlining of the ways in which the rich ruled the poor, a leitmotif in world history that attracted the attention of relatively few American historians.

The corruption of the history profession deeply depressed Beard. He complained to Barnes about Bailey's new book, *Man in the Street: The Impact of American Public Opinion on Foreign Policy*, as an exercise in propaganda for Roosevelt: "Bailey beats Schlesinger a million miles in justifying the lie as a holy instrument of national policy, and ends on sob stuff about how the people must be educated by the professors who do the justifying." The lies as well as the deceptions perpetrated by Roosevelt and documented in *American Foreign Policy in the Making, 1932–1940* became transformed in Bailey's telling into master strokes of statesmanship, according to Beard. He continued in the same letter to Barnes: "I may be young and foolish, but I believe that a lot of sensible people want all the truth they can get about how we were governed in the Roosevelt era." No historian could get the whole truth, but he felt certain that "enough can be got to put us on our guard."[43]

On July 10, 1947, Beard wrote to Barnes: "It is good news that several other books on the great mythology are coming along." He had in mind mainly reports about the soon-to-be-published memoirs by members of the Roosevelt administration. *The Memoirs of Cordell Hull* would appear in 1948. Based on what he was reading in magazines about the forthcoming book by Roosevelt's long-time secretary of state, Beard thought that it would reveal the nastiness and divided counsels within the administration over the war. He had read, too, about the reluctance of Henry Stimson to place his papers in the Library of Congress, "for fear Congress might open them up!"[44] Stimson's *On Active Service in Peace and War* also would appear in 1948, but in his letter to Barnes the previous year Beard thought that nothing could save this inveterate warmonger or his boss from an obliterating judgment before the bar of history. To Villard, Beard wrote on September 8: "I think that the State Department is now our prize madhouse, with all the inmates bawling and gesticulating about hourly as they beat the wind."[45]

Meanwhile, Beard continued to work on a sequel to *American Foreign Policy in the Making, 1932–1940*. He informed Barnes on October 21: "Galley proofs of the Roosevelt book went to the printers yesterday. It will be out early next year."[46] *President Roosevelt and the Coming of the War, 1941: A Study in Appearances and Realities* would be published in February 1948. About this forthcoming book he apologized to Barnes the next month for its limitations. Writing from the Pine Crest Inn in Tryon, North Carolina, where he and Mary had gone to escape the winter cold of New England, he complained about his health: "I am wrestling with a cough and a cold, perhaps God's punishment for my lack of understanding." The FDR book, dealing only with the year 1941, would barely hint at the full enormity of the president's foreign policy. We really needed a book about Tehran, Cairo, Yalta, and Quebec, but, Beard wrote, "I fear that I haven't strength enough to tackle it." He still had to check the new book's page proofs: "After that, well, I can't say."[47]

Gabriel Kolko's *The Politics of War: The World and United States Foreign Policy, 1943–1945* was the "really needed" book that Beard had in mind. In doing research on the history of Tehran, Cairo, Yalta, Quebec, and indeed the entire record of American wartime diplomacy, Kolko found that American leadership had been motivated first and foremost by "an elaborate and highly sophisticated set of economic and political goals it defined as urgently desirable war aims." These economic and political goals connected the discrete events of the war, including and above all the conferences mentioned by Beard to Barnes. The United States, Kolko concluded, consciously and unswervingly sought throughout the war to create "a transformed world capitalist economy."[48] The plan called for America to step forward at war's end to run the new world system with assistance from "allies" more truthfully understood as adjutants. Ultimate responsibility for world order, however, would reside in Washington. As Beard had foretold, the postwar period would be characterized by a dynamic of revolution and counter-revolution, with the United States, in its Sisyphean task as the guardian of a world status quo seething with inequities and injustices, caught in a never-ending spiral of war and terrorism.

On January 6, 1948, Beard predicted to Barnes that with the publication of his new book, "the axemen will begin their bloody work on me. But the myth of the savior is fading!"[49] Not only FDR's reputation, but that of the entire political system in Washington had been destroyed. Surely people now could see how that war-dependent system worked. The war, not the New Deal, had saved American capitalism. War alone would continue to save it. "Can Truman get a Pearl Harbor in the Mediterranean or Palestine?" He would variously describe Truman as "the necktie salesman from Missouri" and "the Mad Hatter," the haberdasher president.[50] Beard clearly anticipated the alarm of C. Wright Mills in *The Power Elite* over "the great structural shift of modern American capitalism toward a permanent war economy."[51]

Something like a perpetual Pearl Harbor frame of mind would be necessary to maintain the economic status quo, what Beard habitually would come to think of as "permanent war for permanent peace." The system could survive in no other way, as first the Depression and then the Second World War had demonstrated. Existential imperatives brought the political parties to a broad consensus about foreign policy. Regarding America's role in the world, it really did not matter in 1948 if the Democratic or Republican candidate won, although he thought Dewey marginally better than Truman. The war economy would drive America's foreign policy in either case. Kinetic energy could be trusted to propel the country into one war after another. Even in their disputes over domestic affairs, it seemed to Beard that the parties steered well clear of any suggestion that might raise questions about serious change. Contentious a figure though FDR continued to be, whether people realized it or not, he was the real father of the country that America had become.

A week later Beard thanked Barnes for sending him a news report: "I missed Bemis's statement in the *Herald Tribune* about FDR's telling him in May 1939 that [the] United States would go into the war against Hitler."[52] Unfortunately, he could not use the story for the book, which had already gone to press. Samuel Flagg Bemis, the Pulitzer Prize–winning Sterling Professor of Diplomatic

History and Inter-American Relations at Yale University, he included among "the vestal virgins who guard the sacred tradition" in American historiography. According to them, the United States played a uniformly heroic role in the world as the foremost champion of liberty. Bemis, who had worked for the United States government during the Second World War, supported the country's postwar internationalist foreign policy. Beard only felt repugnance for the liberal defenders of FDR: "The dirty reviews that I get from the sweet 'liberals' incline me to the opinion that they are about as liberal as Hitler." He asked Merle Curti on January 19, "What about the new idea of Court Historiographers— . . . S. E. Morison and Wm. Langer—favored by the overlords they serve? Am I just old and Victorian in questioning new and enlightened methods?"[53]

In February 1948, Yale University Press published *President Roosevelt and the Coming of the War, 1941: A Study in Appearances and Realities*. Beard's 600-page arraignment of FDR began with a lengthy compilation, under the heading of appearances, of the president's statements in the 1930s and early 1940s about his devotion to neutrality. He had settled all along on an imperialistic policy in collusion with the British Empire. The book traced the steps that he took to execute this plan, beginning with the lend-lease program of late 1940 and culminating in the attack on Pearl Harbor, which Beard believed President Roosevelt, Secretary of State Cordell Hull, and Secretary of War Henry Stimson dearly wanted as the best means of involving the United States in the war.

The Roosevelt administration initially had sought to provoke war with Hitler in the Atlantic. Giving Britain warcraft and munitions in exchange for bases in the Western Hemisphere under lend-lease terms violated the letter and spirit of America's neutrality laws. FDR assured the country in 1941, as he had done previously, how he had in mind only the protection, strengthening, and furtherance of American neutrality. It struck Beard as a sign of the president's charm, charisma, and eloquence that anyone, let alone the majorities in Congress and in the country who went along with the manifestly unneutral lend-lease plan for the promotion of neutrality, would have believed such a specious argument. As Karl Mundt, a Republican representative from South Dakota, approvingly quoted by Beard, expressed his opposition to lend-lease: "We are asked to violate all pretenses of neutrality."[54] The subsequent convoying of munitions ships to England by United States ships and planes constituted an outright act of war, according to Beard. Despite an intermittent shooting war in the Atlantic between Germany and the United States in the spring and summer of 1941, Hitler held his navy in check and did not fall into the trap set for him by Roosevelt. Hitler appeared in these pages as a man of restraint, FDR as a warmonger by subterfuge.

Beard affirmed that at bottom economics, not an alleged struggle against totalitarianism, motivated the president's war plan against Germany. For people at all interested in a factual understanding of the war's causes, the American alliance with Stalin would have been sufficient reason to doubt the administration's explanation for what it was doing. Even before Hannah Arendt wrote her seminal book, *The Origins of Totalitarianism*, in which she described the Soviet Union as a tyranny equivalent to that of Nazi Germany, Beard expressed a similar view of the two dictatorships. He characterized the Soviet Union as "another totalitarian regime no less despotic and ruthless than Hitler's system . . . employing bands of Quislings as terroristic in methods as any Hitler ever assembled, and insistently effectuating a political and economic ideology equally inimical to the democracy, liberties, and institutions of the United States." Indeed, Russia was "one of the most ruthless Leviathans in the long history of military empires."[55] Opposition to the evils of dictatorship did not explain the president's wartime policies. By allying himself with Stalin, the United States was abetting the evils of dictatorship.

Earlier, Beard had expressed doubts to Oswald Garrison Villard about the rectitude of the Nuremberg Trials, because of the Soviet Union's participation in them on the judges' bench: "I should like to know, in view of the Stalin-Hitler pact, the conduct of Russia 1939–1941 in seizing other peoples' countries and murdering right and left, by what 'right' Russian judges sat in the court of 'Reason' and condemned the bloody German cut-throats?"[56] To Beard's mind, the Stalinist quantity in the Allied equation completely undermined the logic of the president's human rights and freedom rationale for the war.

In *The Rise of American Civilization*, Beard explained every war in American history, from colonial times down to the twentieth century, as a consequence shaped and conditioned by economic factors. The Second World War had been no different, as Roosevelt himself had revealed in the Atlantic Charter, the fruit of his August 1941 meeting with Winston Churchill off the coast of Newfoundland. Beard had been thinking about the special significance of the Atlantic Charter ever since Sumner Welles's revelations, in *The Time of Decision* (1944), about that document. Now he committed those thoughts to print.

The two leaders had wanted "to make known certain common principles in the national policies of their respective countries on which they base their hopes for a better future of the world." Beard interpreted their list of common principles as a revised but still recognizable version of Woodrow Wilson's idealistic agenda in the First World War regarding freedom and the self-determination of peoples. Despite its covering of stylized language, he found the Atlantic Charter to be one of the most open documents in the history of diplomacy because right in the text Roosevelt and Churchill made plain the endgame of the Second World War: "'access, on equal terms, to the trade and to the raw materials of the world which are needed for their economic prosperity.'"[57] The section about equal access he thought a politically necessary obfuscation by FDR and Churchill of the way the world would continue to work after the war, as a system for the enrichment of powerful nations at the expense of the hindmost.

Beard claimed to see in the Atlantic Charter "an understanding as to the kind of world policy to be pursued, presumably, by the United States and Great Britain during and after the war." Until the United Nations could be fully established in the postwar period, the Americans and the British would take charge of maintaining order in the world, to protect capitalist structures of wealth extraction and control. All this while, FDR continued to give misleading explanations about his relations with Churchill and duplicitously to assure the nation that no new commitments had been made in violation of American neutrality. In fact, he had committed the country to a new world order of Anglo-American domination. From this point forward, "the domestic affairs of the American people became appendages to an aleatory expedition in the management of the world," leading to the July 6–22, 1944, Bretton Woods conference, where the hegemony of the United States, with the cooperation and assistance of Great Britain, would be established for the postwar international economic system. The Americans and the British would join other "'peace-loving' nations in ordering and reordering the world" by the suasion of sweet reason when possible and by war when necessary, as Beard understood these official pronouncements.[58]

Beard predicted that presidential power in foreign affairs would become virtually sovereign, a process that inevitably would lead to despotism in domestic affairs as well. He thought that as a matter of political practice, constitutional and democratic government had come to an end in America, to be followed inevitably by disorder at home and hostility abroad. Ultimate dissolution likely would be the country's fate: "If wrecks of overextended empires scattered through the centuries offer any instruction to the living present, it is that a quest for absolute power not only corrupts, but in time destroys."[59]

Failing to maneuver Hitler into a war, the Americans next tried their stratagems on the Japanese, according to Beard. Bound to Italy and Germany by treaty as of September 27, 1940, Japan became the target of FDR's war-inducing designs and maneuvers beginning on July 25, 1941, when he froze Japanese assets in the United States. Trade between the two countries stopped. Japanese premier Fumimaro Konoye proposed a conference between the two countries to settle their differences, but the United States rebuffed him, causing his government to fall and to be replaced by the militarist government of Hideki Tojo. An American ultimatum the following month calling for Japan to withdraw its troops from China and Indochina precipitated the December 7, 1941, attack on Pearl Harbor. Beard did not offer any proof of an American plot to maneuver the Japanese into making the move they did at Pearl Harbor or to implicate FDR in foreknowledge of the attack. He did not think that proof was necessary. The logic of the situation in the Pacific and sequence of diplomatic steps leading up to Pearl Harbor made it perfectly obvious what the United States wanted to happen.

Moreover, as Beard was wont to do in his books, he used the words of the historical actors themselves to make his case. A diary entry by Secretary of War Stimson nicely summed up Beard's thesis in *President Roosevelt and the Coming of the War, 1941*: "the question considered by the President and members of the War Cabinet shortly before Pearl Harbor was how to maneuver the Japanese into firing the first shot without allowing too much danger to ourselves." Beard added, "as they were engaged in maneuvering the Japanese into firing the first shot," FDR and his lieutenants obviously knew that an attack was imminent. After the attack, Stimson confided to his diary: "Now the Japs have solved the whole thing by attacking us directly in Hawaii.'" He felt relief that the attack would unite the whole country behind the war. The American people would put behind them "the apathy and divisions stirred up by unpatriotic men."[60]

Beard had been one of the unpatriotic men and so he would remain in the eyes of mainstream historians who condemned his book as the last word in isolationist foolishness. As Walter LaFeber would observe in *America, Russia, and the Cold War, 1945–2006*, "Such dissent from waging the Cold War was not the fashion in 1948 and 1949, and most American historians wanted to be fashionable."[61] Beard, assessing the early attacks on his book, lamented to Villard on April 13, 1948, "[Walter] Millis axed me in the Herald Tribune and young [Arthur M.] Schlesinger in the Times. They are evidently much displeased with my book." In consolation, Yale University Press had ordered a third big printing to keep up with reader demand. Beard took an added measure of consolation from his own assessment of *President Roosevelt and the Coming of the War, 1941*: "If my own part of the book is all 'wet,' as Millis and Schlesinger contend, the documents which I print verbatim are alone enough to show the public how FDR and his associates were operating behind the scenes. The country seems to be in a mood to consider the question of how we were secretly governed by our own great *Fuehrer*."[62]

Beard wrote to Barnes on July 9, 1948, that his critics could not very well deny FDR's dissembling in the months just before Pearl Harbor. Some of them, like Schlesinger and Bailey, justified the president's deep game by claiming how he had been "justified in duping the people for their own good." Others, like Blair Bolles in the *New Republic*, did not go as far as these two "in praising the lie as an instrument of national policy." Still, Bolles faulted the book for Beard's failure "to obliterate the possibility that the United States would have fought in the war anyway 'no matter who was President.'" Beard commented to Barnes, "This is another item for your menagerie."[63]

In that same July 9, 1948, letter to Barnes, Beard related, "I am informed that Professor (excuse me, Captain) Samuel E. Morison is going to bust me up in the August issue of the *Atlantic Monthly*." As a historian of the Second World War, Morison had become, in Beard's opinion, the head cheerleader for America's victorious crusade. His *Battle of the Atlantic, 1939–1943* (1947), an officially inspired and vetted publication with a foreword by Secretary of Defense James V. Forrestal, failed every test of critical history, as Beard understood the term. Morison had compiled, Beard explained to Barnes, "the right kind of history of the naval operations." FDR and former secretary of the navy Frank Knox had handpicked him, and he had been commissioned in the Naval Reserve to do the job: "This hired man is now going to polish me off for the glory of God and others."[64]

The Morison review, "Did Roosevelt Start the War? History through a Beard," holds a prominent place among models of annihilating reviews. It follows the same pattern as Marc Antony's speech in *Julius Caesar*, initially praising Brutus and ultimately damning him. Beard, like Brutus, was an honorable man of many accomplishments, but the review, like the speech, proceeds inexorably to its obliterating indictment. Despite his successes, Beard always had been held back as a historian by his failure to appreciate or to understand great men: "Some are treated with subtle disparagement; others appear as wan products of economic forces." Throughout his career, Beard had done his best to minimize war, to attach little significance to its results and to overlook the importance of military men. Worst of all for a historian, he had become a fanatical isolationist critic of his country: "When Beard set himself up as a preacher and prophet, he was lost as an historian."[65]

Morison deemed Beard's indictment of Roosevelt to be morally offensive and damaging to the psyche of the nation: "He is trying to revive the same masochistic state of public opinion into which he and most of the American people fell at the end of World War I." Just as Wilson had deceived the country in 1917, so had FDR in 1941, and so might Truman at his first opportunity, Beard had reasoned. In his bizarre interpretation of the war, Beard purported to show that the Japanese did not bear ultimate responsibility for their attack at Pearl Harbor. Their actions only had taken place because we had attacked them, according to "the Sage of New Milford." Morison did not attempt to refute the basic charge that Beard had made against Roosevelt. "It is an easy matter to draw a brief of Rooseveltian hypocrisy," he conceded. The president had engaged in deceptions. Yet he had accomplished a worthy aim by his stealth. The American people, still suffering from the disillusionment that had followed the First World War and victimized by the sophistries of isolationists like Beard, had to be guided by a great president to their rendezvous with destiny as the leader of the free world. Roosevelt had answered the call of a higher morality, a plane of being to which materialistic thinkers like Beard could never ascend. If ever the nation had fought a just war against leaders and regimes of irredeemable evil, it was the Second World War. Historians like Beard would find themselves on the wrong side of history.[66]

At the time of Beard's death in New Haven of aplastic anemia on September 1, 1948, at the age of seventy three, Morison's prediction had not yet come true. Beard's last book quickly went through four printings and received some excellent notices. A review in the then enormously influential *Washington Star* newspaper by Senator Homer Ferguson, a Republican from Michigan, was reprinted in the *Congressional Record*. Ferguson had been a member of the Joint Congressional Pearl Harbor Investigating Committee, and he strongly endorsed the thoroughness of Beard's examination of government documents and other pertinent sources. He said that Beard had the incriminating evidence for his thesis about how FDR had concealed his aim of involving the United States in the European war. It was, in the senator's words, "a colossal display of linguistic duplicity." Many factors had led the United States into the war, but "the fateful decisions," Ferguson concluded, "came from the secret commitments and actions of Mr. Roosevelt and his associates who progressively maneuvered, not only for the 'first shot,' but also to shift American public opinion in favor of war, by pronouncements couched in the misleading language of peace and American security."[67]

Predictably, another stellar review for Beard appeared in *The Progressive*. George A. Lundberg, the chairman of the sociology department at the University of Washington, praised "the meticulous and devastating record which Charles A. Beard presents in his new book."[68] With a true historian's precision, he had documented the "sheer deceit" of the FDR administration. In so doing, "Dr. Beard has rendered one more outstanding service in his long, distinguished, and courageous career." Yale University Press conducted an extensive advertising campaign for the book, complete with numerous blurbs that extolled its merits.

Many obituary notices praised Beard as one of the leading historians of the age. As usual, *The Progressive* took the lead in celebrating him. One of his greatest admirers, Oswald Garrison Villard, wrote the commemoration of him for the magazine, "Charles A. Beard, Patriot." Villard began, "Of all the Americans known to me, Charles A. Beard was the one the country could least afford to lose." A patriot of the kind George Washington would recognize, Beard could be called an isolationist only insofar as "he wanted his country to be isolated from futile, needless war, whose outcome, a lost peace, he so clearly foresaw."[69] No other American possessed so profound a knowledge of the Constitution and the history of the United States, or had more courageously braved the manifold forms of intimidation practiced by the country's real power structure.

In its celebratory death notice for Beard, the steadfastly isolationist *Chicago Daily Tribune* commented on how *President Roosevelt and the Coming of the War, 1941* had "brought around his head a storm of criticism from internationalists and admirers of the Roosevelt administration."[70] Yet in May, soon after the book had appeared and in the midst of the furor it had provoked, he had received a gold medal from the National Institute of Arts and Letters for distinction in a body of historical writing, an award presented only once every ten years in any given field. The gold medal had moved Beard deeply. He had written to Villard about the experience: "Like you, I rejoice in the medal as a sign of the times. As to my merits as a writer, I have dour misgivings, but I am truly happy to have won that recognition by a secret ballot of many eminent persons. It bewilders me and makes me to wonder about what people are really thinking in the quiet of their souls."[71] Two days after his death, the *Chicago Daily Tribune* noted that 1948 had been an annus mirabilis for him. In addition to the Roosevelt book, he had published that year the tenth edition of his *American Government and Politics* (1910) and an edited version of *The Federalist Papers*.[72]

Even the often-hostile *New York Times*, Beard's wife informed Barnes, had printed an outstanding article about Beard. This obituary featured his enormous success as a teacher at Columbia University, where, despite the violent controversies that engulfed him from the day that *An Economic Interpretation of the Constitution of the United States* had appeared in print, he always had retained the respect and admiration of students and colleagues. His antiwar views in the 1930s and 1940s had exposed him to even worse recrimination, but the *New York Times* quoted at some length Beard's able defense of his foreign policy ideas. He had denied that critics of FDR's interventionist policy were defeatist and unpatriotic: "They are giving instead evidence of sanity, not cowardice; of adult thinking as distinguished from infantilism." He had insisted that such individuals did not deserve to be called isolationists. They only had proposed to deal with the world as it is, with each nation staying within the limits of its own civilization. No one nation should try to transform all the other nations in its own image, as the United States in a ruinous miscalculation born of hubris had set itself to do. This newspaper had disagreed with Beard when "he went so far as to accuse President Roosevelt of having attempted secretly to bring this country into war," but Mary felt grateful for its obituary of him.[73]

Indeed, Mary's file of obituaries for her husband contained many "wonderful tributes to him published in all parts of the United States." She added, "Comments did not all run one way by any means. Not by any means."[74] Mary paid for a public notice to thank the people across the United States and around the world who had written to extend their condolences to her. She had wanted to thank each one of them personally, "but their volume makes this impossible."[75] The anti-Beard consensus had not yet taken its full shape, but even before his death there could be no doubt about the political and intellectual power of its constituent elements.

The *Congressional Record* contains numerous documents by and about Beard, most of them requested by senators and congressmen who celebrated him for his learning and wisdom. It is significant, however, that for the House session of January 6, 1948, the *Congressional Record* included a letter written by one F. C. Sammons from West Virginia. Representative Hubert S. Ellis of that state described him as "a successful construction contractor and a student of history and world affairs." Sammons, in a December 21, 1947, letter to the editor of the *Herald Advertiser* in Huntington, West Virginia, condemned Beard for his generally disrespectful ideas about the history of the American people. Beard had been the real pioneer among those historians who always looked to tear down America. Worst of all, he had written a book "slandering the motives of our patriot fathers."[76] Cleverly designed to deceive Americans into thinking that their country had been founded by swindlers and shady lawyers, *An Economic Interpretation of the Constitution of the United States* had launched Beard on the most damaging career in the history of American scholarship. It was as if he hated his own country and his own people. Such severe charges reflected the gathering mood about Beard, but they only gave an inkling of what the history profession had in store for this enemy of the people.

CHAPTER 10

Defending Beard after the Fall

Beard did not live to see the full force of the counterattack provoked by *American Foreign Policy in the Making, 1932–1940* and, especially, *President Roosevelt and the Coming of the War, 1941*. Harry Elmer Barnes and Beard's wife, Mary, did. Their correspondence reveals the extent of the posthumous damage to Beard's reputation, as well as the efforts the two of them made to defend him and his intellectual legacy. That the increasingly notorious Barnes would become Beard's foremost champion in the history profession ultimately proved to be a liability for the Beardian legacy.

Mary had begun corresponding with Barnes on July 27, 1948, just as Beard was preparing to enter the hospital in New Haven where he would die. Barnes had sent his friend *The Struggle against the Historical Blackout*, a pamphlet that he had written about the suppression of revisionist history by establishment historians. Mary had found the document amusing and had chuckled over it. She wrote Barnes, "Perhaps today I can read parts of it to CAB. Certainly soon. Then I'll send you his comments."[1] After Beard's death, she wrote to Barnes about the blackout pamphlet, noting that as much as she appreciated it, he had made some mistakes in using Beard's *President Roosevelt and the Coming of the War, 1941* as an example of the campaign against revisionist historiography. She had meant to write to him about this matter sooner: "I failed to carry out my intention to write you a complaint while Charles was too ill himself at New Haven to tell you that your revisions were not far-reaching enough to meet the verifiable facts in the case of the publication of his last book by the Yale Press." Mary thought that she had contacted him about her concerns, but now was writing to apologize for claiming to have done so when in fact she had not. She had been completely absorbed in tending to Beard during his last illness: "But this does not excuse me for claiming that I complained when I did not in truth do it to you."[2]

Barnes had misrepresented in the blackout pamphlet the actual history of the second FDR book, claiming that the commercial publishing world had boycotted it because of its damning indictment of the president. In fact, Mary informed him, Beard had not tried to get the book published anywhere but at Yale. It was wrong, therefore, to give the impression that the book had been rejected by other publishers. Perhaps it would not have been accepted any place else, but Beard did not know this to be true: "So for your own sake and for CAB's it seems imperative to keep within the confines of fact, which is verifiable."[3]

At the same time Mary wanted Barnes to know how much she valued him: "But I also want to assure you of my pride as an American that in our society there is such a spirited thinker-writer as YOU—a person of such basic knowledge, such concern over the fate of our shaky Republic, such daring and self-respect." He had been a magnificent friend to her husband, his greatest ally in the struggle to save the Republic from the imperialists now planning its demise. Among the imperialists, she included many of the country's leading historians. Those among them who had hated her husband and had sought to vilify him she called "the Smearbund," who, happily from her viewpoint, had encountered much competition among the obituary writers for Beard. Yes, there were "hyenas," she told Barnes, men consumed with a vendetta against Beard, but he still had his supporters. She thought that his work would return to favor: "When, as, and if—and I think it will be when and as—we get licked in a new war on a world battle field, then the Smearbund will be such a casualty that the validity of 'Uncle Charley's' position will be accepted by surviving fellow-citizens and the Praisebund will have its day."[4]

Mary wrote to Barnes again, on February 21, 1949, upon receiving the fourth edition of the blackout pamphlet, "so largely devoted to CAB and still heroically defending him against the 'hatchet men.'" Barnes, she said approvingly, wielded a bloody hatchet of his own. She understood the need for such aggressive writing in the cause of defending Beard against scurrilous attacks. She continued to offer corrections regarding Barnes's biographical portrait of Beard, for "untruths only make him vulnerable to more assaults." She especially wanted the story of Beard's consulting work in Japan during the 1920s to be told with absolute fidelity to the truth because "the hostile press has more than insinuated that this made him 'pro-Japanese.'" He had performed similar work in Yugoslavia during the same period, and, given the charged anti-communist climate in the country, she looked "for something vile to be said about his 'advising Belgrade,' but I have seen nothing about it yet."[5] Concerning that story as well, Barnes had to avoid all misrepresentation for dramatic effect.

The pathetic, embarrassingly ignorant indictment of her husband as a Marxist bothered Mary most of all. Just such a "cheap communist interpretation" had been published in the conservative *Human Events* magazine on September 8, 1948. To make a Marxist out of Beard required an intellect entirely unacquainted with his work. Indeed, she was right. Much more important to him were *The Federalist Papers*, where the intimate rapport between economics and politics had been explained with classic exactitude for people with the wit to understand the reasoning of Madison and Hamilton. Marx could have learned something from these two authors, particularly about the way economic power expressed itself throughout all history in the political machinery of every system yet devised by the mind of man. Marx might have learned from them, too, how his own political system was unlikely to reverse the kinetic energy of history and by the magic of a dictatorship of the proletariat result in humanity's long-awaited rendezvous with democracy in its perfected form. In explaining the dynamics of capitalism, Marx had made some excellent points about the power of the economic substructure over political superstructures, echoing many others before him, but, for Beard, he was well to the rear of Madison and Hamilton as an authority even on that subject, let alone their superior insights into the mechanics of political power itself.

As disturbing as the attacks on Beard by such historians as Samuel Eliot Morison had been, Mary professed to be almost as irritated by many of the positive articles about him: "Commendatory comments were frequently ridiculous insofar as they indulged in biographical data for which the writers had no competence." She entreated Barnes in her February 21, 1949, letter to strive always for accuracy in his defense of Beard. The defamers deserved the bludgeoning that Barnes gave them, but his invective-laced style lent itself to exaggerations and distortions. Stick to the facts, she implored, but closed on a grace note: "Truly, truly my deep gratitude to you for your urge to champion our hero so courageously."[6]

Among the defamers Mary singled out was the brilliant historian of literature and architecture Lewis Mumford for a vicious attack on Beard that he had made in the *Saturday Review* on December 2, 1944. In *Herman Melville: A Study of His Life and Vision* (1929), he had been instrumental in reviving the reputation of that long-neglected genius. His *Technics and Civilization* (1934) and *Cul-*

ture of Cities (1938) had established his reputation as a social philosopher possessed of great understanding about the promise and threat of technology. Beard had admired Mumford's talent and had helped him to get started as a writer. After the fine beginning to their relationship, however, they developed diametrically opposed views about American foreign policy. Mumford, a passionate anti-fascist, spoke out vehemently against isolationists, such as longtime friend and idol Frank Lloyd Wright, as appeasers and objective agents of the Gestapo. Beard he put in the same traitor category.[7]

The Mumford attack on Beard to which Mary referred in a March 17, 1949, letter to Barnes concerned a communication that he had sent to the editor of the *Saturday Review of Literature* following an article in that journal about *A Basic History of the United States*. A mildly critical review by Dixon Wecter had not been sufficiently thoroughgoing for Mumford. Though critical of what he called the book's isolationist biases and exaggerations, Wecter had found some merit in it as a respectable textbook. Moreover, he had praised Beard, particularly for *An Economic Interpretation of the Constitution of the United States*: "In fact, that book must rank with Frederick Jackson Turner's first essay on the frontier as pivotal in the writing of our history."[8] Wecter went no farther in his negative comments than saying how in *A Basic History of the United States*, a great historian had written a book of only ordinary merit.

In the fiercely contentious letters to the editor that followed Wecter's review, Mumford's communication stood out for its verbal violence. He gratefully remembered the early kindnesses that he had received from Beard, but very quickly flew to the attack. Wecter had erred on the side of kindness. The trouble with Beard extended far beyond this one book; it concerned his whole life's work, especially during the past dozen years or so. His mechanistic philosophy of economic determinism vitiated everything he ever had written, even before his fatal embrace of isolationism. Mumford, bereaved by the loss of a son in the war, could see nothing redeeming in the isolationist cause. People like Beard who could not understand the need to fight the unparalleled evil of Hitler seemed mindless and soul-dead to him, despite their advanced degrees and bulging publication records. Beard's case partook of the tragic. He had deceived himself and deceived others in turn. His fantastic misconceptions about the war made him a partner to the Nazis and the Fascists: "He has created a mental wall between himself and the real world; and in order to preserve his position he has become a passive—no, active—abettor of tyranny, sadism, and human defilement."[9]

In the letter that Mary wrote nearly five years later to Barnes, she recalled Mumford's shocking words about her husband: "corrupt, an *abettor of schism*, and a defiler of mankind." Schism from which orthodoxy, she wondered:

"These marks [referring to her underlining] are my comment. You will understand." She even underlined her sign-off to Barnes: "Yours *sincerely*."[10] Beard himself never had taken Mumford's thesis, the same one offered by the government, seriously as a convincing explanation for why the United States had entered the Second World War. To argue that this was a war for democracy against tyranny, as Mumford asserted, overlooked an inconvenient fact: the Soviet Union's participation as an ally of the United States. Stéphane Courtois would observe in *The Black Book of Communism* that mass extermination by the state was not restricted to the Nazis. Indeed, Stalin, continuing and augmenting the methods pioneered by Lenin, fully established the "terror as a system of government" model employed by other communist dictators in their world-record slaughter for totalitarian governments of a hundred million people.[11] His collaborator in this book, Nicolas Werth, described America's wartime ally as a vast prison house of torture and death: "The Great Terror was a political operation initiated and carried out from beginning to end by the major organs of the Party, that is to say by Stalin," or "Uncle Joe," as FDR affectionately referred to him.[12]

Courtois, reflecting on Werth's statistics, could see no difference between what Stalin did to the kulaks and Ukrainians and what Hitler did to the Jews: "The mechanisms of segregation and exclusion of class totalitarianism present, therefore, an extraordinary similarity with that of race totalitarianism." The goal of one was a pure race, the other of a pure proletarian society; the methods employed differed only in their technical aspects. Courtois only could speculate about why one of these mass exterminations had received so much more attention than the other in history books, films, and television programs. The Nazis, after all, had murdered only twenty-five million people. Yet, Himmler and Eichmann had become household names, whereas the even bloodier adjutants in Stalin's entourage languished in relative obscurity: "Why has the testimony about communist crimes had such a weak echo in public opinion?"[13] Wartime exigencies from 1941 to 1945, Courtois surmised, explained why Nazism had become branded as the absolute evil while Communism had been allowed to pass into the camp of the good, until the exigencies of the Cold War eventually necessitated a reconfiguration of the Soviet Union as the "evil empire."

Mumford, in the manner of the FDR administration, had kept silent about the Stalin tyranny, even though the crimes of that regime were well known in the 1930s. In *The Passing of an Illusion: The Idea of Communism in the Twentieth Century*, François Furet catalogued and analyzed the books of those years in which the truth of the Soviet Union had been documented and revealed, "a kind of inventory," he called it. A member of the French Communist Party from 1949 to 1956, Furet had been a true believer in the cause. He could find no excuse for himself because for many years before his joining the party the essential truth about Stalin had been reported: "Never had any state in the world taken as its purpose to kill, deport or enslave peasants." Indeed, the pre-war case against him, which research in the state archives subsequent to the fall of the Soviet Union would confirm and strengthen, portrayed Stalinism as the equivalent of Hitlerism in practical outcomes: "They were political systems without fixed rules, with nothing to protect anyone, and with a political police that could arrest and liquidate any of its citizens except for one."[14] From the vantage point of the 1930s, before the Holocaust, Hitler would have seemed a rather minor practitioner of state terrorism compared to Stalin, who just in Ukraine already had piled up millions of corpses.

Furet identified the pre-war writers who presented the truth about the Soviet Union under Stalin: Boris Souvarine in *A Historical Overview of Bolshevism* (1935), Waldemar Gurian in *The Future of Bolshevism* (1935), André Gide in *Return from the USSR* (1937), Walter Citrine in *I Search for Truth in the USSR* (1936), Victor Serge in *From Lenin to Stalin* (1937) and in *Destiny of a Revolution* (1937), and Ante Ciliga in *The Russian Enigma* (1940). Arthur Koestler's classic novel about the Stalin purges and the Moscow show trials, *Darkness at Noon*, appeared in 1940. Prior to America's alliance with the Soviet Union, abundant opportunity existed for English-speaking people to learn about Stalin. Furet wrote, "those who wanted to know could have known. The problem was that few wanted to."[15] The later work of such writers as Aleksandr Solzhenitsyn, Robert Conquest, Dmitri Volkogonov, Edvard Radzinski, and Nadezhda Mandelstam would flesh out the story of Stalin's horrendous regime.[16] The main outline of the story, however, long had been in circulation.

Not only from publications by Europeans could Americans in the 1930s become informed about Stalin's tyrannical rule. In 1937 dissident American Marxist intellectual Max Eastman wrote *The End of Socialism in Russia*, relating the known and documented crimes of the Soviet regime: the state-caused terror famines resulting in the deportation and deaths of millions of peasants, the frame-up Moscow purge trials and mass executions. Stalin's infamous record had made the USSR "a totalitarian state not in essence different from that of Hitler and Mussolini." Eastman had spent nearly two years in the Soviet Union during the 1920s and had observed the consolidation of dictatorial power by Stalin. After leaving the country, he published *Since Lenin Died* (1925) and *Marx and Lenin: The Science of Revolution* (1926), warning of the dangers posed by Stalinism to the democratic aspirations in socialism. *The End of Socialism in Russia* updated his critique of Stalinism, which he characterized as the "concentration of political power and privilege in the hands of a bureaucratic caste supporting an autocrat more ruthless than the tzars had been."[17] Eastman by this time had progressed a long way toward his ultimate ideological position as a severe critic of Marxism and socialism on behalf of the free-market capitalism espoused by Friedrich Hayek, Ludwig von Mises, and Wilhelm Röpke.

Beard, who read widely outside the fields of his research expertise, could not agree with men like Mumford on the fundamental point about the U.S. war effort as a struggle against tyranny in the name of freedom. Mumford never had a word to say about the state-orchestrated famines, purge trials, and death camps in the Soviet Union, as if all the evil in the universe had been concentrated in the being of Hitler radiating outward as far as his malignant power could be extended. Beard thought, anticipating the clear implications of Furet's argument, that in the Nazis we were fighting a tyranny no more depraved than Stalin's, a point that emerges fully in his correspondence and in *President Roosevelt and the Coming of the War, 1941*. At no time did he have any illusions about the USSR. When he described the Soviets as cutthroats who had murdered right and left, he had the whole of Stalin's abysmal record in mind. An American war for democracy on the side of Stalin's tyranny seemed like a contradiction in terms to him. The war had to be about something other than fighting against tyranny.

Much of Mary's correspondence with Barnes touched on her complaints about Beard's antagonists who had attacked him for his evil influence on students. In an August 7, 1949, letter to Barnes, she described an attack of this kind by Ralph Waldo Gwinn, a Republican congressman from New York and a graduate of DePauw University no less: "He has a simple mind and his venom was mixed of piety and the religion of laissez-faire. Plus Republican Party loyalty."[18] Beard always had antagonized individuals of Congressman Gwinn's stamp. Now, however, the liberals in full battle cry had descended upon him as well over his World War II revisionism in general and, especially, his two FDR books.

In a handwritten postscript to her typed August 7, 1949, letter to Barnes, she wrote, "Do read 'The Case of General Yamashita' by A. Frank Reel. I was sent an advance copy. It is an imperative document."[19] The book dealt with many of her husband's ideas about the war and featured a Beardian interpretation of American history. This case concerned the trial by a military commission of General Tomoyuki Yamashita for war crimes in the Philippines. The University of Chicago Press published Reel's book in 1949. He had been one of six American lawyers for Yamashita. In Manila, where many of the war crimes charged in the case had taken place, a military commission of five generals, none of them a lawyer or a combat officer, on December 7, 1945, found

Yamashita guilty of failing to exercise control over his troops and sentenced him to death by hanging. Reel thought the sentencing date highly revealing about the motives of revenge that from the beginning had determined the outcome of the trial.

The war being over, the defense team attempted to have the trial transferred to the civilian courts. They succeeded in placing a petition before the U.S. Supreme Court, which on February 4, 1946, decided against them and upheld military jurisdiction in the case, with Justice Frank Murphy and Justice Wiley Blount Rutledge dissenting on Fifth Amendment grounds that General Yamashita's right to due process had been grossly violated. Justice Murphy's dissent impressed Reel for its eloquence and integrity. Listening to him in the Supreme Court building in Washington, Reel thought, "not only judicial history but English literature was in the making." Only with the utmost insult to American legal practice and values, Justice Murphy reasoned, could the element of personal culpability be disregarded in a criminal case, as it most disgracefully had been in the trial of General Yamashita. The Justice made it clear that he was using the word trial in its loosest sense and ventured the opinion that a better word for it would be farce. About both dissenting opinions, Reel rhapsodized, "here was America's soul."[20] General Douglas MacArthur, the supreme military commander in the Pacific, and President Truman approved the death sentence, denying the defense team's petition for clemency. General Yamashita was hanged on February 23, 1946.

In his book, published nearly four years after the legal proceedings in the case, Reel criticized the military commission for the summary character of its deliberations. The officers had failed to produce any evidence against Yamashita for his personal involvement, direct or indirect, in the war crimes committed by his troops. The commission had decided that through his position of command he had incurred responsibility for the actions of the men under him. This theory of command responsibility would be treated with benign neglect when Americans in government and the military faced similar charges for atrocities in American military history.

What particularly would have interested Mary about *The Case of General Yamashita* was its Beardian spirit in using American history to frame a withering analysis of the legal proceedings. Reel doubted that brutality toward noncombatants was peculiar to the Japanese. He proceeded to cite some American instances of this problem. "An honest reading of United States history must give us pause," in our rush to judgment of General Yamashita. On both sides of the Civil War such crimes had occurred, but as a prime example of brutality against noncombatants General Sherman's destruction of Atlanta might qualify for moral censure on the grounds laid out by the prosecution in the

Yamashita case. Moreover, "our callous extermination of American Indian women and children by flame and shot, often preceded by unconscionable betrayal, is part of an ugly picture." In the same picture belong the American torture practices against the guerrillas and massacres of Filipino noncombatants in the Philippine War of 1899–1902, "bloody pages that have been glossed into innocuous paragraphs in American history books."[21] Beard never had tired of debunking the myth of a peace-loving Unites States.

In the Philippines, Reel continued, the Japanese "were essentially clever imitators" of the Americans. Indeed, General Yamashita had been far more restrained than the American military leaders during the Philippine War, to say nothing of the men who ordered the atomic bombing of Hiroshima and Nagasaki, which had caused over two hundred thousand innocent non-combatant deaths. If brutality toward noncombatants bothered us so much, perhaps we might want to consider putting President Truman and Secretary of War Stimson on trial. Reel could not foresee such a possibility materializing at the expense of the victors and concluded, "Perhaps Yamashita's real crime was that he was on the losing side." He made this same point a second time, only more fully and with additional emphasis: "For Yamashita was not hanged because he was in command of troops who committed atrocities. He was hanged because he was in command of troops who committed atrocities *on the losing side.*"[22]

Mary, and Barnes with her, hoped that such books as *The Case of General Yamashita* would contribute to the revival of revisionism in the writing of American history. They looked to the day when historians would react against the recent wartime propaganda in the manner of what had occurred after the First World War. Barnes had written his "Struggle against the Historical Blackout" pamphlet in the immediate wake of Beard's October 4, 1947, op-ed for the *Saturday Evening Post,* "Who's to Write the History of the War?" In that article, Beard had protested the blackout against revisionist interpretations of the war and had criticized subsidies from the Rockefeller Foundation and the Council on Foreign Relations "in preparing the 'right kind' of history of World War II for the education of the American people." Evidently, the rulers did not want "journalists or any other persons to examine too closely and criticize too freely the official propaganda and official statements relative to our 'basic aims and activities' during World War II."[23] Above all, there should be no return to the debunking fashions of the post–World War I era. This time we had fought the good war about which no question unfriendly to received opinion ever should be raised.

At the initial cost of a $139,000 grant, Beard continued, the reliably patriotic William Langer of Harvard could be trusted to write "for the benefit of 'an American public' a 'clear and competent' history of World War II from 1939 to 'the peace settlements.'" That Langer would be given privileged access to documents denied other scholars seemed to Beard entirely wrong and a precedent likely to produce books deficient in critical rigor. We needed a public debate about the war conducted on equal terms between critics and supporters of government policies, not merely ex cathedra pronouncements from the FDR priesthood. It seemed to him that "subsidized histories of this kind, prepared to serve a purpose fixed in advance, are more likely to perpetuate errors than to eliminate them."[24] Historical research had to be free of political interests and restraints.

In the fifteen-page "Struggle against the Historical Blackout" of late 1947, Barnes followed the lead of Beard's *Saturday Evening Post* article. By 1951, however, he had expanded it to the size of a short book, at nearly a hundred pages. After receiving a copy of this expanded version, Mary wrote to Barnes on January 24, 1951, about how much she appreciated his "Memorial to CAB."[25] Indeed, Barnes presented Beard, "Great eagle, knower of the skies," as the father of World War II revisionism.[26] Beard thus acquired a distinction that, more than anything else, undermined his postwar reputation as a historian.[27] The eagle had to be brought to earth, Barnes explained in his pamphlet. To bring him down, a history profession religiously devoted to the righteousness of America's intervention in World War II and the ideals reputedly at stake in this struggle unleashed its most powerful weapons: Samuel Eliot Morison, Perry Miller, Arthur M. Schlesinger Jr., Thomas Bailey, and numerous other high-caliber figures. Barnes characterized these critics as totalitarian liberals leading the United States into a *1984* pattern of living. Indeed, he likened the American history profession, with very few exceptions, to the Ministry of Truth in Orwell's dystopian novel.

About *1984* Barnes wrote to Merle Curti on February 15, 1950, "As for the world situation, I think the pattern is now clear: we have already moved, perhaps irrevocably, into the *1984* pattern of using war and foreign policy as the means of diverting the fruits of technology from the people." The supreme genius of Orwell's novel lay in his portrayal of war in Oceania as an end in and of itself. Beard had come to the same conclusion about the Cold War against an enemy who only yesterday had been presented to the American people by their rulers as a friend in the crusade for freedom against Nazi tyranny. The ally of yesterday was today's enemy in Oceania, too. With the Nazis no longer a threat to freedom, a new enemy had to be found by Washington and quickly, as Barnes put the matter to Curti, to perpetuate a psychology of fear and to keep defense expenditures flowing, "for the cold war and operations rathole."[28] Orwell had the good taste to describe Big Brother as a Stalin look-alike. *1984*, though written by an avowed socialist, found great favor in the United States on the assumption that the evil it described existed only in the Soviet Union. Beard, on the other hand, made it seem as if America had a Big Brother complex of its own, with the entire world, not just Oceania, as the object of its desire for absolute control. That Beard inspired such plainly subversive thoughts counted against him in a widening circle of opinion.

Journalists and university presidents joined the attack on Beard as an irresponsible guide in understanding America's past and present. Barnes singled out for special mention among the most obstreperous anti-Beard critics in the public sphere the one-time revisionist journalist Walter Millis, FDR zealot Max Lerner, President Harry D. Gideonse of Brooklyn College, and President James Bryant Conant of Harvard University. Before 1939, Beard had been the country's foremost historian, but now, tainted by the charge of isolationism, he became passé and for many an untouchable. All his work, even the books that had nothing to do with American foreign policy, came under unprecedented attack. About the outbursts that followed upon Beard's death, Barnes wrote, "we were treated to an obscene performance which reminded fair observers of jackals and hyenas howling about the body of a dead lion."[29]

The same fate overtook every revisionist who questioned the conventional wisdom about the causes and conduct of World War II: Barnes himself, George Morgenstern, John T. Flynn, William Henry Chamberlin, and Frederic R. Sanborn, among others. They all stood condemned of the same isolationist thought-crimes committed by Beard. Their books only could find outlets in small publishing houses and, upon publication, were either ignored or came under immediate attack by what Barnes, echoing Mary, called the *"Smearbund."* Through such devious means did the historical blackout spread. Nothing could dispel the illusions about the war, thus proving to Barnes "that our propaganda facilities are about as powerful as those depicted in *Nineteen Eighty-four*."[30]

Mary, meanwhile, continued her vigilant supervision of Beard's memory, lashing out in her January 24, 1951, letter to Barnes against commentators who, in her judgment, misrepresented him and his work. She vehemently protested Matthew Josephson's portrait of him, published a little more than a year earlier in the *Virginia Quarterly Review*, "Charles A. Beard: A Memoir." Josephson, a left-wing journalist and historian, had been a great admirer of Beard and under his influence had turned from literary biography to economic history. In *The Robber Barons* (1934), his most famous book, he indicted the great American capitalists of the Gilded Age for their piratical business practices. About Beard, whose student Josephson had been at Columbia before becoming his neighbor in Connecticut, he explained in the *VQR* how the two men always had gotten on well and had become close friends. He wrote in a jocular manner about the Sunday dinner parties at the home of "Uncle Charley" and Mary. Discussions of human affairs became highly animated in the salon-like atmosphere of these occasions. Josephson described Beard as a spirited and sarcastic debater with his guests: "His high, clear voice would rise, his eyes would fairly snap with excitement, and he would gesture vigorously with arm extended and finger pointed, as if accusing and transfixing his adversary." In a similar vein, Josephson recalled the manner of Beard's dying in the New Haven Hospital. There, too, a jesting Beard "would be laughing, jabbing, or thrusting quickly at some adversary, crying out: 'But now there, I have you, sir!'"[31]

Despite the many gracious tributes to Beard in Josephson's article, Mary flew into a protective rage at what she called his falsifications, beginning with the "terrible misrepresentation for the most part of Beard as host." In his portrayal of evenings at the Beard "salon," she did not recognize the man she had been married to for nearly fifty years, nor did she appreciate the role he had given her "as a foil or clown in this play, needing such a figure for a drama of his kind." Even worse, Josephson had done "the unpardonable thing of falsifying Charles' dying. He had been in Italy at that time "and knew absolutely nothing about that end of a great living." He simply had made up an account of the death scene, which had nothing to do with the truth: "Oh Harry, the truth is that Charles died quietly, saying with his last breath, 'Mary, I have found—peace.' During his entire month at the hospital, he was moving gently to this life closure."[32]

Mary also had commented to Barnes in her letter of January 24, 1951, on an anthology of essays about Beard under the editorship of University of Wisconsin historian Howard K. Beale. She called it a disgrace and expressed relief that the publisher had rejected it: "If this volume had been finished and published and presented to CAB, CAB would have felt wretched about it, except for a few good [this last word crossed out] pages. I am so glad that it has never appeared in the market." She had come to read Josephson's contribution to the anthology, when another publisher asked her opinion about the manuscript. He had gotten nearly everything wrong. She explained to Barnes: "You couldn't understand this by hearing what Howard Beale told you, if he was your informer. He has been bitter, I have heard, about the rejection of his essay collection, but naturally it is hard, if not impossible, to a person to believe he could be an incompetent editor."[33]

When *Charles A. Beard: An Appraisal* did at last appear, in 1954, Beale recounted the book's tortuous history, in his editor's introduction, dated November 1, 1952. The origins of the book went back to 1939 or 1940—two festschrift volumes were planned: one in history edited by Louis Hacker and another in political science edited by Arthur Macmahon. Before either of these projected volumes could progress very far, the war came. Beale observed, "Some men who had loved Beard came to dislike him bitterly." The participants lost interest, and both projects died. Another effort to honor Beard got underway during the winter of 1945–1946 with a lunch meeting of potential contributors at the Princeton Club in New York City. The meeting did not go as planned: "Some of those invited expressed such dislike of what Beard stood for that they would have nothing to do with a project to honor him." Yet several of those present went ahead with a modified plan for a single volume, to be ready in time for Beard's seventy-third birthday, November 27, 1947. Failing to meet that deadline, the contributors then aimed at finishing their volume by his next birthday, but he died nearly three months before turning seventy-four. It would take six more years for this star-crossed book, in Mary Beard's characterization of the project, to be completed. When the book did appear, Beale had to acknowledge that it was not at all a festschrift in the ordinary meaning of the word: "Participation in the volume by no means implies agreement with all of Beard's opinions or the absence of emphatic criticism of some of them."[34] Mary thought the whole enterprise too conflicted to be of any value, and her name does not appear in the acknowledgments.

Even Barnes came under fire in Mary's January 24, 1951, letter, for comments he had made in *The Struggle against the Historical Blackout* about the publisher who had turned down the Beale anthology. She admired the publisher and agreed with his editorial decision. Barnes had gotten the story all wrong in claiming that this rejection was part of the historical blackout: "But when you shoot an atomic bomb at the 'leading publisher who had in previous years craved even the smallest crumbs from Beard's literary table'—not in the least true, dear Harry Barnes—I feel that I must inform you that you should not have used that bomb." As Mary so often did in her letters to Barnes, she urged him to avoid exaggerating, which was his worst vice as a writer, in her opinion: "You have so much wisdom and power, dear friend Harry, that I am zealous for you to stick to truths which you can verify—in all instances."[35]

After receiving yet another edition of *The Struggle against the Historical Blackout*—there would be nine in all—Mary wrote to Barnes again, on April 5, 1951. She judged the pamphlet to be "still red-blooded with hand and heart devotion to CAB and truths of history." Although concerned about certain factual inaccuracies in it, she wanted him to know, "Your loyalty to Charles Beard, based on your own loyalty to the revisionist positive learning about Roosevelt's operations and your personal acquaintance with CAB, is a magnificent satisfaction to me." She revered him for his "integrities" and "keeping Beard's memory alive."[36]

Mary wanted more information from Barnes about an experience that he had described in the new edition of *The Struggle against the Historical Blackout*, regarding his participation at the December 1950 American Historical Association (AHA) convention in Chicago. "I had heard," she wrote, "that this meeting was full of fire and rejoiced that it was not death-like—again."[37] In the pamphlet, Barnes had explained how at the previous AHA convention, in 1949, his views about World War I revisionism had come under attack in two different papers. He was given a chance to respond at the 1950 convention, but in a manner that set off in bold relief the inferior position, within the professional establishment, of the revisionist school. He lamented in the pamphlet, "Between the invitation to prepare the paper and the printing of the program the writer was switched, without his knowledge, to the role of discussing papers read by others." The original address could not be given. He noted in the pamphlet that the AHA program for President Samuel Eliot Morison's address featured him in his admiral's uniform, "not in the lowly and pacific garb of a scholar."[38] The profession, it seemed to him, had entered its twilight. Mary agreed: "All any of us can do, it appears, is to foster the revisionist principles. That is vital for this day and may be revitalized in the days to come when societies of the current forms have destroyed themselves."[39]

Barnes's next pamphlet, *The Court Historians Versus Revisionism*, appeared in 1952. Mary wrote to congratulate him on February 27. The letter began, "Dear Revisionist Harry Barnes."[40] The pamphlet had given her "unqualified joy." She wanted a dozen copies for distribution to people capable of appreciating a serious historical argument. In a letter of August 3, she exclaimed, "'Masterpiece' seems to me positively a hackneyed word for this unqualifiedly second and enlarged edition of *The Court Historians*." She most appreciated his continuing tributes to Beard: "Your high appraisal of my nobleman's 'Giddy Minds and Foreign Quarrels' . . . gives me rapture."[41] Twelve days later, she wrote again to tell him that Fola La Follette and her husband, George Middleton, had come to visit her: "They read your Court Historians with joy in your treatment and said they would like to help circulate it—as their own instant reaction." She asked for two dozen more copies, some of which would be sent to Fola, who would pass them out in Washington, D.C. Mary promised to "get mine going with delight."[42]

Barnes indeed did celebrate Beard in *The Court Historians*, using once again his "Who's to Write the History of the War" article for the *Saturday Evening Post* as a point of departure. The recent publication, Barnes wrote, of *The*

Challenge to Isolation, 1937–1940 by William L. Langer and S. Everett Gleason "fully confirms Dr. Beard's estimate and prophecy." An extreme example of mythologizing court history celebrating the higher wisdom and brilliant statesmanship of FDR in guiding the United States into the war, the book had earned Langer and Gleason high posts in the Orwellian Ministry of Truth that the history profession had become. Barnes deemed the Langer-Gleason book to be "the most impressive product of court historiography in the whole course of historical writing from the late Paleolithic Cave of Font-de-Gaume to 1952." Langer's résumé included a wartime stint in the Office of Strategic Services, the forerunner of the CIA, and the experience had completed his transition from revisionism, of which he had been a leading proponent in the 1920s and 1930s, to the professional safety of four-square American interventionism and internationalism. That many other American historians had similar or related wartime involvements and enthusiasms insulated FDR's foreign policy from critical inquiry, however raucous the debates about the New Deal might continue to be. To Barnes, however, "the two magisterial volumes by Charles Austin Beard on Roosevelt's foreign policy" already had destroyed the foundation of the Langer-Gleason thesis about FDR's pacifism and integrity.[43]

In their introduction, the coauthors described Beard as "[a] prominent American historian, who was at the same time one of the intellectual leaders of what he chose to call 'nationalism.'" They used his characterization of isolationism as a convenient summation of what the movement represented in American foreign policy. In their words, Beard had called for "rejection of membership in the League of Nations; non-entanglement in the political controversies of Europe and Asia; non-intervention in the wars of those continents; neutrality, peace and defense for the United States through measures appropriate to those purposes; and the pursuit of a foreign policy friendly to all nations disposed to reciprocate."[44] Beard, however, had reasoned in the abstract, overlooking the concrete threat posed by the Nazi and Fascist dictatorships. Langer and Gleason regretted that a large public audience for such aberrations had been created by the post–World War I revisionists and the Nye Committee.

Barnes wrote to Langer on February 14, 1952, and sent him a copy of the review he had written about *The Challenge to Isolation, 1937–1940*. He began, "It has seemed to me the decent and honorable thing for you to receive your first copy of the enclosed review direct from me." Remembering their past friendship and Langer's support for the revisionist cause between the wars, he had taken no personal pleasure in writing the review: "Since, however, I regard Roosevelt's foreign policy after 1937 as the great public crime in human history (which covers quite a lot of ground), I could not very well ignore your book."[45] Langer had possessed the means and the opportunity to become a great historian, but he had thrown the opportunity away to support a corrupt power structure, Barnes lamented. A few months later, he further explained to Curti that Langer had not been "bought," but had succumbed to a combination of fear and ambition.[46] Harvard University, where Langer taught under the interventionist president James Bryant Conant, had become a fertile recruiting ground for scholars disposed toward civic engagement in Washington. As Barnes explained in *The Court Historians*, by the late spring and summer of 1940 Harvard was "going wild" for war. Barnes surmised that Langer, for nearly twenty years the most resolute of revisionists, did not want to be marooned on the wrong side of history.

Herbert Feis, the other leading court historian examined in Barnes's pamphlet, had just published *The Road to Pearl Harbor: The Coming of the War between the United States and Japan*. He had been an important official in the State and War departments. Based at the prestigious Institute for Advanced Study at Princeton, New Jersey, Feis parroted the official government propaganda about Japan. In passing, he condemned Beard's *Giddy Minds and Foreign Quarrels* for its virulence. Barnes, on the other hand, thought it "the most cogent and penetrating explanation of the revolution in our foreign policy, and the motives lying behind it, which has ever been set down."[47]

Feis meticulously had detailed acts of Japanese aggression, without ever noticing the impressive American record for engaging in wars of territorial expansion. The FDR administration had set unreal and hypocritical standards for the Japanese, never acknowledging that they were doing in their own sphere of influence what the United States had done in Latin America and elsewhere. With solemn mien, Feis had written about American foreign policy in the Pacific as if it had not been permeated throughout by well-documented deceit and double-crossing, as if it had been a simple case of American morality against Japanese perfidy. Naturally, Feis had dismissed as irrelevant the smoking gun that had shot his thesis to death, the statement by Secretary of War Henry L. Stimson: "the question was how we should maneuver them [the Japanese] into the position of firing the first shot without allowing too much danger to ourselves." As Beard had shown irrefutably in his last two books, the United States was committed to war in the Pacific with or without an attack by the Japanese. Barnes added: "Roosevelt and his top-level associates expected and desired a Japanese attack on Pearl Harbor."[48] For this book of FDR worship to have received by acclamation the endorsement of reviewers in the leading newspapers, magazines, and journals confirmed Barnes's view that the profession had entered its final agony.

Mary urged Barnes, in a letter on April 11, 1953, "Don't stop writing comments on the show which does not pass . . . alas!"[49] The following month, she thanked him for sending a copy of the 679-page anthology of essays that he had edited, *Perpetual War for Perpetual Peace*. "I am glad you keep strong for the fray," she told him in her thank-you letter.[50] The book, which was dedicated to the memory of Beard, thrilled her. She wrote to Barnes again in September about it: "Though you had written me that the book was dedicated to CAB, I could not have dreamed that it would be such a sweeping tribute. It is like a veritable monument, certainly a great aid in revisionism. I am all for it and grateful to you."[51]

In his editor's preface, Barnes recalled that the title for the book had come from Beard. In their last conversation, which had taken place in June 1947, Beard had summed up the foreign policy of FDR and Truman as an exercise of perpetual war for perpetual peace.[52] The United States had a war economy now. National prosperity would depend on wars and rumors of wars, the better to keep American citizens in a constant state of anxiety and ever more willing to pay exorbitant sums for "defense." Barnes observed that "events since that time have further reinforced Beard's sagacity and insight in this respect." He likened Beard to George Orwell for perceptiveness in showing "how a new political order throughout the world may be erected on the premises and implications of this goal of perpetual war, presented in the guise of a global struggle of free peoples for perpetual peace."[53]

Beard had taken the lead among American historians in calling for a sane foreign policy based on the country's traditional pre-1917 values, involving primarily a cessation of government support for capitalists' manipulation of the global economy and their supplementary strategy for expanding military budgets. Beard clearly saw the link between imperialism and militarism: the financiers would need a collection agency of well-armed soldiers and sailors. Barnes presented the anthology's contributors as the outstanding revisionist historians following in Beard's wake: Charles Callan Tansill, Frederic R. Sanborn, William L. Neumann, George Morgenstern, Percy L. Greaves Jr., William Henry Chamberlin, and George A. Lundberg. Such men did Barnes have in mind when he had written to Merle Curti earlier about "the few sane and honest historians left."[54]

Summing up the significance of the volume, Barnes observed in its concluding section that the work of the contributors had shown how the two world wars "have converted the libertarian American dream of pre-1914 days into a nightmare of fear, regimentation, destruction, insecurity, inflation, and ultimate insolvency."[55] The country would not survive a foreign policy that made global meddling intrinsic to its way of relating to the rest of the world.

Already in 1953 American military bases around the world proclaimed the existence of a great new empire, despite the denials and obfuscations of the court historians now serving as the scholarly spokesmen for the hegemony. As with all previous empires, the American empire would go down to defeat. The only hope for the country consisted of the chance that the American people could be taught the truth about their government and the financial interests that controlled it.

Mary Beard had a second reason for taking delight in *Perpetual War for Perpetual Peace*. Besides all the praise showered on her husband, she found in the book a long quotation by William R. Matthews, the editor of the *Arizona Daily Star* in Tucson. Mary had written to Barnes about him on February 27, 1952. She had been spending the winter in Tucson. During her stay, she had developed a high opinion of Matthews's editorials for what she called his fight against "'Humbuggery,' frankly calling deceits by that name, with thrusts day by day." She added, "He knows by long and extensive travels, as direct observation of the world which the U.S seeks to dominate, whereof he speaks, as well as by his refined judgments."[56] She had sent some of his editorials to Barnes, and he began his editor's conclusion to *Perpetual War for Perpetual Peace* by quoting from one of them. It began: "I charge that the articulate publicists of our country, by their semi-hysterical words in print and speech in which they champion extremes of diplomatic and military policy, are driving us rapidly into a war of unlimited and unattainable objectives which will bring on a gigantic catastrophe of ruin and revolution at home and abroad."[57]

The Harry Elmer Barnes archive contains no further correspondence between him and Mary Beard after 1953. She continued to work on her own scholarship in the field of women's history, publishing that year *The Force of Women in Japanese History*. Two years later Mary's short biography of her husband appeared, *The Making of Charles A. Beard*. The biography dealt almost entirely with the formative influences in Beard's life and his work as a consultant during the 1920s in Japan and Yugoslavia. She did not mention the battles that the couple fought together in furtherance of World War II revisionism. For evidence of Mary's passionate devotion to that cause, it is necessary to consult her correspondence. She is remembered today primarily as Beard's collaborator and for her own research and writing on the history of women. A 1946 book, *Women as Force in History: A Study in Traditions and Realities*, remains her most influential publication. She died on August 14, 1958, at the age of eighty-two.

Barnes persevered with his World War II revisionist endeavors, always in the name of Beard. The zenith of that revisionist campaign, in Barnes's estimation, occurred with the publication in 1961 of A. J. P. Taylor's *Origins of the*

Second World War. The book thrilled Barnes for its challenge to the orthodox "good war" interpretation of that conflict. Taylor began by noting a historical oddity: everyone was happily agreed about Hitler as the sole cause of the Second World War. As a rule, however, historians did not agree about anything. Why should the Second World War be such a conspicuous exception to the rule? For his own part, after considering the historical record of the events leading up to the German invasion of Poland on September 1, 1939, Taylor concluded that the Treaty of Versailles, not Hitler, had ignited the passions that brought on the war. It was inconceivable that the Germans could accept this treaty as a permanent settlement. They believed that all their troubles stemmed from it. Hitler's diplomacy did not differ from that of his predecessors in wanting to liberate Germany from the restrictions of Versailles, a perfectly reasonable foreign policy objective for him, given the virtual unanimity of the German people on this question. He had no plans for world conquest. Seeking legitimate redress against a treaty that even British leaders found lacking in moral validity, Hitler is seen in *The Origins of the Second World War* as a rational statesman on the same moral plane as his counterparts among the other leaders of Europe. For Taylor, "this is a story without heroes; and perhaps even without villains."[58] Knowledge of later events had made it impossible to see prewar developments in their proper historical perspective.

Barnes hailed Taylor's book as a decisive breakthrough against the historical blackout of revisionist writing about the Second World War. "It gives me particular pleasure," he rejoiced in a forty-two-page pamphlet-review, "to pay tribute to the courage and integrity of Professor Taylor in producing this book."[59] One of Britain's most famous and esteemed historians, Taylor had undertaken to write *The Origins of the Second World War* in full possession of his well-known anti-German sentiments and personal hostility to Hitler. His research showed, however, that the conventional assumption of Hitler's sole responsibility for the war, derived entirely from Allied propaganda, had no support in the historical record. Hitler comported himself with caution and moderation, not at all as the fanatical and bellicose psychopath Taylor had expected to find in the historical sources.

Barnes, who had been saying as much for years, had the advantage of not putting a career at risk. The history profession had rid itself of Barnes long ago, in the manner of free and open societies, by ignoring him. Once a favorite of New York commercial presses like Knopf, he now had to resort to private printers in Caxton, Idaho, and the like to get his work before an ever-shrinking audience. Taylor, in contrast, stood on the heights of a profession that responded to his book with shock, anger and vehement condemnation. Any British historian with the temerity to present the Munich agreement of 1938 as an instance of comprehensible statesmanship in the necessary revision of the Versailles Treaty, when everyone had been taught to view its architect, Neville Chamberlain, as the human symbol of appeasement and cowardly refusal to stand up to a mad dictator, could expect the maximum sentence for heresy against the holy of holies in the catechistical teachings about the Second World War. For Barnes, therefore, Taylor's achievement "must be regarded as one of the most courageous acts in the whole history of historical writing."[60]

The pamphlet-review regarding *The Origins of the Second World War* dealt as much with Barnes's ideas as with Taylor's. In view of the later charges against him of anti-Semitism, it is pertinent to discover that in this piece Barnes sought to defend the Jews against the charge that they had played a large role in maneuvering the United States into the war. Surrounded by communist sympathizers and an array of progressive Gentile interventionists, "Roosevelt did not need any pressure from the Jews to create his interventionism and war policy." The Jews could not be saddled with the responsibility for FDR's foreign policy from 1937 to Pearl Harbor. They did have a role in the postwar creation and spread of anti-German literature, but "it is unfair, as so many do, to attribute this flood of smear literature against Germany wholly to Jews and Jewish pressure." As for the Holocaust, without mentioning the term he claimed to be "personally still quaint enough to hold it to be reprehensible to exterminate either Jews or Gentiles." Hitler's anti-Semitism and treatment of the Jews he denounced as "a piece of folly which I have condemned for nearly thirty years in numerous articles, books, and lectures."[61]

On May 9, 1961, Barnes wrote to former president Herbert Hoover about what he called the strategic importance for the revisionist cause of *The Origins of the Second World War*. He had thought of Taylor as "one of the Shirers of Britain," a reference to William Shirer's *The Rise and Fall of the Third Reich: A History of Nazi Germany* (1960), which Barnes dismissed as a sodden lump of Allied propaganda distortions about Hitler. For a nemesis of Germany to write *The Origins of the Second World War*, "it is almost as though the Pope had come out for Luther's *Ninety-five Theses*."[62] To maximize its impact, he hoped that an American publisher would bring out the book as well.

Barnes's interest in Jews became increasingly negative. He faulted Jewish publishers, editors, writers, and filmmakers for their alleged part in the historical blackout of revisionist writing about the Second World War. Claiming to see a similarity between the campaign to promote awareness about the Holocaust in World War II and the German atrocity stories in World War I, he gravitated to the works of Paul Rassinier, a Frenchman who disputed that there ever had been a German extermination policy against the Jews. He formed a close relationship with David L. Hoggan, whose *Myth of the Six Million* (1969) would pioneer Holocaust denial in English-language publications. In 1956, Barnes had written to Curti about Hoggan as "a real prize" for any history department looking to hire a stellar Europeanist and praised his writing for its professional excellence.[63] Only much later did he recognize Hoggan as "a complicated mental case," whose psychological instability had undermined his academic career.[64] He held in high regard Hoggan's 1961 book, *Der erzwungene Krieg* (translated into English as *The Forced War*), despite reports of the author's association with neo-Nazi groups. Barnes had endorsed Hoggan's thesis, that Germany in fact had been maneuvered into the war by a collusive arrangement between Britain and Poland. For the book, he had written a glowing blurb. Barnes's mental life now increasingly consisted of conspiracy theories about the war. In the minds of some critics, his defense of Beard would become interpolated with the questions of anti-Semitism and Holocaust denial.

Barnes tried to be subtle in his writing about the Holocaust. Full-throated Holocaust deniers, like Lewis Brandon of the Institute for Historical Review, admired him but criticized his lack of forthrightness on this question. Regarding the Barnes pamphlet *Revisionism and Brainwashing* (1963), which the Institute for Historical Review republished in 1979 in *The Barnes Trilogy*, Brandon apologized: "One regrettable aspect of the booklet is that Barnes did not at this stage feel confident enough to openly challenge the Holocaust in its entirety." Instead, Barnes rested content with innuendo and "ambiguous tongue-in-cheek writing." Compensating somewhat, Brandon reported, "in private, Barnes was more convinced than ever that the entire Holocaust was a sham." Brandon hoped that if the myth of the Holocaust at last can be exposed, "Harry Elmer Barnes will not have struggled in vain."[65]

Brandon's criticisms notwithstanding, Deborah Lipstadt identifies Barnes as "one of the seminal figures in the history of North American Holocaust denial."[66] In *Denying the Holocaust: The Growing Assault on Truth and Memory*, she describes him as the link between two leading European Holocaust deniers, Paul Rassinier and Maurice Bardèche, and their American counterparts, chiefly David L, Hoggan, Austin J. App, and Willis Carto, the founder of the Institute for Historical Review. Lipstadt concedes that Barnes, though filled with animosity toward Jews and revulsion toward Israel, did not actually deny the existence of the gas chambers. What Lewis Brandon had said in criticism of Barnes she said in modest mitigation of the part that he played in the history of American Holocaust denial.

For more on the infamy of Barnes, Lipstadt recommends Peter Novick's *That Noble Dream: The "Objectivity Question" and the American Historical Profession*. Novick, she said, knew well the Barnes archive at the University of Wyoming. He did, indeed, portray Barnes as a paranoiac and a fanatic whose career as a scholarly historian had been badly damaged by his reputation for unseemly controversy in the debates over World War I revisionism. After the Second World War, he became a pariah in the profession, churning out his broadly derided pamphlets and using money provided by extreme right-wing funders to commission covertly other works of revisionism, which in their turn had almost no impact beyond a fringe of Roosevelt haters.[67] Nonetheless, Novick mentioned nothing about Barnes as a Holocaust denier.

The question of Beard and the Jews is an important and easily answered one. It can be said with certainty that he had nothing to do with anti-Semitism and was very well-known in the historical profession for his sentiments in opposition to bigotry of this kind. Three examples among many that could be cited here will illustrate where he stood on anti-Semitism.

At the beginning of the Red Scare following the Bolshevik Revolution, Beard came to the defense of three left-wing Jewish teachers at De Witt Clinton High School in New York City. Samuel Schmalhausen, Thomas Mufson, and A. Henry Schneer had been found guilty of "holding views subversive of good discipline and of undermining good citizenship in the schools."[68] At a school meeting held to discuss the case of the three teachers, John Dewey likened the proceedings against them to "an inquisition, to use the term of antiquity." Beard, who recently had resigned from Columbia University over free speech cases on that campus, sent a letter that was read at the De Witt Clinton High School meeting. The problem for the three teachers, as he saw it, certainly had to do with their politics, but there had been "no little anti-Semitic feeling in the case. . . . This is denied, but it is a fact."[69] For Beard, schools either honored free speech or they did not, regardless of the politics or ethnic background or religion of the faculty members.

Throughout his professional career, Beard enjoyed a reputation as an enemy of racism in all its forms. When on the eve of the Second World War, the American Historical Association sought speakers to address the theme of "The Historian and the Present World Crisis," the program committee extended an invitation to Beard. A member of the program committee, Paul Lewinson of the National Archives, explained to Beard what the AHA wanted from him. He would be one of three speakers at a luncheon meeting. The other two would be from Nazi Germany and the Soviet Union. Beard would speak last: "the committee knows that you can at once paint the lurid picture of historical scholarship in the totalitarian states as soberly as it can be, and also give this picture its proper setting and draw the necessary morals." Lewinson continued, "to be confidentially frank, we are arranging a set-up or perhaps even a pushover for you."[70]

That the AHA program committee clearly had in mind as one of its top concerns for the luncheon addresses Nazi anti-Semitism can be deduced from Lewinson's correspondence with the American University historian Ernst H. Correll. He asked him for help in recruiting a Nazi speaker: "My ancestry is such . . . that I could not, I think, get very far with the German Embassy." It really did not matter to Lewinson who the other two speakers were, "as long as Mr. Beard speaks last."[71] He could be counted on absolutely to hold forth with an unrivaled authority against the desecration of history and morality by the Nazis and the Communists.

The planned exchange at the December 1939 Washington meeting of the AHA never took place. Lewinson explained to Beard a little more than a month after the outbreak of the war, "History has gotten ahead of us so far that our American Historical Association luncheon session has had to be jettisoned."[72] Beard agreed with the decision to give up the luncheon: "Neither the Germans nor the Russians have any interest in telling the truth about anything. Moreover, they are devoid of any sense of humor as stark lunatics."[73] The anti-Semitic essence of Nazism disgusted Beard, as Lewinson and everyone else on the AHA program committee well understood.

Finally, the part that Beard played in an episode that took place at Johns Hopkins University during his 1940–1941 teaching stint there gives us another glimpse of the non-racist way that he thought about Jews. In 1935, Isaiah Bowman became the president of that institution. Thinking that there already were too many Jews at Johns Hopkins, he instituted a formal Jewish quota at the school in 1938. A few years later, he refused to reappoint the young historian Eric Goldman, despite the history department's unanimous backing of him. Recounting in *FDR and the Jews* this clear case of anti-Semitic prejudice, Richard Breitman and Allan J. Lichtman note "the intervention of Charles Beard" on Goldman's behalf.[74] Beard had developed a high opinion of Goldman and said so. Neither race nor religion affected his judgment in this case, or in any other such instance for which records remain.

Yet Beard's intimate connection with Barnes established ample grounds for guilt by association. Lipstadt specifically removed Beard from the dock where she relegated Barnes and his Institute for Historical Review ilk: "Citing Beard for a purpose that would have appalled him, Holocaust deniers' journals and publications argue that the war against Hitler was not just folly but counterproductive to American interests."[75] He is a background figure in Lipstadt's account, a kind of intellectual accessory, for his work as a revisionist historian, in the crime of Holocaust denial. As Lewis Mumford had remarked in his slashing 1944 attack, "Our pro-Nazis, our so-called nationalists, will use Beard as their respectable front."[76] The historical revisionists, over whom Beard presided as an exemplar, made it look as if America, even more than Germany and Japan, had something to answer for regarding the real causes of the Second World War. To be charged with the offense of intellectually aiding and abetting, even if unintentionally, Holocaust deniers did not do Beard's reputation as a historian any good.

Beard, in fact, tried to think in realistic terms about war. He claimed that a cold look at the motives of both sides in any conflict best served the cause of historical scholarship. In recounting the Civil War, for example, he had refused to take sides; the conflict, in his view, arose irrepressibly from economic forces, not from a struggle between good and evil over slavery. He doubted very much that leaders in the North seriously concerned themselves about the fate of black people. Even the good war had its economic side, which would explain, he insistently argued, the conflict's aftermath and the need for America to become the champion of global capitalism and the protagonist in perpetual war for perpetual peace. There were no good wars, he believed. They were all evil, the consequence of greed, pride, and self-deception. With their victory in World War II, the Americans had vanquished the manifold evils of German Nazism, Italian fascism, and Japanese militarism. These victories, however, had been only incidental to the real purposes of the American leaders—the establishment of their own empire, which in the end Beard predicted would decline and fall, as all such constructs did. In triumphalist postwar America, no historian could make such claims and get away with them, as the fate of Beard's postwar reputation vividly illustrates.

CHAPTER 11

Beard's Philosophy of History and American Imperialism

Beginning in his late fifties and continuing for more than a decade, Beard reeducated himself about what it meant to be a historian. Long after the time of life when most historians settle into a routine way of thinking about the past, he kept on exploring new ground in his search for the truth about American history. It was a field, he thought, full of vulgar myths, which had brought about a scholarly culture immersed in trivial concerns and therapeutic reassurances about the country's exceptionally virtuous past, present, and future. He expressed contempt for the way American historians as a class, with only a handful of honorable exceptions past and present, deceived themselves and their fellow countrymen about the real meaning of the United States for the world. Beard became famous early for his economic interpretation of the American past, but he did not develop a true philosophy of history until the 1930s.

Personal humiliation and mortification precipitated the crisis in Beard's thinking. The moral and intellectual collapse of the history profession during the First World War killed his faith in the self-sufficiency of the norms by which historians traditionally had done their work. The canon had not proved out. While maintaining the formal norms of scholarship, historians had unleashed a flood of propaganda justifying American intervention in a war caused not solely by German perfidy, but by the greed of all the powers involved in it, including the United States. How could such a conspicuous truth have escaped the notice of scholars ostensibly trained to test evidence for its validity? How could he have failed to see it? These questions motivated him to start over again, to reequip himself for the historian's craft. His training had been defective and had betrayed him. He wanted to do the job right this time.

Three articles that Beard wrote for the *American Historical Review* (AHR) in that decade reveal important stages of his growth as a philosopher of history. The first of these articles, the notorious "Written History as an Act of Faith," was his presidential address delivered before the American Historical Association convention on December 28, 1933, in Urbana, Illinois. He began by disputing the possibility of ever writing history objectively: "Every student of history knows that his colleagues have been influenced in their selection and ordering of materials by their biases, prejudices, beliefs, affections, general upbringing, and experience, particularly social and economic." Every written history, Beard continued, "is a selection and arrangement of facts, of recorded fragments of past actuality."[1]

Beard's opening remarks cleared the way for his assault on Leopold von Ranke whose *wie es eigentlich gewesen* (to show the actual past) philosophy had come as a defining revelation for American historians. The founding of the American Historical Association in 1884 coincided with the acme of Ranke's influence in Europe and the United States. That same year he was made the first honorary member of the AHA. Many of its founders had studied in German universities. They had returned home aflame with Rankean ideas about historical research as an activity undertaken at its most exalted level in archives and requiring a strict objectivity in the presentation of document-based facts. The historical profession in America became the fulfillment of Ranke's ideals. Beard, however, doubted that the historian could be "a disembodied spirit as coldly neutral to human affairs as the engineer to an automobile." It seemed more probable to him that "any written history inevitably reflects the thought of the author in his time and cultural setting," much as Ranke himself had gone about his business as a conservative historian affiliated with the ruling classes in Germany.[2]

The objectivity problem went deeper than Ranke's baleful influence, Beard concluded. The historian "must cast off his servitude to the assumptions of natural science and return to his own subject matter—to history as actuality." The intellectual formulas of natural science had cramped and distorted the exercise of historical analysis. History, in fact, was made up of "imponderables, immeasurables, and contingencies," the securely documented portion of the past scarcely constituting a visible surface fleck on the forbidding totality of a human experience almost entirely submerged in unknown elements. The history that can be known is always partial and never "actual" in the Rankean sense. Therefore, "all written history is relative to time and circumstance." Here Beard came to his main point: "The historian who writes history, therefore, consciously or unconsciously performs an act of faith." Certainty is denied him. Surveying the past and trying to explain it, he makes choices, always "with respect to some conception of the nature of things." This faith Beard described as the historian's "conviction that something true can be known about the movement of history and his conviction is a subjective decision, not a purely objective discovery."[3]

Beard made it clear that he wanted historians to go on with their work as researchers guided by empirical standards of science. Accurate knowledge of historical facts constituted a good in the support it gave to the life of a democracy: "The scientific method is, therefore, a precious and indispensable instrument of the human mind; without it society would sink down into primitive animism and barbarism." In keeping with his abiding interest in the power of money as a determining factor in history, he called for "no abandonment of the tireless inquiry into objective realities, especially economic realities and relations." Nevertheless, the limitations of the scientific method had to be acknowledged. The writing of history is not an objective science. Many subjective elements come into play: "Any selection and arrangement of facts pertaining to any large area of history, either local or world, race or class, is controlled inexorably by the frame of reference in the mind of the selector and arranger."[4] Whatever philosophy of history a historian espouses, class and a welter of other prejudices affect his thinking.

The "Written History as an Act of Faith" address concluded with Beard's confession about his own faith as a historian. He believed that history was moving toward a collectivist democracy. This was his "guess," he called it, "founded on a study of long trends and on a faith in the indomitable spirit of mankind." He might be wrong, but so might every other historian: "one is more or less a guesser in this vale of tears."[5]

On February 19, 1950, Howard K. Beale wrote to Merle Curti, his colleague in the University of Wisconsin history department, about his impressions of the 1933 AHA convention. He described how Beard's presidential address went "over the heads of members of the AHA." Beard always had enjoyed a reputation for plain, clear speech as befits a midwestern farm boy. "Written History as an Act of Faith," however, completely mystified the convention goers. They had no idea what Beard was talking about. It was as if to them he had become the worst kind of German philosophy professor, unable to speak understandably to normal people. Beale further observed, "the address dealt grandly with fundamental problems of the historian."[6] Hardly anyone in Beard's audience, however, so much as suspected the existence of such problems. Hence the address not only mystified his fellow historians; it shocked them as well.

Indeed, German philosophy provided the theoretical foundation of Beard's argument in "Written History as an Act of Faith," but as interpreted by philosopher and historian Benedetto Croce, the most learned man of his time in Italy. Beard cited him repeatedly in the address. He had invited Croce to attend the convention in Urbana. Instead, Croce had sent a letter on the present state of historiography. The letter was read at the convention and then published in the *AHR*.

In his letter, Croce grimly noted that the writing of history had shared in the West's general lowering of moral and spiritual values. The most pressing issue in the profession today concerned the need for historians to raise the standards of their craft. It was not as if they would have to invent anything or to develop new theoretical insights. Good history writing, like good poetry, had existed from time immemorial, but it constantly had to be revivified: "In its eternal essence, history is the story of the human mind and its ideals insofar as they express themselves in theories and works of art, in practical and moral actions." History included politics, economics, and every form of human activity, but the catalyst for effective history writing was to be found in the moral consciousness of the historian. Without being overly specific, Croce condemned the false historical schools of the past fifty years. He limited himself to a general denunciation of materialistic interpretations of history and the equally egregious ethnic or racial interpretations—"two forms of historical insensibility," he called them. They must be attacked, Croce concluded: "in the intellectual tendencies they generate, in the prejudices they introduce . . . they misguide and enfeeble thought and distort the course of historical narrative."[7] The problems facing historians affected modern society generally.

In *History: Its Theory and Practice*, a book that more than any other work influenced Beard's philosophy of history, Croce wrote with much greater specificity about the historians who had led the profession into a wilderness of errors and deformations. Based mainly on articles that Croce had written in 1912 and 1913, *History* had appeared in 1917 and then in English in 1923. "Every true history is contemporary history," Croce began.[8] Historians, thoroughly conditioned by their own life experiences and values, write to answer questions of the present, not the past. Some other species of the future might be capable of writing history objectively, but not the men who had appeared on earth thus far.

In Croce's survey of the great historians, in the sense of their being greatly influential and not necessarily greatly perceptive, he celebrated Giambattista Vico as the field's most original genius. In his *Scienza nuova* (1725), Vico recognized "the unfolding of the human mind in history" as the supremely significant theme in all human experience. Croce called this insight the "intellectual backbone" of modern historiography insofar as the field plays a serious role in cultural life.[9] This was another Croce argument that Beard adopted, and it deeply influenced *The Rise of American Civilization*, as well as many other subsequent books, most conspicuously *The American Spirit: A Study of the Idea of Civilization in the United States* (1942).

It took Croce several hundred pages to make his way to Ranke, but the German historian was his real target all along. Even the relentlessly materialistic Marx, for whom Croce had scant regard as a historian, had done less damage than Ranke to the history profession overall. Early in the book, he stated, with obvious reference to Ranke, that for any historical event, "no one can know how it really happened." In a chapter called "The Historiography of Positivism," Croce sarcastically commented about the famous objective style of Ranke: "a form of exposition conducted in the tone of a presidential summing up, where careful attention is paid to the opinions of opposed parties and courtesy is observed toward all." In Ranke, elegance of style went hand in hand with a careful concealment of the author's convictions and a habitual evasion of anything like a definite resolution. Consummately moderate, the ever tactful and cautious Ranke met with resounding success "among the moderately disposed."[10]

One had to praise the industry of a scholar who had published fifty-four books, and Croce did acknowledge his enormous and fruitful industry. He also gave Ranke credit for great intelligence and finesse as a writer. Nevertheless, Croce could not take seriously his pretenses as an objective historian: "The boasted impartiality and objectivity, which was based on a literary device of half-words, of innuendoes, of prudent silences, was also equally illusory."[11] Respect and caution are undesirable traits, Croce averred in language that stirred Beard, for the crucial moral judgments that history must make.

In October 1935, Beard published the second of his historiographical articles for the *AHR*, "That Noble Dream." At the most recent convention of the AHA, Theodore Clark Smith had read a paper in which he had spoken of "a noble dream" as the quest for objective truth by historians. Such a dream, now deemed to be an illusion by the likes of Beard, had been the inspiration for the founding of the AHA, Smith claimed. Beard responded in his article that Smith had implied how opposition to the noble dream was ignoble. Smith's charge triggered an aggressive counterblast from Beard. Just as this second *AHR* article was appearing, he acerbically observed to James Harvey Robinson, his former colleague at Columbia University and the New School for Social Research: "What the hell do the historians think they are doing when they are selecting ten facts out of millions and gluing them together with adverbs?"[12]

In "That Noble Dream," Beard continued his critique of Ranke and once again used Croce as his point of departure. Beard castigated Ranke as a propagandist on retainer for the Prussian establishment "against which so many 'impartial' historians in the United States wrote vigorously in 1917–1918." Ranke had contributed powerfully to the noble dream in America, and Beard saw in mainstream American historiography an all-but-irresistible proclivity toward celebratory writing born of the German connection. In fact, the impartiality of Ranke entailed a completely incurious attitude toward the assumptions of the Prussian power structure, in the service of which he became a cherished intellectual adornment. Claiming to be objective, he in fact helped to preserve the status quo by uncritically accepting the premises of its rule. Objective historians did not pass moral judgments. They simply recorded the facts of the past and let them stand without critical comment. Beard could not conceive of a more effective method for the intellectual defense of an existing order than to muzzle the moral conscience of historians in the name of science. He rejected the Rankean philosophy of history for its complete lack of self-awareness about its real hegemonic function in society: "Persistently neglecting social and economic interests in history, successfully avoiding any historical writing that offended the most conservative interests in the Europe of his own time, Ranke may be correctly characterized as one of the most partial historians produced by the nineteenth century." Beard wondered, was he "totally unaware of the fact that he might be writing from the point of view of the conservative reaction in Europe?"[13]

An even more pertinent question for Ranke-inspired American historians concerned the pro-establishment bias of their work. By not questioning the methodological assumptions ordained by Ranke, American historians presided over a scholarly culture in which the defects of his approach to writing history had coalesced into a formidable orthodoxy. Beard noted that vigorous challenges to Ranke's ideas had emerged in Europe, with Croce serving as one of his foremost contemporary critics. Even some Americans had questioned the wisdom or the possibility of an objective methodology in writing history. In the United States, however, the academic world generally lay under a Rankean pall. There "slight attention has been given to the intellectual problems involved in the choice of subjects, the selection of facts, and the construction of monographs and many-volumed works."[14] American historians, he lamented, for the most part have not concerned themselves with the assumptions of their research and writing. Europeans, led by Croce and others, largely had freed European historiography from its thrall to Ranke.

Beard in "That Noble Dream" commented extensively about Marx's influence on him. He began by comparing Marx favorably with Ranke. Professor Smith had claimed that the economic interpretation of history had its origin in Marx's theories. Beard understood that with this polemical shaft Smith once again had targeted him. He replied: "I cannot speak for others, but so far as I am concerned my conception of the economic interpretation of history rests upon documentation older than Karl Marx—Number X of the *Federalist*, the writings of the Fathers of the Republic, the works of Daniel Webster, the treatises of Locke, Hobbes, and Machiavelli, and the *Politics* of Aristotle—as well as the writings of Marx himself." Here he praised Marx: "Yet I freely pay tribute to the amazing range of Marx's scholarship and the penetrating character of his thought." A deeply learned man with a highly impressive training in languages, philosophy, and history, he had led a life completely devoted to the service of his moral vision for the world. Possibly, he concluded, we may be able "to learn a little bit, at least, from Karl Marx."[15] This was much more than he expected to obtain from Ranke.

Between Beard's second and third theoretical articles for the *AHR*, he wrote *The Discussion of Human Affairs*, in part a summary of "Written History as an Act of Faith" and "That Noble Dream." He also used the book to explain the origins and nature of imperialism in the light of his evolving philosophy of history. Economics, he now conceded, could not be said to account for everything in the history of imperialism. He cited Joseph Schumpeter, who in a classic 1919 essay, "The Sociology of Imperialisms," had sought to refute John A. Hobson and other left-wing critics for arguing that capitalism served as the source of modern imperialism. Schumpeter had countered with the dictum that modern imperialism is an atavistic survival of past ages when warrior elites fought wars of objectless military expansion. Such predacious elements continued to exist, and every society had them. Militarism and imperialism could and did acquire capitalist support, but the propulsive force of aggression on an international scale originated and still drew its animating force from pre-capitalist survivals into the modern age. Schumpeter wrote, "it is a basic fallacy to describe imperialism as a necessary phase of capitalism, or even to speak of the development of capitalism into imperialism." Under capitalism, it was not the businessman and industrialist who fomented imperialism, "but the intellectual, and the content of his ideology is explained not so much from definite class interests as from chance emotion and individual interest."[16]

Beard read Schumpeter appreciatively and thought there was "something" to his theory about imperialism as "a hangover from feudalism." Schumpeter certainly had identified a significant element in the phenomenon of imperialism, but Beard brought up the recently concluded Nye Committee investigation into the munitions industry and Wall Street financial community to suggest that the claims in "The Sociology of Imperialisms" had the effect of obscuring the crucial war-making role of businessmen and industrialists. "The history of imperialism," Beard continued to insist, "is in large measure the story of government protection and promotion of economic interest in distant places." The Great War had been fought over empire. Economic motives in the war remained incompletely understood, but business, financial, and munitions interests "cannot escape some responsibility for the actions which eventuate in war." The actions he had in mind were the war scares, armament rivalries, and bank pressures on government leading to American intervention that the Nye Committee had documented. Modern war he thought "closely related to the forms and distribution of wealth and to the struggle over resources and trade opportunities of the earth."[17]

Though still strongly committed to the economic interpretation of history, Beard now adopted an increasingly subtle and variegated way of writing about it. Much of history really had nothing or relatively little to do with economics, and, besides, people had been shown to look after their economic interests in ways both ignorant and self-destructive. As he would write to Merle Curti some years later, "There certainly is something in economic determinism, more than most people suspect, but there is a lot of sheer folly in the world that is no-sense or chaos."[18] He no longer spoke with any confidence about cause and effect in history. The enormous complexities of the past and the tight, limitless mesh of influences shaping it made him think in terms of conditioning forces rather than specific historical causes. Forays into what Beard called the "highly technical literature about historiography" had a humbling effect on him, as he explained at considerable length in *The Discussion of Human Affairs*. He wanted his fellow American historians to try reading some of this literature. "It was not to be read casually by laymen," Beard warned, "any more than the technical literature on higher physics."[19] He did not see how professional historians in the United States, however, could do serious work anymore without catching up to the Europeans.

In an *AHR* article that Beard wrote with his son-in-law, Alfred Vagts, for the April 1937 issue, "Currents of Thought in Historiography," American historians came in for some particularly rough handling because of their general ignorance about theory. Born in Germany and a European-trained historian, Vagts and his wife, the former Miriam Beard, had fled Germany when the Nazis took power in 1933. He would go on to a distinguished scholarly career in the United States at Harvard and at the Institute for Advanced Study in Princeton. Vagts in 1937 had published *The History of Militarism*, a term he defined as denoting a culture not focused on the winning of wars but on the narcissistic promotion of a nation's armed forces to gain financial support for them. He also was extremely well informed about the theoretical developments of the utmost interest to Beard.[20]

The coauthors lamented, "Upon American historical scholarship all this continental searching and exploring has had little apparent effect." They summed up the attitudes of American historians toward the philosophy of history this way: "American historians have no philosophy of history; they want none; they distrust it; they regard anyone who bothers with it as an intruder or a mystic who is trying to impose something on them." Yet American historians do have "some philosophy or scheme of controlling values," only they do not acknowledge it. Dutiful children of Ranke, they tell themselves that they are writing objective history as neutral observers. "Taking notes and pasting them together with innocent assurance," few of them ever had bothered to question their operating assumptions, which Beard judged to be principally the democratic character of the United States and the country's beneficent role in the world.[21]

German historians, on the other hand, could no longer afford to indulge themselves in their national clichés, which had helped produce the calamities of 1914 to 1933. Ranke had received his most thoroughgoing repudiation in Germany. He still had German followers, such as Friedrich Meinecke, but the new history was in the ascendant, at least in Europe. Beard and Vagts mentioned numerous German critics of Ranke, singling out for special importance Karl Heussi, whose *Die Krisis des Historismus* (1932) they praised as an excellent overview of the new theoretical literature.

"Currents of Thought in Historiography," however, derived its main insights from the Budapest-born Karl Mannheim, who had studied in Berlin and Heidelberg. Beard long had admired Mannheim. He and Mary had concluded the second edition of *The Rise of American Civilization* with a reference to Mannheim's book: "So, Thought, weary Titan, continued to climb as for two thousand years the rugged crags between Ideology and Utopia," as if American history up to that point, in the millennial context of the Western world, could be boiled down to two words—ideology and utopia.[22] In *Ideology and Utopia*, which had appeared in English in 1936, Mannheim presented these terms as the poles of human political and intellectual interaction from which the historical process derived its deepest meaning. All power establishments resorted to ideological mystifications about the motives for their policies. Government always involved deception on a grand scale. The leaders desired to be seen dispensing justice and furthering the common good, not promoting a self-serving agenda for an elite class to which they themselves belonged.

Mannheim had credited Karl Marx with the discovery of how political rhetoric is used as a cover for power. He called this insight the most original and greatest intellectual achievement of Marxism. Yet Marxists conspicuously had failed to apply their supreme insight to themselves, preferring to think of Marxism as the purest science conceivable and communist societies as immune to the corruption of government power. In this preference, Marxists adhered to what Mannheim called the law of all utopian thinkers, to envisage their alternative to the status quo as reason itself. Opposition groups unfailingly indulged in utopian thinking about their aims and motives. History for Mannheim lay between ideology and utopia. Using the relational categories of analysis that he called the sociology of knowledge, the historian would be able to rise above the subjective claims of the ideologues and the utopians and thus explain the dynamics of the power struggles that propelled history forward. The discipline of history, properly conceived in the humility of recognizing that the historian is part of the historical process and, therefore, essentially conditioned by it, furnished a method to compensate for subjectivity without doing the impossible of eliminating it. Mannheim presented his method as the best chance that historians had for understanding how societies have come to be what they are and work the way they do.

Mannheim's book came much more as a confirmation of what Beard had been doing from nearly the beginning of his career than as a revelation, but *Ideology and Utopia* gave him a new way to think about the American version of the human struggle for preeminence. Even in America, the power elites controlling government routinely employed ideological mystifications regarding their rule, which had as its abiding aim the manipulation of the disorganized masses for the benefit of the politically conscious and connected elites. Just as invariably, American adversaries of the status quo developed utopian fantasies about themselves. Whenever the utopians won, as with the American revolutionaries of 1776, the agrarian party of Jefferson in 1800, and the Republicans of 1860, they became new elites, and the process of corruption by power started all over again.

Mannheim had shown, too, that historians write from one of four basic viewpoints: liberal, conservative, socialist, and reactionary.[23] In keeping with the overall theme of their article, Beard and Vagts called these viewpoints "schemes of reference."[24] Their habitual assumptions, predilections, preferences, and affections would influence the ways in which historians chose topics to write about, selected facts, and structured arguments. Historians had the obligation to be scrupulous in research and argument, but they always would be arguing from a preconceived viewpoint. History, therefore, would be an eternal argument with no final resolution, only provisional judgments susceptible to revision or overthrow as evidence accumulated and viewpoints changed. Beard and Vagts thought that it would take another thirty or forty years at least for American historians to realize that the scholarly culture of the even-handed neutral observer had been the profession's grand illusion.

Also in the late 1930s, Beard began to reread Brooks Adams, who became his supreme master among American historians during this period of questioning and reevaluating what it means to write history. One of Beard's most perceptive and admiring commentators, William Appleman Williams, claimed, "every major piece of historical writing that Beard published after 1940 bore the impact of Brooks Adams' two major volumes: *The Law of Civilization and Decay* and *The Theory of Social Revolutions*."[25] Williams referred to the many passages in Beard's books, including and perhaps above all the final two indictments of FDR, where the influence of Adams is manifest. He convincingly made his case regarding Beard's heavy reliance on Adams for understanding the general dynamics of the historical process. The Europeans helped Beard to frame his *AHR* articles about the relativism of all historical arguments, but Adams taught him more than anyone else did to think of American history in comparative and even universal terms. The great disabling limitation of American historiography, Beard and Adams pronounced, lay in its remorseless provincialism.

Beard wrote a long introduction for the 1943 reprint edition of Adams's *Law of Civilization and Decay: An Essay on History*.[26] From the standpoint of historical theory, he ranked him higher than his vastly more famous brother, Henry, another Beard favorite. Beard particularly admired Henry for the essays collected in *The Degradation of the Democratic Dogma* (1920), which he had reviewed very favorably for the *New Republic*.[27] According to Beard, though, Brooks's ideas had transformed Henry's writing.[28] The introduction began with the claim that *The Law of Civilization and Decay* is "among the outstanding documents of intellectual history in the United States and, in a way, the Western world." Through prodigious research, a conceptual framework of genius, and brilliant writing, Adams analyzed plutocratic and imperialistic tendencies in historical development. Applied to the United States, Beard thought, Adams's thesis made sense of the complex forces that had led to its plutocracy and empire—all this work coming well before Thorstein Veblen's *Theory of the Leisure Class* and John A. Hobson's *Imperialism: A Study*.

Perhaps most important for Beard, Adams had been the chief exception to the anti-theory rule in American historiography. Until Adams's book, Beard observed, there had been little speculation in the United States about the operating assumptions of historians. Adams, however, attempting to develop a philosophy of history, had anticipated many of Oswald Spengler's ideas in *The Decline of the West*. Beard judged Adams by far the better historian of the two.

Like Spengler, Adams thought in comparative historical terms in time and space. For both historians, the single most important question in the sweep of history concerned why civilizations rise and fall. Reacting to the devastating panic of 1893 and the economic depression that followed when the financial security of the Adams family appeared to be dissolving, he had begun a search for the deep historical causes of this disaster. He traced its origins back to ancient times. *The Law of Civilization and Decay* unfolded as a survey of pivotal episodes in world history foreshadowing the calamitous events of the present. With a strong note of approval, Beard pointed out the governing power of money in the Adams interpretation of history. In the cyclical movement from the chaos of barbarism to high civilization and then dissolution— the invariable long-term trajectory of history for empires—greed figured as the paramount negative force. Men intermittently had worked together in building prosperous and stable societies capable of producing original art and thought. Adams defined civilization as the rare consequence of such intervals between long periods of chaos. Inevitably, though, greed had destroyed every past civilization.

In modern civilization, according to Adams, the greed-driven process of decay had reached an advanced stage. The economic man had become dominant in society. Beard in his introduction explained how Adams had focused on "the driving greed of the usurer or finance capitalist never able to satiate his lust for money and power."[29] Money as an agency of exploitation and dominion gave the financial elites of the West effective economic control of all countries and cultures. As the center of the world's exchanges, London served as the primary conduit for the West's economic imperialism in subjugating backward peoples and appropriating their resources. The British, consequently, had the biggest empire. Other Western nations jostled for position in the imperialist sweepstakes. As a locus of power, industrial capitalism had been superseded by finance capitalism. The bankers and the financiers ruled the earth, but not in unison. Their greed-stoked rivalries, artfully concealed by all the usual demagogic stratagems of deception and disinformation plus many brand-new ones, already had brought the Western world face-to-face with its mortality. Spengler was not more pessimistic in his post–World War I best-seller, *The Decline of the West*, than Brooks Adams in *The Law of Civilization and Decay*, written during the alleged belle époque of the late nineteenth century.

For Beard, Adams's book took the mystery out of American statecraft past and present. William Appleman Williams was right to identify the late 1930s and early 1940s as the period when Adams's influence decisively shaped Beard's understanding of American history. Adams's name never appears in *The Rise of American Civilization* (1927). In *A Basic History of the United States*, published the year after Beard's introduction, he repeatedly used Adams to explain the country's turning points. In the chapter on the post–Civil War centralization of the United States economy, Beard observed: "If, as Brooks Adams declared in *The Law of Civilization and Decay*, published in 1895, the movement of energies in society is inexorably toward centralization, the course of economic and political affairs in the United States certainly provided illustrations." Moreover, with astonishing accuracy Adams had predicted the terrible agonies of war and economic disarray that would overwhelm Europe and shape American history after 1914. He had not been deceived or confused by "the rosy exposition of individualism or of social meliorism" in the American creed, which he ridiculed as a classic example of the country's flabby thinking about itself. As "a prophecy of the death of civilization under the heel of capitalistic usury," Adams's book had left a lasting mark on American intellectual and political life, but on no one more than Beard.[30]

The world still worked, Beard believed, in accordance with the thesis advanced in *The Law of Civilization and Decay*. Throughout the book, Adams specified the central role of money in dictating power relationships. With the ancient Romans, he wrote, "money was to take its ultimate form in a standing army." Great oligarchies would form the core elements of all the empires to come. In sixteenth-century England "wealth reached the point where it could lay the foundation of the paid police, the crowning triumph of the monied class." In their rise to imperial power, the English followed the program of the ancient Romans, who had "amassed the treasure by which they administered their Empire through the plunder and enslavement of the world."[31] This was the good old plan, which Beard thought Washington, D.C., now in 1943 was busily implementing for its own emoluments, to the thoroughly deceptive accompaniment of FDR's spellbinding rhetoric about a war being fought on behalf of freedom.

The Theory of Social Revolutions, the second Adams book that pervaded Beard's thinking as he tried to formulate a philosophy of history, appeared in 1914, twenty years after the publication of *The Law of Civilization and Decay*. Adams continued to think about history from ancient times to the present as a sequence of exploiting empires. Since 1815, Britain had possessed the most powerful empire, but now, a hundred years later, had begun to decline, its rule no longer equal to the task of maintaining world economic order. Indeed, Adams detected everywhere in the West the suspicion "that the principle of authority has been dangerously impaired."[32]

As the emerging financial colossus of the world, the United States merited special attention. A powerful anxiety had taken hold in America, "with its unwieldy bulk, its heterogeneous population, and its complex government." American capitalism he thought a particularly degenerate economic phenomenon, and its imposition on the world could only bring about the complete subjugation of mankind to the money power. Already the relationship between the financiers and the citizenry had assumed a master-slave character, in the sense that capital totally controlled the means of earning a livelihood. There was no appeal from the decision of the capitalist, "an unaccountable superior," about what he would do with his money or where he would send it in search of ever-greater profits, a point Adams already had made in the ominous closing pages of *The Law of Civilization and Decay*.[33] Now he warned about an unparalleled concentration of money in Wall Street and what this imperious wealth would mean for the American people and eventually for all peoples. Obviously, such a situation would mean war, as it always had, for the protection and augmentation of assets.

In the year when *The Theory of Social Revolutions* appeared, the European struggle for imperialist supremacy produced the Great War. In 1902, Adams had devoted an entire book to a positive reevaluation of imperialism, *The New Empire*, which William Appleman Williams in his account of Adams's influence on Beard did not mention. Yet any writing by Adams would have attracted Beard's notice. His abiding fascination with the subject of imperialism and great respect for Adams as a historian would have made *The New Empire* required reading for him, though he did not mention it in his 1943 introduction for *The Law of Civilization and Decay*. Beard did tell Merle Curti in a November 24 letter that year how for the introduction he had done extensive research in "a lot of Henry and Brooks Adams manuscripts and found an unknown story."[34] It safely can be presumed that *The New Empire* was one of the Adams manuscripts read by Beard.

Around the time of the Spanish-American War, three years after the publication of *The Law of Civilization and Decay*, Adams began to undergo a political and intellectual conversion to the cause of empire.[35] The victory of the United States in this war inspired him to think that something like an "American Century" might be dawning.[36] The prospect excited Adams and drew him to the imperialist statesmen eager for an American empire. He would not have been the first historian to be dazzled by the prospect of gaining access to power. Even before the war, he had been on friendly terms with Theodore Roosevelt, who had reviewed *The Law of Civilization and Decay* and, despite some criticisms of its somber tone and conclusions, praised the book for its profound research, vivid writing, and as "a distinct contribution to the philosophy of history."[37] Their relationship deepened after Roosevelt became president in 1901.[38] He made Adams one of his chief foreign policy advisers and relied heavily on him regarding Asian affairs in particular. Adams fit right in with the president's plans for an expanded American presence in Asia and offered him gratefully received advice about the need for a military buildup.

Although *The New Empire* appeared the same year as John A. Hobson's *Imperialism: A Study* and both authors shared an interest in the connections between economics and foreign policy, the two books emanated from different mental universes. Hobson argued that the manipulation of foreign policy by capitalist oligarchs in their relentless pursuit of profit had led to the imperialist rivalries then, in 1902, menacing the peace of the world. In his vehemence against the machinations of these economic elites, he wrote *Imperialism: A Study* as a moral reproach.

For Adams, in *The New Empire*, the ineluctable laws of history made moral judgments futile. Unlike Hobson—and Beard—Adams at this time held classic Darwinian views, without any mitigating values, about the historical process: "Competing nations seek, along the paths of least resistance, the means which give them an advantage in the struggle for survival."[39] The United States had been cast into the struggle for world economic supremacy, not by Wall Street, but by the dialectical forces of historical evolution, which condemned weakness and quiescence while exalting warlike energy.

Far from denouncing imperialism as a scourge in the manner of Hobson, Adams embraced it as a higher calling to which only the strongest and healthiest nations could respond. He would change his mind about imperialism, as he did about many of his views, and in such later books as *The Theory of Social Revolutions* and in his long introduction to Henry Adams's *The Degradation of the Democratic Dogma* (1920) revert to the critical viewpoint found in *The Law of Civilization and Decay*. For some years after 1898, however, he provided intellectual support for the American war party against the Spanish and the Filipinos.[40] It is most likely that Beard, inveterately hostile to the first Roosevelt occupant of the White House, would have considered *The New Empire* a perversely brilliant book because of its prophetic insights regarding the future of America.

In its appendices, Adams cited a book he had written two years earlier, *American Economic Supremacy*, as the indispensable preamble for understanding *The New Empire*. The 1900 book consisted of a series of essays he had written for various magazines the previous two years. He advanced an unvarnished Darwinian thesis about America as the replacement empire for an exhausted England, whose lackluster performance in the Boer War and reliance on American capital to finance it, among numerous other instances of British inability to lead effectively, left little uncertainty about the shift of power westward to New York and Washington. The Spanish-American War provided additional evidence, Adams contended, for the claim that the United States stood poised to take Britain's place as the new balance point in the world order. About that war he wrote, "The present outbreak is, probably, only premonitory, but the prize at stake is now what it always has been in such epochs, the seat of commercial exchanges—in other words, the seat of empire." To compete for world markets and resources, Adams explained, "the United States has been converted from the most pacific of nations into an armed and aggressive community."[41] In his explanation of American capitalism's existential need to find outlets for its large agricultural and industrial surplus, he reached the same conclusion uncritically that Hobson did as a latter-day Jeremiah.

America's immense wealth and extremely energetic population impelled the country toward its imperial destiny. It possessed the wherewithal and the desire to lead. All the alternatives to American world leadership Adams found fatally flawed, because of either their threat to American interests or lack of sufficient power for the task. He concluded in *America's Economic Supremacy*, "the expansion of the United States is automatic and inevitable." The fate of Latin America, which had become a satrapy of Wall Street, would overtake the rest of the world, as the United States developed the greatest empire in all history. He thought the main significance of the Spanish-American War lay in Commodore George Dewey's conquest of Manila. The Philippines would be the strategic center of the American presence in the Pacific. The fabulously rich resources and market of China, "this mass of undeveloped wealth," would be in play. It followed, then, that "America must more or less completely assume the place once held by England, for the United States could hardly contemplate with equanimity the successful organization of a hostile industrial system on the shores of the Pacific, based on Chinese labor, nourished by European capital, and supported by the inexhaustible resources of the valley of the Ho-hang-ho." The United States would be obliged "to enter upon the development of Eastern Asia and to reduce it to a part of our economic system." For the accomplishment of such a daunting task, Adams saw no alternative to the creation of a large American army and navy "in being armed and organized against all emergencies."[42] He was the most corroborative of advisers to President Theodore Roosevelt.

It is worth noting here that a reprint edition of *America's Economic Supremacy* appeared in 1947, just as the Truman Doctrine promising assistance to all countries resisting communist tyranny was becoming the foundation of America's Cold War foreign policy. The implacably interventionist author and journalist Marquis W. Childs wrote a long introduction for the book, which he described as a prescient analysis of the compelling reasons for America's full involvement in the world as a necessary consequence of the country's economic supremacy. With the implementation of Truman's plan to have the United States assist Greece and Turkey for the present, and for the future any other country seeking to repel communist subversion, it could be seen, Childs happily announced, "Even those who have persisted in blind isolationism seem to be accepting the necessity of action, although with a kind of churlish reluctance."[43] He might have had Beard in mind as one of the churls, except that the historian had lacked the grace even to give his reluctant acceptance to this Magna Carta of the American military-industrial complex.

In *Architects of Illusion: Men and Ideas in American Foreign Policy, 1941–1949,* Lloyd C. Gardner also took note of the strong effects generated in Washington by the postwar republication of *America's Economic Supremacy*. George F. Kennan, the guru of America's Cold War "containment" strategy, hailed Adams as a prophet who with an astonishing clairvoyance had predicted the future of America as the leader of the world and even the role of Russia as a hegemonic Washington's paramount adversary. War had come in 1941 not primarily because of Pearl Harbor. That attack constituted only one variable in the complex sweep of history for which *America's Economic Supremacy* furnished the indispensable historical prologue. Gardner deftly summed up the essential meaning of the prologue, World War II, and the Cold War: America had inherited world leadership from Great Britain, as Adams had foretold, "and that meant responsibility for world capitalism."[44]

Beard's interest in *The New Empire* touched not on the Darwinian philosophy held over from *America's Economic Supremacy*, or on Adams's repeated assertions about the inevitable succession of the United States as the ruler of an empire mightier than Britain's at its imperial peak. The sections of the book dealing with the Pacific pertinently addressed the questions of foreign policy and war dominating Beard's thinking in the early 1940s as he tried to fathom the real reasons for the Second World War and its likely outcome for the United States. Adams, who admired the military and economic prowess of the Japanese, hoped for cooperation between them and the Americans in what he imperturbably called the administration of Chinese resources and business affairs. The two nations already had demonstrated their capacity to work together toward this end during the Boxer Rebellion of 1899–1901 when Chinese nationalists sought to expel all foreign occupying powers. The Europeans had wanted to solidify their spheres of influence and to extinguish Chinese independence. The United States and Japan had resisted the partition plan in favor of maintaining the territorial integrity of the country. He could not resist noting, "The President of the United States took the lead and led to the end." Adams at once understood the real import of the open-door policy, much vaunted in the press as a characteristic instance of American fair play and concern for the underdog: "The New Empire had stretched its arm over north-ern China."[45]

Yet the following comment by Adams about Japan put the entire twentieth-century history of the Pacific in a context that to Beard made more sense of the Second World War than any pronouncement by Theodore Roosevelt's fifth cousin, Franklin: "Nor can the Japanese well afford to remain passive. Were they to abide within their islands while their competitors opened the richest mineral beds of the world at their doors, their very existence as an independent people would be endangered."[46] To compete with its rivals, Japan would have to expand, just as they all had done. Without some accommodation for the Japanese, war would be inevitable.

Adams observed in *The New Empire*, "To supply themselves with what they lack men must trade or rob, and on the whole trading has been cheaper." Reasoning from this principle and without recourse to any euphemisms about freedom, Adams concluded that the United States and Japan should work to find a way to share the Pacific. He lacked the flexibility of mind to substitute a quadripartite division of freedom for the ideologically unadorned word "rule" and would have been a verbally insensitive adviser to Franklin Roosevelt. "War," Adams asserted, "is economic competition in its sharpest aspect."[47] He admitted of no exceptions to this rule in all recorded history, a point to which Beard gave his vigorous assent, the Second World War, most especially, included. From Adams the intellectually retooled Beard learned to think of the military operations then taking place in the Pacific as a trade war in the interminable sequence of struggles for world power.

Some principles in the reeducated Beard's thinking did not change from before. Beard remained staunchly committed to empirical research as the professional ideal for historical investigation. The economic power relationships that determined the fate of nations and civilizations could be uncovered in no other way. The famous Beard economic interpretation of history remained central to the way he thought about the past. Among his educators of the 1930s and 1940s, Adams confirmed and reinforced Beard's "act of faith" as a historian. *The Law of Civilization and Decay*, with its eloquent appeal to moral suasion soon to be silenced in Adams's pro-imperialist tracts, identified predatory ruling classes as the single most important cause of imperialism and the wars necessary for its implementation. Beard took Adams's thesis in *The Law of Civilization and Decay* as the starting point for understanding the world in the twentieth century. Adams's dictum about the ultimately ruinous impact made on foreign policy by economic elites ever retained its validity for him.

Beard nevertheless became increasingly mindful during the 1930s of the many other factors that influenced history. He especially recognized the importance of government power and the commanding figures, such as FDR, who exercised it. Charismatic individuals of this world-historical type could embody a culture and reflect its deepest yearnings, thereby inserting themselves decisively into the stream of events. Hobson in *Imperialism: A Study* had not taught Beard this lesson. To Hobson, politicians stood on a plane with liveried footmen, doing as they were told by the lords of finance. Such an image conveyed some important truths about the prime movers of domestic and foreign policy, but left completely unaccounted for the enormous manipulative energy generated by modern governments.

Adams had come closer to understanding government power as a collusive but independent variable in the modern capitalist order. He had seen Theodore Roosevelt work the levers of power. He knew from first-hand experience how an intellectually nimble and charismatic leader could initiate and advance a political agenda of his own, involving, for example, wars of expansion. From Adams, as well as from the 1934–1936 Nye Senate Committee investigation of the munitions industry, Beard drew the lesson that in some of his writings he had oversimplified the relationship between politics and economics by not understanding fully its reciprocal character. In periods of the maximum stress and tension brought on by war, politics even could subsume and predominate over economics. Beard's final two books, dealing wholly with FDR as the chief conditioning influence for America's entry into the Second World War, could not have taken shape in his mind the way they did without the labors of Adams and the Nye Committee.

The most startling innovation resulting from Beard's historical reeducation had to do with the strong emphasis that he placed on morality. On the need for a rigorously moral approach to history, Beard the archetypal economic historian dutifully took instruction partly from the early and late Adams books, but mainly from Croce.[48] After reading and fully absorbing Croce, Beard came to understand that a work of history derives its true meaning from the historian's moral foundation. By his own Croce-inflected reasoning, the fundamental question for historical philosopher Charles Austin Beard concerned the moral values that he brought to his work.

Beard's experience with religion provides one possible source for investigating his moral outlook. Religion was a somewhat ambiguous theme in Beard's life. He had an irregular Protestant upbringing about which he did not write very much. From ages six to sixteen, he attended a private elementary and secondary Quaker school, Spiceland Academy.[49] For college he went to a Methodist institution, DePauw University. The Beard family, however, never joined any religious denomination and did not go to church.[50] It is impossible to measure precisely but unwise to disregard the leavening effect of religious instruction, however fitful it may have been, in his understanding of morality.[51]

In a broad cultural sense, Beard may be said to have absorbed Christian conceptions of morality without, so far as the record shows, expressing himself in overtly religious terms. In his youth, the ecstatically devout John Ruskin made a life-changing impression on him. Hobson, however, permanently redirected his thinking toward the entirely secular ends described in Beard's long introductory essay for the American publication, in 1932, of *The Idea of Progress* (1920) by Cambridge University historian J. B. Bury. In that essay, the fifty-seven-year-old Beard wrote in evident sympathy about the idea of progress as "the conquest of the material world in human interest, of providing the conditions for a good life on this planet without reference to any possible hereafter."[52] He regarded the idea of material progress as the driving force and leading principle of American society.

Mary may have revealed in a letter to Northwestern University political scientist and family friend Kenneth Colegrove the essential character of what religion meant to them when she commented on the purging from religious observance in postwar Japan of the Sun Goddess. She understood why that country's American rulers had made such a decision: "To overcome Emperor worship there this is necessary, I know." She wondered, however, if this change would result "in the enthronement of the Hebraic God Jehovah, a God of War made to sanction the divine rights of kings and emperors for so long in the Occident. I can only hope that the gentler Jesus Christ imbued with the concept of Love will make a place in Japanese religious perceptions and hold it more firmly than it has been held in the West."[53] As the Beards had argued in *The American Spirit*, Christianity possessed ethical and moral properties highly conducive to civilization, a claim they made with equal fervor for the Enlightenment.

Albert Jay Nock, the libertarian journalist and magazine editor, offered perhaps the most suggestive way of thinking about Beard and religion. In his *Memoirs of a Superfluous Man*, Nock described the religious discussions that he had with "my able and distinguished friend, Mr. Charles A. Beard."[54] Beard always had an ally in him. For example, he had hailed *The Rise of American Civilization* for its "superabundant, almost incredible excellence." The Beards had the distinction, according to him, "of being the first to write their country's history as it should be written."[55]

A fervent Beardian particularly in his convictions about the oligarchic character of the United States throughout its history and the country's involvement in the Second World War as a means of escaping the political consequences of Roosevelt's failed domestic policies, Nock wrote in his memoirs: "I remember too, one day when Charles Beard and I were in one of what he used to call humorously our Meditations on the New Testament." The key word in Nock's account is "humorously." The exchange between the two men that he then recounted does not rise to the level of devotional literature. He quoted Beard on the subject of his relationship with God: "I believe if you approach God in a perfectly frank, self-respecting manner, as one gentleman to another, He will meet you half-way and do the decent thing by you." Treated in a cringing and sniveling way, "he will wait till you get real close up, and then kick the seat right out of your pants."[56] They had a good time over such discussions, but based on Beard's published work and surviving letters, secular values, quite possibly superimposed on earlier beliefs, governed his thinking about morality.

In "Written History as an Act of Faith," Beard succinctly described the cause of genuine democracy as his ultimate concern. The paramount struggle throughout American history down to today involved the thwarting of democracy by oligarchy. Once again Hobson led the way for Beard. In his 1918 book *Democracy after the War*, Hobson dramatically described the world situation as a struggle of humanity with the powers and principalities of capitalism. He had written about the irony of the then-concluding war for democracy, understood realistically by its architects as the prelude for a world order made safe for investors, and the actual plight of democratic institutions, which had undergone the authoritarian transformations made inevitable in wartime. Hobson predicted that the postwar period would witness the most pitiless and treacherous campaign ever waged against the common people of the earth: "All the intellectual and moral as well as the financial resources of the ruling and possessing classes that hate and fear democracy (though doing lip service) will be used so as to control and dope public opinion as to prevent the formation and emergence of a popular will reasonable enough to master the state, and through the state to reform property, industry, and social institutions." The most extreme and varied measures would be employed "to check the intellectual and moral growth of democracy."[57] The revisionist Beard thought so, too, and viewed the world he lived in as confirmation for the timeliness of Hobson's warnings.

In Beard's final public address, on the theme of "Neglected Aspects of Political Science," he spoke at the American Political Science Association convention, in Washington, D.C., on December 29, 1947, and summed up his historical philosophy. In his opening statement he lamented "our general disregard of the primary truth that in thinking and writing about government or any aspect thereof all of us necessarily proceed upon some presupposed and controlling theory of knowledge, certainty, probability, possibility, and conviction."[58] In effect, he stated for the audience the principles outlined in his historiographical articles published in the *American Historical Review* during the 1930s and in his *Discussion of Human Affairs* from the same period.

Beard then lamented the divorce between political science and history as a great moral and intellectual disaster, resulting as it had in work both scholarly and popular of "unreality and formalism." About the real world of politics, foreign policy, and war, the American people had been deprived of the realistic guidance and instruction that in the manner of Brooks Adams should have been the province of historians and political scientists. Instead of providing realism, the scholars by and large engaged in the preservation of a national mythology about the United States as a democratic country standing for peace and security in the world: "Indeed the business of expounding and writing commentaries on projects for ordering up the world and its several parts on correct principles has become a heavy industry in academic circles, and those who engage in it zealously can count on rewards and applause." He feared that political science would become "subservient to vested interests and politicians temporarily in power."[59]

The serious study of foreign affairs, Beard continued, had become a risky and even dangerous occupation in America today. Universities had fallen victim to an invincible conformity on questions pertaining to America's role in the world. He took for his example the devoutly proclaimed insistence on the peace-loving character of the American people and their proud record of waging wars for moral purposes: "Any professor who challenges the truth of it is likely to be treated as a rude and wanton disturber of a prayer meeting." Professors of gilt-edged reputation at the country's foremost institutions of higher learning taught that wars are forced on the United States "by aggressive foreigners." Wars of self-defense were the only kind that we ever did or could fight, our exceptional democratic values systemically shielding us from unjust aggressive acts. We were a land fated to wage wars only "for enduring peace, world democracy, and the rights of suppressed peoples."[60]

The implications for domestic politics of a world-saving foreign policy could be guessed at with a fair degree of confidence, Beard supposed. People who commented critically on the deficiencies of American life for vast numbers of our fellow citizens were "likely to be charged with indifference to our world obligations." Already it was starkly evident how "the exigencies of foreign commitments and preparedness for the next war have acquired a terrific preponderance over domestic requirements, whatever they may be." To stave off the complete subversion of the Republic by the imperialists and militarists now leading the country, political scientists and historians would have to revive their critical faculties and courage. They had a cause, to enlighten their fellow citizens about the dangers lying in wait for a country that had proved to be tragically eager for self-deception. He concluded: "We might contribute a little to the advancement of learning and good will among peoples by trying to see ourselves as other nations see us, to think of them as far as possible in terms of their thought of themselves, and to get rid of the insidious idea that the United States has been designated by God as a kind of cosmic committee for the Americanization of mankind and the final revision of universal history."[61]

Mary recalled how at the end of Beard's address, the hall had erupted in a thunderous applause. After Beard's death, she wrote to Merle Curti about the event. A turn-away crowd had come to hear him, and people stayed in the doorway listening as best they could. She thought that he had spoken brilliantly and handled the entire occasion with "esthetic skill."[62] In that same letter, though, she recognized that the trend in the profession already had made Beard an anachronism. His pro-war and internationalist adversaries had gained a decisive victory.

In their correspondence, Mary and Curti had identified the Second World War as the turning point. The glorification of that war and the policies that had led to America's intervention in it ruled out a genuinely critical examination of the actual motives behind the fighting. Curti became despondent about the corrupting effects on the profession of such a gag order. Mary sought to console him: "if you will consider my advice, you will work on, irrespective of what the profession is like, does or does not do, with your own integrity as your guide and let the chips fall where they will."[63] Her husband had lived that way for his entire career. She could not imagine a more noble way to live and gloried in sharing his struggles. A little more than a year earlier, though, Mary had told Curti that she was glad Beard had not lived to see the absolute triumph in Washington of a culture based on "war hopes and plans amid the verbalism of peace."[64] He at least had escaped that grief.

Conclusion

The Sad Historian of the Pensive Plain

Toward both ends of a long career, Beard gained extreme notoriety for iconoclastic assaults on America's myth making about itself. He envisaged *An Economic Interpretation of the Constitution of the United States* as an essay in critical thinking about the patriotic myths that over time had enveloped the fundamental law of the land. *President Roosevelt and the Coming of the War, 1941: A Study in Appearances and Realities* Beard presented as a valedictory challenge to the country's unexamined assumptions about the Second World War. Actualized legends drove the dominant narrative for both cases, he believed. Historians, in his view, were supposed to liberate history from myths, not to celebrate them. Human nature in all times and places being as it is, neither events nor peoples honestly could be given a unique place in the history of goodness. Americans had lived their history under the same mark of Cain that every other people had. History generally proceeded by wrong turns, and in the end for earthly powers always did.

Beard very precisely identified where American history appeared to have taken the wrong turn that had led to major national predicaments: the defeat of John Quincy Adams in the presidential election of 1828. He made this point emphatically and at length in *The American Spirit*. Adams's defeat meant the repudiation of his American System idea of federal leadership in developing the country's resources for the common good. Instead of adopting a wise planned system of economic development, Americans decided to build up the nation by a process that a historian much admired by Beard, Henry Adams, likened to the pillaging of an immense ore bed stretching from sea to shining sea. Andrew Jackson became for Beard the paramount human symbol of the plundering operation that defined American history. Extending the sphere, in the picturesque expression of James Madison, had been the driving force of American history all along, but Beard thought that the election of 1828 had produced a frank avowal of greed as the dominant American philosophy in the country's political and economic life. Jackson would have many successors, the country's foremost political and economic figures among them. Destiny after 1828 beckoned the country to a defining Gilded Age.

The implications of such a philosophy for American foreign policy pointed in the direction of empire. Once the national ore bed had been staked out and the bulk of its contents distributed to the oligarchs who ran the country, it would be time to extend the sphere abroad. The nation's wars from 1898 to 1948, the year of Beard's death, had been fought and were being fought for many different reasons, but economic gain always seemed to him to have a place of systemic importance in the calculation of the leaders or to result as an inescapable consequence of their world view. The Cold War, only in its earliest phase when Beard died, he judged to be the most fully realized example of how the United States had come to envisage itself as the world's guardian and promoter of corporate capitalism and consumer society. All the invocations to democracy and human rights as the motives for American foreign policy diverted attention from economic fundamentals, which had to be seen operating in a broad cultural context, not simply and narrowly in the form of Wall Street knavery. Campaign financing did give economic elites an overwhelming advantage in American political life, but their capacity to manipulate the system extended far beyond election-cycle funding.

Ironies abound in the intellectual biography of Beard. Conservative thinkers shaped the critical sensibilities of this famous left-wing historian to an extent that never has been properly understood. Although he was a man of the left politically, thanks to the far-reaching influence on his thinking of John Atkinson Hobson, Beard at the very beginning of his serious mental development found in cultural conservative John Ruskin a model social critic. Our first loves leave their marks on us. Ruskin's work quickened into full development Beard's appreciation of modern history as a perennial struggle between corrupt business elites and subordinate populations. He did not understand this process as a Marxist dialectic guaranteeing a communist outcome, but as something permanent, an open-ended extension of the battle fought between the rich and the poor throughout history.

Every aspect of life suffered from the economic and political institutions created by modernity, culture most of all, Ruskin taught. Beard analyzed American civilization in the cultural terms laid down by Ruskin in *Unto This Last*, meaning fundamentally that the prerogatives of financial elites without moral compunction have an overmastering and debilitating effect on the collective. To save culture from the domination of concentrated wealth, a resistance movement had to be undertaken by artists and writers. Young Charles Beard responded to Ruskin's call, which gave him his general intellectual and moral direction in life.

Beard viewed American history in a way akin to Oliver Goldsmith's story of Auburn, the name the English poet and novelist chose for the community described in "The Deserted Village." In that poem, which Goldsmith wrote in 1770, he depicted scenes of the decay and desolation that had befallen Auburn. Once it had been a thriving community of healthy-natured people fulfilled in their work and strivings, the kind of citizens later admired by Ruskin as the unfailing sign of authentic national wealth. Free of luxury's temptations, they enjoyed a benevolent relationship with nature and each other. The contagious greed of economic tyrants spoiled everything for the people of Auburn:

> Thus fares the land, by luxury betray'd
> In nature's simplest charms at first array'd
> But verging to decline, its splendours rise,
> Its vistas strike, its palaces surprise.

The working people had no place there anymore and departed. One last inhabitant of the ruined community remained to tell the tale of woe, "the sad historian of the pensive plain." Beard gave himself this same assignment in recording what he felt increasingly certain were the causes and the agents of America's Auburn-like fate: "'Tis yours to judge how wide the limits stand / Between a splendid and a happy land."[1]

Beard never abandoned his vocation for social criticism. He took his place in the ranks of the dissident Americans he most admired. To him a cardinal virtue of American civilization lay in its capacity to produce critical intellectuals and activists. He filled his books with vignettes of such people. The critical mind understood how power tended to corrupt any person or group that held it. Beard did not believe in class conflict in any Marxist sense. His study of history, particularly in reading Brooks Adams's *The Law of Civilization and Decay: An Essay on History*, had taught him that the people with money and power always want more of what they already possess in a superabundance.

The health and sanity of society required critical intellectuals and activists to oppose these elites by a reflex action, always responding to their rhetorical declamations and proposed policies with skepticism and, as a rule, opposition. Democracy dies when the critics desert their posts.

Beard took a prominent place in the defining debate of American historiography about the country's true character and meaning for humanity. Was America the light of the world or more like its extinguishing shadow? Two archetypal figures in American historiography representing this divide between celebrators and critics were George Bancroft and Richard Hildreth, both nineteenth-century historians. Bancroft, by far the more famous and successful of the two, hailed America as a beacon of liberty, in the vanguard of God's unfolding purposes for humanity. He celebrated U.S. expansion in the Mexican-American War as a just policy for extending the area of freedom. Hildreth, by contrast, thought that slavery and the complicity of the entire nation in it destroyed all American claims, past or present, about the creation in God's country of a city upon a hill. The slaughter of Native Americans and the theft of their lands also called into serious question the culture of patriotic self-laudation, to use his term, among American historians. Hildreth had a difficult time of it trying to convince his countrymen that the proper moral attitude for them should be one of conscience-stricken atonement. Both these men established precedents for the historians who followed them, with Bancroft in the role of pacesetter. For family likeness, the historical revisionist minority took after Hildreth.

In the case of Beard, the historical revisionism that he espoused contained much that was original with him. He also borrowed a lot, but it was the way that he borrowed, significantly from European sources, that made him an American original. Ruskin, Hobson, Gibbs, Croce, Mannheim, and numerous other Europeans gave him a unique pedigree by the normal standards of American historical scholarship. The Italian realists—Mosca, Pareto, and Michels—also strongly appealed to him. He brought European styles of questioning and reasoning to the study of American history. He also found inspiration in the example of Hildreth and the genius of the Adams brothers, Henry and Brooks. His reading of these European and American historians as well as the life experiences he had in England, at Columbia University, and in the revisionist movements after both world wars taught him to trust the wisdom of the classical authors about the relentless drive of power ever to expand and to exceed all limits until fatally overreaching itself. No nation could expect an exemption from these laws of history.

Beard thought that FDR had brought the United States to the point of no return in its history. From then on only a war economy could keep the American capitalist system operating. In this chief executive, Wall Street and what would become known as the military-industrial complex had found their ideal collaborator and patron. Their collaboration meant "perpetual war for perpetual peace," an agenda that carried a death sentence for the country, be it near or far, Beard believed. The Second World War's terrible outcome unmistakably proved to him that the leaders in Washington either did not know what they were doing or, more likely, did know and did not care about the destructive shock waves they had unleashed in society. He placed the blame primarily on the president. To Beard, FDR seemed to be creating a military empire as a way of covering up the failure of the New Deal to overcome the Depression. Roosevelt had discovered that capitalism could not cure itself by peaceful means. His discovery meant that war remained as the system's only option for survival. The country would be saddled with the responsibility of keeping a lid on the capitalist status quo—an utter impossibility, given the sordid fate of the billions living in squalor, want, and degradation who subsisted in the deep shadows of the world system.

Beard published at war's end his two big Roosevelt books: *American Foreign Policy in the Making, 1932–1940* and *President Roosevelt and the Coming of the War, 1941*. They buried his reputation as a historian. Beard did not disdain the good opinion of mankind. He wanted to be well regarded as a man and a historian. Beard's letters to his closest friends, Oswald Garrison Villard, Edwin Montefiore Borchard, Merle Curti, and Harry Elmer Barnes, underscore this need in his nature. Mary Ritter Beard repeatedly made the same point about her husband's chagrin over the insulting treatment that he received. Bad reviews he grew accustomed to, but public attacks injured him. He did not court the onslaught that befell him at the end.

Beard thought that he was being careful and cautious in writing about FDR, but none of his defensive strategies shielded him from the attacks that came in the last six months of his life. The accusation of his having been an objective ally of Fascists and Nazis did not seem unjust to a broad spectrum of intelligent American opinion. For many learned people in America, even among those who once had been Beard's friends and admirers, his intellectual influence in retrospect began to seem baleful. He gasped at such comments and concluded that there might be a large element of fantasy in America about its claims to honor freedom of expression. You could express yourself here, so long as you agreed with everyone about what really mattered, such as the unflawed goodness of the American cause in the Second World War.

The problem that Beard foresaw with a non-critical approach to the history of the Second World War concerned the obstacles that such dogmatism would create for our understanding of the postwar period. To comprehend the international scene of 1945, a person would have to know, first, that World War I and World War II comprised one war with a twenty-year armistice in between. World War II had been fought primarily to maintain the status quo ordained by the victors after World War I. The obsessive focus by FDR apologists on Hitler as the supreme incarnation in earthly form of all iniquity, and as the most self-evident of reasons for American intervention on the side of the Allies, Beard dismissed as a distraction from the real history of the war. Stalin, as of 1941, was infinitely worse than Hitler. Beard never got past the Stalin problem in his effort to understand the logic of Washington in branding the war as a crusade for freedom. He believed that no one could get past it trusting merely to facts and evidence. To do so required a certain kind of mystical faith in the leader. Beard once had possessed such a faith, in Wilson. The Treaty of Versailles, however, permanently had reprogrammed him.

World War II did nothing to revive Beard's lost faith in the American government. A postwar world writhing in agony would not be healed by the oligarchs who ran the United States. They had not succeeded in solving the social, economic, educational, and health problems of the American people. It was unrealistic to expect these individuals suddenly to acquire the knowledge, expertise, and human concern that would be equal to the far greater challenge of world peace, stability, and prosperity. Based on the record of American elites in their own country, it safely could be concluded that they did not care about such objectives and, even if they did, would not know how to achieve them. Their objectives had to do with extending the sphere. All American history, including the years 1941 to 1945, had been about sphere extension. After the war, he told Curti that Russia and the United States were playing a straight imperialist game, just as they had done during the Second World War. They would go on playing it, and the postwar period would be defined by its outcome, with an imperialist order the result, whichever side won.

Beard found in the beginnings of the Cold War the true meaning of the Second World War and thus a reliable indication about where the United States would be headed long-term. He did not think that the stated official concerns about the Soviet Union fundamentally had anything to do with the Cold War. Washington treated Russia as a malleable commodity: a friend of democracy and the Four Freedoms one day and a totalitarian monster the next, with no primary concern about the realities in that country. American foreign policy seemed to him involved with a good deal of hocus-pocus, for the facilitation of cash flow into the military-industrial complex or what he, still using the old-fashioned term, called the munitions industry. For Beard, the postwar establishment of American military bases in Europe and elsewhere abroad had an entirely different purpose from the one announced by American leaders. The Soviets, he argued, served as a pretext and a means to American imperialist ends.

Beard, therefore, would not have been at all surprised by what happened at the end of the Cold War. The fall of the Soviet Union in 1991 and its subsequent disappearance from the world map scarcely registered as a pause in the American military buildup worldwide. Although the Soviet threat had been presented as the justification for the bases, they continued in existence and soon increased in number, even when the stated reason for them had vanished. He had expected that replacement threats, should any be needed in the future, would never be in short supply.

The specific threat did not matter, according to Beard, because the bases and the vast support network supplying them had a permanent supervisory purpose. He connected the military tactics to an overarching strategy of keeping the American economic system preeminent in the world, which far more than the promotion of the Four Freedoms had been the main American objective in the Second World War. The war ended, as planned, with the victors in command of the world's resources. This actual outcome, as opposed to the fictitious triumph of democracy and human rights touted by people mistaking government propaganda for historical analysis, made the Second World War a problem requiring serious study. Instead, historians mistakenly treated it as a nonproblem presenting no ambiguity in its causes or consequences.

In a way resembling Hildreth's systematic critique of nineteenth-century American society, Beard called for a complete examination of twentieth-century America's operating assumptions. It would not be enough, according to him, to expose the crimes and follies of FDR, necessary as that research task was. Beard wanted Americans to retrace their steps back to John Quincy Adams. By this he meant that they would have to gain democratic control of their government and to use it for the public good, not for the promotion and protection of oligarchic wealth. Foreign policy Beard believed to be an extension of domestic politics. Oligarchic control at home would be extended abroad. War would be the perpetual result. At the very least, his ideas about contemporary American history and foreign policy possessed a prophetic character.

Like Hildreth, Beard experienced crushing difficulties in trying to put over a revisionist program for the whole of the country's history. To argue, as he did, that the premises of American political and economic life needed not overhaul but replacement put him at a disadvantage in the post–World War II period when the people by and large became persuaded that all was for the best in the best of all possible countries. Beard as a revisionist had been fortunate, from a professional standpoint, to live most of his life when he did, through the depression of the 1890s, the social and political crises of the Progressive era, the disillusionment following World War I, and the Great Depression of the 1930s. Beard's crisis historiography caught the spirit of those anguished times. His revisionist historical instruction and radical social criticism have exerted an ongoing and steady appeal on the left; however, with a growing and multi-faceted discontent abroad in the land today, Beard might be due for a return to the popular favor he once enjoyed.

Beard deplored American corporate capitalism as a destructively revolutionary force seeking always to transform the entire world into its own investment field and causing endless social and cultural dysfunction to achieve its nefarious end. Tradition and morality could not withstand an engine of such enormous power and under the control of amoral profit takers. He thought that this economic system had failed every test of history, insofar as the past is measured by the way societies meet the requirements of a high civilization.

It took Beard a long time to come to such drastic conclusions, and he reached them only in the last letters that he wrote to his intimates and in his final addresses. The process of his piecing them together really began with the slow conversion that he underwent to World War I revisionism, the central claim of which held that this conflict had been brought on by the relentless pursuit of empire on the part of all the Great Powers. Senator Robert La Follette's instinct about the slaughter pens of this war as an equal-opportunity looting operation had proved right, Beard later and with the highest admiration acknowledged. The militarism and imperialism spawned by a vulpine corporate capitalism had been the downfall of Europe. A fate identical to the one that already had befallen Europe eventually would overtake America. The eye-opening Nye Committee had shown the same imperialistic and militaristic forces at work in the United States. Like the ghouls and vultures fluttering over the carnage in Goya's *Disasters of War*, the big moneymen at J. P. Morgan had torn flesh and drunk blood. They had fed money to the war machines. Without such men, there would have been no war machines.

Whenever in his later years Beard made a pronouncement about capitalist elites, it was in implacable opposition to everything that Wall Street represented. *America in Midpassage*, written at the end of the depression-wracked 1930s, was the most impassioned of his books on the theme of corporate capitalism's unsuitability for a democratic society. He mocked the bankers, financiers, and businessmen whose greed, ignorance, and callousness had brought bread lines, shantytowns, and mass unemployment to the country. In discussing the overall record of American capitalism in peace and war, he veered sharply in the direction of Thorstein Veblen's *Theory of the Leisure Class* and even wrote sympathetically about that economist's later and more radical work. He regarded Veblen, though on the left, as a prize intellectual heir of Ruskin. Beard himself drew on the left and the right in formulating his indictment of the status quo, which by the late 1930s he predicted would not survive. It did not deserve to survive. For the country to become a genuine commonwealth, Americans would have to build *ex novo* a workers' republic. Nothing could save the country but a renewed sense of collective purpose in achieving the common good.

With the failure of the New Deal, Beard completely gave up hope for a successful adaptation of corporate capitalist economics to the democratic political system. FDR's response to his failure consisted not of a serious plan to transform the American system's iron oligarchy. Instead he decided to take the country into war to save the oligarchy. Thus, Beard began the final stage of his political education. This war, too, came down to profit share, only now the United States wanted to control it all. Naturally, there would be allowances doled out to right-thinking allies endowed with the suppleness of mind to conceal their subservience with rhetoric befitting loyal adjutants. This was what Beard meant by his remark to Curti about the straight imperial game played by the United States and Russia in the Cold War. It could not have been any straighter, but the rhetoric on both sides of the Atlantic made it necessary to have a sound historical education to understand the real nature of things.

Some of the most important lessons in Beard's fully formed political education came from *The Progressive* magazine. He not only contributed to this publication, he learned from it, most notably arresting details about the economic subtext of the American war effort against the Axis. The reporting in *The Progressive* pointed toward the protection and reinforcement of existing international cartel arrangements, in which American corporations were dominant stakeholders. Such economic connections tended to be an overlooked incentive for Washington's waging of the good war. The mirage of freedom arising from the Atlantic Charter faded as it became clear that the Allies did not intend to dismantle their empires in Asia or in Africa. Things would go on as before, minus the imperialists of Germany, Japan, and Italy. The world's victorious imperialists expected to be thanked for their democratic services to all mankind, a task in which, Beard lamented, their historians and film makers eagerly would participate.

Beard claimed that documents and counsel he had received from Herbert Hoover had completed his education about the Second World War. It was the most unexpected friendship of Beard's life. The former president believed in the free market and had opposed the New Deal as a monstrous government intrusion where it did not belong. He likened FDR to Hitler and Stalin. Viewing them all as totalitarian rulers, Hoover thought that the only difference between FDR and the other two was the relatively slower pace of America's transformation into a dictatorship. Beard, too, in time condemned the New Deal, but only because it had not gone far enough or quickly enough in transforming the allegedly free market into a workers' republic. When they met and corresponded, there could be no common ground between Beard and Hoover for a discussion of domestic issues. As an underlying problem responsible for everything wrong with America, capitalism occupied the central place in Beard's thinking as he pondered the postwar period. The immediate problem with the potential to bring down the country, however, concerned its empire.

About the American empire, Hoover and Beard came to an agreement on a fundamental point: the sinister part performed by FDR. It was the most brilliantly successful performance in the history of American politics and the most tragic. This tragedy for Beard eclipsed all others in American life. To expose its diabolical character, he overlooked his old political and economic biases against Hoover. He focused instead on the help that this Republican conservative could give him regarding documents and contacts. Moreover, with the passing years and in the light of the two presidents who followed him, Beard reasoned that on the big existential issue of American imperialism, Hoover had displayed astounding wisdom and forbearance. He lacked the hubris imperialism required and thus likely passed into history as America's last great president.

Beard's career as a public intellectual in the promotion of peace and democracy mattered to him as much as—if not more than—the work that he did as a research historian. No American historian has ever surpassed him for volume and influence as a commentator on current affairs and national questions. He did with his scholarship and activism what Ruskin had done a century earlier in tackling the great social issues of the day. His dream of a workers' republic did not come as an anticipation of the peoples' democracies of communist Eastern Europe in the post–World War II period, but as a product of Ruskin's influence. The workingmen studying at Ruskin Hall made a permanent impression on him. The young graduate student found his true calling while organizing a workers' movement and giving lectures and speeches in the West Midlands of England. The Ruskin Hall experience explains Beard's inner life and what he most wanted to do in his career after returning to the United States. He only wrote two scholarly monographs based on archival research—the gold standard in the moral economy of academic historians.

Neither of the last two Roosevelt tracts fell into that category, and nearly all the rest of his vast output concerned textbook writing for students at all levels and works of social criticism and policy analysis for his fellow citizens. Beard, thinking that he had a country to save, devoted most of his time and energy to public affairs. He wanted to be a historian in the real world and rushed out to engage it, come what may.

Notes

1. Discovering the Economic Taproot of Imperialism

1. Returning to DePauw for an honorary degree, Beard told Weaver: "I am glad to have the privilege of thanking you again as one of my most revered and respected teachers." Merle Curti, "A Great Teacher's Teacher," *Social Education* 13, no. 6 (October 1949): 263.

2. Mary R. Beard, *The Making of Charles A. Beard* (New York: Exposition Press, 1955), 14–15. The historian Eric Goldman, who as a student at Johns Hopkins University knew Beard the year he taught there, in 1940–1941, remembered from conversations with him how important the experience at Hull House was in his "moving further from the certitudes of Knightstown." "The Origins of Beard's Economic Interpretation of the Constitution," *Journal of the History of Ideas* 13, no. 2 (April 1952): 235. Beard himself explained in a memoir article, "I had made a special study of labor and social problems in college and had spent a season in a social settlement in Chicago where I had come into first-hand contact with them." Burleigh Taylor Wilkins, ed., "Charles A. Beard on the Founding of Ruskin Hall," *Indiana Magazine of History* 52, no. 3 (September 1956): 279. This article contains two different accounts by Beard about his time in England as a graduate student.

3. Charles A. Beard to Lionel Elvin, December 18, 1945. Elvin was then the principal of Ruskin Hall. This is the second of the two Beard accounts in Wilkins, "Charles A. Beard on the Founding of Ruskin Hall." In the same account to Elvin, Beard strongly identified with his English heritage, noting that ancestors of his had left England in the seventeenth and eighteenth centuries. He qualified his "colossal" ignorance in the following way: "From my immediate forebears I had acquired a deep interest in England and I was more than casually acquainted with the great classics in English history and letters. I wanted to learn more and was willing to pay the price of hard work."

4. Mary R. Beard, *The Making of Charles A. Beard*, 19.

5. John Ruskin, *Unto This Last and Other Essays on Art and Political Economy* (London: J. M. Dent & Sons, 1907), 24, 58.

6. Ibid., 109, 116.

7. Ibid., 141, 142, 143–144, 144.

8. Ibid., 149, 146, 193, 160.

9. Ibid., 168, 171, 184, 185.

10. The Vroomans divorced in 1903, and she then became Amne Grafflin. Vrooman died in 1909 at the age of forty. John Braeman gives Vrooman credit for conceiving the original ideas behind Ruskin Hall, which Beard, with extraordinary

energy and a talent for organization, then made a reality, in "Charles A. Beard: The English Experience," *Journal of American Studies* 15, no. 2 (August 1981): 165–189.

11. Harold Pollins, *The History of Ruskin College* (Oxford: Ruskin College Library, 1984), 9.

12. Memorandum and Articles of Association of Ruskin College Incorporated, registered June 11, 1900, Ruskin College Archive, Charles Beard folder.

13. Memorandum from Executive Committee, undated, Ruskin College Archive, Charles Beard folder.

14. For the history of the school's political and ideological disputes, see Pollins, *The History of Ruskin College*, especially about "the very radical 1930s" and the student revolts of the 1960s accompanied by "a new interest in marxism and a proliferation of marxist sects" (42, 52).

15. Charles A. Beard, "Ruskin and the Babble of Tongues," *New Republic* (August 5, 1936): 372. Writing in the depths of the Depression, Beard recommended, "Perhaps in the crisis in thought that now besets us it will do some good to take up again 'Unto This Last,' and read it without anger or tears" (372). Four years later, Beard wrote, "The name Ruskin Hall was chosen by Mr. Vrooman on my suggestion, after many long debates." Charles A. Beard to A. Barrett Brown, July 7, 1940, 280. Brown served as the principal of Ruskin Hall from 1926 to 1945. This is the first of the two Beard accounts of his time in England as a graduate student, in Wilkins, ed., "Charles A. Beard on the Founding of Ruskin Hall." The Charles Beard folder in the Ruskin College Archive contains this account as a separate paper by Beard and a note to Brown. In the note, he states, "with your request I have written the enclosed paper dealing with the early days of Ruskin Hall."

16. Beard, "Ruskin and the Babble of Tongues," 372. About his devotion and that of Vrooman to Ruskin, Beard wrote to A. Barrett Brown: "We were both students of that great moralist and, while we dissented from many of his opinions we came to the conclusion that Ruskin had laid the best foundation for a humane labor program." Wilkins, ed., "Charles A. Beard on the Founding of Ruskin Hall," 280.

17. Beard, "Ruskin and the Babble of Tongues," 372.

18. In a January 26, 1900, letter to Moses Coit Tyler, Beard expressed appreciation for his time in Ithaca, New York: "I shall always have pleasant memories of my short but delightful stay at Cornell." Merle Curti Papers, Charles Beard material microfilm, State Historical Society of Wisconsin. To long-time Cornell University history professor Carl Becker, Beard described himself "as a kind of quasi-Cornellian." Beard to Carl Becker, March 28, 1944, Merle Curti Papers.

19. Letter from unknown addressee, undated, Department of History archives at the University of Wisconsin, Madison; cited by Wilkins, ed., "Charles A. Beard on the Founding of Ruskin Hall," in the second of two letters that Beard wrote to Lionel Elvin, December 18, 1945.

20. Mary Beard, *The Making of Charles Beard*, 19ff.

21. "In Memory of John Ruskin," *Young Oxford: A Monthly Magazine Devoted to the Ruskin Hall Movement* 1, no. 5 (February 1900): 14, 15.

22. Mrs. Alfred Vagts (Miriam) to David Horsfield (Ruskin College Librarian), December 10, 1975, Ruskin College Archive, Charles Beard folder.

23. Charles A. Beard, "Self-Education," *Young Oxford* 1, no. 1 (October 1899): 17.

24. Charles A. Beard, "A Living Empire," *Young Oxford and the Ruskin Hall News* 3, no. 25 (October 1901): 24. The name of the magazine changed in March 1901.

25. Ibid., 25.

26. Charles A. Beard, "A Living Empire" (second installment), *Young Oxford and the Ruskin Hall News* 3, no. 25 (October 1901): 39, 40.

27. Arthur W. Macmahon, "Charles Austin Beard as a Teacher," in Mary Beard, *The Making of Charles Beard*, 92.

28. Frederick York Powell, "John Ruskin," in Oliver Elton, *Frederick York Powell: A Life and a Selection from His Letters and Occasional Writings*, 2 vols. (Oxford: Clarendon Press, 1906), vol. 2, 325, 333.

29. For Powell's collaborative relationship as a translator and editor with Gudbrand Vigfússon in promoting Icelandic scholarship in the English-speaking world, see Elton, *Frederick York Powell*, vol. 1, chap. 2, "Vigfússon: 1875–1883."

30. Frederick York Powell to Mrs. Marriott Watson, March 13, 1901, in Elton, *Frederick York Powell*, vol. 1, 314.

31. Frederick York Powell to W. P. Kerr, March 10, 1904, in Elton, *Frederick York Powell*, vol. 1, 394.

32. Elton, *Frederick York Powell*, vol. 1, 307.

33. Thomas Hardy, *Jude the Obscure* (Oxford: Oxford University Press, 1985), 316, 301, 308, xlv.

34. George Bernard Shaw to Charles A. Beard, May 1, 1899, Ruskin College Archive, Charles Beard folder.

35. In a follow-up letter on May 20, 1899, to James Dennis Hird, the Warden of Ruskin College, Shaw wrote, "The baneful influence of Oxford is apparent in every line of your letter. Had I known that Ruskin Hall had already come to giving breakfasts to '8 ladies of considerable distinction, literary and otherwise,' I should have used much stronger language." He thought that the school would be "a lark whilst it lasts; so I wish you plenty of fun." Letter found in Ruskin College Archive, Charles Beard folder. Hird would become the principal of Ruskin College in 1903.

36. Frederick York Powell, prefatory note to *The Industrial Revolution*, by Charles Beard (New York: Greenwood Press, 1969; London: George Allen & Unwin, 1927), vii. Citations refer to the George Allen & Unwin edition.

37. Ibid., xiv.

38. Frederick York Powell to Charles A. Beard, January 12, 1901, in Elton, *Frederick York Powell*, vol. 1, 314.

39. Beard, *The Industrial Revolution*, xvi, 102.

40. Charles A. Beard to Lionel Elvin, December 18, 1945, in Wilkins, ed., "Charles A. Beard on the Founding of Ruskin Hall," 283.

41. For an illuminating introduction to the Oxford School of historians, see Burleigh Taylor Wilkins, "Frederick York Powell and Charles A. Beard: A Study in Anglo-American Historiography and Social Thought," *American Quarterly* 11, no. 1 (Spring 1959). One of the most interesting figures treated by Wilkins is Oxford University's John Richard Green, whose classic book *A Short History of the English People* offered a view of politics in the context of broader social factors. Wilkins counts Green, who had died fifteen years before Beard's arrival in Oxford, as a forerunner of the "New History" championed by Beard in *An Introduction to the English Historians* (New York:

Macmillan, 1906). Beard praised Green's book as "doubtless the most vivid and inter-esting account" of the Anglo-Saxon conquest and settlement period (12). Moreover, Green also had written about the religious history of England, particularly Puritanism, "with great sympathy and insight" (321).

42. Miriam Vagts to David Horsfield, December 15, 1977, Ruskin College Archive, Charles Beard folder.

43. Edwin R. A. Seligman, *The Economic Interpretation of History* (New York: Mac-millan, 1902), 3, 108, 165.

44. Scott Nearing, *The Making of a Radical: A Political Autobiography* (New York: Harper & Row, 1972), 62.

45. Ellen Nore, *Charles A. Beard: An Intellectual Biography* (Carbondale: Southern Illinois University Press, 1983), 31.

46. Charles Beard, *An Introduction to the English Historians*, v.

47. Cited by Beard in ibid., 241.

48. Eugene D. Genovese, "Beard's Economic Interpretation of History," in *Charles Beard: An Observance of the Centennial of His Birth*, ed. Marvin C. Swanson (Greencas-tle, Ind.: DePauw University, October 11–12, 1974), 36.

49. Miriam Vagts to David Horsfield, undated, November 1975, Ruskin College Archive, Charles Beard folder.

50. "Ruskin the Reformer," *Young Oxford* 1, no. 8 (May 1900).

51. John Atkinson Hobson, *John Ruskin, Social Reformer* (Boston: Dana Estes, 1898), 40, 49.

52. Ibid., v–vi.

53. John Atkinson Hobson, *Confessions of an Economic Heretic* (London: George Allen & Unwin, 1938), 42.

54. For the influence of Richard Cobden's radical ideas on Hobson, see Bernard Semmel, *Imperialism and Social Reform: English Social-Imperial Thought 1895–1914* (Lon-don: George Allen & Unwin, 1960), 137.

55. For Hobson's own account of his career, see *Confessions of an Economic Heretic*. After reading this book, John Maynard Keynes wrote to him: "You have been not only a heretic able to see much which at the time was concealed from others, but you have not even belonged to any heretical school or clique, so that you have not even had that support. No academic environment, no orthodoxy, and not even a personal clique have been there to support you. But it remains a fine record, and I do not get the impression from reading the book that you are really discontented with it." John Maynard Keynes to John A. Hobson, March 20, 1938, JMK/CO3, Personal Papers of John Maynard Keynes, King's College Library, Cambridge.

56. Hobson, *John Ruskin, Social Reformer*, 51.

57. Thomas Carlyle, *Past and Present* (London: J. M. Dent & Sons, 1912), 5, 14.

58. Ibid., 240, 243, 254.

59. William Appleman Williams, "Charles Austin Beard: The Intellectual as Tory Radical," in *American Radicals: Some Problems and Personalities*, ed. Harvey Goldberg (New York: Monthly Review Press, 1957), 298.

60. Hobson, *John Ruskin, Social Reformer*, 176, 176–177, 180, 204, 202.

61. Ibid., 213, 214, 215, 220.

62. Ibid., 223, 224, 226.

63. Ibid., 295.

64. Ibid., 341.

65. Ibid., 342, 345.

66. "Ruskin on War," *Young Oxford* 1, no. 12 (September 1900): 27.

67. Beard, *An Introduction to the English Historians*, 423.

68. Powell, "John Ruskin," in Elton, *Frederick York Powell*, 333.

69. John Atkinson Hobson, *Imperialism: A Study*; cited in Beard, *An Introduction to the English Historians*, 626.

70. Ibid., 633.

71. Beard, "Ruskin and the Babble of Tongues," 372.

72. Charles A. Beard and Mary R. Beard, *The Rise of American Civilization* (New York: Macmillan, 1935), vol. 2, 407.

2. Two Contrasting Progressive Views of the Great War

1. Charles A. Beard to Robert La Follette, January 11, 1911, RML Sr. Papers, box I: B 66, Library of Congress (hereafter LOC). For the historical context of the Beard–La Follette correspondence, see Richard Drake, *The Education of an Anti-Imperialist: Robert La Follette and U.S. Expansion* (Madison: University of Wisconsin Press, 2013), chap. 6, "The Wilson Era Begins."

2. Robert La Follette to Charles A. Beard, January 13, 1911, RML Sr. Papers, box I: B 106, LOC.

3. John J. Hannan (secretary) to Charles A. Beard, January 27, 1911, RML Sr. Papers, box I: B 106, LOC.

4. Belle Case La Follette and Fola La Follette, *Robert M. La Follette: June 14, 1855–June 18, 1925* (New York: Macmillan, 1953), vol. 1, 472.

5. "What Washington Said," *La Follette's Weekly Magazine* 5, no. 8 (February 22, 1913): 3.

6. George Middleton, "Snap Shots," *La Follette's Weekly Magazine* 5, no. 21 (May 24, 1913): 7.

7. Editor's introduction for Charles Zueblin, "Political Snapshots," *La Follette's Weekly Magazine* 5, no. 46 (November 15, 1913): 11.

8. Charles Zueblin, "Political Snapshots: A Discussion of American Beliefs," *La Follette's Weekly Magazine* 5, no. 43 (October 25, 1913): 8.

9. Zueblin, "Political Snapshots: A Discussion of American Beliefs," *La Follette's Weekly Magazine* 5, no. 47 (November 22, 1913): 8.

10. Charles A. Beard, *An Economic Interpretation of the Constitution of the United States* (New York: Macmillan, 1962), 153. For an update, with some modifications, of the Beard thesis, see Woody Holton, *Unruly Americans and the Origins of the Constitution* (New York: Hill and Wang, 2007). For a more characteristically Beardian approach, see Terry Bouton, *Taming Democracy: "The People," the Founders, and the Troubled Ending of the American Revolution* (New York: Oxford University Press, 2009) and Michael McDonnell, *The Politics of War: Race, Class, and Conflict in Revolutionary Virginia* (Chapel Hill: University of North Carolina Press, 2007).

11. Beard, *An Economic Interpretation*, 161.

12. Beard, *Economic Origins of Jeffersonian Democracy* (New York: Free Press, 1915), 9. Beard claimed that the economic divisions in American life did not disappear after the Constitution had gone into effect, but continued into the Jeffersonian era and defined its politics: "Whoever takes the trouble to examine the newspapers and correspondence of the period of presidential and congressional elections will find the same partisan flavor that characterized the constitutional struggle" (94). Summing up the controversies over the Jay Treaty of 1794, which resolved a series of economic and territorial issues between England and the United States, Beard wrote: "In short, it was the same battle over again, or rather another battle in the long campaign begun with the adoption of the Constitution" (276).

13. For a penetrating analysis of Beard's economic interpretation of history and "the Marxism with which it has often been confused," see Eugene D. Genovese, "Beard's Economic Interpretation," in *Charles A. Beard: An Observance of the Centennial of His Birth*, ed. Marvin C. Swanson (Greencastle, Ind.: DePauw University, October 11–12, 1974), 25. Genovese contended that Beard stressed "the parasitism and greed of specific economic interests rather than the class exigencies of capitalism as a whole" (36).

14. Leonardo Bruni, *History of the Florentine People*, ed. James Hankins (Cambridge, Mass.: Harvard University Press, 2001), vol. 1, 349.

15. Karl Marx, *Selected Writings*, ed. David McClellan (Oxford: Oxford University Press, 1977), 341.

16. Beard, *An Economic Interpretation*, xiii.

17. Robert La Follette, *La Follette's Autobiography: A Personal Narrative of Political Experiences* (Madison, Wis.: Robert M. La Follette, 1913), 269, 352, 760, 784.

18. Robert La Follette to Charles A. Beard, May 10, 1913, RML Sr. Papers, box I: B 107, LOC.

19. Charles A. Beard to Robert La Follette, May 14, 1913, RML Sr. Papers, box I: B 73, LOC.

20. Ibid.

21. Ibid.

22. Ibid.

23. Ibid.

24. Ibid. William Edward Dodd, a Jefferson expert, in 1908 began a twenty-five-year teaching career in the history department at the University of Chicago. From 1933 to 1938 he served as the American ambassador to Nazi Germany.

25. Editorial postscript following Middleton, "Snap Shots."

26. Robert La Follette to Mary R. Beard, January 17, 1914, RML Sr. Papers, box I: B 109, LOC.

27. Charles A. Beard and Mary R. Beard, *The Rise of American Civilization* (New York: Macmillan, 1927), vol. 2, 631.

28. For La Follette's embrace of Hobson's theory of imperialism, see Drake, *The Education of an Anti-Imperialist*, especially 157–162.

29. Joseph Freeman, *An American Testament: A Narrative of Rebels and Romantics* (New York: Farrar and Rinehart, 1936), 107. He praised him as a professor: "In the classroom, we found Dr. Beard a teacher of great intellectual vigor and integrity. He was a dramatic and concise lecturer" (106).

30. Nicholas Murray Butler to Charles A. Beard, November 28, 1916, Nicholas Murray Butler Papers, Arranged Correspondence, box 27, Columbia University Rare Book and Manuscript Library.

31. "What Professor Beard Said," letter to the editor, *New Republic* (May 6, 1916): 188. Fifty-four Columbia graduate students signed a letter in defense of Beard's integrity and innocence in this case.

32. "Dr. Beard Attacks Columbia Trustees," *New York Times* (December 28, 1917): 8. Beard considered his spring 1916 clash with the trustees to be the beginning of the process that led to his resignation the following year.

33. Charles A. Beard, "Letter to the Editor," *New Republic* (June 2, 1917): 136–138.

34. Charles A. Beard, "German Annexations and Indemnities," *New Republic* (July 14, 1917): 309–310.

35. "Columbia Ousts Two Professors, Foes of War Plans," *New York Times* (October 2, 1917): 1.

36. Ibid.

37. Ibid. In this article, the newspaper published the full text of Butler's 1917 commencement address.

38. In his memoirs, *Across the Busy Years: Recollections and Reflections* (New York: Charles Scribner's Sons, 1939–1940), 2 vols., Butler omits all mention of the events at Columbia involving Dana and Cattell. Beard also fails to make an appearance in the book. In *A World in Ferment: Interpretations of the War for a New World* (New York: Charles Scribner's Sons, 1919), Butler adheres to a Wilsonian view of America's role in the conflict, which he described as "a war for a new international world, and a war for a new intranational world" (5). He dated the introduction for this book, July 14, 1917, just a month after his commencement address of that year.

39. James McKeen Cattell to Robert La Follette, March 31, 1917, RML Sr. Papers, box I: B 80, LOC.

40. James McKeen Cattell to Robert La Follette, April 12, 1917, RML Sr. Papers, box I: B 80, LOC.

41. James McKeen Cattell to Robert La Follette, August 25, 1917, RML Sr. Papers, box I: B 80, LOC.

42. Robert La Follette, stenographer's transcript of extemporaneous speech delivered at St. Paul, Minnesota, September 20, 1917, RML Sr. Papers, box I: B 219, LOC.

43. "La Follette Attacks War and Government," *New York Times* (September 24, 1917): 1. In *The Making of a Radical: A Political Autobiography* (New York: Harper & Row, 1972), 173, Scott Nearing writes about his work in 1917 as the chairman of the People's Council for Peace and Democracy.

44. Nearing, *The Making of a Radical*, 104.

45. "The Expulsions at Columbia," *New York Times* (October 3, 1917): 12.

46. Robert La Follette, Toledo speech, September 23, 1917, typescript of speech, RML Sr. Papers, box I: B 221, LOC.

47. "An Arch Malcontent," *Seattle Post Intelligencer*, September 26, 1917, RML Sr. Papers, box I: B 164, LOC.

48. "Dr. Butler Wants La Follette Ousted," *New York Times* (September 28, 1917): 11.

49. Ibid.

50. "Columbia Ousts Two Professors," *New York Times* (October 2, 1917): 1. See note 35 above.

51. Ibid.

52. "The Expulsions at Columbia," *New York Times* (October 3, 1917): 12. See note 45 above.

53. Charles A. Beard to Nicholas Murray Butler, October 12, 1917, "Professor Beard Resigns," Historical and Biographical Files of Columbia University, box 25, folder 13, Rare Book and Manuscript Library, Columbia University. The full text of Beard's resignation letter appeared in "Quits Columbia; Assails Trustees," *New York Times* (October 9, 1917): 7.

54. Ibid.

55. By December, the *New York Times* would be quoting him as saying, "it was the evident purpose of a small group of Trustees, unhindered, if not aided, by Mr. Butler, to take advantage of the state of war to drive out or humiliate or terrorize every man who held progressive, liberal, or unconventional views on political matters in no way connected with the war." Beard continued, "Mr. Butler cannot conceive of a scholar's entertaining progressive ideas." "Dr. Beard Attacks Columbia Trustees," *New York Times* (December 28, 1917): 8.

56. Joe A. Jackson, "Professor Beard—Pacemaker," *Columbia Alumni News*, March 26, 1915.

57. Arthur Macmahon, "Charles Austin Beard as a Teacher," originally published in the *Political Science Quarterly* 65, no. 1 (March 1950) and reprinted in Mary Beard, *The Making of Charles Beard* (New York: Exposition Press, 1955), 91.

58. "Columbia Students to Appeal to Butler," *New York Post*, October 10, 1917.

59. "Committee of Nine for Columbia Peace," *New York Times* (October 11, 1917): 18.

60. "Quits Columbia; Assails Trustee," *New York Times* (October 9, 1917): 1. See note 53 above.

61. Ibid.

62. "Committee of Nine for Columbia Peace," 18.

63. Ibid.

64. "Columbia's Deliverance," *New York Times* (October 10, 1917): 10.

65. Ibid.

66. Ibid.

67. Annie Nathan Meyer, "The Issue at Columbia: A Trustee's Reply to the Attack of Professor Beard," *New York Times* (October 13, 1917): 11.

68. "Committee of Nine for Columbia Peace," 18.

69. "Loyal Columbia Men Check the Radicals," *New York Times* (October 16, 1917): 10.

70. "Egg Shower Stops Columbia Radicals," *New York Times* (October 18, 1917): 5.

71. "Columbia Alumni Back Up Trustees," *New York Times* (October 28, 1917): 17.

72. "A Statement by Charles A. Beard," *New Republic* (December 29, 1917): 249–251.

73. Ibid.

74. Beard, "The End of the War," *New Republic* (July 6, 1918): 297–299.

75. Frederic A. Ogg and Charles A. Beard, *National Governments and the World War* (New York: Macmillan, 1919), v, 13.

76. In November 1914, *La Follette's Weekly Magazine* became a monthly publication. For an analysis of La Follette's pro-war editorials in 1918, see Drake, *The Education of an Anti-Imperialist*, 217–221.

77. Ogg and Beard, *National Governments and the World War*, 556, 570.

3. Becoming a Revisionist

1. Charles A. Beard to Munro Smith, December 2, 1907, *Political Science Quarterly* Collection, Cataloged Correspondence, Columbia University Rare Book and Manuscript Library.

2. John Atkinson Hobson, *Confessions of an Economic Heretic* (London: Allen & Unwin, 1938), 57, 61.

3. Ibid., 95, 103.

4. John Atkinson Hobson, "Why the War Came as a Surprise," *Political Science Quarterly* 35, no. 3 (September 1920): 337–359.

5. Ibid.

6. Philip Gibbs, *The Realities of War* (London: William Heinemann, 1920), v. Harper & Brothers published the American edition that same year with the title *Now It Can Be Told*.

7. Paul Fussell, *The Great War and Modern Memory* (Oxford: Oxford University Press, 1975), 169.

8. Gibbs, *The Realities of War*, v, 429.

9. Charles A. Beard and Mary R. Beard, *The Rise of American Civilization* (New York: Macmillan, 1927), vol. 2, 673.

10. Sidney Bradshaw Fay, "New Light on the Origins of the World War, II, Berlin and Vienna, July 29 to 31," *American Historical Review* 26, no. 1 (October 1920): 37–53.

11. Sidney Bradshaw Fay, "New Light on the Origins of the World War, I, Berlin and Vienna, to July 29," *American Historical Review* 25, no. 4 (July 1920): 616–639.

12. Sidney Bradshaw Fay, "New Light on the Origins of the World War, III, Russia and the Other Powers," *American Historical Review* 26, no. 2 (January 1921): 225–254.

13. Charles Beard, "The Recent War," *New Republic* 25, no. 316 (December 22, 1920): 114–115. The review dealt with *A Brief History of the Great War* by Carlton J. H. Hayes, his former colleague at Columbia. About Hayes's Roman Catholic viewpoint, Beard wrote, "The present reviewer not being versed in theology feels unable to enter this domain, but he was not aware that the Ouija board had made any serious inroads upon excess profits since the war broke out. Neither is he able to see how Professor Hayes can record, almost on the same page, the grand triumph of economic imperialism and the grand triumph of those who look to the Sermon on the Mount for their inspiration and strength." Ibid.

14. Charles A. Beard, "Light on the Franco-Russian Alliance," *New Republic* 29, no. 377 (February 22, 1922): 375–376.

15. John Maynard Keynes, *The Economic Consequences of the Peace* (London: Penguin, 1971), 6, 39, 52.

16. Ibid., 216, 228, 297.

17. Charles A. Beard, *Cross Currents in Europe Today* (Boston: Marshall Jones Company, 1922), 103.

18. Charles A. Beard, review of *La Guerre Absolue*, by Georges Batault, *New Republic* 28, no. 355 (September 21, 1921): 109–110.

19. Beard, *Cross Currents in Europe Today*, 3–4, 6.

20. Ibid., 133, 245, 246, 133.

21. Charles A. Beard, "Transitions in Politics," review of *Political Systems in Transition: Wartime and After*, by Charles G. Fenwick, *The Nation* 116, no. 2903 (February 23, 1921): 297–298.

22. Charles A. Beard and William C. Bagley, *The History of the American People*, rev. ed. (New York: Macmillan, 1923), 628.

23. Raymond Beazley, preface to "The Secret History of a Great Betrayal," by E. D. Morel, *Congressional Record*, 68th Cong., 1st Sess., presented by Senator Robert Latham Owen, February 7, 1924 (Washington, D.C.: Government Printing Office, 1924), iii, v, iii.

24. E. D. Morel, "The Secret History of a Great Betrayal," 2, 5.

25. Ibid., 6, 16, 31, 32.

26. Ibid., 16, 25, 27.

27. Ibid., 15, 22, 19.

28. Ibid., 28, 31–32, 32.

29. Charles A. Beard, "Viscount Grey on War Guilt," *New Republic* 44, no. 566 (October 7, 1925): 172–175.

30. Ibid.

31. Ibid.

32. Ibid.

33. Ibid.

34. Count Max Montgelas, *The Case for the Central Powers: An Impeachment of the Versailles Verdict* (New York: Alfred A. Knopf, 1925), 23.

35. Ibid., 110.

36. Ibid., 113, 164.

37. Harry Elmer Barnes to Roger Butterfield, March 31, 1966, Merle Curti Papers, Charles Beard material microfilm, State Historical Society of Wisconsin.

38. Harry Elmer Barnes to Edwin Montefiore Borchard, February 16, 1926, Edwin Montefiore Borchard Papers, box 1, folder 12, Manuscripts and Archives, Yale University Library.

39. Harry Elmer Barnes to Edwin Montefiore Borchard, February 24, 1926, Edwin Montefiore Borchard Papers, box 1, folder 12, Manuscripts and Archives, Yale University Library.

40. Harry Elmer Barnes, *The Genesis of the World War: An Introduction to the Problem of War Guilt* (New York: Alfred A. Knopf, 1926), xi.

41. Ibid., xix.

42. In a letter to Borchard, Barnes complained that in his review of Lord Grey's memoirs, Beard appeared "to be below form," November 2, 1925, Edwin Montefiore Borchard Papers, box 1, folder 12, Manuscripts and Archives, Yale University Library. Barnes hoped that Montefiore would "jump on Lord Grey's Memoirs."

43. Barnes, *The Genesis of the World War*, 735.

44. Ibid., 643.

45. Ibid., 646.

46. *The Intimate Papers of Colonel House*, arranged as a narrative by Charles Seymour (Boston: Houghton Mifflin, 1926), epigraph.

47. Charles A. Beard, "Colonel House's Papers," *New Republic* 46, no. 589 (March 17, 1926): 109–111.

48. Ibid.

49. Ibid.

50. Ibid.

51. Ibid.

52. Ibid.

53. Beard and Beard, *The Rise of American Civilization*, vol. 1, 255, 338.

54. Ibid., vol.1, 682, 710, 632.

55. Ibid. vol. 2, 172, 528, 532.

56. Ibid., vol. 2, 617, 618.

57. Ibid., vol. 2, 631, 640.

58. Ibid., vol. 2, 635.

59. Ibid., vol. 2, 650, 651, 650, 658.

60. Beard, "A Frenchman in America," *New Republic* 51, no. 653 (June 8, 1927): 75–76.

61. Ibid.

4. Washington and Wall Street Working Together for War

1. Helmuth Carol Engelbrecht and Frank Cleary Hanighen, *Merchants of Death: A Study of the International Armament Industry* (New York: Dodd, Mead, and Company, 1934), vi.

2. Ibid., 118.

3. Ibid., 173.

4. Ibid., 176.

5. Ibid., 260.

6. Charles Beard, *The Navy: Defense or Portent?* (New York: Harper & Brothers, 1932), 2.

7. Ibid., 46.

8. Ibid., 63.

9. Ibid., 197.

10. Charles Beard, "Hitlerism and Our Liberties," address at the New School for Social Research, Tuesday, April 10, 1934, Charles Austin Beard Letters, 1929–1939, Beard, Charles Austin Collection, Correspondence between Charles A. Beard and George S. Counts, Rare Book and Manuscript Library, Columbia University.

11. Charles Beard, *The Devil Theory of War: An Inquiry into the Nature of History and the Possibility of Keeping Out of War* (New York: Vanguard Press, 1936), 12.

12. Beard's estimate of the Nye Committee's historical significance by and large differed from that of subsequent scholars in the field. In *John T. Flynn and the Transformation of American Liberalism* (New York: New York University Press, 2005), John E. Moser observed, "Most historians have taken a dim view of the Nye Committee's investigation, claiming that they operated from the ridiculous premise that arms merchants and international bankers had lured the country into World War I" (57).

Flynn, trained as a lawyer before beginning a career in journalism, had served as the legal adviser to the Nye Committee. For his dismissive assessment of the Nye Committee, which Moser likens to the McCarthy hearings of the 1950s, he cited support from the following historians: John E. Wiltz, *In Search of Peace: The Senate Munitions Inquiry, 1934–1936* (Baton Rouge: Louisiana State University Press, 1963); Samuel Lubell, *The Future of American Politics* (Garden City, N.Y.: Doubleday, 1956); Robert David Johnson, *The Peace Progressives and American Foreign Relations* (Cambridge, Mass.: Harvard University Press, 1995); and Robert A. Divine, *Second Chance: The Triumph of Internationalism in America during World War II* (New York: Atheneum, 1967).

13. Charles A. Beard to President Roosevelt, January 1934, an enclosure in a letter from Beard to fellow historian Merle Curti, January 20, 1934. Beard lamented to Curti, "The storm gathers. Capitalist henchmen will give intelligence no choice but communism, it seems. The New Freedom gave us war. The New Deal may, too." Found in Merle Curti Papers, Charles Beard material microfilm, State Historical Society of Wisconsin.

14. Wayne S. Cole, *Senator Gerald P. Nye and American Foreign Relations* (Minneapolis: University of Minnesota Press, 1962), 80.

15. Thomas W. Lamont, January 8, 1936, Hearings before the Special Committee Investigating the Munitions Industry, part 25, January 7 and 8, 1936 (Washington: United States Government Printing Office, 1937), 7568.

16. Lamont, January 9, 1936, Hearings, part 26, 7808 and 7815.

17. Gerald P. Nye, January 9, 1936, Hearings, part 26, 7819.

18. Senator Bennett Champ Clark, January 9, 1936, Hearings, part 26, 7832.

19. Lamont, January 9, 1936, Hearings, part 26, 7866.

20. J. P. Morgan, January 10, 1936, Hearings, part 26, 7873.

21. Clark, January 10, 1936, Hearings, part 26, 7884.

22. Charles Beard, "Railroad Reorganization-Statement on Behalf of Independent Bondholders' Committee," *Congressional Record*, vol. 79, part 6, April 17–May 4, 1935, 6519.

23. Clark, January 10, 1936, Hearings, part 26, 7885.

24. Morgan, January 10, 1936, Hearings, part 26, 7893.

25. Nye, January 10, 1936, Hearings, part 26, 7893.

26. Ibid.

27. Senator Arthur H. Vandenberg, January 10, 1936, Hearings, part 26, 7918.

28. Vandenberg, January 10, 1936, Hearings, part 26, 7921.

29. Senator James P. Pope, January 16, 1936, Hearings, part 28, 8634.

30. Nye, January 16, 1936, Hearings, part 28, 8635.

31. Clark, January 15, 1936, Hearings, part 28, 8487.

32. Ibid.

33. Clark, January 15, 1936, Hearings, part 28, 8498.

34. Walter Millis, *The Road to War, 1914–1917* (Boston: Houghton Mifflin, 1935), 221.

35. Clark, January 15, 1936, Hearings, part 28, 8509.

36. Quoted by Clark, January 15, 1936, Hearings, part 28, 8509.

37. Quoted by Clark, January 15, 1936, Hearings, part 28, 8514.

38. Clark, January 15, 1936, Hearings, part 28, 8515.

39. Stephen Raushenbush, February 4, 1936, Hearings, part 29, 9009. He adopted an Americanized spelling of the family name.

40. Vandenberg, January 16, 1936, Hearings, part 28, 8636.

41. Charles A. Beard to Oswald Garrison Villard, January 26, 1936, Oswald Garrison Villard Papers, Houghton Library, Harvard University.

42. Oswald Garrison Villard to Charles A. Beard, January 23, 1936, Oswald Garrison Villard Papers, Houghton Library, Harvard University.

43. Charles Beard, "Dr. Beard Warns United States against Seeking to Profit by any War," *Washington Daily News*, February 6, 1936. Printed in the *Congressional Record*, vol. 80, part 2, January 30–February 18, 1936, 2021.

44. Ibid.

45. Beard, *The Devil Theory of War*, 15.

46. Ibid., 27.

47. Ibid., 104.

48. Ibid., 105.

49. Ibid., 118.

50. Ibid., 120.

51. Ibid., 122.

52. Charles Beard, with the collaboration of G. H. E. Smith, *The Open Door at Home: A Trial Philosophy of National Interest* (New York: Macmillan, 1934), 230.

53. Sidney L. Jackson, "An Open Letter to Dr. Charles A. Beard," *Social Frontier*, May 4, 1935, Charles Austin Beard Letters, 1929–1939, Beard, Charles Austin Collection, Correspondence between Charles A. Beard and George S. Counts, Rare Book and Manuscript Library, Columbia University.

54. When later asked by Oswald Garrison Villard for the name of a military expert who could comment authoritatively about the practical prospects for foreign invasion of the United States, Beard mentioned Smedley Butler. Charles A. Beard to Oswald Garrison Villard, February 22, 1938, Oswald Garrison Villard Papers, Houghton Library, Harvard University.

55. Beard, *The Devil Theory of War*, 119.

56. Smedley D. Butler, "America's Armed Forces 2 'In Time of Peace': The Army," *Common Sense* 4, no. 11 (November 1935).

57. Ibid. (emphasis in original).

58. Charles Beard, "The Hire Learning in America," review of *The Higher Learning in America*, by Thorstein Veblen, *The Dial* 65, no. 779 (December 14, 1918): 553–555.

59. Smedley D. Butler, *War Is a Racket* (Los Angeles: Feral House, 2003), 23.

60. Ibid., 41.

5. Isolationism versus Internationalism

1. This is the same title used by David George Kin, a pseudonym for David George Plotkin, in an alleged exposé of Montana isolationist Senator Burton K. Wheeler, who also plays a dastardly role in Roth's novel. The full title of Kin's book is *The Plot Against America: Senator Wheeler and the Forces behind Him* (Missoula, Mo.: John E. Kennedy, Publishers, 1946). The chapter "Wheeler Becomes Hitler's Handyman" foreshadows Roth's thesis about the senator in his novel as a species of American quisling.

2. Philip Roth, *The Plot Against America* (Boston: Houghton Mifflin, 2004), 178. Susan Dunn made the same case against the isolationists as a motley collection of

anti-British, anti-Jewish, anti-FDR, and anti-Wilson fools and knaves in *1940: FDR, Willkie, Lindbergh, Hitler—the Election amid the Storm* (New Haven, Conn.: Yale University Press, 2013). The king of the knaves is Lindbergh, an anti-Semite and apostle of Aryanism who embodies "the fiercest, most virulent brand of isolationism" (48). Her book and Roth's echo the wartime indictment of the America First Committee by John Roy Carlson (a pseudonym for Arthur Derounian). In his luridly titled bestseller, *My Four Years in the Nazi Underworld of America—The Amazing Revelations of How Axis Agents and Our Enemies Within Are Now Plotting to Destroy the United States* (New York: E. P. Dutton, 1943), readers learned how "the America First Committee had become the voice of American Fascism and the spearhead aimed at the heart of Democracy" (260).

3. Wayne S. Cole, *America First: The Battle Against Intervention 1940–1941* (Madison: University of Wisconsin Press, 1953), 8.

4. In his sympathetic biography, *Charles A. Lindbergh and the Battle Against American Intervention in World War II* (New York: Harcourt Brace Jovanovich, 1974), Cole continued his defense of Lindbergh against the charge of anti-Semitism, emphasizing instead the philo-Semitic elements in his thinking about Nazi persecution of the Jews and his rejection of conspiracy theories about hidden Jewish influence in American political life (173).

5. John E. Moser, *John T. Flynn and the Transformation of American Liberalism* (New York: New York University Press, 2005), 121.

6. Kingman Brewster Jr. to R. Douglas Stuart Jr., July 1940, in *In Danger Undaunted: The Anti-Interventionist Movement of 1940–1941 as Revealed in the Papers of the America First Committee*, ed. Justus D. Doenecke (Stanford, Calif.: Hoover Institution Press, 1990), 88.

7. Charles Beard, "Radio Address by Dr. Charles Beard on March 29, 1937," *Congressional Record*, vol. 81, part 9, appendix, 75th Cong., 1st Sess., April 19, 1937, 868.

8. Charles Beard, "Roosevelt's Place in History," article quoted by Senator Henry F. Ashurst of Prescott, Arizona, in the Senate on March 17, 1938, *Congressional Record*, vol. 83, part 4, 75th Cong., 3rd Sess., 3561. About Beard's judgment of the president, Ashurst declared in his speech, "This is the deliberate conclusion of an authoritative historian contemporaneous with our times."

9. Charles A. Beard and Mary R. Beard, *America in Midpassage*, 2 vols. (New York: Macmillan, 1939), vol. 1, 3.

10. Ibid., vol. 2, 890.

11. Ibid., vol. 1, 326.

12. Ibid., vol. 1, 409; vol. 2, 915.

13. Ibid., vol. 2, 885.

14. In a review of Hobson's *Imperialism: A Study*, Veblen approvingly described the book as an examination of "a social pathology, and no endeavor is made to disguise the malignity of the disease." He agreed with Hobson that the most important factor relating to imperialism concerned "the influence relating to investments." *Journal of Political Economy* 11, no. 2 (March 1903): 311–314.

15. Beard and Beard, *America in Midpassage*, vol. 2, 888.

16. Ibid., 887, 888.

17. William Shakespeare, *Henry IV, Part II*, Act IV, Scene V, in *Shakespeare's Histories*, ed. Peter Alexander (London: Collins, 1951), 260.

18. Justus D. Doenecke, *Storm on the Horizon: The Challenge to American Intervention, 1939–1941* (Lanham, Md.: Rowman & Littlefield, 2000), 8.

19. Charles A. Beard, *Giddy Minds and Foreign Quarrels: An Estimate of American Foreign Policy* (New York: Macmillan, 1939), 49, 53, 54.

20. Ibid., 58–59, 61.

21. Ibid., 63.

22. George Washington, "Farewell Address," Avalon Project: Documents in Law, History, and Diplomacy, Yale Law School, http://avalon.law.yale.edu/18th_century//washington.asp.

23. Beard, *Giddy Minds and Foreign Quarrels*, 67–68, 71, 80.

24. Ibid., 82.

25. Ibid., 83.

26. Ibid., 86.

27. Charles A. Beard, "Neutrality: Shall We Have Revision?—The President's Policy and the People's," *New Republic*, January 18, 1939. Senator Nye included this article as an extension of his January 23, 1939, remarks in the U.S. Senate, *Congressional Record*, vol. 84, part 11, 76th Cong., 1st Sess., appendix, 260.

28. Charles A. Beard, "America Cannot 'Save Europe,'" *Common Sense*, February 1939. Senator Rush D. Holt of West Virginia included this article as an extension of his February 27, 1939, remarks in the U.S. Senate, *Congressional Record*, vol. 84, part 11, 76th Cong., 1st Sess., appendix, 723. Other contributors to this issue of *Common Sense* were Bertrand Russell, John Dewey, John T. Flynn, and Harry Elmer Barnes.

29. Charles Beard, "We're Blundering into War," *American Mercury*, April 1939. Senator Arthur Capper of Kansas included this article as an extension of his March 27, 1939, remarks in the U.S. Senate, *Congressional Record*, vol. 84, part 11, 76th Cong., 1st Sess., appendix, 1171.

30. Charles A. Beard, *A Foreign Policy for America* (New York: Alfred A. Knopf, 1940), 3, 62, 67.

31. Ibid., 84, 85, 147.

32. Ibid., 94 (emphasis in original).

33. Ibid., 114.

34. Ibid., 121.

35. Ibid., 148.

36. Ibid., 148–149.

37. Charles A. Beard to Merle Curti, February 6, 1948, Merle Curti Papers, Charles Beard material microfilm, State Historical Society of Wisconsin.

38. Beard, *A Foreign Policy for America*, 151, 152, 153.

39. Doenecke, *Storm on the Horizon*, 52.

40. Justus D. Doenecke, ed., *In Danger Undaunted*, Document 23, "America First Book List," Page Hufty, Bulletin 476, August 7, 1941, 121.

41. Hugh S. Johnson, "One Man's Opinion," *San Francisco News* 38 (May 7, 1940): 14.

42. Gerald P. Nye, *Congressional Record*, Senate, Friday, June 21, 1940, 8792.

43. Allan Nevins, "Two Views of America's Past: Mr. Buell Argues Our Responsibility—Professor Beard Upholds Isolation," *New York Times Book Review*, May 26, 1940, 20.

44. Charles A. Beard, *Public Policy and the General Welfare* (New York: Farrar & Rinehart, 1941), 5, 19.

45. Ibid., 25, 47.

46. Ibid., 132.

47. Ibid., 65.

48. Thomas E. Mahl, *Desperate Deception: British Covert Operations in the United States, 1939–1944* (Dulles, Va.: Brassey's, 1999), xi–xii.

49. Ibid., 195.

50. Ibid., 103.

51. Ibid., 68.

52. Gore Vidal, *Screening History* (Cambridge, Mass.: Harvard University Press, 1992), 41.

53. The German lobbying effort in America, led by the chargé d'affaires in Washington, Hans Thomsen, paled by comparison with that of the British. The FBI constantly investigated Germany's embassy and consulates, which also came "under the suspicious watch of the Special Committee to Investigate Un-American Activities, chaired by Texas congressman Martin Dies." See Dunn, *1940*, 234. Chapter 16, "The Fifth Column," presents a sharply contrasting picture to the one found in Mahl's book.

54. Albert Eisele, "Death of Senator from Minnesota Still Shrouded in Mystery," *Minnpost*, September 3, 2009.

55. Mahl, *Desperate Deception*, chap. 8, "'We Want Willkie.'"

56. Dunn, *1940*, 149, 150.

57. Mahl, *Desperate Deception*, 178.

58. In *America First! Its History, Culture and Politics* (Amherst, Mass.: Prometheus Books, 1995), Bill Kauffman traces the movement's cultural antecedents back to the populists of the late nineteenth century and identifies elements of its legacy in the writing of Sinclair Lewis, Edgar Lee Masters, Edmund Wilson, Robinson Jeffers, J. P. Marquand, Edward Abbey, Jack Kerouac, Murray Rothbard, and Gore Vidal, as well as in the political careers of Robert A. Taft, William Fulbright, Eugene McCarthy, John McLaughrey, Pat Buchanan, Ross Perot, and Jerry Brown. Despite a noble literary and political lineage, isolationism remains "that most insidious word" in American politics, to use Gore Vidal's phrase in his foreword to *America First!* (10).

6. A Wartime Trilogy

1. Mary R. Beard to Merle Curti, May 24, 1938, Merle Curti Papers, Charles Beard material microfilm, State Historical Society of Wisconsin.

2. Mary R. Beard to Merle Curti, December 2, 1947, Merle Curti Papers, Charles Beard material microfilm, State Historical Society of Wisconsin.

3. Charles A. Beard and Mary R. Beard, *The American Spirit: A Study of the Idea of Civilization in the United States* (New York: Macmillan, 1942), v.

4. Ibid., 36, 3.

5. Ibid., 51–52.

6. Ibid., 158, 159, 161.

7. Ibid., 376–377.

8. Ibid., 483, 538.

9. Ibid., 547.

10. Henry R. Luce, "The American Century," *LIFE* (February 17, 1941): 61–65 (emphasis in original).

11. Ibid.

12. Ibid. (emphasis in original).

13. Ibid.

14. Ibid.

15. Ibid.

16. Beard and Beard, *The American Spirit*, 609.

17. Charles A. Beard, *The Republic: Conversations on Fundamentals*, 6th printing (New York: Viking Press, 1945; originally published 1943), 12.

18. Ibid., 26, 82.

19. Ibid., 103.

20. Ibid., 215.

21. Ibid., 262.

22. Ibid., 264, 309.

23. Ibid., 328.

24. Ibid., 338, 340.

25. Ibid., 342, 343.

26. Alan Brinkley, *The Publisher: Henry Luce and His American Century* (New York: Alfred A. Knopf, 2010), 265–266. For Lippmann's influence on Luce's argument in "The American Century," see James L. Baughman, *Henry R. Luce and the Rise of the American News Media* (Baltimore, Md.: Johns Hopkins University Press, 1987), 132.

27. Robert E. Herzstein, *Henry R. Luce: A Political Portrait of the Man Who Created the American Century* (New York: Charles Scribner's Sons, 1994), 159.

28. Inside description of *LIFE*'s cover (January 17, 1944).

29. Editors' note to Charles A. Beard, "We the People," first installment from *The Republic*, *LIFE* (January 17, 1944): 46.

30. Pvt. Peter J. Frank, Camp Hood, Texas, letter to the editors, *LIFE* (February 7, 1944): 2.

31. Hayden L. V. Anderson, principal of Gorham Normal Training School, Gorham, Maine, letter to the editors, *LIFE* (February 14, 1944): 4.

32. Max L. Berges, Los Angeles, California, letter to the editors, *LIFE* (March 20, 1944): 8.

33. Charles A. Beard, Tryon, North Carolina, letter to the editors, *LIFE* (March 6, 1944): 4, 6.

34. "Beard's *Republic*," editorial, *LIFE* (March 20, 1944): 36.

35. Ibid.

36. Ibid.

37. John K. Jessup, ed., *The Ideas of Henry Luce* (New York: Atheneum, 1969), 15. Luce's irrepressible wife, Clare Boothe Luce, also found inspiration in Beard's historical writing done later in the 1940s. See Sylvia Jukes Morris, *Price of Fame: The Honorable Clare Boothe Luce* (New York: Random House, 2014), 472–473.

38. "American Foreign Policy," *LIFE* (March 27, 1944): 32.

39. Ibid.

40. Clark Foreman, Black Mountain, North Carolina, letter to the editors, *LIFE* (March 27, 1944): 6.

41. Charles A. Beard and Mary R. Beard, *A Basic History of the United States* (New York: Doubleday, Doran & Company, 1944), prefatory note.

42. Ibid., 464.

43. Ibid., 463.

44. Ibid., 480, 482.

45. Ibid., 485.

46. Charles A. Beard to Merle Curti, September 28, 1944, Merle Curti Papers, Charles Beard material microfilm, State Historical Society of Wisconsin.

47. Edwin Montefiore Borchard to Charles A. Beard, August 14, 1944, Edwin Montefiore Borchard Papers, box 1, folder 15, Manuscripts and Archives, Yale University Library.

48. David S. Brown, *Richard Hofstadter: An Intellectual Biography* (Chicago: University of Chicago Press, 2006), chap. 1, "Radical Roots." Brown notes the importance of Hofstadter's "life-long dialogue with scholars of the conflict school," notably Beard (16).

49. Richard Hofstadter, *The American Political Tradition and the Men Who Made It* (New York: Alfred A. Knopf, 1948), viii, x.

50. Richard Hofstadter, *The Progressive Historians: Turner, Beard, and Parrington* (New York: Alfred A. Knopf, 1968), 299, 344. For a compilation of negative judgments about Beard and his legacy, see Pope McCorkle, "The Historian as Intellectual: Charles Beard and the Constitution Reconsidered," *American Journal of Legal History* 28, no. 4 (October 1984).

51. Richard Hofstadter, "Charles Beard and the Constitution," in *Charles A. Beard: An Appraisal*, ed. Howard K. Beale (Lexington: University of Kentucky Press, 1954), 90.

52. Ibid., 91.

53. Charles A. Beard, "The Constitution and the Courts," Cosmos Club address, January 13, 1936, extracts reprinted by request on February 6, 1936, by Senator Elbert D. Thomas of Utah in *Congressional Record*, vol. 80, part 2, 74th Cong., 2nd Sess., 1560.

54. Beard, "The Constitution and the Courts," 1561.

55. Irving Howe to Richard Hofstadter, undated, Richard Hofstadter Papers, Cataloged Correspondence, Rare Book and Manuscript Library, Columbia University (emphasis in original).

56. Cited by Walter LaFeber in "The Impact of Fred Harvey Harrington," paper for delivery at the Organization of American Historians Meeting, Minneapolis, April 19, 1985, found in William Appleman Williams Papers (MSS Williams), Oregon State University Special Collections and Archives Research Center, Oregon State University, Walter LaFeber file, box 1.001, Correspondence A–M.

57. Yet, the consensus theory of American history would cling vigorously to life. For example, John Patrick Diggins attempts to defend Beard against the charge of vulgar economic determinism, but concludes that in a crucial respect: "Beard's critics are correct: consensus, not conflict, explains the 'uniqueness' of American history," in "Power and Authority in American History: The Case of Charles A. Beard," *The American Historical Review* 86, no. 4 (October 1981): 730.

58. Richard Hofstadter to Arthur M. Schlesinger Jr., March 1, 1968, Richard Hofstadter Papers, Cataloged Correspondence, Rare Book and Manuscript Library, Co-

lumbia University. In this same letter, he claimed not to be very fond of the work by Daniel Boorstin, another paragon of the consensus school.

59. Richard Hofstadter to Arthur M. Schlesinger Jr., April 1, 1968, Richard Hofstadter Papers, Cataloged Correspondence, Rare Book and Manuscript Library, Columbia University.

60. Richard Hofstadter to Dumas Malone, May 7, 1969, Richard Hofstadter Papers, Cataloged Correspondence, Rare Book and Manuscript Library, Columbia University.

61. Hofstadter, *The Progressive Historians*, 282.

7. Waging War for the Four Freedoms

1. Charles A. Beard to Harry Elmer Barnes, September 2, 1943, Harry Elmer Barnes Papers, box 29, folder 2, August 2–September 30, 1943, American Heritage Center, University of Wyoming.

2. Patrick J. Maney, *Young Bob: A Biography of Robert M. La Follette, Jr.*, 2nd ed. (Madison: Wisconsin Historical Society, 2003; 1st ed. University of Missouri Press, 1978), 130.

3. "Solons Pleased as Neutrality Wins," *The Progressive* 4, no. 144 (September 7, 1935): 1.

4. Smedley D. Butler, "Lobbying for Another War," *The Progressive* 4, no. 148 (October 5, 1935): 3, reprinted from *Common Sense* magazine.

5. Ibid.

6. "Bankers Seeking to Deny War 'Pressure,'" *The Progressive* 4, no. 162 (January 18, 1936): 1, 5.

7. "'War Racket' Is Denounced by General Butler," *The Progressive* 4, no. 168 (February 29, 1936): 6.

8. "Congress, High Court Blistered: Beard, Lewis Hit as Dodging Duties," *The Progressive* 4, no. 163 (January 25, 1936): 5.

9. Robert M. La Follette Jr., "Keep America Out of War," *The Progressive* 4, no. 166 (February 15, 1936): 1.

10. Maney, *Young Bob*, 228.

11. Robert La Follette Jr., speech in the U.S. Senate, October 12, 1939, *Congressional Record*, vol. 85, part 2, 76th Cong., 2nd Sess., 325.

12. Ibid., 327.

13. Ibid., 329.

14. Ibid., 331.

15. Ibid., 332.

16. Ibid., 333.

17. John Alan Ziegler, "*The Progressive*'s Views on Foreign Affairs, 1909–1941: A Case Study of Liberal Economic Isolationism," unpublished PhD dissertation, Syracuse University, 1970, 280.

18. "New, Militant Progressive Takes the Field," *The Progressive* 40, no. 26 (June 29, 1940): 1.

19. "Charles Beard Urges U.S. Stay Out of Europe," *The Progressive* 4, no. 38 (September 21, 1940): 3.

20. R. Douglas Stuart Jr. to Robert M. La Follette Jr., September 24, 1940, Robert M. La Follette Jr. Papers, box I: C18, Library of Congress.

21. Charles A. Beard to Frederic A. Ogg, January 1, 1941, Kenneth Colegrove Papers, Herbert Hoover Presidential Library.

22. Charles A. Beard to Frederic A. Ogg, January 20, 1941. APSA officers hoped that Beard would attend their executive council session at the New York convention on December 28, 1941, when they would discuss the issue that he had raised regarding renting space to propaganda organizations. To their invitation he replied from Aiken, South Carolina, where he and Mary had gone for the winter: "As you can see I have already fled from the wintry blasts, and it will be impossible for me to attend the sessions of the Association, pleasant as it would be to see all the saints again!" Charles A. Beard to Kenneth Colegrove, December 15, 1941, Kenneth Colegrove Papers, Herbert Hoover Presidential Library. Colegrove taught political science at Northwestern University and long served as the secretary-treasurer of APSA.

23. Burton K. Wheeler, extension of remarks in the U.S. Senate, February 13, 1941, *Congressional Record*, vol. 87, part 10, 77th Cong., 1st Sess., appendix, A625.

24. Charles Beard, testimony before the Senate Committee on Foreign Relations, extension of remarks in the U.S. Senate by Burton K. Wheeler, February 13, 1941, A626.

25. Ibid.

26. Ibid., A627.

27. Ibid.

28. Senator Arthur Capper, "A Statement Concerning the Granting of Unlimited Aid to Great Britain," speech in the U.S. Senate, February 22, 1941, *Congressional Record*, vol. 87, part 2, 77th Cong., 1st Sess., 1274.

29. Charles A. Beard, "Counting the Consequences," *The Progressive* 5, no. 9 (March 1, 1941): 2.

30. Ibid.

31. Frank Lloyd Wright, "America! Wake Up!" *The Progressive* 5, no. 25 (June 21, 1941): 2.

32. Oswald Garrison Villard, "'America Is Not God,'" *The Progressive* 5, no. 25 (June 21, 1941): 5.

33. Norman M. Clapp to Richard Neuberger (for the *Portland Oregonian*), August 15, 1941, Robert M. La Follette Jr. Papers, box I: C18, LOC.

34. Philip La Follette, "Secret Covenants, Secretly Arrived At," *The Progressive* 5, no. 34 (August 23, 1941).

35. Herbert Hoover, "The Wells of Freedom," *The Progressive* 5, no. 39 (September 27, 1941): 9.

36. Hoover's restraint in foreign policy led William Appleman Williams to hail him as a statesman vastly superior to FDR. Taking a Beardian view, Williams wrote, "It may be that Hoover is one of the few tragic figures in American history." *The Tragedy of American Diplomacy*, 50th anniversary edition (New York: W. W. Norton, 2009), 140. Hoover tried to control the bankers and rejected calls for big military appropriations. Such a leader was bound for oblivion. An American president resolutely opposed to economic imperialism and militarism has not been seen since. According to Williams, "More than any other twentieth-century American's Hoover's reputation is the prod-

uct of misinformation and distortion." *The Contours of American History* (New York: W. W. Norton, 1988), 426.

37. Harry Elmer Barnes, "The War and World Revolution," *The Progressive* 5, no. 46 (November 15, 1941): 9.

38. Harry Elmer Barnes, "World Trends and the War," *The Progressive* 5, no. 47 (November 22, 1941): 9.

39. Ibid.

40. Harry Elmer Barnes, "No War with Japan," *The Progressive* 5, no. 49 (December 6, 1941): 9.

41. "Nation United Against Aggression," *The Progressive* 5, no. 50 (December 13, 1941): 1.

42. Morris H. Rubin, "The Last Column," *The Progressive* 5, no. 50 (December 13, 1941): 12.

43. Charles A. Beard to Robert M. La Follette Jr., January 11, 1942, Robert M. La Follette Jr. Papers, box I: C19, LOC.

44. Charles A. Beard to Robert M. La Follette Jr., January 27, 1942, Robert M. La Follette Jr. Papers, box I: C 19, LOC.

45. Robert M. La Follette Jr. to Charles A. Beard, February 4, 1942, Robert M. La Follette Jr. Papers, box I: C19, LOC.

46. FDR to Robert M. La Follette Jr., February 20, 1942, Robert M. La Follette Jr. Papers, box I: C20, LOC.

47. Ibid. (emphasis in original).

48. Harry Elmer Barnes, "How the Bad Boy Got Started," *The Progressive* 6, no. 9 (February 28, 1942): 5.

49. In the more restrained language of academic scholarship, Thomas J. McCormick reached the same conclusion about the economic causes of the war in the Pacific: "Compelled by the exigencies of depression, fearful of the rising tides of Chinese nationalism and radicalism, and resentful of bearing the brunt of political responsibility while others reaped most of the economic reward, Japan dissolved the partnership with the United States and struck out on her own." Thomas J. McCormick, *China Market: America's Quest for Informal Empire, 1893–1901* (Chicago: Quadrangle Books, 1967), 194. The partnership, dating back to the turn-of-the-century Open Door initiative in China, had been based on their shared interest in the economic exploitation of Chinese markets and resources.

50. Harry Elmer Barnes, "The Challenge to Democracy," *The Progressive* 6, no. 13 (March 28, 1942): 9.

51. Harry Elmer Barnes, "Science to the Aid of Government," *The Progressive* 6, no. 14 (April 4, 1942): 4.

52. Harry Elmer Barnes to Edwin Montefiore Borchard, February 4, 1943, Edwin Montefiore Borchard Papers, box 1, folder 12, Manuscripts and Archives, Yale University Library.

53. Edwin Montefiore Borchard to Harry Elmer Barnes, February 23, 1943, Edwin Montefiore Borchard Papers, box 1, folder 12, Manuscripts and Archives, Yale University Library.

54. Edwin Montefiore Borchard to Harry Elmer Barnes, March 5, 1943, Edwin Montefiore Borchard Papers, box 1, folder 12, Manuscripts and Archives, Yale University Library.

55. Morris H. Rubin, "The Last Column," *The Progressive* 6, no. 18 (May 2, 1942): 12.

56. Morris H. Rubin, "The Last Column," *The Progressive* 6, no. 22 (May 30, 1942): 12.

57. James T. Patterson, *Mr. Republican: A Biography of Robert A. Taft* (Boston: Houghton Mifflin, 1972), 286–291.

58. Ronald Radosh, *Prophets on the Right: Profiles of Conservative Critics of American Globalism* (New York: Simon and Schuster, 1975), 129.

59. For historical background on "the fabled Far Eastern markets" and the imperialist rivalries that they caused in the Pacific, see Thomas J. McCormick, *China Market: America's Quest for Informal Empire 1893–1901* (Chicago: Quadrangle Books, 1967), 18.

60. John Williams to Robert M. La Follette Jr., April 6, 1942, Robert M. La Follette Jr. Papers, box I: C20, LOC.

61. John Williams to Robert M. La Follette Jr., January 19, 1943, Robert M. La Follette Jr. Papers, box I: C21, LOC.

62. John Williams to Robert M. La Follette Jr., January 26, 1943, Robert M. La Follette Jr. Papers, box I: C21, LOC.

63. Robert M. La Follette Jr. to John Williams, January 27, 1943, Robert M. La Follette Jr. Papers, box I: C21, LOC.

64. John Williams to Robert M. La Follette Jr., January 30, 1943, Robert M. La Follette Jr. Papers, box I: C21, LOC.

65. John Williams to Robert M. La Follette Jr., February 4, 1943, Robert M. La Follette Jr. Papers, box I: C21, LOC.

66. Robert M. La Follette Jr. to John Williams, March 6, 1943, Robert M. La Follette Jr. Papers, box I: C21, LOC.

67. John Williams to Robert M. La Follette Jr., June 1, 1943, Robert M. La Follette Jr. Papers, box I: C21, LOC.

68. Robert M. La Follette Jr. to John Williams, June 2, 1943, Robert M. La Follette Jr. Papers, box I: C21, LOC.

69. Enclosure, John Williams to Robert M. La Follette Jr., September 7, 1943, Robert M. La Follette Jr. Papers, box I: C21, LOC.

70. For a withering indictment of Harris and LeMay as war criminals for their terror bombing tactics against civilian populations, see John Keegan, *The Second World War* (London: Penguin, 1989), chap. 22, "Strategic Bombing," esp. 420–421.

71. Enclosure, John Williams to Robert M. La Follette, Jr., September 7, 1943.

72. John Williams to Julia Emory, day after Thanksgiving, 1943, Robert M. La Follette Jr. Papers, box I: C21, LOC.

73. C. Wright Mills, *The Power Elite* (New York: Oxford University Press, 1959), 100. He further observes, "During World War II, the merger of the corporate economy and the military bureaucracy came into its present-day significance" (212).

74. John Williams, "America Is Britain's Rubber Stamp," *The Progressive* 9, no. 27 (July 2, 1945): 9–10.

75. John Williams to Robert M. La Follette Jr., July 5, 1945, Robert M. La Follette Jr. Papers, box I: C23, LOC.

76. John Williams to Robert M. La Follette Jr., October 8, 1945, Robert M. La Follette Jr. Papers, box I: C23, LOC.

77. Robert M. La Follette Jr., "Breeding the Next War," *The Progressive* 8, no. 21 (May 22, 1944): 1.

78. Frank C. Hanighen, "The Forgotten Man in North Africa," *The Progressive* 7, no. 5 (February 1, 1943) 4.

79. Many other Hanighen columns for *The Progressive* touched on the theme of economic imperialism as the fundamental motive of the Allies in the Second World War, including "Saving the Imperialists," May 17, 1943; "The Tin Cartel Does Business as Usual," May 24, 1943; "1919 and 1943—A Deadly Parallel," October 25, 1943; "France and the Seeds of World War III," December 6, 1943; and "The Patterns of Imperialism in the Middle East," July 30, 1945.

80. Frank C. Hanighen, review of *U.S. Foreign Policy* by Walter Lippmann, *The Progressive* 7, no. 32 (August 9, 1943): 10.

81. Morris H. Rubin, "The Last Column," *The Progressive* 6, no. 45 (November 9, 1942): 12.

82. Max Otto, review of *The American Spirit*, January 4, 1943; William B. Hesseltine, review of *The Republic: Conversations on Fundamentals*, November 22, 1943; and William B. Hesseltine, review of *A Basic History of the United States*, August 7, 1944. In a November 29, 1943, letter to Merle Curti, Beard expressed appreciation for *The Progressive* review of *The Republic*: "If you see Hesseltine, tell him that I am simply overjoyed to learn from his review of *The Republic* . . . that he thinks so highly of my poor labors." Merle Curti Papers, Charles Beard material microfilm, State Historical Society of Wisconsin.

83. Charles A. Beard, "Our Irresponsible Government," *The Progressive* 8, no. 10 (March 6, 1944): 1.

84. Beard feared that an overweening executive branch would extinguish as a practical matter the constitutional prerogatives of Congress, a point he developed in a November 1942 article for the *American Mercury*, "In Defense of Congress—We Cannot Hamstring Congress without Hamstringing Our Own American Civilization." Beard warned, "We cannot kill off Congress without committing suicide as a democratic nation." This article was included as an Extension of Remarks of Guy L. Moser of Pennsylvania in the House of Representatives, October 29, 1942, *Congressional Record*, vol. 88, part 10, 77th Cong., 2nd Sess., appendix, A3850.

85. Beard, "Pearl Harbor: Challenge to the Republic," *The Progressive* 9, no. 36 (September 3, 1945): 1–2. Requesting to have this article printed in the *Congressional Record*, Clare Booth Luce declared, "Mr. Speaker, the American people are demanding the truth about Pearl Harbor. The reasons why the truth must be given them are brilliantly and succinctly set forth in an article in *The Progressive* by Charles A. Beard, eminent American historian." Extension of Remarks by Hon. Clare Booth Luce of Connecticut, in the House of Representatives, September 5, 1945, *Congressional Record*, vol. 91, part 12, 79th Cong., 1st Sess., appendix, A3759.

8. Beard Finds an Ally in Herbert Hoover

1. Ray Lyman Wilbur to Charles A. Beard, August 30, 1944, Herbert Hoover Papers, Beard file, Manuscript Biographies Collection, Herbert Hoover Presidential Library.

2. Ibid.

3. Ray Lyman Wilbur to Charles A. Beard, October 9, 1944, Herbert Hoover Papers, Manuscript Biographies Collection, Herbert Hoover Presidential Library.

4. Colonel Truman Smith to Herbert Hoover, October 26, 1945, Herbert Hoover Papers, Manuscript Biographies Collection, Herbert Hoover Presidential Library. For Smith's extraordinary career, see Robert Hessen, ed., *The Memoirs and Reports of Truman Smith* (Stanford, Calif.: Hoover Institution Press, 1984).

5. Herbert Hoover to Truman Smith, October 29, 1945, Herbert Hoover Papers, Manuscript Biographies Collection, Herbert Hoover Presidential Library.

6. Truman Smith to Herbert Hoover, November 6, 1945, Herbert Hoover Papers, Manuscript Biographies Collection, Herbert Hoover Presidential Library.

7. Herbert Hoover to Truman Smith, November 8, 1945, Herbert Hoover Papers, Manuscript Biographies Collection, Herbert Hoover Presidential Library.

8. Herbert Hoover to Charles A. Beard, November 15, 1945, Herbert Hoover Papers, Manuscript Biographies Collection, Herbert Hoover Presidential Library.

9. Charles A. Beard to Herbert Hoover, November 17, 1945, Herbert Hoover Papers, Manuscript Biographies Collection, Herbert Hoover Presidential Library.

10. Herbert Hoover, "America's Position—III," memorandum to unnamed cabinet officers, May 15, 1945, Herbert Hoover Articles, Addresses and Public Statements #2836, Herbert Hoover Presidential Library.

11. Ibid.

12. Edgar Rickard, diary entry, May 30, 1945, in *Herbert Hoover and Harry S. Truman: A Documentary History*, ed. Timothy Walch and Dwight M. Miller (Worland, Wyo.: High Plains Publishing Company, 1992), https://www.trumanlibrary.org/hoover/documents.php.

13. Herbert Hoover to Harry S. Truman, May 30, 1945, in *Herbert Hoover and Harry S. Truman*, ed. Walch and Miller.

14. Herbert Hoover to Harry S. Truman, "Memorandum on Ending the Japanese War," May 30, 1945, in *Herbert Hoover and Harry S. Truman*, ed. Walch and Miller.

15. Ibid.

16. Joseph Grew to Harry S. Truman, June 13, 1945, in *Herbert Hoover and Harry S. Truman*, ed. Walch and Miller.

17. Ibid.

18. Hoover, "Memorandum on Ending the Japanese War."

19. Herbert Hoover to Harry S. Truman, "Memorandum on Reorganization of the War Food Agencies," May 30, 1945, in *Herbert Hoover and Harry S. Truman*, ed. Walch and Miller.

20. Herbert Hoover to Harry S. Truman, "Memorandum on War Economic Policies and Their Organization," May 30, 1945, in *Herbert Hoover and Harry S. Truman*, ed. Walch and Miller.

21. Quoted in a letter from Bernice Miller (writing for Hoover) to Charles A. Beard, January 3, 1946, Herbert Hoover Papers, Beard File, Manuscript Biographies Collection, Herbert Hoover Presidential Library.

22. Charles A. Beard to Herbert Hoover, November 17, 1945, Herbert Hoover Papers, Manuscript Biographies Collection, Herbert Hoover Presidential Library.

23. George H. Nash, "Editor's Introduction: Herbert Hoover's Mysterious Magnum Opus," in *Freedom Betrayed: Herbert Hoover's Secret History of the Second World War and Its Aftermath*, ed. George H. Nash (Stanford, Calif.: Hoover Institution Press, 2011), lxii.

24. James A. Healy to Herbert Hoover, July 5, 1944, Herbert Hoover Papers, Beard File, Manuscript Biographies Collection, Herbert Hoover Presidential Library.

25. Herbert Hoover to James A. Healy, July 10, 1944, Herbert Hoover Papers, Beard File, Manuscript Biographies Collection, Herbert Hoover Presidential Library.

26. Nash, "Editor's Introduction," lviv.

27. Ibid., lxxiv.

28. Herbert Hoover, Document 20, "Preface to Lost Statesmanship, July 1, 1957," appendix: "A Selection of Documents Pertaining to *Freedom Betrayed*," 888.

29. Herbert Hoover, Document 16, "Mr. Winston Churchill," *circa* 1950–1953, appendix to *Freedom Betrayed*, 866.

30. Herbert Hoover, Document 14, "Churchill," May 10, 1949, appendix to *Freedom Betrayed*, 861–862.

31. Ibid., 861.

32. Nash, editor's introduction to Document 13, "The Results of World War II to the United States" and "A Review of Franklin Roosevelt's Foreign Policies," 1947, appendix to *Freedom Betrayed*, 850.

33. Nash, editor's introduction to Document 17, "Hoover Assesses Franklin Roosevelt's Wartime Record," 1953, appendix to *Freedom Betrayed*, 871.

34. Nash, editor's introduction to Document 18, "A Review of Lost Statesmanship—19 Times in 7 Years," 1953, appendix to *Freedom Betrayed*, 875.

35. "RJ to American Academy of Arts and Letters," in *The Collected Letters of Robinson Jeffers with Selected Letters of Una Jeffers: Volume Three, 1940–1962*, ed. James Karman (Stanford, Calif.: Stanford University Press, 2015), 425.

36. Cited in "The Last Word: A Record of the Auxiliary Library at Tor House" (1998), containing a list of the holdings in the personal library of Jeffers and his wife Una. I am indebted to Robinson Jeffers scholar James Karman for this information.

37. Robinson Jeffers, "The Double Axe," in *The Double Axe and Other Poems* (New York: Liveright, 1977), 7.

38. Ibid., 18.

39. Ibid., 40.

40. Jeffers, "Teheran," in *The Double Axe and Other Poems*, 128.

41. Jeffers, "Historical Choice," in *The Double Axe and Other Poems*, 129.

42. Jeffers, "So Many Blood Lakes," in *The Double Axe and Other Poems*, 132.

43. Jeffers, preface to *The Double Axe and Other Poems*, xxii.

44. Publisher's note to *The Double Axe and Other Poems*, xxiii.

45. William Everson, foreword to *The Double Axe and Other Poems*, xi.

46. Editor's note, *The Collected Letters of Robinson Jeffers with Selected Letters of Una Jeffers: Volume Two, 1931–1939*, ed. James Karman (Stanford, Calif.: Stanford University Press, 2011), 1043.

47. James Karman, "The Life and Work of Robinson Jeffers: An Introduction," in *The Collected Letters of Robinson Jeffers with Selected Letters of Una Jeffers: Volume One, 1890–1930*, ed. James Karman (Stanford, Calif.: Stanford University Press, 2009), 76–77.

48. Herbert Hoover, Document 13, "The Results of World War II to the United States" and "A Review of Franklin Roosevelt's Foreign Policies," 1947, appendix to *Freedom Betrayed*, 852.

49. Herbert Hoover, Document 17, "Hoover Assesses Franklin Roosevelt's Wartime Record," 1953, appendix to *Freedom Betrayed*, 872.

50. Hoover, Document 13, 857.

51. Ibid., 858.

52. Hoover, Document 17, 873.

53. Ibid.

54. Herbert Hoover, Document 18, "A Review of Lost Statesmanship—19 Times in 7 Years," 1953, appendix to *Freedom Betrayed*, 875.

55. Ibid., 878.

56. Hoover, Document 13, 855.

57. Hoover, Document 18, 882.

58. Hoover, Document 13, 854.

59. Hoover, *Freedom Betrayed*, 566.

60. The Right Honorable Lord Hankey, *Politics, Trials and Errors* (Chicago: Henry Regnery Company, 1950), 46–47, quoted in Hoover, *Freedom Betrayed*, 568.

61. Nash, "Editor's Introduction," xvi, lxxx, lxxxii.

62. For an appreciative account of Beard's role in the foreign policy debates of the 1930s, see James J. Martin's *American Liberalism and World Politics, 1931–1941: Liberalism's Press and Spokesmen on the Road Back to War between Mukden and Pearl Harbor*, 2 vols. (New York: Devin-Adair Company, 1964). Reflecting Beard's view of the era, Martin concluded, "There was to be no history of the propaganda on the coming of the Second World War because the propaganda of the Allied side was to become the official history of the coming of the war and the war itself, to survive for a period longer than the interim between the wars without any significant adjustment or revision" (vol. 2, 1202).

63. Scholars debate the identity of the person who wrote "The Art of Political Lying," long attributed to Swift. His friend and fellow satirist John Arbuthnot was involved in its composition. Both are identified as authors in the 2013 Editions Dupleix publication of the pamphlet.

64. Jonathan Swift, "The Art of Political Lying," https://en.wikisource.org/wiki/The_Works_of_the_Rev._Jonathan_Swift/Volume_17/On_the_Art_of_Political_Lying. The pamphlet is thought to have been written around 1712.

65. James J. Martin, *Revisionist Viewpoints: Essays in a Dissident Historical Tradition* (Colorado Springs, Colo.: Ralph Myles Publisher, 1971), 180, 191.

66. Ibid., 192, 193. For a diametrically opposed interpretation of interwar revisionism and of Beard's role in the movement, see Warren I. Cohen, *The American Revisionists: The Lessons of Intervention in World War I* (Chicago: University of Chicago Press, 1967). About Beard and other leading revisionists, he wrote, "Their one great error was their belief that the United States could remain out of war simply by willing to stay out; they had underestimated the totalitarian threat" (240). Evidently, the totalitarian threat, for Cohen, did not include Stalin.

9. Attacking "the Saint"

1. Edwin Montefiore Borchard to Charles A. Beard, March 15, 1945, Edwin Montefiore Borchard Papers, box 1, folder 15, Manuscripts and Archives, Yale University Library.

2. Charles A. Beard to Edwin Montefiore Borchard, April 7, 1945, Edwin Montefiore Borchard Papers, box 1, folder 15, Manuscripts and Archives, Yale University Library.

3. Charles A. Beard to Edwin Montefiore Borchard, June 25, 1945, Edwin Montefiore Borchard Papers, box 1, folder 15, Manuscripts and Archives, Yale University Library.

4. Charles A. Beard to Harry Elmer Barnes, September 2, 1945, Harry Elmer Barnes Papers, box 31, folder July 1–September 26, 1945, American Heritage Center, University of Wyoming.

5. Charles A. Beard to Harry Elmer Barnes, September 15, 1945, Harry Elmer Barnes Papers, box 31, folder 1, July 1–September 26, 1945, American Heritage Center, University of Wyoming.

6. Ibid. (emphasis in original).

7. Charles A. Beard to Harry Elmer Barnes, September 26, 1945, Harry Elmer Barnes Papers, box 31, folder 1, July 1–September 26, 1945, American Heritage Center, University of Wyoming.

8. Charles A. Beard to Harry Elmer Barnes, December 13, 1945, Harry Elmer Barnes Papers, box 80, folder December 1–December 13, 1945, American Heritage Center, University of Wyoming. This letter is to be found in the "Undated Letters" section of the collection, but internal evidence plainly indicates a 1945 date.

9. Kenneth Colegrove to A. Gayle Waldrop, December 29, 1945, Kenneth Colegrove Papers, Herbert Hoover Presidential Library.

10. Oswald Garrison Villard to Charles A. Beard, February 6, 1946, Oswald Garrison Villard Papers, Houghton Library, Harvard University.

11. Charles A. Beard to Oswald Garrison Villard, February 9, 1946, Oswald Garrison Villard Papers, Houghton Library, Harvard University.

12. Charles A. Beard to Edwin Montefiore Borchard, January 18, 1946, Edwin Montefiore Borchard Papers, box 1, folder 15, Manuscripts and Archives, Yale University Library.

13. Sumner Welles, *The Time for Decision* (New York: Harper & Brothers Publishers, 1944), 55–56, 56.

14. Ibid., 174. Two years later, he would expand on his account of the Atlantic Charter, calling it "the beacon which the English-speaking democracies held aloft to the peoples struggling for liberty, to light them forward to peace, to human progress and to a free world," in *Where Are We Heading?* (New York: Harper & Brothers Publishers, 1946), 3, esp. 6–18. This second book appeared several months after Beard wrote his letters to Borchard and Villard in January and February 1946.

15. Charles A. Beard to Harry Elmer Barnes, February 18, 1946, Harry Elmer Barnes Papers, box 32, folder 2, January 2–April 29, 1946, American Heritage Center, University of Wyoming.

16. Carolyn Woods Eisenberg, *Drawing the Line: The American Decision to Divide Germany, 1944–1949* (Cambridge: Cambridge University Press, 1996), 17, 31, 416, 492.

17. Beard, *American Foreign Policy in the Making, 1932–1940: A Study in Responsibilities* (New Haven, Conn.: Yale University Press, 1946), 62, 113.

18. Ibid., 136.

19. Charles A. Beard to Herbert Hoover, November 17, 1945, Beard File, Manuscript Biographies Collection, Herbert Hoover Presidential Library.

20. Beard, *American Foreign Policy in the Making, 1932–1940*, 135.

21. Warren I. Cohen describes *The Idea of National Interest* as "probably the dullest book Beard ever wrote," likening it to an encyclopedia, in *The American Revisionists: The Lessons of Intervention in World War I* (Chicago: University of Chicago Press, 1967), 129.

22. Charles A. Beard, *The Idea of National Interest: An Analytical Study in American Foreign Policy*, with the collaboration of G. H. E. Smith (New York: Macmillan, 1934), 14.

23. Ibid., 416, 435.

24. Ibid., 546, 547.

25. Beard, *American Foreign Policy in the Making, 1932–1940*, 142.

26. Ibid., 184.

27. Ibid., 212.

28. Ibid., 226.

29. Ibid. 256.

30. Ibid., 261, 268.

31. Ibid., 314, 316.

32. Charles A. Beard to Harry Elmer Barnes, August 7, 1946, Harry Elmer Barnes Papers, box 32, folder 1, May 1–August 31, 1946, American Heritage Center, University of Wyoming.

33. Charles A. Beard to Edwin Montefiore Borchard, August 15, 1946, Edwin Montefiore Borchard Papers, box 1, folder 15, Manuscripts and Archives, Yale University Library.

34. Charles A. Beard to Harry Elmer Barnes, August 7, 1946, Harry Elmer Barnes Papers, box 32, folder May1–August 31, 1946, American Heritage Center, University of Wyoming.

35. Charles A. Beard to Harry Elmer Barnes, May 5, 1947, Harry Elmer Barnes Papers, box 33, folder April 1–July 31, 1947, American Heritage Center, University of Wyoming.

36. Oswald Garrison Villard to Charles A. Beard, August 14, 1946, Oswald Garrison Villard Papers, Houghton Library, Harvard University.

37. Oswald Garrison Villard, "Dr. Beard Reviews the Record," *The Progressive* 10, no. 42 (October 28, 1946): 10.

38. Oswald Garrison Villard to Charles A. Beard, October 16, 1946, Oswald Garrison Villard Papers, Houghton Library, Harvard University.

39. Charles A. Beard to Oswald Garrison Villard, January 24, 1947, Oswald Garrison Villard Papers, Houghton Library, Harvard University.

40. Charles A. Beard to Oswald Garrison Villard , April 15, 1947, Oswald Garrison Villard Papers, Houghton Library, Harvard University.

41. Charles A. Beard to Harry Elmer Barnes, May 23, 1947, Harry Elmer Barnes Papers, box 33, folder April 1–July 31, 1947, American Heritage Center, University of Wyoming (emphasis in original).

42. Ibid.

43. Ibid.

44. Charles A. Beard to Harry Elmer Barnes, July 10, 1947, Harry Elmer Barnes Papers, box 33, folder April 1–July 31, 1947, American Heritage Center, University of Wyoming.

45. Charles A. Beard to Oswald Garrison Villard, September 8, 1947, Oswald Garrison Villard Papers, Houghton Library, Harvard University.

46. Charles A. Beard to Harry Elmer Barnes, October 21, 1947, Harry Elmer Barnes Papers, box 33, folder October 3–December 31, 1947, American Heritage Center, University of Wyoming.

47. Charles A. Beard to Harry Elmer Barnes, November 27, 1947, Harry Elmer Barnes Papers, box 33, folder October 3–December 31, 1947, American Heritage Center, University of Wyoming.

48. Gabriel Kolko, *The Politics of War: The World and United States Foreign Policy, 1943–1945* (New York: Random House, 1968), 4, 620.

49. Charles A. Beard to Harry Elmer Barnes, January 6, 1948, Harry Elmer Barnes Papers, box 34, folder January 6–March 31, 1948, American Heritage Center, University of Wyoming.

50. Charles A. Beard to Harry Elmer Barnes, January 14, 1948, Harry Elmer Barnes Papers, box 34, folder January 6–March 31, 1948, and Charles A. Beard to Harry Elmer Barnes, February 14, 1948, box 36, folder March 1–May 31, 1950, American Heritage Center, University of Wyoming.

51. C. Wright Mills, *The Power Elite* (New York: Oxford University Press, 1959), 215. The strongly marked tendency in postwar America would be "to define the reality of international relations in a military way" (220). No effectively competing world view to the one offered by "the warlords" and their corporate and political allies in the power elite would trouble the status quo: "There is no effective countervailing power against the coalition of businessmen . . . and the ascendant military men" (267).

52. Charles A. Beard to Harry Elmer Barnes, January 14, 1948, Harry Elmer Barnes Papers, box 34, folder January 6–March 31, 1948, American Heritage Center, University of Wyoming.

53. Charles A. Beard to Merle Curti, January 19, 1948, William Appleman Williams Papers (MSS Williams), Oregon State University, Special Collections and Archives Research Center, Corvallis, Oregon, box 1.001, Correspondence A–M. This letter was on a mimeographed sheet in the Merle Curti file. The historians referred to in the letter were Samuel Eliot Morison and William Langer.

54. Charles A. Beard, *President Roosevelt and the Coming of the War, 1941: A Study in Appearances and Realities* (New Haven, Conn.: Yale University Press, 1948), 26.

55. Ibid., 577.

56. Charles A. Beard to Oswald Garrison Villard, November 8, 1946, Oswald Garrison Villard Papers, Houghton Library, Harvard University.

57. Beard, *President Roosevelt and the Coming of the War, 1941*, 119, 120.

58. Ibid., 453, 580, 590.

59. Ibid., 593.

60. Ibid., 349, 357, 419.

61. Walter LaFeber, *America, Russia, and the Cold War, 1945–2006*, 10th ed. (Boston: McGraw-Hill, 2008), 101.

62. Charles A. Beard to Oswald Garrison Villard, April 13, 1948, Oswald Garrison Villard Papers, Houghton Library, Harvard University (emphasis in original). Arthur M. Schlesinger Jr. wrote *The Vital Center: The Politics of Freedom* in the fall and

winter of 1948–1949. In this liberal call for America to glory in its global responsibilities, he accorded Beard a slight measure of regard. After announcing that "History has thrust a world destiny on the United States," thus ending the debate between interventionists and isolationists, Schlesinger observed, "with the death of Professor Beard, isolationism lost its last trace of intellectual respectability" (219).

63. Charles A. Beard to Harry Elmer Barnes, July 9, 1948, Harry Elmer Barnes Papers, box 34, folder July 2–September 30, 1948, American Heritage Center, University of Wyoming.

64. Ibid.

65. Samuel Eliot Morison, "Did Roosevelt Start the War? History through a Beard," *Atlantic Monthly* (August 1948): 91–97.

66. Ibid.

67. Senator Homer Ferguson, "Roosevelt and History," extension of remarks by Hon. Lawrence H. Smith of Wisconsin, in the House of Representatives, Monday, April 12, 1948, *Congressional Record*, vol. 94, part 10, 80th Cong., 2nd Sess., appendix, A2254.

68. George A. Lundberg, "The Road to War," *The Progressive* 12, no. 5 (May 1948): 36–37.

69. Oswald Garrison Villard, "Charles A. Beard, Patriot," *The Progressive* 12, no. 10 (October 1948): 21–22.

70. "Dr. C. A. Beard Dead at 73, Critic of FDR," *Chicago Daily Tribune* (September 2, 1948): B5.

71. Charles A. Beard to Oswald Garrison Villard, February 10, 1948, Oswald Garrison Villard Papers, Houghton Library, Harvard University.

72. "Charles A. Beard," *Chicago Daily Tribune* (September 4, 1948): 8.

73. "Charles A. Beard, Historian, Is Dead," *New York Times* (September 2, 1948): 23.

74. Mary R. Beard to Harry Elmer Barnes, February 21, 1949, Harry Elmer Barnes Papers, box 35, folder January 7–March 30, 1949, American Heritage Center, University of Wyoming.

75. Mary Beard, "Charles A. Beard," public notice, September 1948, Kenneth Colegrove Papers, Herbert Hoover Presidential Library.

76. F. C. Sammons, letter to the editor of the *Herald Advertiser* (West Virginia), December 21, 1947, extension of remarks by Hon. Hubert S. Ellis of West Virginia in the House of Representatives, January 6, 1948, *Congressional Record*, vol. 94, part 9, 80th Cong., 2nd Sess., appendix, A5.

10. Defending Beard after the Fall

1. Mary R. Beard to Harry Elmer Barnes, July 27, 1948, Harry Elmer Barnes Papers, box 34, folder July 2–September 30, 1948, American Heritage Center, University of Wyoming.

2. Mary R. Beard to Harry Elmer Barnes, November 19, 1948, Harry Elmer Barnes Papers, box 34, folder October 1–December 31, 1948, American Heritage Center, University of Wyoming.

3. Ibid.

4. Ibid.

5. Mary R. Beard to Harry Elmer Barnes, February 21, 1949, Harry Elmer Barnes Papers, box 35, folder January 7–March 30, 1949, American Heritage Center, University of Wyoming.

6. Ibid.

7. Donald L. Miller, *Lewis Mumford: A Life* (New York: Grove Press, 1989), 398.

8. Dixon Wecter, "A Farewell to the Republic," *Saturday Review of Literature* 27, no. 45 (November 4, 1944): 7–8.

9. Lewis Mumford, "Mr. Beard and His 'Basic History,'" letter to the editor, *Saturday Review of Literature* 27, no. 49 (December 2, 1944): 27.

10. Mary R. Beard to Harry Elmer Barnes, March 17, 1949, Harry Elmer Barnes Papers, box 35, folder January 7–March 30, 1949, American Heritage Center, University of Wyoming.

11. Stéphane Courtois et al., *Il libro nero del comunismo: crimini, terrore, repressione* (Milan: Mondadori, 1998), "I crimini del comunismo," 4 (my translation).

12. Nicolas Werth, "Violenze, repressione, terrori nell'Unione Sovietica," in Courtois et al., *Il libro nero del comunismo*, 187.

13. Courtois, "I crimini del comunismo," 17, 18.

14. François Furet, *The Passing of an Illusion: The Idea of Communism in the Twentieth Century* (Chicago: University of Chicago Press, 1999), xi, 148, 202.

15. Ibid., 146.

16. For Aleksandr Solzhenitsyn, see especially *The Gulag Archipelago*, 3 vols., 1973–1978. Robert Conquest's *Harvest of Sorrow: Soviet Collectivization and the Terror Famine* (1986) analyzes Stalin's destruction of Ukraine's peasant culture. For studies of Stalin based on research in the Soviet archives, see Dmitri Volkogonov's *Stalin: Triumph and Tragedy* (1991) and Edvard Radzinsky's *Stalin: The First In-Depth Biography Based on Explosive New Documents from Russia's Secret Archives* (1997). Volkogonov's *Lenin: A New Biography* (1994) makes the case that Vladimir Ilyich Lenin paved the way for Stalinism and cannot be presented as a Soviet leader who was tragically betrayed by his successor. Richard Pipes offers the same indictment in *The Unknown Lenin: From the Secret Archive* (1999). Nadezhda Mandelstam's *Hope against Hope: A Memoir* (1970) is the best primary-source account of daily life in Stalinist Russia and one of the greatest autobiographies ever written.

17. Max Eastman, *The End of Socialism in Russia* (Boston: Little, Brown and Company, 1937), 23, 6.

18. Mary R. Beard to Harry Elmer Barnes, August 7, 1949, Harry Elmer Barnes Papers, box 35, folder July 2–September 29, 1949, American Heritage Center, University of Wyoming.

19. Ibid.

20. A. Frank Reel, *The Case of General Yamashita* (Chicago: University of Chicago Press, 1949), 222, 248.

21. Ibid., 108, 125.

22. Ibid., 109, 111, 245.

23. Charles A. Beard, "Who's to Write the History of the War?," *Saturday Evening Post* 220, no. 14 (October 4, 1947): 172.

24. Ibid.

25. Mary R. Beard to Harry Elmer Barnes, January 24, 1951, Harry Elmer Barnes Papers, box 37, folder January 1–February 28, 1951, American Heritage Center, University of Wyoming.

26. Eugene Davidson, "Tribute to Charles Austin Beard," cited by Harry Elmer Barnes in *The Struggle against the Historical Blackout* in Barnes, *Selected Revisionist Pamphlets*, 9th and enlarged ed. (New York: Arno Press & New York Times, 1972), 2.

27. Even so fervent and well-informed an admirer of Beard as Clyde W. Barrow conformed to the consensus about his "egregious factual mistakes" in misinterpreting the Second World War. Misreading the perils of fascism and Nazism, "he misled himself," wrote Barrow in *More than a Historian: The Political and Economic Thought of Charles A. Beard* (New Brunswick, N.J.: Transaction Publishers, 2000), 227.

28. Harry Elmer Barnes to Merle Curti, February 15, 1950, Merle Curti Papers, State Historical Society of Wisconsin.

29. Barnes, *The Struggle against the Historical Blackout*, 26.

30. Ibid., 50.

31. Matthew Josephson, "Charles A. Beard: A Memoir," *Virginia Quarterly Review* 25, no. 4 (Autumn 1949): 589, 602.

32. Mary R. Beard to Harry Elmer Barnes, January 24, 1951, Harry Elmer Barnes Papers, box 37, folder January 1–February 28, 1951, American Heritage Center, University of Wyoming.

33. Ibid.

34. Howard K. Beale, ed., *Charles A. Beard: An Appraisal* (Lexington: University of Kentucky Press, 1954), vi, v.

35. Mary R. Beard to Barnes, January 24, 1951.

36. Mary R. Beard to Harry Elmer Barnes, April 5, 1951, Harry Elmer Barnes Papers, box 37, folder March 12–April 30, 1951, American Heritage Center, University of Wyoming.

37. Ibid.

38. Barnes, *The Struggle against the Historical Blackout*, 75, 84.

39. Mary R. Beard to Barnes, April 5, 1951.

40. Mary R. Beard to Harry Elmer Barnes, February 27, 1952, Harry Elmer Barnes Papers, box 38, folder February 1–February 29, 1952, American Heritage Center, University of Wyoming.

41. Mary R. Beard to Harry Elmer Barnes, August 3, 1952, Harry Elmer Barnes Papers, box 39, folder July 1–August 31,1952, American Heritage Center, University of Wyoming.

42. Mary R. Beard to Harry Elmer Barnes, August 15, 1952, Harry Elmer Barnes Papers, box 39, folder July 1–August 31, 1952, American Heritage Center, University of Wyoming.

43. Harry Elmer Barnes, *The Court Historians versus Revisionism*, in *Select Revisionist Pamphlets*, 2nd and rev. ed. (New York: Arno Press and New York Times, 1972), 3, 6, 11.

44. William L. Langer and S. Everett Gleason, *The Challenge to Isolation, 1937–1940* (New York: Harper & Brothers Publishers, 1952), 14–15.

45. Harry Elmer Barnes to William Langer, February 14, 1952, Merle Curti Papers, Charles Beard material microfilm, State Historical Society of Wisconsin. Barnes sent this letter to Curti without comment.

46. Harry Elmer Barnes to Merle Curti, May 24, 1952, Merle Curti Papers, State Historical Society of Wisconsin.

47. Barnes, *The Court Historians versus Revisionism*, 24.

48. Ibid., 28, 30. With what delight would Barnes have welcomed the publication of Robert Stinnett's *Day of Deceit: The Truth about FDR and Pearl Harbor* (New York: Touchstone, 2000), replete with its illustrations of the revisionist thesis. About the American government's foreknowledge of the Pearl Harbor attack, he concludes, "the major secrets of Pearl Harbor are at last out in the open. After years of denial, the truth is clear: we knew" (263). Stinnett's book, although confirming the suspicions of Beard and Barnes, has failed to still the debate over Pearl Harbor. Synthesizing a pro-FDR consensus regarding Pearl Harbor, Susan Dunn explains, "Conspiracy theories would later emerge, suggesting that the president had wanted and planned the attack, but, as historian James MacGregor Burns wrote, a better explanation is a 'complacency theory' that takes into account the lazy security in Pearl Harbor and the poor communications arrangements of the American command," in *1940: FDR, Willkie, Lindbergh, Hitler—the Election amid the Storm* (New Haven, Conn.: Yale University Press, 2013), 308.

49. Mary R. Beard to Harry Elmer Barnes, April 11, 1953, Harry Elmer Barnes Papers, box 40, folder April 1–April 30, 1953, American Heritage Center, University of Wyoming.

50. Mary R. Beard to Harry Elmer Barnes, May 17, 1953, Harry Elmer Barnes Papers, box 40, folder May 1–May 31, 1953, American Heritage Center, University of Wyoming.

51. Mary R. Beard to Harry Elmer Barnes, September 27, 1953, Harry Elmer Barnes Papers, box 41, folder September 1–September 30, 1953, American Heritage Center, University of Wyoming.

52. Beard attributed the authorship of this phrase to Yale University law professor and implacable American foreign policy critic Edwin Montefiore Borchard. As the Second World War was ending, Beard summed up American foreign policy as a formula for our incessant interference in the affairs of other nations: "If any country does anything we do not like we must jump on it." Such a business could only lead to ruin. Beard added, "as you say: perpetual war in the name of permanent peace." Charles A. Beard to Edwin Montefiore Borchard, March 4, 1945, Edwin Montefiore Borchard Papers, box 1, folder 15, Manuscripts and Archives, Yale University Library.

53. Harry Elmer Barnes, ed., *Perpetual War for Perpetual Peace: A Critical Examination of the Foreign Policy of Franklin Delano Roosevelt and Its Aftermath* (Caldwell, Idaho: Caxton Printers, 1953), viii.

54. Harry Elmer Barnes to Merle Curti, December 4, 1948, Merle Curti Papers, State Historical Society of Wisconsin.

55. Barnes, *Perpetual War for Perpetual Peace*, 629.

56. Mary R. Beard to Harry Elmer Barnes, February 27, 1952, Harry Elmer Barnes Papers, box 38, folder February 1–February 29, 1952, American Heritage Center, University of Wyoming.

57. Cited by Barnes, *Perpetual War for Perpetual Peace*, 627.

58. A. J. P. Taylor, *The Origins of the Second World War* (London: Hamish Hamilton, 1961), 17.

59. Harry Elmer Barnes, "Blasting the Historical Blackout: Professor A. J. P. Taylor's *The Origins of the Second World War*, Its Nature, Reliability, Shortcomings, and Implications," *Selected Revisionist Pamphlets* (New York: Arno Press and New York Times, 1972), 4.

60. Ibid., 4.

61. Ibid., 30, 31, 35.

62. Harry Elmer Barnes to Herbert Hoover, May 9, 1961, Herbert Hoover Papers, Beard File, Manuscript Biographies Collection, Herbert Hoover Presidential Library.

63. Harry Elmer Barnes to Merle Curti, July 22, 1956, Merle Curti Papers, State Historical Society of Wisconsin.

64. Harry Elmer Barnes to Merle Curti, November 7, 1965, Merle Curti Papers, State Historical Society of Wisconsin.

65. Lewis Brandon, introduction to Harry Elmer Barnes, *The Barnes Trilogy: Three Revisionist Booklets* (Torrance, Calif.: Institute for Historical Review, 1979), v, vi, vii.

66. Deborah Lipstadt, *Denying the Holocaust: The Growing Assault on Truth and Memory* (New York: Free Press, 1993), 22.

67. Peter Novick, *That Noble Dream: The "Objectivity Question" and the American Historical Profession* (Cambridge: Cambridge University Press, 1988), 208–223, 308–309.

68. "Arraigns Methods in Trying Teachers," *New York Times* (December 16, 1917): 5.

69. Ibid.

70. Paul Lewinson to Charles A. Beard, March 29, 1939, Charles Austin Beard Letters, 1929–1939, Beard, Charles Austin Collection, correspondence between Charles A. Beard and George S. Counts, Manuscript Collection, Rare Book and Manuscript Library, Columbia University.

71. Paul Lewinson to Ernst H. Correll, April 22, 1939, Charles Austin Beard Letters, 1929–1939, Beard, Charles Austin Collection, correspondence between Charles A. Beard and George S. Counts, Manuscript Collection, Rare Book and Manuscript Library, Columbia University.

72. Paul Lewinson to Charles A. Beard, October 12, 1939, Charles Austin Beard Letters, 1929–1939, Beard, Charles Austin Collection, correspondence between Charles A. Beard and George S. Counts, Manuscript Collection, Rare Book and Manuscript Library, Columbia University.

73. Charles A. Beard to Paul Lewinson, October 15, 1939, Charles Austin Beard Letters, 1929–1939, Beard, Charles Austin Collection, correspondence between Charles A. Beard and George S. Counts, Manuscript Collection, Rare Book and Manuscript Library, Columbia University.

74. Richard Breitman and Allan J. Lichtman, *FDR and the Jews* (Cambridge, Mass.: Harvard University Press, 2013), 127.

75. Lipstadt, *Denying the Holocaust*, 39.

76. Lewis Mumford, "Mr. Beard and His 'Basic History,'" *Saturday Review of Literature* 27, no. 47 (December 2, 1944): 27.

11. Beard's Philosophy of History and American Imperialism

1. Charles A. Beard, "Written History as an Act of Faith," *American Historical Review (AHR)* 39, no. 2 (January 1934): 220.

2. Ibid., 221.

3. Ibid., 222, 225, 226.

4. Ibid., 227.

5. Ibid., 228, 222.

6. Howard K. Beale to Merle Curti, February 19, 1950, Merle Curti Papers, State Historical Society of Wisconsin.

7. Benedetto Croce to Charles A. Beard, June 24, 1933, *AHR* 39, no. 2 (January 1934): 229–231.

8. Benedetto Croce, *History: Its Theory and Practice*, trans. Douglas Ainslie (New York: Harcourt, Brace, and Company, 1923), 12.

9. Ibid., 269, 270.

10. Ibid., 54, 290, 292.

11. Ibid., 300.

12. Charles A. Beard to James Harvey Robinson, September 21, 1935, Merle Curti Papers, State Historical Society of Wisconsin. Peter Novick provides a masterly analysis of the epistemological challenge mounted by Charles Beard and Carl Becker against the objectivist orthodoxy in writing history. He places himself on the side of Beard and Becker in this dispute: "in general and on the whole, I have been persuaded by the critics of the concept; unimpressed by the arguments of its defenders," in *That Noble Dream: The "Objectivity Question" and the American Historical Profession* (Cambridge: Cambridge University Press, 1988), 6.

13. Charles A. Beard, "That Noble Dream," *AHR* 41, no. 1 (October 1935): 78.

14. Ibid., 81–82.

15. Ibid., 85.

16. Joseph Schumpeter, "The Sociology of Imperialisms," in *Imperialism and Social Classes* (New York: Meridian, 1951), 89, 95.

17. Charles A. Beard, *The Discussion of Human Affairs* (New York: Macmillan, 1936), 74, 78.

18. Charles A. Beard to Merle Curti, November 6, 1943, Merle Curti Papers, State Historical Society of Wisconsin.

19. Beard, *The Discussion of Human Affairs*, 82.

20. For an assessment of Beard's knowledge of German critical theory, see Lloyd R. Sorenson, "Charles A. Beard and German Historiographical Thought," *Mississippi Valley Historical Review* 42, no. 2 (September 1955): 274–287. Sorenson wrote, "Beard knew better than any leading American historian the great significance of recent German historiography." Nevertheless, in a one-eyed man in the land of the blind judgment, he assessed Beard's knowledge in this field to be quite limited, superficial, and often wrong.

21. Charles A. Beard and Alfred Vagts, "Currents of Thought in Historiography," *AHR* 42, no. 3 (October 1937): 464, 466, 480.

22. Charles A. Beard and Mary R. Beard, *The Rise of American Civilization* (New York: Macmillan, 1935), vol. 2, "The Industrial Era," 837.

23. Karl Mannheim, *Ideology and Utopia: An Introduction to the Sociology of Knowledge* (New York: Harcourt, Brace & World, 1936), 118. He allotted the conservatives two separate categories, bureaucratic and historicist, but Beard did not make any such distinction when he wrote about conservatism in an American context.

24. Beard and Vagts, "Currents of Thought in Historiography," 480.

25. William Appleman Williams, "A Note on Charles Austin Beard's Search for a General Theory of Causation," *AHR* 42, no.1 (October 1956): 59–80. In an undated letter to James W. Groshong, Williams expressed his own admiration for Brooks Adams and his grandfather, John Quincy Adams, "two men who in their dedicated ways did try to speak the truth (and act on it) about the character of America . . . especially what price was paid for Empire." William Appleman Williams Papers (MSS Williams), Oregon State University Special Collections and Archives Research Center, Corvallis, Oregon, box 1.001 Correspondence A–M. Groshong was a professor in the Department of English at Oregon State University. Paul M. Buhle and Edward Rice-Maxim describe the way in which Williams felt drawn to "the immensely alluring observations of Brooks Adams," in *William Appleman Williams: The Tragedy of Empire* (New York: Routledge, 1995), 58.

26. A version of Beard's introduction also appeared as an article for the *Atlantic Monthly* in April 1943, "Historians at Work: Brooks and Henry Adams."

27. Charles A. Beard, review of *The Degradation of Democratic Dogma*, by Henry Adams, *New Republic* 22, no. 278 (March 31, 1920): 162–163. About Henry Adams, Beard wrote that he deserved praise as a historian for rising above the pedestrian level of mere chronicle. Instead, he sought to uncover the basic law governing human events and to give a genuinely historical account of the forces responsible for the degradation of America's democracy and the general crisis of Western civilization.

28. Timothy Paul Donovan analyzed the intellectual relationship between the two brothers, in *Henry Adams and Brooks Adams: The Education of Two Historians* (Norman: University of Oklahoma Press, 1961). While criticizing Brooks as a historian of only amateur attainments, Donovan recognized the importance of his thought for Henry. In response to Brooks's work, Henry's "research received a significant impulse" (100).

29. Charles A. Beard, introduction to *The Law of Civilization and Decay: An Essay on History*, by Brooks Adams (New York: Knopf, 1943), 3, 37.

30. Charles A. Beard and Mary R. Beard, *A Basic History of the United States* (New York: Doubleday, Doran & Company, 1944), 303, 367, 378.

31. Adams, *The Law of Civilization and Decay*, 68, 231, 286.

32. Brooks Adams, *The Theory of Social Revolutions* (New York: Macmillan, 1914), 1.

33. Ibid., 2, 14.

34. Charles A. Beard to Merle Curti, November 24, 1943, Merle Curti Papers, State Historical Society of Wisconsin.

35. For the details of Adams's political reversal and its consequences in his career, see Arthur F. Beringause, *Brooks Adams: A Biography* (New York: Alfred A. Knopf, 1955), esp. chap. 6, "Even Greater."

36. Daniel Aaron, who viewed Brooks Adams as an arrogant, eccentric, and neurotic anti-Semite, judiciously placed his writings from the late 1890s to about 1910 in a special category: "his utterances took on a magniloquence, a bellicosity, and a fervor that he showed neither before nor after," in *Men of Good Hope: A Story of American Progressives* (New York: Oxford University Press, 1951), 268.

37. Theodore Roosevelt, "The Law of Civilization and Decay," *The Forum* 22 (January 1, 1897): 575.

38. William Appleman Williams, "Brooks Adams and American Expansion," *New England Quarterly* 25, no. 2 (June 1952): 217–232. Williams describes the relationship between Adams and Roosevelt as one of "warm understanding." The article is included in an anthology: Thomas J. McCormick and Walter LaFeber, eds., *Behind the Throne: Servants of Power to Imperial Presidents, 1898–1948* (Madison, Wisconsin: University of Wisconsin Press, 1993).

39. Brooks Adams, *The New Empire* (New York: Macmillan, 1902), 189.

40. For an analysis of Adams's contribution to the late nineteenth-century intellectual ferment justifying American expansion in the Pacific, see Walter LaFeber, *The New Empire: An Interpretation of American Expansion 1860–1898* (Ithaca, N.Y.: Cornell University Press, 1963). He linked Adams with Frederick Jackson Turner, Josiah Strong, and Alfred Thayer Mahan as highly influential proponents of the new American empire in the 1890s "watershed period of American history" (101).

41. Brooks Adams, *America's Economic Supremacy* (New York: Macmillan, 1900), 12, 27.

42. Ibid., 81, 195, 197–198, 221, 222.

43. Marquis Childs, "Evaluation," introduction to *America's Economic Supremacy* by Brooks Adams (New York: Harper & Brothers, 1947), 49.

44. Lloyd C. Gardner, *Architects of Illusion: Men and Ideas in American Foreign Policy, 1941–1949* (Chicago: Quadrangle Books, 1970), 319.

45. Adams, *The New Empire*, 193.

46. Ibid., 195.

47. Ibid., 197, 113.

48. In the prefatory essay for his brother Henry's *The Degradation of the Democratic Dogma* (New York: Macmillan, 1920), "The Heritage of Henry Adams," Brooks Adams delivered a moral preachment, in the manner of *The Law of Civilization and Decay* and *The Theory of Social Revolutions*, about the causes of the Great War, which he called "an effect of competition" among the economic elites of the imperialist powers: "This fact, which has been patent from the outset to every observant mind, was at first hotly, not to say angrily, denied by the banking fraternity, lest they should be held responsible therefore, and thereby restrained in their action" (116). About the postwar settlement, he wrote, "of this we may be certain, it will be an arrangement which will conduce to the further dominance of the great moneyed interests" (118).

49. Peter A. Soderbergh, "'Old School Days' on the Middle Border, 1849–1859: The Mary Payne Beard Letters," *History of Education Quarterly* 8, no. 4 (Winter 1968): 497–504.

50. Ellen Nore, *Charles A. Beard: An Intellectual Biography* (Carbondale: Southern Illinois University Press, 1983). She comments about "his family's unorthodox religious background" (4).

51. Regarding the importance of Beard's Quaker heritage, Cushing Strout wrote, "he celebrated the early American Quaker John Woolman as the spiritual father of American radicals who attacked the passion for acquisition as the root of evil," in *The Pragmatic Revolt in American History: Carl Becker and Charles Beard* (New Haven, Conn.: Yale University Press, 1958), 88. Though smoothly engaging in some diplomatic niceties

about Beard the man, Strout in this famous study dismissed his historical relativism as "fatal to the integrity of history as a discipline" (59), his economic interpretation of history as inept, tendentious, and "invidiously ambiguous" (96), and his critique of FDR as sensationalist and the last word in conspiracy theories. In the October 17, 1955, article "In Retrospect: Charles Beard's Liberalism" (*New Republic* 133, no. 16), Strout wondered if Beard had revealed himself to be a parochial midwestern historian caught up in a Manichaean prejudice against Eastern financial interests. Passionately committed to democratic collectivist ideals, Beard had turned "the historian into a utopian astrologer" (17–18).

52. Charles A. Beard, introduction to *The Idea of Progress* by J. B. Bury (New York: Macmillan, 1932), xi.

53. Mary R. Beard to Kenneth Colegrove, October 20, 1946, Kenneth Colegrove Papers, Herbert Hoover Presidential Library.

54. Albert Jay Nock, *Memoirs of a Superfluous Man* (New York: Harper & Brothers, 1943), 49.

55. Albert Jay Nock, "A Model History," review of *The Rise of American Civilization*, by Charles A. Beard and Mary R. Beard, *Saturday Review of Literature* 3, no. 50 (July 9, 1927): 957.

56. Nock, *Memoirs of a Superfluous Man*, 294.

57. John A. Hobson, "A World Safe for Democracy," *La Follette's Magazine* 10, no. 7 (July 1918): 6, 12. This article originally appeared in *Survey*, June 29, 1918, and was a précis of his recently published book *Democracy after the War*.

58. Charles A. Beard, "Neglected Aspects of Political Science," *American Political Science Review* 42, no. 2 (April 1948): 212.

59. Ibid., 217, 218, 222.

60. Ibid., 219, 220.

61. Ibid., 220, 221.

62. Mary R. Beard to Merle Curti, January 3, 1950, Merle Curti Papers, State Historical Society of Wisconsin.

63. Ibid.

64. Mary R. Beard to Merle Curti, November 16, 1948, Merle Curti Papers, State Historical Society of Wisconsin.

Conclusion

1. Oliver Goldsmith, "The Deserted Village," in *English Prose and Poetry, 1660–1800*, ed. Odell Shepard and Paul Spencer Wood (Boston: Houghton Mifflin Company, 1934), 724, 722.

Index

Aaron, Daniel, 304n36
Abbey, Edward, 284n58
academic freedom, 35, 39–41, 44, 255, 276n55. *See also* freedom of speech
Adams, Brooks, 120, 128, 255, 260; Aaron on, 304n36; Donovan on, 304n28; on financial elites, 245–49; on imperialism, 245–52, 305n40; on Spanish-American War, 247–49; Williams on, 304n25
Adams, Henry, 121, 244, 248, 258, 260, 304n28
Adams, John Quincy, 119–20, 257, 263, 304n25
Addams, Jane, 7, 121, 269n2
Alcoa Corporation, 159, 161–62
Alien Registration Act (1940), 126
America First Committee, 98–100, 107, 116; Beard and, 99–100, 148; Brewster and, 99–100; Castle and, 171; dissolution of, 117; Nazi sympathizer charges against, 282n2; as supporter of World War II, 155
America First movement, 147, 284n58
American Century, 5, 96, 115; Adams on, 247; Luce on, 122–24, 129–32; Villard on, 152
American Historical Association (AHA), 223, 231–32, 235–37
American Indians, 13, 29, 218, 260
American Political Science Association (APSA), 148–49, 187, 254–55, 288n22
American Union Against Militarism, 44
Angell, Norman, 50
anti-Catholicism, 277n13
Anti-Imperialist League, 152
anti-Semitism, 97–99, 229–33, 282n2, 304n36
App, Austin J., 230
Arendt, Hannah, 203
Aristotle, xii, 29, 128, 240
Asquith, H. H., 58
Atlantic Charter (1941), 97, 121, 157–62, 188, 203–4, 265, 295n14

Bagley, William C., 56, 175
Bailey, Thomas A., 189–90, 199–200, 206
Baldwin, Stanley, 174
Bancroft, George, 260
Barbusse, Henri, 52
Bardèche, Maurice, 230
Barnes, Harry Elmer, 61, 73–74, 166; Charles Beard and, 63–65, 142, 145, 186, 261; Mary Beard and, 210–23, 226–27; on Cold War, 219; on Holocaust, 229–31; on Langer, 224–25; as *Progressive* columnist, 154–57; revisionism of, 210–11, 218–31
Barnes, Harry Elmer, works of: *The Court Historians Versus Revisionism*, 223–24; *Genesis of the World War*, 63–65; *The History of Western Civilization*, 119; *Perpetual War for Perpetual Peace*, 226–27; *Revisionism and Brainwashing*, 230; *The Struggle against the Historical Blackout*, 210–11, 218–23
Barrow, Clyde W., 300n27
Beale, Howard K., 221–22, 236
Beard, Charles Austin, 7–12, 231–33, 252–53; death of, 3, 4, 173, 207, 210, 221; dissertation of, 17; festschrifts for, 221–22; on historiography, 234–45, 251–52, 255–56, 260; obituaries of, 207–9, 211; at Oxford University, 7–26; teaching style of, 41–42; writing style of, 238
Beard, Charles Austin, works of: *America in Midpassage*, 100–102, 175, 264; *American Foreign Policy in the Making*, 5, 164, 167, 171–73, 185–94, 197–200, 203, 261; *American Government and Politics*, 208; *The American Spirit*, 118–22, 128, 129, 238; *The Balkan Pivot*, 64; *A Basic History of the United States*, 118, 134–39, 165–66, 213, 246; *Cross Currents in Europe Today*, 54; "Currents of Thought in Historiography," 241–44; *The Devil Theory of War*, 73, 80, 87–93; *The Discussion of Human Affairs*,

Beard (*continued*)
240–41, 255; *An Economic Interpretation of the Constitution of the United States*, 1–2, 27–33, 34, 43–44, 209, 213; *Economic Origins of Jefferson Democracy*, 274n12; *A Foreign Policy for America*, 108, 110–12; *Giddy Minds and Foreign Quarrels*, 104–8, 146, 153, 172, 179, 223, 225; *The History of the American People*, 56, 175; *The Idea of National Interest*, 108, 191–94, 296n21; *The Industrial Revolution*, 14–16; *An Introduction to the English Historians*, 18, 25; *National Governments and the World War*, 48; *Open Door at Home*, 91–92; *President Roosevelt and the Coming of the War*, 5, 175, 192, 200–202, 205, 208–11, 261; *Public Policy and the General Welfare*, 113–15; *The Republic*, 118, 125–32, 138, 291n82. See also *The Rise of American Civilization*
Beard, Mary Ritter (Charles's wife), 11–12, 208–9, 253, 256, 261; Barnes and, 210–23, 226–27; on collaborating, 118; death of, 227; La Follette and, 33; Reel and, 216–18
Beard, Mary Ritter, works of: *America in Midpassage*, 175; *The American Spirit*, 118–22; *A Basic History of the United States*, 134–39; *The Force of Women in Japanese History*, 227; *The Making of Charles A. Beard*, 7–8, 227; *The Rise of American Civilization*, 1–2, 67–71, 90, 242; *Women as Force in History*, 227
Beard, Miriam (Charles's daughter), 11, 12, 17, 241
Beard, William (Charles's son), 128
"Beardianism," 3–4; Hofstadter and, 138; La Follette Jr. and, 146; Ruskin and, 8
Beazley, Raymond, 56, 57
Becker, Carl, 270n18, 303n12
Belgium, 66, 168, 177
Bellamy, Edward, 121
Bemis, Samuel Flagg, 201
Berchtold, Leopold, 53
Bethlehem Steel, 74, 159
Bethmann-Hollweg, Theobald von, 53
Beveridge, Albert, 191
Bliven, Bruce, 65
Boer War (1899–1902), 25, 49–50, 248
Bolles, Blair, 206
Bolshevism, 70–71, 152
Boorstin, Daniel, 287n58
Borchard, Edwin Montefiore, 64, 137, 157, 185, 261, 301n52
Bowman, Isaiah, 232

Bracken, Brendan, 160
Brandon, Lewis, 230
Breitman, Richard, 232
Bretton Woods Conference (1944), 204
Brewster, Kingman, Jr., 99–100
Bricker, John W., 172
British Empire, 155, 160; Adams on, 245–50; American Revolution and, 68; Beard on, 59, 69, 106, 121; Bracken on, 160; FDR on, 156, 194, 196; Hoover on, 168; La Follette Jr. on, 147, 153, 156; Montgelas on, 62; positive aspects of, 13, 24–25; John Williams on, 158–60
Brown, Jerry, 284n58
Brown, John, 14
Bruni, Leonardo, 30
Bryan, William Jennings, 88–89
Buchanan, Pat, 284n58
Burke, Edmund, 21
Burma, 158–59
Burns, James MacGregor, 301n48
Bury, J. B., 253
Butler, Nicholas Murray, 5, 34–35, 37–41, 45–46, 275n38
Butler, Smedley Darlington, 92–95, 110, 144–45

capitalism, 245, 258; Adams on, 246–52; communist monopolies and, 168; free trade and, 121; Great Depression and, 100–101, 264; Hofstadter on, 137–38; La Follette on, 30; laissez-faire economics and, 99, 102, 114, 137, 216; C. Wright Mills on, 161; postwar Germany and, 189; public policy and, 113–14; Ruskin on, 20–22; Schumpeter on, 240; Seligman and, 18; World War I and, 34, 36, 38–39, 55–56
Capper, Arthur, 148, 150–51
Carlyle, Thomas, 8, 91–92; Engels and, 21; Ruskin and, 21–23, 113–14; Veblen and, 102
Carto, Willis, 230
Castle, William R., Jr., 171
Cattell, James McKeen, 36–38, 40–41, 45–46
Cattell, Owen, 40
Chamberlain, Neville, 174, 180, 229
Chamberlin, William Henry, 220, 226
Childs, Marquis W., 249–50
China, 72, 150, 169, 249; Japan and, 155, 158–59, 190–91, 205, 250–51; open-door policy toward, 155, 250–51, 289n49

World War I, 27, 34–72, 262; Beard on,
34–36, 46–47, 55–56, 69–71, 108;
financiers' profits from, 74–95; freedom
of speech during, 35–41, 44–45, 126; as
"good war," 47–48; Great Depression
and, 264; La Follette on, 38–39, 70, 127,
264; propaganda of, 55, 59–63, 66, 71;
revisionism of, 56–57, 61, 64–69, 72,
144–45, 183, 223; submarine warfare of,
65, 76, 84
World War II, 4–5, 118–41, 127–28, 262;
famine relief after, 171; freedom of
speech during, 136, 155; as "good war," 2,
5, 96; Luce on, 122–23; C. Wright Mills

on, 161; outbreak of, 108, 146–47;
revisionism of, 173–75, 178–84, 198,
210–11, 218–31; U.S. economy after,
136–37; U.S. isolationism about, 96,
104–17; war crime trials after, 203,
215–18
Wright, Frank Lloyd, 152, 213

Yalta Conference (1945), 180, 200
Yamashita Tomoyuki, 216–18
Yugoslavia, 64, 212

Ziegler, John Alan, 147
Zueblin, Charles, 28–29, 32

CPSIA information can be obtained
at www.ICGtesting.com
Printed in the USA
LVHW111455090119
603298LV00003B/20/P